THE LINGUISTIC CONDITION

Also Available from Bloomsbury

Inventing Agency: Essays on the Literary and Philosophical Production of the Modern Subject, ed. Claudia Brodsky and Eloy LaBrada
Words' Worth: What the Poet Does, Claudia Brodsky
Apperception and Self-Consciousness in Kant and German Idealism, Dennis Schulting
Red Kant: Aesthetics, Marxism and the Third Critique, Michael Wayne
The Bloomsbury Companion to Kant, ed. Gary Banham, Dennis Schulting, and Nigel Hems

THE LINGUISTIC CONDITION

Kant's *Critique of Judgment* and the Poetics of Action

Claudia Brodsky

BLOOMSBURY ACADEMIC
LONDON • NEW YORK • OXFORD • NEW DELHI • SYDNEY

BLOOMSBURY ACADEMIC
Bloomsbury Publishing Plc
50 Bedford Square, London, WC1B 3DP, UK
1385 Broadway, New York, NY 10018, USA
29 Earlsfort Terrace, Dublin 2, Ireland

BLOOMSBURY, BLOOMSBURY ACADEMIC and the Diana logo are
trademarks of Bloomsbury Publishing Plc

First published in Great Britain 2021
This paperback edition published in 2023

Copyright © Claudia Brodsky, 2021

Claudia Brodsky has asserted her right under the Copyright, Designs and Patents Act, 1988, to be identified as Author of this work.

Cover design by Charlotte Daniels
Cover image: Morris Louis, Beta Lambda 1961 © 2020 Maryland Institute College of Art (MICA), Rights Administered by Artist Rights Society (ARS), New York, All Rights Reserved

All rights reserved. No part of this publication may be reproduced or transmitted in any form or by any means, electronic or mechanical, including photocopying, recording, or any information storage or retrieval system, without prior permission in writing from the publishers.

Bloomsbury Publishing Plc does not have any control over, or responsibility for, any third-party websites referred to or in this book. All internet addresses given in this book were correct at the time of going to press. The author and publisher regret any inconvenience caused if addresses have changed or sites have ceased to exist, but can accept no responsibility for any such changes.

A catalogue record for this book is available from the British Library.

Library of Congress Cataloging-in-Publication Data.

Names: Brodsky, Claudia, 1955– author.
Title: The linguistic condition : Kant's Critique of judgment and the poetics of action / Claudia Brodsky.
Description: London; New York: Bloomsbury Academic, 2021. |
Includes bibliographical references and index. |
Identifiers: LCCN 2020049464 (print) | LCCN 2020049465 (ebook) |
ISBN 9781350144378 (hb) | ISBN 9781350144385 (epdf) | ISBN 9781350144392 (ebook)
Subjects: LCSH: Kant, Immanuel, 1724–1804. Kritik der Urteilskraft. | Judgment (Logic) | Language and languages–Philosophy.
Classification: LCC B2784.B76 2021 (print) | LCC B2784 (ebook) | DDC 121—dc23
LC record available at https://lccn.loc.gov/2020049464
LC ebook record available at https://lccn.loc.gov/2020049465

ISBN: HB: 978-1-3501-4437-8
PB: 978-1-3502-1735-5
ePDF: 978-1-3501-4438-5
eBook: 978-1-3501-4439-2

Typeset by RefineCatch Limited, Bungay, Suffolk

To find out more about our authors and books visit www.bloomsbury.com and sign up for our newsletters.

For Chloe and Rebecca, with love and admiration
Toni Morrison, dearest friend, clearest mind, in Memoriam

Alles Menschliche ist voll von Urteilen, weswegen es nicht verwunderlich scheint, wenn einmal ausgesprochen wurde, daß ohne Urteil kein Bewußtsein möglich sei.

Everything human is replete with acts of judgment, for which reason, once it has been articulated, the statement that without judgment no consciousness would be possible does not seem remarkable.

—H. G. Adler, *Eine Reise.*

CONTENTS

Acknowledgements   xi
Preface: Acting upon Condition   xiii

Chapter 1
INTRODUCTION: BEFORE JUDGMENT: DOING WITHOUT KNOWING
IN KANT AND DIDEROT   1

Part I
LINGUISTIC CONDITIONS

Chapter 2
THE "CONDITION" OF JUDGMENT: "COMMON SENSE," OR
THE ORIGIN OF LANGUAGE IN KANT'S *THIRD CRITIQUE*   23
1. "Common Sense" and Signification, or What is Not Tautology   23
2. "Technique"   42
3. "Free"   51
4. "Feeling"   59
5. Speech Act and "Communicability"   64
6. Rousseau's Nouns   72
7. Diderot's Adjectives   92
8. Kant's Predicates: "Synthetic Judgments *A Priori*" and "A General Voice"   109
9. "The Schema," or Language Inside   121
10. What is Articulation?   130
11. World Without Words: Wordsworth   138

Part II
MISSING SENSES AND POETICS

Chapter 3
"JUDGMENT" AND THE GENESIS OF WHAT WE LACK: "POETRY,"
"SCHEMA," AND THE "MONOGRAM OF IMAGINATION" IN KANT   147
1. "Judgment" in the "Age of Critique"   147
2. Judgment and "Indifference:" the "Common Sense" of Imagination in Arendt and Kant   157
3. The Schema and the Language of Poetry   168
4. Poetry and the Judgment of Critique   189

Chapter 4
KLEIST'S MERE FORMALITIES — 193
1. Kant and Kleist: Representation and Irony — 193
2. What happened: Misrepresentation and Missed Representation in "Die Marquise von O …" — 198
3. Contesting "Judgment" in "The Duel" — 210

Bibliography — 227
   Primary Bibliography — 227
   Secondary Bibliography — 229
Index — 235

ACKNOWLEDGEMENTS

I would like to express my gratitude to the Morris Louis Estate for having granted me permission on an exceptional basis to feature Louis' "Beta Lambda" (1961) on the cover of this work. From my first conception of this project and all across the years of its development, as my understanding of its thesis of a "free" "linguistic condition" of judgment grew, Louis' unparalleled "Unfurled" series, of which "Beta Lambda" is a touchstone I have had the fortune to view my life long, appeared directly before my mind's eye. More than any other individual work I know, it concretely represents the centrality of the act of judgment to Kant's tripartite Critique, i.e., the absolute necessity of judgment, precisely because lacking "any proper realm of its own," to the opposing realms of knowledge and moral action so forcefully delineated in the First and Second Critiques. "Beta Lambda" enacts the very condition, of an unprescripted realm of perception actively enabling opposing forces to hold together, at whose description this book aims. My thanks to the Morris Louis Estate for enabling me to bring it before the reader's eye as well.

PREFACE:
ACTING UPON CONDITION

Talking – as actors in Harold Pinter plays typically do – in repetitive fragments of "small talk" shorn of contextualization and response, the principal speaker in "The Room" lets fall an unobtrusive non sequitur: "At least you stand a chance."

In a sense, when all is "said and done," this book explores what such "standing" means. A semantically flexible noun derived from a present tense gerund denoting a singular gravitational orientation or physical motion, "standing," in the abstract sense of access to a "right" conferred upon it in English, denotes a "condition," "position" or "status" independent of existential being of any description, and, at least in a negative sense, its meaning is not new. A function of positioning rather than identity, "standing" designates an acknowledged capacity to act within a representational – social and historical, and thus legal and political, no less than dramaturgical – context. Like the "subject-position" in syntactic structures representing actions and situations of every perceptible and imperceptible kind, "standing" stands for no particular content nor predicts any particular predicate or outcome. To "have standing" is, thus, by definition, nothing more nor less than "to stand a chance:" to possess nothing *per se* but a "standing" relation to possibility.

Like the syntactic production of the subject position within the representational context of the sentence, and the mediated production of subjects by their shared means of articulation, "standing" – the common rather than privative status of subjecthood as *inter*-subjective access to action – is inextricable from the unpredictability by which specifically human activity is defined. While its operative "presence" may be as presumed as that of grammar within language (and of language itself), absences and deprivations of "standing" have been the stuff of cultural imaginaries since the inception of poetics. From the inaugural narratives of the bases of ancient civilization in epic, tragedy and explanatory myth, through the sustaining fables and folklore of every community and continent, to the modern generation of self-reflective cultural traditions and contemporary transformations of the definition of culture across media, the want or disabling of the capacity for communicative interaction has haunted the arts of expression historically. Homer's enchanting sirens and speechless sailors live on in the apparently timeless comic genre of blissfully stupefied men (perennially on view at a theater near "you"), but so does his doubly defeated Trojan princess, Cassandra, cursed by Apollo, son of Zeus and god of song who desired her, with both prophetic power and the ineluctable inability to convey what she knows to anyone – central female figure and subject of tragedy in Aeschylus, Euripides, and Virgil, made metaphor for the general, negative condition of modern lyric composition by Hölderlin, Keats, Baudelaire, Mallarmé, Mandelstam, Celan, and Wolff, among others. Myths of mimetically dissembling statues and automata fashioned by Daedalus and Hephaestus, mortal and god alike, and the endless echoes of Ovid's Narcissus and Echo, and Pygmalion and Galatée, in fictional and theoretical accounts of desire stuck mistaking self for other, find their inverted confirmation in explicitly "alien" models of the subject in which reflexive self-projection is instead short-circuited: La Méttrie's simulacrum of man, or *homme-machine*, incapable not only of desire but of the "imagination" desire requires; Diderot's *homme horloge, homme automate,* and wished-for "decomposition of a man," theoretically imagined, like Condillac's statue, as artificial aids in isolating present and absent sensations from our *nonsensory* ability to represent them. The dummy of Hoffman's *Sandman* whose fatal allure "lives" on in Offenbach's gorgeously scored Olympia and Delibes' Coppélia, along with the many mail-order mannequins figuratively and literally embraced in current cinematic iterations of the medieval romance genre; the singing sea creatures silenced by the same magic spells that grant them limbs, and the myriad denizens of erotic, mytho-fantastic and science-fiction scenarios descended from them – in short, all the beautiful "body doubles" that "people" nightmare narratives of life limited to "going through the motions," semblances of subjects doomed to remain – as Dvorák's *Rusulka* perfectly, paradoxically, describes – "a silent echo of the elements," themselves all *stand for* an uncanny absence of "standing," the invisible yet acknowledged "condition" that, independent of the merely phenomenal materiality and false effigies of *aesthesis*, alone constitutes the capacities for experience and action that produce a subject as such.

Rendered incapable of self-articulation in exchange for coveted human corporal form alone, Dvorák's mythic Rusulka, returned to her watery element, elects to regain both eros and voice at the cost of the life of the human subject with whom she most desired to communicate. The sense of horror with which she recognizes the state of living death to which her future existence is thus consigned, is not shared, ironically enough, by the voluble spokesmen for just such inert animism that have propelled the tide of bizarrely spiritualist – "post-philosophical" and "post-Marxist" – "materialisms," which, echoing neo-Cartesian echoes of neo-Platonic mysticisms, have increasingly submerged all articulated "grounds" for "standing" – for the very possibility of possible action – over recent years. Overlapping conflations of the empirical with the ontological, ontology with a sensation-based aestheticism, *aesthesis* as such with the political, and the political, thus, ultimately, with the nonpolitical, "divine" or "sacred," all describe, in one figurative vocabulary or another, an autotelic status quo rendering any notion of action, rather than predetermined reaction, *per force*, "immaterial."[i] Once objects of understanding themselves, critical theories of

---

i. Among the most widespread of such – now commonplace – figurations of "life" mysteriously liberated from articulation, historicity, disparity, relationality and discursive mediation of any kind are Deleuze's traceless "nomadic" motions in space and predetermined monadic entelechies; Rancière's "politics" of evanescent aesthetic sensations and equations of

understanding that, beginning with Kant's self-"critical" "revolution" in metaphysics, derive not from positivist presumptions, but rather the critical differences and distinctions between real and presumed grounds they draw, are dismissed, whether in traditional noncritical or "postcritical" historicist fashion, for failing *both* to mirror a particular, historically predetermined empirical reality *and* to indicate, without contradiction, an historically independent (aesthetic and/or political) means of overcoming or reversing "history" as such.

In short, the quandary created by noncritical confusions of material *physis* with material forms and objects of our own making replicates the death by *aesthesis* of desiring a lifeless creation represented by Ovid – as well as Homer, Shakespeare, Dryden, Goya, Bronzino, Boucher, Rameau, Rousseau, Hawthorne, Keats, Kleist, Schiller, Balzac, Donezetti, Browning, James, Shaw, Borges, Mandelstam, Brodsky, and innumerable other formative authors and artists of ancient through contemporary, classical and popular culture. For the narcissistic double bind represented by Ovid in Pygmalion's passion for his sculpture dramatizes the confounding basis of any subject's wish that the external world both reflect and remain spatially distinct from – and thus perceptible to – the self that perceives it. Experiential desire of any kind requires external objects upon which to pose its affections, but only by maintaining resolutely ambiguous relations to all bodies "outside" it – by persisting in "viewing" these both as self-contained entities and as props of a scenario it contrives – can the self-sustaining "theater" ("contemplation," or "speculation:" θεωρία) staged by subjective narcissism thrive. It too feeds upon objects, with the significant difference that the *data* of its desire are acknowledged only insofar as they play the mechanical part, which is to say, already fully prescribed roles, to which their perception has assigned them. Thus, while perception and *eros* both require the "objective" resistance of a certain material opacity, the "otherness" of the material embraced by contemporary Pygmalions is of their own making.

---

sensations with "poetics;" the apocalyptic sensationalism and "charismatic" "sacralization" of the "sovereign" uniting Agamben's "glory" of a return to preconscious "infancy" in the "bare life" of a "mute" "bio-politics" with a post-historical, post-philosophical (and post-political) sensory "utopia" projected to realize and replace all terrestrial "politics" with the "sacred" manifestation of a cosmic (Catholic) "theology," and all such purely metaphoric, modern reincarnations of medieval creeds of "the incarnate" in popular oxymoronic notions of a "politics of sensation" See in particular Jacques Rancière, *Aesthetics and its Discontents* (Cambridge: Polity Press, 2009), esp. pp. 19–44: "Aesthetics as Politics" (orig. *Malaise dans l'esthétique* [Paris: Galilée, 2004]. For one of the most trenchant, deeply informed critiques of Agamben's evacuation of all possibility of any, even Heideggerian "ontological" or Benjaminian "historical," let alone politically effective, kind, in adopting the "nihilism" of "absolute utilitarianism" espoused by Carl Schmitt, see Antonio Negri, "The sacred dilemma of inoperosity. On Giorgio Agamben's *Opus Dei*," tr. J. F. McGimsey, *UniNomade* Sep. 9, 2012 (orig. pub. Feb. 2, 2012). See Secondary Bibliography for source texts for Agamben's key themes.

No relations may be more opaque and thus *productive* of culture, in its ever-changing, often oppositional historical forms – from the "intellectual" forms of philosophical concepts and inquiry, logic, law, science, and allegory to the "aesthetic," sensuous, referential and material forms of artistic fiction and representation, and ritual and belief of every kind – than those proposed to span the difference in kind between material existence and conscious life. This book and its companion volume, *Words' Worth: What the Poet Does*,[ii] examine how we *act* in filling that gap. The philosophical and literary works on which they focus attempt to describe actions that are qualitatively different, both in source and potential outcome, from "reactions," i.e., either naturally *or* historically determined results. Unlike the leveling waves of "new," anthropomorphizing "materialisms" leaving an indiscriminate flotsam of living and dead in their wake, the active formation of modes of representation and communication described by Diderot on the model of the stand-ins for sensation performed by the partially sensorily deprived; Kant's formulation of a distinctive "power" or "faculty" for translating the "feeling" of a perceiving subject into the impersonal predications he calls "judgment;" Rousseau's account of language itself originating in one's first encounter with "others" and, therein, with oneself; the temporal transformation of the "sacred" into the exigency of judgment in Kleist; and the "material difference" from codified "poetic diction" that, for Wordsworth, defines the "real language" of "poetry," all work to differentiate inert existence from the capacity to act, or "standing," in both the immediate and historical sense. "Agency" – the unparalleled capacity designated by Locke to underlie his central verbal concept of "consent," and by Rousseau as the basis of any equalizing social "convention" or "contract" – is another name for "standing" in the pivotal sense of "standing a chance." Neither a biological matter nor spiritual power, agency is the ability to act in differentiation – indeed to constitute difference – from a given context, and it can do so because, like the grammatical differentiation of the "subject-position" within a sentence, its own basis, at once "free" in origin *and* conventional in operation, is, for these very reasons, communicable, *rather than* contextual or innate. This book explores the fundamental relation between "material" shaped by "convention" to carry meaning, and unconventionally meaningful, and thus historically *productive* action, which is to say, between "standing" and the condition for action that alters the *status quo* or "state of things," both immediately, in their actuality, and with causally undetermined consequences. To "be" an "agent" "is" to "act" as one (among many), and such representational activity is irreducible both to sensory experience and the mechanics of physical action. It constitutes instead a relational position between "material" shaped to

---

ii. See Brodsky, *Words' Worth. What the Poet Does* (London: Bloomsbury, 2020), for an extended case study of Wordsworth's theory and practice of the thesis presented in this study – in the poet's words, that "the only purpose" of poetics "worthy of the name," no less than the development "likewise of society itself," depends on "the language really used by men" (Wordsworth, "Preface to *Lyrical Ballads*," in W. J. B. Owen and Jane Worthington Smyser, eds. *The Prose Works of William Wordsworth*, 3 vols, I: 121, 124, *et passim*).

carry meaning, and differently meaningful, and thus historically *productive* action, which is to say, between "standing," as the "positioning" of a "subject" as such, and as the condition of any subject's predication, i.e., action that alters the content of subject-object relations, including conditional – social, political and epistemological – definitions of the qualities to which subjecthood refers.

For, to "stand a chance" is to occupy an unpredictable position – in a word, *the position to act* with actual and future, historical and material results unscripted by known past and present circumstance – and "standing," in the necessarily figurative sense that the conceptual substantivization of any transitive or intransitive verb conveys, is a condition unconditioned by the physically empirical. Its basis is the specifically human capacity for self- *and* material invention through productive labor, opposing vampiric evacuations of both by capital accumulation, that Locke's *Second Treatise* called "free agency," the same capacity to act not in fantasized supernatural or magic defiance of natural mechanics but in independence, or "free" of both the real and apparent dependencies whose false conflation Rousseau's *Discourses* analyzed in turn. Like the capacity for "fiction" and "hypothetical reasoning" on which, Rousseau freely acknowledges, his own necessarily "speculative" counter-"history" of the formative, necessarily materially unlocatable "foundations of inequality among men," exposed in the *Discourse* named for them, must rely, the "inalienable" capacity for "free agency" theorized in tandem with that critical history is tied to the ability *not* to replicate an already artificially instituted *status quo*. That ability is afforded Rousseau, acting in his capacity to narrate a logical "fiction" of the "real" history and bases of social relations, by "discourse" itself, fitting generic title of his conceptually revolutionary, internationally outlawed text on the joint trajectory of society and inequality, as well as of its internationally celebrated predecessor, the prize-winning *Discourse on whether the Arts and Sciences Improve Morals*. Because discourse, too, "*is*" only its enactment, rather than a positive object or historical fact, it has the inalienable ability to enable the kind of "change" and empirically untethered "exchanges" (of appearance for reality, and inequality for equality) that the Second Discourse demystifies and so acts, on pain of exile for its author, against. Just as nothing – including its own entirely differential materiality – within or about discursive activity is natural, the only "natural" condition of discourse, language, is the condition of history itself.

The choice, then, is not and can in fact never have been between language and matter, language and history, language and "difference," or language and politics and political theory, or, in a larger hermeneutic sense, text and context. Indeed, in that they frame inherently conjoined subject matters as opposed, such choices are "false" or, at best, "Solomonic" to begin with, the exclusion of one or the other side of their proposal resulting in the demise of both, which is to say, the whole.

The theorists and authors of agency – of "standing a chance" – investigated in this study and its companion volume not only undermine such dichotomous understandings but underscore why understanding as such is sidelined by their pursuit. Chief among these is Kant, who, long relegated to "the dustbin of history" by most (while, significantly, not all) neo-Marxian materialist and post-Marxist cultural–social or "anthropomorphic" theory, first hypothesized that both historical agency and the capacity for "judgment" with which it is intertwined depend upon a self- and empirically alienating "faculty" for speech. Just as no language is purely ideational, void of externalization or materialization of some kind, so no language is "individual:" all languages require what Kant calls the "unresearchable" "common" "ground" of more than one mind. Not only the capacity for, but the actual acts of speech that, according to Kant, the specifically *non*cognitive activity we call "judgment" entails, are described as inherently shared by the subject who articulates them with all other potential speakers. Kant disingenuously calls this heretofore untheorized, intersubjective capacity a "faculty" of "common sense" whose own either experiential or *a priori* origin he does not pretend to know, and asserts he "neither can nor want[s] to investigate at present."[iii] Yet the capacity for "common sense" on which, Kant states in the *Critique of Judgment*, his thoroughly revolutionary theory of judgment (counter-intuitively) depends, is anything but the familiar recourse to platitudinous, "commonsensical" prejudice that Kant consistently derided as anti-philosophical and regressively anti-critical throughout both his metaphysical (or, in Kant's terms, "speculative") and historical and political writings.

The first, introductory Chapter of this book, "Before Judgment: Doing without Knowing," describes Diderot's and Kant's necessarily hypothetical accounts of actions undertaken by subjects forced to constitute a common means of communication (be it experiential and "nominal," or "real," i.e., for Kant, mathematical or moral, in purport) from epistemologically inadequate sensations. By contrast, Chapter Two, "The 'Condition' of Judgment: Kant's 'Common Sense,' or the Origin of Language in the *Third Critique*," analyzes the active interrelation of noncognitive phenomenal experience with subjective feeling at the origin of what Kant calls the "power" of aesthetic judgment, the "faculty" within each subject for producing the particular *intersubjective* sense communicated uniquely by linguistic predication. Rather than prescribing rules for aesthetic judgment, Kant instead describes it as a "free" act of articulation. The Chapter includes a comparative analysis of the related role of *negative* – missing or alienating – phenomenal experience in the differing accounts of the "origin" of language hypothesized by Rousseau and Diderot, and concludes with a preliminary discussion of Wordsworth's representations of the alienation of the human power of linguistic articulation itself, the eclipses of both knowledge and judgment in which Wordsworth's purposeful excursions into the phenomenal world repetitively result.

In contrast to the "common," *signifying rather than sensible* "sense" theorized as the "condition" ("Bedingung") of judgment by Kant, the second Part of this study, "Missing Sense and Poetics," analyzes how the absence of immediate, perceptible "sense" explicitly results in the active engagement with signification we call poetics. In this it follows Kant's own lead. For, when Kant self-critically acknowledges, at

---

iii. Kant's longstanding criticism and thoroughly original repurposing of the well-worn term, "common sense," are discussed in detail in Chapter Two below. For his demurral to investigate the temporal origin of the faculty he calls by that same name, see Chapter Two, Section One, n. 57.

the opening of the Second Book of the *Critique of Pure Reason,* that his theory of "representation[al]" knowledge of perceived phenomena lacks an explanation of how we produce representations capable of "synthesi[zing]" "heterogeneous" – "sensory" and "intellectual" – capacities for perception in the first place, he proceeds to posit a new "internal," non-sensory capacity precisely to fill that lack. He calls that capacity "the schema," and his invention and extraordinary representation of the schema in a purely graphic figure, that of an identifying sign or "monogram of the imagination *a priori*" (*Kritik der reinen Vernunft* B 181), is not only a practical act of poetic production in its own right. It is one Kant links explicitly to how all "poets" do what they do.

For "poetry," Kant states in the *Critique of Judgment,* occupies "the highest rank among all the arts" specifically because of the active "use" to which "poets" put the perceptible world we all regularly represent to ourselves. "Poets," he remarks, purpose those sensible givens into a sign or "schema for the supersensible" (*Kritik der Urteilskraft* B 215), and thus, by implication, into a sign of just such an (imagined) "*a priori*" "imagination" itself. Furthermore, just as the "schema" that enables our capacity to make cognitions out of perceptions can find no basis in external objects and contexts outside itself, so the faculty for judgment that, like poetry, Kant states, lacks a "field of objects of its own" (*Kritik der Urteilskraft* BXXII–XXIII), also apprehends any and all objects differently, which is to say, not cognitively but imaginatively, with experiences of "feeling" *a posteriori* rather than schematic "representations" *a priori* operative at its base. Kant's description of the "schema" as the imprint of an *a priori* power of "pure imagination" acting upon experience in the *Critique of Pure Reason,* and of the "schema"-like use of "nature" by "poetry" in the *Critique of Judgment,* thus effectively and fundamentally crosses his theory of cognition with poetics.

In this Kant's theory of judgment also critically illuminates the otherwise unfathomable basis of what we may instead call cognitive criminality, too real consequence of the material negation of agency that the second Part of this book next explores. Chapter Three includes an analysis of Arendt's infamous description of Adolf Eichmann as someone who, above all, "lacked imagination" – for Arendt, the basic ability to view those "outside" him as other than external material bodies. Obscured in the controversy resulting from Arendt's unconventional account, the Chapter argues, is the basis of its formulation, her analysis of the way in which acts of judgment (and their absence) both manifest themselves and prove immeasurably consequential. Arendt attended Eichmann's trial as a reporter, and she came to her conclusion based not on the detailed documentation of his deeds that made the trying of the accused a mere formality in the juridical sense, but on the words in which Eichmann, speaking, so to speak, "on the stand," described them and himself. Arendt listened to the words Eichmann chose, and what she heard in his representation of himself, as "mere" executor rather than agent of industrial deportation and mass murder, was someone entirely capable of organizing and executing the functional logistics of international genocide because he saw no difference between genocide and insecticide, between the methodical destruction of elementary organisms and of living human bodies equally classed as pestilent matter. Eichmann felt no guilt for his actions because he had, in short, no concept of agency; in the same terms of Kant's *Third Critique* that would later be investigated by Arendt herself, he lacked the apparently banal faculty for enacting universally shared or "common sense" required for "think[ing] from the standpoint of somebody else." In making her logically paradoxical argument for the "banality" of Eichmann's absolute amorality, it is to that "lack of imagination," of any capacity to see more than what meets the eye – to regard other persons not merely as the stuff of disposable objects but as subjects composed of lives undergone and made, with thoughts, experiences, recognitions, understandings and abilities of their own – that she attributes Eichmann's equally absolute inability to "judge his actions in the very sense that understanding requires imagination for judgment." The key to understanding and judging Eichmann's actions in turn lies not in replacing the interaction of understanding and imagination by sensationalism, the same conceptual leveling of persons with matter that enabled acts of mass murder in the first place, but in the radically non-sensationalist notion of a capacity for shared or "common sense," or, in the commonplace terms in which Pinter's first-person speaks in *non propria* persona to an other, the "standing" by which, "*at least, you stand a chance.*"

Kant's and Arendt's central conceptions of the dependence of judgment upon imagination bring the "common" "ground" on which both philosophy and literature "stand" into relief. Rather than reify or naturalize that "ground," both the second Part of this study and its companion volume, *Words' Worth*, examine literary works in which internal as well as sensible bases of judgment are directly put to the test. First among these are Kleist's unparalleled narratives of unaccountable actions whose unfolding parameters defy all available evidence, "The Marquise of O . . ." and "The Duel" ("Der Zweikampf"). Comparing Kant's critical theory of limited representational cognition with the critique of just such knowledge effectively dramatized by all of Kleist's fictions, Chapter Four proceeds to analyses of how the actors of the stories manage to get so much wrong for so long. Not only the agent but actual occurrence of the punctual act from whose "unwitting conception" the story of "The Marquise von O—" devolves, remain intractably difficult to identify, both for the Marquise directly affected and altered by that action and for the reader of Kleist's inimitable prose. By direct contrast, although "The Duel," like "The Marquise . . .," owes its narration to a pointedly transgressive event, the empirical vehicle, occurrence and impact of that event are all graphically represented in its very first sentence. What the ensuing story instead represents is a highly entailed history of how the ascription of agency to that event, its "judgment," eventually, indeed involuntarily takes place: how the subject of agency is not only mis-taken and the actions that are the objects of judgment, switched, but the empirical attention of those judging them is disastrously distracted from one theater of judgment to the next before recognizing the literally legible marks of agency for what they are. Named for a ceremonially sanctified ("göttlich") "contest" or "conflict" ("Kampf") between "two" combatants ("Zwei"), entered so as to determine the truth or falsity of contradictory testimony in a capital case, Kleist's *sui generis* "Zweikampf" instead piles uncertainty upon uncertainty, as the outcome of a duel designed specifically to manifest the verdict of God, too, comes, with time, into doubt. Even the conflicting first-person accounts of events that spur the duel are ultimately re-enacted by the duel itself, for this is a physical fight to the death of which, with every passing day narrated, no certain victor can be sensibly discerned. The story of "the duel" thus makes of every reader a "critical" reader of the actions it represents, presenting in the realist terms of a mimetic or worldly fiction the precise quandary, of non-communication between knowledge and action, conceptual understanding and "feeling," to which Kant's theory of "judgment" responds. Rather than delaying, in the mode of a mystery story, the revelation of the agent responsible for a particular event, both "Die Marquise ..." and "The Duel" compel their confounded subjects and readers alike to *question* "where" – in what intellectual or sensory capacity – and "when" (whether "a priori" or "a posteriori" to experience), the common basis (or, in Kant's terms, "condition") of acts of judgment lies.

Finally, the complementary volume to this study, *Words' Worth: What the Poet Does,* examines the active effects of language upon the capacity for human agency itself. The "real" relations between perception, action, "feeling," and language, taken full-circle by Wordsworth's definitions and practice of the production of poetry, tie the extended discussion of the poet's explicit poetic theory to analyses of some of his most dynamic "scenes" of action in *The Prelude,* in Part One of that study, and to individual "Lucy poems" and the invocation of "Imagination" and subsequent "Gondo Gorge" description at the highpoint of *The Prelude* (Bk VI) in Part Two. In Part Three, these analyses of poetic texts find their counterpart in fictive and speculative accounts, by Rousseau, Diderot, Hegel, Wordsworth, and Proust, of the "real" limit (or, in Proust's and Wordsworth's words, "horizon") enabling both internal *and* material experience to occur. As for Wordsworth, writing as theorist of poetics, so for these ineffaceably effective analysts of the historical production of meaning, neither given objects nor self-crediting subjects but actions relating them within the world – the "acting and re-acting" of "man and the objects that surround him" – define not only the poet's "subject matter" but the subject, any otherwise undefined woman or man. While the purposefully "prosaic" language and settings of his poetry have led to his own construal as complacent "nature poet," Wordsworth emphasizes, with a specificity perhaps only matched by Kant, that "poets" can only be identified by what they "*do*." "What then does the Poet?" he asks directly, in the "Preface to *Lyrical Ballads*," and his response, that poets act to "construct," for re-enactment in the reader's mind, "complex scene[s]" of interaction between subjects and objects, further specifies that the "language" in which they "do" this must be as integral to the act of representation as objects and subjects are to experience itself. Rather than reiterate the inert inventory of an "inherited," "pre-coded" lexicon, any poet "worth" the name will write in the active, consequential, and thus "more permanent," "real" and "philosophical language of poetry," which is not only *not* opposed to the "prosaic," but indeed indistinguishable from the "common" language shared by all.

In this, words most resemble not each other, but rather what they are not, name and describe. Wordsworth's celebrated defense of the "language really used by men," and rejection, in theory and in practice, of stilted "poetic diction," reflect his explicit view that the active "interest" which "the mind attaches to words" owes to their status "not only as symbols ..., but as *things*, active and efficient ... themselves." In reconceiving and employing the everyday "real language of men," as Kant's theory of judgment employs the prosaic predicative language he calls "common sense," Wordsworth's poetic theory indicates that the "inter-acti[ons]" "the Poet considers" are those in which words are co-participants. His ordinary language representations not only set the physical, geometrically delineable "scene" for individual acts staged to conflict with their own scenography – with localization of any kind – but communicate the "sense" of profound disorientation they enact both outwardly and inwardly, rendering every imaginative thwarting of imagination, like "winds thwarting winds" (*Prelude* VI: 631), the perceptible object of its own "contemplation" in "thought."

Like Wordsworth, all the authors discussed in *Words' Worth* understand the *representational* relation between experience and "communicability" to be as conflicted (or, as Hegel writes, "essentially ambiguous") as it is opaque. And, like Wordsworth's, the extraordinary power of their individual descriptions of that relation owes in part to their fundamental recognition that any "sense" of experience, no matter how banal or particular, depends upon a "common" faculty or ability which, first made operative by way of "words" or some other equally common means of potentially unlimited semantic scope, is itself enabled by its own formative delimitation from other kinds of activity. For, unlike either traditional ideas of existential "Being" considered "pure" of either embodiment or effect, or their "new" sensualist replacement by appeals to "energies" of "emotion" or "affect," action effected upon "condition" is consequential because defined *against* something else, and the non-naïve, or consciously impure understanding of experience and materiality these authors share keep that conditionality – like Proust's "real horizon" – in view.[iv]

---

iv. By contrast, for unstintingly naïve conflations of poetics and a "utopian" politics revealed in "political-poetic transport[s]" of "feeling" and "sensation," see the breathless pronouncements of their entirely metaphoric unification in Rancière, *Flesh of Words: The Politics of Writing*, trans. Charlotte Mandell (Palo Alto: Stanford University Press, 2004 [*La chair des mots. Politique de l'écriture* (Paris, 1998)]), pp. 14–21, esp., in which "nature, " "liberty," "the Revolution," "revelation," "humanity," "lyric subjectivity" and "community" are all rapidly synthesized within an "immediate meaning of the sensory" purportedly "recognized" by (of all people) Wordsworth. Cf. Rancière, "Aesthetics as Politics," in *Aesthetics and its Discontents*, in which "politics" and "art" are not only both loosely equated with an entirely undefined "reframing of a material and symbolic space," but "the 'politics' of art," wholly figuratively defined as "suspending the normal coordinates of sensory experience," similarly distinguishes something called "'politics'" from something called "art" only by a euphemistic use of quotation marks (24–25) – whether to the greater detriment of politics or of art seems, from their empty *emboîtement* here, moot.

When, repeating the popular truism, "truth will out," we implicitly discount our ability to effect either conceptual or material difference, we also unwittingly make ourselves the punchline of an otherwise pointless joke, the sadistic prank played on his blind father by one of Shakespeare's more minor fools. In reciting, with all the gravity of received wisdom, the words of this conspicuously nonheroic "Launcelot" (surname "Gobbo"), we (unlike Shakespeare, *Merchant of Venice* [II. ii.74]) effectively confuse "truth" with nature. For it is nature that "will" always "out," of its "own" "accord:" no matter how forcefully compelled to serve other ends, nature "can" only and so will always remain true to its own causal physical laws. "Standing," the non-natural "condition" or "position" on the sole basis of which "you stand a chance," directly implies, by contrast, the act of "standing" apart: of declining or refusing to "sing from the same hymnal," to "sound" *like* a string of natural matter strung upon a supernatural universal lyre of purely sensory accord. In so declining, in "sounding" differently, agency departs from mere *aesthesis*. In place of the sensational, it composes problems of "sense." But departures of any kind depend upon the pivotal position represented by "standing" in the first place, the non-natural "ground" and possibility of action that alone links any, always only partially material subject – any "you" – to another, fully absent of determination, that is, "chance."

Pinter, who knew a thing or two about political as well as dramaturgical discourse and action, knew that the basis and object of both is "standing a chance:" that nothing can happen, in the most consequential sense of the possible, without actors or agents whose words and actions stand apart from their self-replicating context, whether that context be the mind-numbing "non-sense" of space-filling, time-killing "small talk," equally nonsensical conceits bearing the trademark stamp of "poetic diction" – materiality without meaningful, because lacking actively "differ[ing]," significance – or the wholly reactive, mechanical mutations of purely material *physis* itself.

If, to paraphrase Wordsworth's "Preface" together with Kant's, the only "purpose" of "critique" "worthy of the name" is to bring its own basis and object into relief, so as to make their own effectivity known, their and others' pivotal works written during the "time" of reflection Kant dubbed "our" "age of critique" – which is to say, any "time" "we" participate in the unprescripted "realm" of judgment, or in Wordsworth's words, that we "communicate" the "material difference" enacted in "the language really used by men" – have themselves formed the basis and object of the present work, producing actions whose ongoing effects this study can only preface.

Chapter 1

INTRODUCTION:
BEFORE JUDGMENT: DOING WITHOUT KNOWING IN KANT AND DIDEROT

The double participial phrase, "doing without knowing," can be understood in at least two principal ways. First and most obviously, doing without knowing means doing something without actively knowing it or without knowing *what* it is one is doing. However, when the second of the present participles, "knowing," is understood as a substantive rather than an active verb, then "doing without knowing" means doing without the thing, state or capability we call knowing *while* knowing one is doing so, acting, carrying on, in spite of and in the face of this lack. In proverbial English, "doing without" may, of course, also be used alone, or without object, to mean "making do without," in the sense of *faire suffire*, or "getting on with it," persevering in whatever one is doing, even while knowing that one is missing a key ingredient, an otherwise essential part of the process involved.

In the case of "doing without," then, "getting on *with it*" means "getting along" *without* something. Understood as action undertaken in the face of partial deprivation and real uncertainty as to its outcome, the expression, "doing without," carries *with* it the implication of something more: the ability to substitute something else for the elemental something one is missing. To do without is, in other words, to act effectively but to do so through indirection, to bring something about, to accomplish or arrive at, rather than directly cause a result by putting something to work in the place of something else one does not possess. In short, it is to act in the presence, and on the basis, of a representation: not a representation already ready to hand, whose use value, previously determined by past usage, is part of the practical, cognitive repertoire upon which the mind unreflectively relies, but a representation made to stand for something excluded from – unavailable or lost to – that repertoire, the knowledge, whether primary and empirical, or secondary, i.e., symbolic or semiotic, that one is missing.

Thus to do without knowing is not simply to continue on in the same course but rather to continue on in a course that we ourselves have altered by adding something extra and previously external to it. In that it causes us to "figure out" – determine or shape and bring to bear – the extra means that the act of "doing without" can do the most *with*, the mode of indirection whose natural ground is deprivation and whose product is a representation may provide us with our own grounds for reflection, for arriving at an understanding of the acquisition of knowledge itself. For what we do when we do without knowing produces knowledge that, rather than directly reflecting a foregone conclusion, comes about unforeseeably, *without* causal or conventional determination, and *with* the presence of something that effectively negates the negation or absence of something, a representation.

Thus, "doing without knowing" may mean living ignorance, pure and simple, an ongoing practice of accidental hit or miss, or it may mean, in a purposeful, constructive sense, acting so as to achieve an aim or bring something about despite the absence of the direct knowledge, means, or data that would facilitate, if not predetermine action in the first place. "Doing without knowing" may be as commonplace as ignoring what one does – as most of us, unconsciously or consciously, gracefully or catastrophically, do most of the time – but it may also be doing something different from the norm, something that, in its precise contours, cannot have been done before in that it requires, among other things, the real absence of positive information, whether apprehended by the senses in the present or passed along by an already mediated tradition (or "prejudice"), an absence that alone enables the real presence of ignorance, as well as its positively negative effects. Uncertain not only as to what he or she knows, but as to what one *can* know, and in possession of no "fall-back" position or perceptible path forward, the subject contrives another way of proceeding by putting another sensible form or object in position: the subject, any subject, in other words, represents.

Such uncertainty should be sharply distinguished from the all-too-handy refrain of self-exculpation, "Had I known then what I know now." This disclaimer of disastrous, typically vainglorious action implies that empirical ignorance, rather than personal interest and duplicity, at once causes our acts and exonerates us from all future responsibility for their consequences. Yet knowing this – that one can always plead former ignorance at a later date – is not to know nothing but, indeed, to know something, something of not only personal and calculable but historical and incalculable consequences, and to proceed or to continue to act, on the basis of it, is to shadow, if not eclipse the content of such an alibi with the conscious foreknowledge of its future rhetorical, exculpatory effect. Acting on the knowledge that one can always claim one acted out of ignorance is to clothe one's acts in the costume of a *Bildungsroman*, a ready-to-wear trope of self-serving de-indemnification passing itself off as innocence after the fact. Oriented instead, in their distinctive approaches to knowledge, toward our response to and responsibility for what we *do with experience*, as partial or limited as that experience may be, Kant and Diderot – distinct theorists of doing without knowing in their own right – refuse equally to confuse ignorance with innocence and the pursuit of self-interest with uncertainty, to tailor morality to the limits of cognition.

Before Kant theorized *judgment* as a specifically noncognitive activity directly dependent (as described in Part One of this study) upon our ability to communicate and be understood by others, and thus to speak, in effect, not merely for oneself but for "any" and "everyone" ("jedermann"), both Kant and Diderot related *cognitive* impasses to purposeful acts of representation. And while both Kant and Diderot divide such representations into markedly different kinds, each with its own referential title and mode, and while the two-sided (or, as Diderot might say, *amphibological*) subject matter of this introduction to a study of the internal relations linking judgment with poetics and action could likewise bear such bilateral subtitles as, "the Blind *and* the Deaf," "Metaphor *and* Gesture," "Hypothesis *and* Image," and "'Whatever-His-Name-Is' and 'Saunderson'" as well, any individual analysis of doing without knowing must begin with the frankly – because necessarily – figurative account in Kant's own prefatory description of all just such activity, his distinctly non-causal narrative, in the Second Preface to his First Critique "Vorrede zur zweiten Auflage," *(Kritik der reinen Vernunft,* 1787), of the impasses and blind "gropings" ("herumtappen") that, extending over millenia of scientific and mathematical ignorance, could only be interrupted by being radically disrupted, all then operative presumptions overturned, in the unforeseeable, because unprecedented intellectual actions that Kant calls "revolution[s] in mode of thinking" ("Revolution der Denkart").[1] To do without knowing in any of the senses that knowing has had before is what Kant repeatedly calls not a blunder or blindspot but, on the contrary, the necessary condition of each of the irreversible "revolution[s]" in our most fundamental powers of conception represented by Kant in the, by turns, retrospective and prospective narration of the history of ignorance and knowledge, from ancient thought onwards, with which his "Preface" begins. As Kant recounts it, the initial step undertaken in the first of these "revolution[s]," from recursively self-reinforcing ignorance into a practically constructive doing *without* knowing, was the turning of reason outward from its own internally formulated rules, the "formal," autonomous laws of "logic," or "rules of all thinking" ("die formalen Regeln alles Denkens"[2]). "Validated" as it is "bound" by "its limitation" to "abstract[ing] from all objects of knowledge and their differences" ("ihrer Eingeschränkung ..., dadurch sie berechtigt, ja verbunden ist, von allen Objekten der Erkenntnis und ihrem Unterschiede zu abstrahieren"), logic is "understanding having to do with nothing more than itself and its form" ("...der Logik, wo der Verstand es mit nichts weiter, als sich selbst und seiner Form zu tun hat").[3] The "revolution in mode of thinking" Kant first describes itself first turns outward, in an act neither logical nor illogical in

---

1. Immanuel Kant, *Werkausgabe*, 12 vols., ed. Wilhelm Weischedel (Frankfurt: Suhrkamp, 1977); *Kritik der reinen Vernunft* (hereafter *KrV*) B VII, XI, XIV, XV, XVI, XXII, XXX, III: 20, 22–25, 28, 33. See also, within the same 1787 Preface, the synonymous phrases: "Umänderung der Denkart" ("reversal" or "transformation in mode of thinking"); *KrV*, B XVI, III: 25, B XXIII, III: 28n; "Veränderung der Denkart" ("change in mode of thinking"), *KrV*, B XX, III: 27, B XXXII, III: 34; "veränderte Methode der Denkungsart" ("altered mode of thinking"), *KrV*, B XIX, III: 26; "gänzliche Revolution" ("total," "all-embracing revolution"), *KrV*, B XXIII, II: 28.

All further quotations from Kant in this study are from this edition. All translations from the German in this study are my own.

2. Kant, *KrV*, B IX, III: 21.
3. Kant, *KrV*, B IX, III: 21.

basis, toward precisely those heteronomous, empirical objects with which logically coherent understanding not only has "nothing to do," but *knows* that to be so in a positively negative (i.e., self-critical) sense. Yet, the orientation of reason toward the empirical world would have constituted a mere change of direction rather than "revolution," if it had not taken the further step of turning its outward trajectory – inflecting or angling it, so to speak – back toward the mind. Rather than merely reversing its own autonomous course, reason ,submitted to what Kant calls "critique" turns back upon itself *in conjunction with or relation to something else*. What returns to the purview of logic is not more, but something different from, logic, the content of which is specifically *not* the absence of content, or "abstraction from objects," that is the binding (negative) condition of logical positivism, but rather something positive that is also something negative, or positive only in part: something whose own "limited" relation to that which is outside and otherwise unrelated to the mind allows it to come under the purview of logic in the first place. Critically limited to "representations" (of experiential objects) that can be submitted to logic – even as the absence of any relation between things as such (or "in themselves") and the purely "formal rules of logic" remains intact – investigations of the empirical can begin to produce what Kant specifically calls "scientific" "*knowledge*," rather than an "inevitable" skepticism toward all epistemogical claims: a new "mode of thinking" according to which "reason," now "occupied not merely with itself, but also with objects" ("wenn [die Vernunft] nicht bloss mit sich selbst, sondern auch mit Objekten zu schaffen hat"), finally "forge[s] for itself the sure path of science" ("den sicheren Weg der Wissenschaft einzuschlagen").[4]

Perhaps most significantly, such "revolution[s] in mode of thinking" are *both concrete and conceptual* for Kant. They seamlessly join mind and world by laws both rational *and* sensuously perceptible, describing an actual revolution (or upending) of "method," by moving in two opposing trajectories at once.[5] Yet what is remarkable about the first of the individual "revolution[s]" whose story Kant tells, is that Kant knows he doesn't really know, and makes clear he doesn't really care to know, whom it is he is writing about: the actual name, historical circumstances and identity of the single subject ("eines einzigen Mannes") who carried this "endlessly extensive" ("in unendliche Weiten"), irreversible or "transhistorical" ("für alle Zeiten") movement out.[6] Well known for describing "genius" in the *Critique of Judgment* in terms directly reflecting those he reserves for poets, as the revolutionary ability to change the "rules" by which one's own and future work is judged, all Kant has to say about the first individual to "forge the sure path" of mathematical and scientific knowledge, and so to change forever the relationship, or lack thereof, between intellect and the world, is that he was (or turned out to be) a "fortunate fellow" ("Glückliche[r]") – some lucky guy.[7] This

4. Kant, *KrV* B IX, III: 21.
5. Kant, *KrV* B XXII, III: 28.
6. Kant, *KrV* B XI, III: 22.
7. Kant, *KrV* B XI, III: 22. On Kant on "genius," see Chapter Three, Section Three, n. 356; Section Four, n. 366.

historically speculative passage from the Second Preface to the First Critique is worth quoting at some length not only for its rare, explicitly narrative account of the relationships – between ignorance and representation, construction and knowledge, and forgettable and unforgettable time – involved in our comprehension of matters, real and abstract, to which judgment does not apply, but also because of its own unvarnished, widely unrecognized admission of ignorance on Kant's part. The pointed assertion, by its author, himself, arguably, the greatest epistemologist in history, of neither knowing nor caring to know how and to whom the inaugural "revolution" in conceptual history he is describing occurred, makes Kant's narrative of the first imperishable, intellectually and historically transformative "mode of thinking" one whose reading should also always give pause:

> From the earliest times from which the history of human reason reaches forward, in the admirable people of the Greeks, mathematics has taken the sure path of a science. Yet one should not think that it was as easy for mathematics as it was for logic to find, or rather, forge that royal path in which reason has only to do with itself. I believe rather that – especially under the Egyptians – things long remained at a [blind] groping about [*ein Herumtappen*], and that this transformation is to be ascribed to a *revolution* which the lucky notion [*der glückliche Einfall*] of a single man brought into existence in one attempt [or 'experiment:' *Versuch*], from which, going forward, the path that one had to take was no longer to be missed, and the sure way of science was struck and marked for all times and into endless expanses. The history of this revolution in mode of thinking, which was far more important than the discovery of the passage around the Cape of Good Hope, and of the happy [or "the fortunate:" *Glücklichen*] one who brought it into being, is not preserved for us. Still the legend, transmitted to us by *Diogenes Laertius*, that names the supposed inventor of the smallest elements of geometrical demonstrations – which, according to common judgment, did not even necessitate proof – indicates that the memory of the change effected with the first trace [*Spur*] of the discovery of this new way must have seemed so extremely important to mathematicians that it thereby became unforgettable. A *light* went on in the one who demonstrated the equilateral *triangle* (whether Thales or whatever one wishes to call him); for he found that he must not trace after that which he saw in the figure, or take away, so to speak, its characteristics from the mere concept of it, but bring [these] forward, through that which he, according to concepts that he himself *a priori* thought into it and represented (through construction); and that, in order to know something *a priori* with certainty, he must not include in the thing anything other than that which necessarily follows from what he himself has put in it according to his concept.
>
> [Die *Mathematik* ist von den frühesten Zeiten her, wohin die Geschichte der menschlichen Vernunft reicht, in dem bewundernswürdigen Volke der Griechen den sichern Weg einer Wissenschaft gegangen. Allein man darf nicht denken, dass es ihr so leicht geworden, wie der Logik, wo die Vernunft es nur mit sich

selbst zu tun hat, jenen königlichen Weg zu treffen, oder vielmehr sich selbst zu bahnen; vielmehr glaube ich, dass es lange mit ihr (vornehmlich noch unter den Ägyptern) beim Herumtappen geblieben ist, und diese Umänderung einer Revolution zuzuschreiben sei, die der glückliche Einfall eines einzigen Mannes in einem Versuche zu Stande brachte, von welchem an die Bahn ... und der sichere Gang einer Wissenschaft für alle Zeiten und in unendliche Weiten eingeschlagen und vorgezeichnet war. Die Geschichte dieser Revolution der Denkart, welche viel wichtiger war als die Entdeckung des Weges um das berühmte Vorgebirge, und des Glücklichen, der sie zu Stande brachte, ist uns nicht aufbehalten. Doch beweiset die Sage, welche Diogenes der Laertier uns überliefert, der von den kleinsten, und, nach dem gemeinen Urteil, gar nicht einmal eines Beweises benötigten, Elementen der geometrischen Demonstrationen den angeblichen Erfinder nennt, dass das Andenken der Veränderung, die durch die erste Spur der Entdeckung dieses neuen Weges bewirkt wurde, den Mathematikern äusserst wichtig geschienen haben müsse, und dadurch unvergesslich geworden sei. Dem esten, der den gleichseitigen *Triangel* demonstrierte (er mag nun Thales oder wie man will geheissen haben), dem ging ein *Licht* auf; denn er fand, dass er nicht dem, was er in der Figur sahe, oder auch dem blossen Begriffe derselben nachspüren und gleichsam davon ihre Eigenschaften ablernen, sondern durch das, was er nach Begriffen selbst a priori hineindachte und darstellte (durch Konstruktion), hervorbringen müsse, und dass, er, um sicher etwas a priori zu wissen, er der Sache nichts beilegen müsse, als was aus dem notwendig folgte, was er seinem Begriffe gemäss selbst in sie gelegt hat.[8]]

"The first one (whether Thales or whatever one wants to call him) in whom a light went on ...": Kant has managed to transmute the founding "legend" of geometry into a story about some whatever-his-name-is into whose head at some unknown time, following successive centuries of groping or tapping blindly about ("Herumtappen"), a lucky notion ("glückliche[r] Einfall") happened to fall. What fell, the content of that singular event ("Einfall" literally: "single" or "one fall," or, in its anglicized Latin equivalent, "singular case"), was, to be more exact, nothing less than the first equilateral triangle, a form born neither of what whatever-his-name-is "saw in the figure" of such a triangle with his own eyes ("nicht dem, was er in der Figur sahe") nor what he derived or took away from the mere concept of such a form ("oder auch dem blossen Begriffe derselben nachspüren und gleichsam davon ihre Eigenschaften ablernen ... müsse"). Rather, the production of this form joined together, for the first, and at one and the "same" time, two radically heterogeneous modes of bringing (mathematical) knowledge about: intellectual, or object-independent conceptualization *and* linear or physical representation, "what he himself according to concepts thought into it *and* represented (through construction)" ("was er nach Begriffen selbst a priori hineindachte und darstellte [durch Konstruktion]"). The term by which the "single man" we "call" "Kant"

8. Kant, *KrV* B XI–XII, III: 22 (emphasis in text)

designates the heterogeneous action he describes here is itself no less simultaneously conceptual *and* representational, which is to say, irreducibly *figural*. For the "revolution" ("in mode of thinking") to which Kant refers repeatedly in the Second Preface comprises the same double movement definitive of an actual "revolution" (in space). All revolutions revolve around a fixed countervailing force, a limit holding its purely dynamic – undelimited and nonfigurative, and thus formally violent – motion in check. A figure representing a movement outward that is thus simultaneously oriented inward, Kant's "revolution in mode of thinking" is a turn to the empirical constrained by its equal footing in something unmoving, an equivocal grounding in a subject that both produces that motion, or "change," in the first place and is the unequivocal condition for its "memory" thereafter, the necessary basis for the "extensive" reception, imprinting and transmission of its "trace" "for all time," without which it would be lost, among innumerable motions, to time and mind in space. The "revolution" called "critique" that Kant introduces into "thinking," the "unprecedented notion," "*casus*" or case that happened to occur or "fall" not in space but within him, as thinking subject, produces a conscious "construction" of something external defined only by what he (or any "what's-his-name") can "th[ink] into it *a priori*," that is, to begin with: a "representation," rather than merely notional conjecture or misplaced logical projection, made of reason 'applied' ("angewandt") to what, by definition, is not homogeneous with reason, the "temporally extant" ("Dasein in der Zeit"), "external" ("ausser"), rather than purely ideational, empirical world.[9]

Now Kant is, of course, well known for declaring the supposedly 'rationalist' Enlightenment dictum that reason must somehow take itself in hand, or rather – in the actual terms of Kant's non-rationalist, critical view – in both, heterogeneous, or at least nonidentical hands: that it must go to nature ("an die Natur gehen") with "its principles" "in one hand" ("in einer Hand") and "the experiment" ("mit dem Experiment"), that it has "thought out" ("ausdachte") according to these principles, "in the other" ("in der anderen").[10] Less well known, if indeed even acknowledged, is the apparently endless *Herumtappen* that precedes such ventures: the many centuries ("so viel Jahrhunderte") – themselves neither strictly rational nor irrational in character – of feeling one's way, of tapping blindly about, trying out this potential path or that, this or that hypothetical approach to knowing the external world, before, for no apparent reason, reason appears, to an undetermined individual at an undetermined moment in time, in the "construction" of a concrete "representation" of the laws governing it *and* the external world. Kant offers no step-by-step, rational-analytic account of a progressive development toward Enlightenment, to reason revealing, and revealed by, the sensory world in a representation pertaining to both. Instead, he repeatedly names this abrupt, two-sided illumination ("dem ging ein Licht auf") of our internal capability to cognize the external world "eine Revolution," employing that word at least six times in the first few pages of the Second Preface, just as he uses the pointedly prosaic

9. Kant, *KrV* B XL–XLI, III: 38–9.
10. Kant, *KrV* B XIV, III: 23.

"Herumtappen" four times, beginning in the first paragraph, and the even more philosophically heterodox "Einfall," at least twice.[11] Rather than a developmental, step-by-step process, that sudden "insight" or "fall" into representation and out of ignorance obviously owes a debt to ignorance, a real absence of knowledge that cannot be papered-over "unter blossen Begriffen" ("under mere concepts"), merely conceptualized – or as Kant might say, "erdichtet" ("fictionalized") – away. It is a doing *without* knowing, and, what is the same for Kant, *with no known language*, neither *Reden* ("speeches") nor *Ausreden* ("excuses") ready to hand, that finds itself compelled outward to the physical world, forced to commit perceptible forms of representation that remove the problem from the inadequate province of the mind alone, so that an "Einfall" becomes simultaneously – following Kant's rotational model – what one might call a kind of "Ausfall," something heretofore invisible that falls instead from the mind outward. An exteriorization as external as a source of light, this revolutionary combination of conceptual with material form, in the graphically visible "construction" of a new basis for mathematics and physics alike, presents the inside of thinking turned out.

That centuries of blind missteps precede moments of "enlightenment" is the shared, barely narrative characteristic of the history not only of mathematics but of natural science and metaphysics on Kant's account, centuries of *Herumtappen* interrupted by periodic "revolution[s] in mode of thinking." And these inexplicable inventions of new and effective modes of knowledge are expressed by Kant in terms as graphically prosaic as any his or any language may possess – that of "a light" "going on in whomever-it-is" who spontaneously realizes and, in so doing, composes that mode. In Kant, knowledge itself is no incremental transition of a thinking subject out of the ignorance we call darkness, but the sudden availability to mind, composed by the mind, of a form, "path" or "mode" for thinking itself.

Precisely when and why the light dawned on whatever-his-name-is, we do not know; we don't know the nature of its origin, the "what" that could have caused it, nor the "who" that perceived it, the certain, historical identity of him in or upon whom it first shone. Indeed, Kant makes light of the "legendary" account of such particulars, claiming instead, both in significant agreement with and no less significant divergence from Husserl 150 years later,[12] that "the first trace" ("die erste

---

11. "Revolution": *KrV* B XI, III: 22 (twice); B XIII; III: 23 (twice); B XVI, III: 23; B XXII, III: 28; likewise "Umänderung der Denkart": *KrV* B XVI, III: 25; B XXIII, III: 28; "Herumtappen": *KrV* B VII, X: 20; B XI, III: 22; B XXV, III: 24 (twice); "Einfall": *KrV* B XI, III: 22; B XIII, II: 22.

12. See Edmund Husserl, "Die Frage nach dem Ursprung der Geometrie als intentional-historisches Problem," ed. Eugen Fink, *Revue internationale de la philosophie* 1, 1939, pp, 203–225 (written 1936); *L'origine de la géométrie*, trans. Jacques Derrida, Paris, 1962; reprinted as "Beilage III," in *Die Krisis der europäischen Wissenschaften und Phänomenologie*, ed. Walter Biemel, *Husserliana* 6 (The Hague: Martin Nijhoff, 1954), pp. 365–86; *The Crisis of European Sciences and Transcendental Phenomenology*, trans. David Carr (Evanston, IL: Northwestern University Press, 1970), pp. 353–78.

Spur") of the origin of geometry "must have appeared [so] extremely important to mathematicians" ("den Mathematikern äusserst wichtig geschienen haben müsse) as to "become unforgettable" ("und dadurch unvergesslich geworden sei"); that is, the origin of geometry, the "change that ... was effected" ("d[ie] Veränderung, die ... bewirkt wurde') with the first external "marking" ("vorgezeichnet") of its "founding principle" ("Grundsatz") and principal form, never required, thanks to that original externalization, either additional reasoning or external recording to be reborn (Husserl, by contrast, ultimately arguing instead that the origin of geometry must be repeated – and can only be repeated – in its written form).[13]

By contrast, we *do* know that Kant's *own* "revolution in mode of thinking" is now known as his "Copernican turn" after the comparative model he provides of Copernicus' conceptual turning of the tables between heaven and earth, his successful mental "experiment" of "turning the spectator outward" and "leaving the stars in peace" (*"Kopernikus* ... der ... versuchte, ob es nicht besser gelingen möchte, wenn er den Zuschauer sich drehen, und dagegen die Sterne in Ruhe liess").[14] Whenever and however "a light came on for" Kant remains as unknown as ever, but the known name he attaches to its advent "by analogy" (with "the examples of mathematics and natural science") provides the manner in which it will be imagined thence.[15] Kant's references to "Copernicus" and "whatever-his-name-is" stand for the two different versions – the former, necessarily entirely theoretical or intellectual (or, as Kant repeatedly states, "hypothetical" in origin[16]), the latter, specifically sensuously "represented," a graphic "construction" – of "revolution[s] in mode of thinking" that the theoretical hypothesis of Kant's own *Critique* combines. For Kant's *Critique* employs hypothetical, philosophical means to replace not-knowing with knowing by redefining knowledge itself *as* the construction of *discursive* representations. While non-hypothetical and non-discursive linear constructions of purely logical geometrical figures can be transmitted discursively only by "legend," Kant observes, since they are realized in independence of the impure "logic" of discourse to begin with, so Kant's own critical hypothesis, transmitted in this narrative and explanatory "Preface" to his First Critique, enacts a "revolution" in the history of thinking about thinking, or philosophy. The difference between a partly sense-dependent, logically developed scientific or philosophical hypothesis and a non-sense-based, intellectually realized mathematical construction, then, is the difference between employing the discursive language at hand – an already codified, signifying and empirically referential system of representation – and inventing a newly configured language

---

13. Kant, *KrV* B XI, III: 22.
14. Kant, *KrV* B XVI, III: 25.
15. *Ibid.*
16. Kant, *KrV* B XXII, III: 28n: "what Copernicus took only as an hypothesis to begin with ... in this Preface I pose the transformation in mode of thinking put forth in the Kritik also only as an hypothesis analogous to that hypothesis" ("was *Kopernikus* anfänglich nur als Hypothese annahm...Ich stelle in dieser Vorrede, die in der Kritik vorgetragene, jener Hypothese analogische, Umänderung der Denkart auch nur als Hypothese auf").

or significant form for which, like the first equilateral triangle, there were no empirical referents. A language which positively replaces something *missing* – whether the indubitable laws governing a mathematical figure, or the "synthetic judgment[s] *a priori*" upon which a theory of knowledge impervious to empirical skepticism must be based – might also be called, in the strictest sense, a language of poetry. For poetic language, by definition, effects a cognitive "revolution" in that it replaces not-knowing by a partly conceptual, partly formal, and thus always in some way analogizing knowledge inseparable from the acts of inaugural representation that produce it: a language that names the "change" in conception it itself effects – that, as all "poetic" language by definition does, *does what it says*. Before judgment, in Kant's words, "speaks for everyone" on the basis of *non*cognitive sensory experience – the subject of Part One of this book – the dependence of knowledge upon the formation of language in the *absence* of any otherwise available means of cognition, which is to say, by indirected or "reflected" means of "metaphor" ("réfléchie de la métaphore"[17]), is explored at the limit of sensory experience by Diderot.

Dr. Nicholas Saunderson (1682–1737), Professor of Mathematics at Cambridge, is Diderot's Copernicus, a real historical figure, blind from birth, creator of a tactile algebraic calculator, author of *The Elements of Algebra* (orig. pub. 1740), and imputed originator of Bayles' Theorem (of dual factor probability), but perhaps most widely known posthumously in his largely fictive role as the ventriloquized speaker of Diderot's "Lettre sur les aveugles à l'usage de ceux qui voient" (1749) ("Letter on the blind as used by those who see"). In a fabricated deathbed colloquoy with a similarly fictional stand-in for another actual historical figure, the Reverend Gervaise Holmes, Diderot's "Saunderson" espouses the Lucretian, or Diderotian, view of nature as a series of accidental combinations devoid of higher purpose or plan (which is to say, of a beneficent God), a world "rapidly" composed and decomposed of random beings, monstrous more often than not, that destroy each other in successive "revolutions:" "What is this world, Mr. Holmes? ... a rapid succession of beings," "monsters [that] are successively annihilated," "a composite subject to revolutions, all of which indicate a continual tendency to destruction" ("Qu'est-ce que ce monde, monsieur Holmes? ... une succession rapide d'êtres," "des monstres [qui] se sont anéantis successivement," "un composé sujet à des révolutions, qui toutes indiquent une tendance continuelle à la destruction"[18]). Entirely scripted by Diderot, "Saunderson"'s (necessarily) hypothetical description of the infinite and transitory permutations of life, "revolutions" that destroy as they compose the world we see, and the myriad, imperfect "worlds" that, produced by those revolutions, are as invisible to the sighted as they are impalpable to his own sense of touch – "[h]ow many misshapen, failed worlds have been dissipated, reformed, and dissipate every

17. Denis Diderot, *Oeuvres complètes* (hereafter *OC*), 25 vols, ed. H. Dieckmann, J. Fabre, J. Proust, with J. Varloot, (Paris: Hermann, 1975–), IV: 41. All translations from the French in this study are my own.
18. Diderot, *OC*, IV: 48–52.

instant in distant spaces which I do not touch and you do not see" ("Combien de mondes estropiés, manqués, se sont dissipés, se reforment et se dissipent peut-être à chaque instant dans des espaces eloignés, où je ne touche point, et vous ne voyez pas"[19]) – proved so imaginatively and logically convincing as to jump the bar between reality and fiction and land its real author in the Vincennes prison.

More than the immediately preceding work, *Pensées philosophiques* (1746), or the subsequent *De l'interprétation de la nature* (1753), it is in the "Lettre sur les aveugles," in which an historically known blind person is made to speak for Diderot, articulating the limits – indeed, the anti-empirical "blindness" – of religious dogma no less than the anti-philosophical "blindness" of reductive empirical positivisms, that Diderot represents the possibility of worlds to which direct sensory perception does not pertain. What better speaker than a sensorily deprived mathematician to hypothesize the logical probability of unknown "spaces" of living matter's constant transformation, arguing persuasively, to his author's own peril, for knowledge constituted on the basis of experiment or experience: "expérience" that always knows itself, however, to be inexhaustive, which is to say, to be, at every moment, historical, situational, limited.

And it is a blind mathematician who, knowing he must do without knowledge based entirely and directly on sense perception, invents the analogue in language to Kant's "happy notions:" "happy expressions" that "proper to one sense ... are at the same time metaphorical to another" out of necessity ("des expressions heureuses ... propre à un sens ... et métaphorique en même temps à un autre sens"), and thus shed a "reflected" "double light" ("la lumière réfléchie;" "une double lumière"[20]) – i.e., a light revealing at once both the activity of the subject and materiality of the object – to the mind of anyone who hears or reads it. It is in this "double," hybrid or Kantian cognitive sense that those compelled to fabricate a mode of substitution for a missing sense most successfully represent the incomplete nature of all human experience, supplementing, through a combination of logic and the always partly analogical work of imagination, the absolute knowledge that we, as human subjects, must lack, not in spite but because of our always incomplete experience of any sensible object or context.

By contrast with his "Saunderson," Diderot's *muet de convention*, and *sourd et muet de naissance* ("mute by convention" and "deaf and mute from birth"), fictive subjects of a fictional and real sensory deprivation, respectively, in his "Lettre sur les sourds et muets, à l'usage de ceux qui entendent et qui parlent" (1751) ("Letter on the deaf and mute as used by those who hear and speak"), do not articulate (or rather, are not "used," in dramatic deathbed fashion, to articulate) a materialist theory of the unending, destructive "revolutions" of nature. Lacking a given language they can, of course, express to others no view of the universe, or of the mind – any hypothesis of any kind – and, in this second "Letter," they are also given no name. Their discursive treatment, as agents of knowledge, could hardly be more different than Diderot's fictionalized first-hand account of the parting words of

---

19. *Ibid.*
20. Diderot, *OC*, IV: 41. Full passage cited in following Chapter, n. 31.

"Saunderson." While the discourse delivered by Diderot's "Saunderson" combines (its real author's) speculative hypotheses with the (fictive) representation of a real historical person, the nominal identity of the subjects of the second "Letter" is implicitly rendered insignificant by their own inability to express themselves verbally, their self- as well as knowledge-defeating ignorance of discourse itself.

Yet "[i]gnorance," Diderot states in the "Letter on the Deaf and Mute," "is less far removed from truth than prejudice" ("l'ignorance est moins éloignée de la vérité que le préjugé"[21]), underscoring, therein, the paradoxical – *necessary yet negative* – relation of knowledge to the senses, and the combined relation of both to representation in Diderot. For the blind, who have immediate access to sound and so make free use of verbal language, also provide us with no knowledge about it, and the deaf, who have immediate, visual access to the external world and make free use of visible movement within it, provide us with no knowledge about *it*. Each provides us with knowledge of that of which they can have no knowledge, except by way of representation. Thus, in the second "Letter," Diderot uses (fictional) deaf and mute subjects to speculate not on the visible forms of nature but on the formation of language or, what we like to call, human nature. Diderot's word for that nature we cannot see, peculiarly human nature, is the "soul," and his own remarkable description of the "soul" or "spirit" (*âme*) as infinitely complex seat of experience makes it not only impossible to see directly and distinctly at once – think of Frenhofer's continually changing painting, in Balzac's aptly entitled, "Chef d'oeuvre *inconnu*" ("*Unknown Masterpiece*" [emphasis added]), minus the single, still discernible detail of the painted subject's protruding foot – but makes it, for that very reason, both a name for the complex ability to combine experience and intellect that is language and the invisible subject of its own continuing representation by discourse. Much as the ability to see impedes one's ability to reason and imagine the possibility of forms and relationships one cannot see, so one's ability to hear and to speak impedes one's ability to articulate that which does not already take the form of speech (two positives can indeed result in negatives, or positive *absences* of positives, in Diderot).

Such, for Diderot, is the "soul," from which all knowledge, action, and representation spring, closest to language but never defined *by* language, whose "simultaneous movements," consisting of "sensations" as well as "ideas" experienced all at once ("tout[es] à la fois"), must be subjected to their own analytic "decomposition" in order to be known at all: to the "successive," rather than synchronous, structure of discourse that is the given of any linguistic form, the "distribution" by the "precision of language" of a "total impression" into "parts."[22] It is in the act of representing the actions of those deprived of a codified language that the "soul," name of the never already fully codified nor empirically visible seat of poetry, can be brought, according to Diderot, into view:

> The state of our soul is one thing; another is the account we render of it, whether to ourselves, or to others; one thing, the total and instantaneous sensation of this

21. Diderot, *OC*, IV: 142.
22. Diderot, *OC*, IV: 161.

state; another thing, the successive and detailed attention that we are forced to give it to analyze it, make it manifest and make ourselves understood. Our soul is a moving *tableau* after which we paint without cease: we employ a great deal of time to render it with fidelity: but it exists in its entirety, and all at once: spirit does not proceed, like expression, by counted steps.

[Autre chose est l'état de notre âme; autre chose, le compte que nous en rendons, soit à nous-même, soit aux autres; autre chose, la sensation totale et instantanée de cet état; autre chose, l'attention successive et détaillée que nous somme forcés d'y donner pour l'analyser, la manifester, et nous faire entendre. Notre âme est un tableau mouvant, d'après lequel nous peignons sans cesse: nous employons bien du temps à le rendre avec fidélité: mais il existe en entier, et tout à la fois: l'esprit ne va pas à pas comptés comme l'expression.[23]]

Articulate knowledge – a "compte rendu" – of the soul requires ignoring the original composition of what one articulates, substituting for it our analytic "decomposition" of it, a "decomposition of the simultaneous movements of the soul" ("décomposition des mouvements simultanés de l'âme") in accordance with the "successive development of discourse" ("développement successif du discours").[24] Thus, any true knowledge of the soul, that indecipherable amalgam of intellectual and sensory experience, would, on the one hand, *require* knowledge of language, the means we use to decipher and express the indecipherable heterogeneity of a soul inflected by but not reflective of discourse. Yet, on the other hand, if knowledge of the soul, and of language, is to be obtained, it would have to be not through language as given but language as it is being made: not through the linguistic "decomposition" of complex experience, which we commit nearly every moment of every day, but through the decomposition of everyday decomposition, that is, of language itself, the necessary negation of an analytic negation – strange hybrid of syntheses *a priori* and *a posteriori* – such as may be made available to the hearing and speaking by those who must first represent language to themselves. For, "deprived" of the immediately language-bearing "faculties of understanding speech and speaking" ("privé de la faculté d'entendre et de parler"[25]), those who are, by nature, "decomposed" must actively compose representations everyday.

Deprived of the sense most conducive to the second nature of verbal communication, the deaf – as Diderot's anonymous stories in the Letter represent them – instead communicate graphically, through gesture. No history-making revolution in mode of thinking is recounted or indeed possible here; instead the light goes on as it goes out, as, unapprehended, and without self-defining laws, it flickers, in situation after situation, from one empirically given moment to the next. This flickering signal, emitted without external correspondence, could well be called the first light of language according to Diderot, an origin preceding the

23. *Ibid.*
24. Diderot, *OC*, IV: 158.
25. Diderot, *OC*, IV–142.

institutionalization of language, the birth pangs of which are immediately apprehensible sensory qualities untethered to specifically identified objects. On this fictive, experimental account, long preceding Nietzsche's theoretical genealogy of language in "Wahrheit und Lüge im aussermoralischen Sinn" ("Truth and Lie in the extramoral sense") (1872), the substantive, central linguistic unit of analytic logic, is not the founding unit of language itself. Instead of naming things, language first spoke sensations, according to Diderot, and, thus, once subordinated in real time to the communicative exigencies of successive, temporal discursivity, it was the adjective that syntactically preceded the substantive. We now "imagine," Diderot argues (as will Nietzsche), "that the adjective was really subordinated to the substantive, even though the substantive is not properly anything and *the adjective is everything*" ("*l'adjectif soit tout*"[26]). In the first, half-light of language, Diderot argues, the adjective *was* everything, and the so-called "inversion" of adjective before substantive that occasionally occurs in spoken French is in fact a reversion to an earlier, natural order that institutional and scientific French had inverted first, according to Diderot. This is Diderot's foray into the famous "bonnet blanc" or "blanc bonnet" controversy of the grammarians, in which a supposed historical priority was thought to mirror an equally putative precedence of logic within the development of thought, or not, and that historical and/or logical priority, to underpin the syntactic precedence of substantive or adjective, respectively. Yet Diderot enters the fray only to put the grammarians' distracting dispute, over which codified part of language exercises priority over the other, to rest (as he does with most intra-institutional debates), so as better to discover what language in general can tell us about who and how we are and how and what we know.

And what it tells us about us, according to Diderot, is that it is peculiarly human nature to know by representing what we don't know – experience *unattainable by the senses* and thus unavailable to abstract conception – *by way of another material medium*, just as the simultaneous yet ever "moving tableau" of the "totality of impressions" that "is" the soul must instead be represented sequentially by discourse, "painted after the fact." Thus the "natural" subjects of Diderot's account of knowledge are not naturally "enlightened," let alone, as – curiously self-blinding – historicist clichés about "the Enlightenment" would have it, "universal" or "transcendent," but the sensorily deprived for whom the necessity of representation is not the exception but the rule. It is these subjects, *lacking* in the direct means of knowing, that provide Diderot with a *supplemental* model for representing the unknown. For even as they are subjected to others' clichéd assumptions – prejudices or 'pre-judgments' – regarding their own intellectual and moral capacities *as* subjects *before* developing or learning a symbolic mode of action of their own, it is these subjects that most conclusively indicate every subject's general capacity to communicate acts of conception by means that are necessarily internal in origin and material in medium. It is those, for whom certain sensory experience and its corresponding, institutionalized medium are unavailable to begin with, whose

---

26. Diderot, *OC*, IV-135.

circumvention, by expressive substitution, of the blockage of one means of sensory reception and sign production or another, shines an occult light upon the mind's ability to produce knowledge of which it has, so to speak, no knowledge, for theirs is a knowledge *a priori* non-identical with the data that senses deliver directly. Diderot's "Letter on the Deaf and Mute" was not only the direct predecessor to l'Abbé de l'Epée's formalization of the "sign language" he had witnessed in action among the deaf in Paris into the instructional "method" (*Institution des sourds et muets, par la voie de signes méthodiques* [pub. 1776]) that would then be literally institutionalized by the Institut des sourds et muets founded by the Abbé in 1760. In the most universally 'literal' sense, unlimited by specific institutional *or* sensory capacity, Diderot's representation (via dramatized actors of his own invention) of the invention of "signs" or "symbols"[27] "uses" the sensorily deprived not as limit case or exception to the norm but as fitting substitute for us all, for the sense of things and/or the ability to express such a sense that we *all* lack, more *or* less, at different times.[28] Another name Diderot gives such inevitable representers is "poet," and his description of "the spirit" that "passes in the discourse of the poet," an undefined spirit that makes do by doing what it does with language, without our ever *knowing* what it itself is ("what is this spirit? I have sometimes felt its presence but all I know of it . . . is [its actions]") is itself well known:

There passes then in the discourse of the poet a spirit that moves and animates all syllables. What is this spirit? I have sometimes felt its presence; but all that I know of it is that it is it that acts so that things are said and represented at the same time; that at the same time that understanding understands them, the soul is moved, the imagination sees them and the ear hears them, and that discourse is nothing but a concatenation of energetic terms which expose thought with force and nobility, but that it is also a tissue of hieroglyphs piled one on the other that paint it. I could say, in this sense, that all poetry is emblematic.

[Il passe alors dans le discours du poète un esprit qui en meut et vivifie toutes les syllabes. Qu'est-ce que cet esprit? J'en ai quelquefois senti la présence; mais tout ce que j'en sais, c'est que c'est lui qui fait que les choses sont dites et représentées tout à la fois; que dans le même temps que l'entendement les entend, l'âme en est

---

27. Diderot, *OC*, IV: 34.
28. For a compelling investigation of states of physical incapacitation or "dis-ability" as just that, states to which all bodily subjects are subject in time, see Paul Kelleher's excellent "'The Man Within the Breast': Sympathy, Deformity, and Moral Subjectivity in Adam Smith's *The Theory of Moral Sentiments*," in *Inventing Agency: Essays on the Literary and Philosophical Production of the Modern Subject*, ed. C. Brodsky and E. LaBrada (NY: Bloomsbury, 2017), pp. 173–200 (see esp. 188–94, on the 'unavoidable [disabling] effects of . . . our temporal bodily implication in the world" [193–194]). For an overview and analysis of historically acknowledged states of disability, see Jacques Striker, *A History of Disability*, trans. William Sayers (Ann Arbor: University of Michigan Press, 1999).

émue, l'imagination les voit et l'oreille les entend, et que le discours n'est plus seulement un enchaînement de termes énergiques qui exposent la pensée avec force et noblesse, mais que c'est encore un tissu d'hiéroglyphes entassés les uns sur les autres qui la peignent. Je pourrais dire, en ce sens, que toute poésie est emblématique.[29]]

Of what and in what "sense" a stack of hieroglyphs "can be said" to "be emblematic" is knowledge that the simultaneously internal ("l'imagination les voit") and external ("l'oreille les entend") quality of poetic representation alone can provide, knowledge that, without the indirection of poetry – of the spirit passing *through* the poet – we, even when enjoying the full complement of our senses, are missing.

Diderot's epistemological poets – revolutionaries out of sensory necessity – are those whom, for the most part, history is missing. Yet, Kant's historical series of *Revolutionen* is more Diderotian than at first appears, for revolutions in knowledge occur randomly on his account, their agents acting less like the masterminds than the mere vehicles of mental *Einfälle*, notions falling into individual minds from who-knows-where. In other words, not determinative historical contexts but history-making events determine the history Kant tells. Unpredictable occurrences, these *Einfälle* punctuate periods of blind groping that may last hundreds of years, centuries of efforts that can offer no adequate external expression – explanation, 'excuse' or *Ausrede* – for an enduring failure or lack of intellectual "vision" that can only be characterized metaphorically – so Kant's *Herumtappen* – as sensorily deprived. So it is that in Kant, as in Diderot, the sighted can appear blinder than the blind, precisely by identifying knowledge uniquely with the evidence of their senses, taking the temporally and spatially proximate – the "momentary" outcomes and visible identities of ongoing material permutations – either as sufficient proof of an "eternal" "order" (in the words of Diderot's "Saunderson"), or as sufficient disproof of the possibility of knowledge whatsoever (in the presumptively skeptical view of the sighted, or should we say, near-sighted Hume).

Similarly, the difference in Diderot's accounts of "Saunderson" and anonymous deaf subjects illuminates the critical difference between the modes of "revolution" in mathematics and metaphysics recounted by Kant. For, while the revolution now known as geometry ensues from an *a priori* act of "construction" – the composition, according to Kant's *Logik*, of some "thing" that is "real" in itself[30] – Kant's 'Copernican turn' is instead a *discursive hypothesis a priori*, a theoretical reconception of human actions that understands itself as "analogous" to the scientist's reversal of the long-standing conception of our relation to the stars. In hypothesizing such a reversal in how we understand the mind's relation to all objects, based on an equally "revolution[ary]" conception of how empirical knowledge itself is composed, Kant's "Copernican turn," like Copernicus's, is not a figure of geometrical construction but an intellectual figure or theoretically necessary metaphor, one

---

29. Diderot, *OC*, IV: 169.
30. Kant, *Logik* §203, A 219, VI: 573.

doubling, in Kant's case, as a metaphor for the intellect itself. For, in the "case" of Kant's "turn," the "tenor" or basic sense to be conveyed (knowledge of the world), and the "vehicle" for its conveyance (knowledge of the subject) *are exchanged*, rendering the "real" object of knowledge not *what* we know but *how* it is that we *can* know (objects in the first place) – in which, in short, the basis not of externality but of knowledge of the external is the cognitive mode the metaphor exposes.

In contrast with theoretical or metaphorical "Copernican turn[s]," the gestures of Diderot's deaf and mute are turns in *deed*, physical movements, actual doings without knowing in any given discursive sense. Although not synchronous with the thought they embody, in the unique mode of a geometrical figure, like discursive language "painting after" the "moving tableau of the soul," their movements aim to imitate sequentially, bodily, graphically, sensorily, the simultaneous occurrence of sensations and ideas. The speeches of Diderot's "Saunderson," on the other hand, are, of necessity, verbal through and through: like their philosophy, their mode is anti-mimetic. Diderot notes that they are reputed instead for what, akin to Kant's "happy notions" (as described above), he calls their "happy expressions," observing:

> Those who wrote an account of [Saunderson's] life say that he was fertile in happy expressions, and that is highly probable. But what do you mean by happy expressions, you will perhaps ask? I reply ... that they are those which are proper to one sense, to touch, for example, and metaphoric at the same time to another sense, such as the eyes, from which results a double light for him to whom one speaks; the true and direct light of expression, and the reflected light of metaphor.
>
> [Ceux qui ont écrit sa vie dissent qu'il était fecund en expressions heureuses, et cela est fort vraisemblable. Mais qu'entendez-vous par des expressions heureuses, me demanderez-vous peut-être? Je vous répondrai ... que ce sont celles qui sont propre à un sens, au toucher par example, et qui sont métaphoriques en même temps à un autre sens, comme aux yeux, d'où il résulte une double lumière pour celui à qui l'on parle; la lumière vraie et directe de l'expression, et la lumière réfléchie de la métaphore.[31]]

Although the "language of gestures" is also called "metaphoric"[32] by Diderot, the strong communicational purpose, mimetic content and successive structure of such physical substitutions would place them not only at the opposite end of the spectrum from the language of poetry, described as an illegible stack of hieroglyphs, but in opposition to the "double light" of Saunderson's "happy expressions." For, deprived of the direct experience and confirmation of external evidence, Saunderson must shed a second light with the same necessity as Copernicus and Kant, which is to say, the purely internal necessity of replacing empirical ignorance with hypothetical knowledge by speculatively – again,

---

31. Diderot, *OC*, IV: 41.
32. Diderot, *OC*, IV: 144.

necessarily metaphorically – "turning things around." Unlike his own "Copernican turn" and the overturning of the presumed supremacy of the senses to cognition enacted by Diderot's sensorily deprived, whether these be mimetic and *a posteriori*, or hypothetical and *a priori* to experience in mode, the revolution in mathematics recounted by Kant does not reverse the bases of our understanding of sensible things but alone constructs that impossible thing, the fully symbolic, entirely nonexperiential, and so nonmetaphoric, purely graphic "language" of self-identical geometrical forms in space. As such it requires no explanatory language to become a permanent foundation of mathematical knowledge, and as such its initial mortal vehicle may as well remain unnamed.

In Rossellini's surprisingly sober *Cartesius* (1974) – non-dramatic depiction of a studious, itinerant, and publication-shy Descartes sleeping most of the day after reading all night, his small quarters a mess – as in Percy Adlon's necessarily sober *Céleste* – *huit clos* depiction of Proust's eponymous real-life housekeeper meticulously carrying out the duties of her kitchen-bound nocturnal routine, watching the clock for the precise moment to begin pouring boiling water over coffee painstakingly pressed into a cloth filter – any external view of "revolutions of mode of thinking" in the making must indeed limit itself to the few things and people that surround the subjects in which they occur. Any biopic of Kant courageous enough to "represent" the "life" of the "revolution" his *Critique* effects would have to restrict itself to the hour and repeated rounds of his daily walk (leaving to Herder the "picture" of the teacher and the man). But the "revolution in mode of thinking" that "constructs" its own external representation in, say, an equilateral triangle, would have to remain without further, even metonymic illustration, a subject of material and historical ignorance.

In this, it would most "resemble" the kind of agency, involving neither judgment nor knowledge, narrated in Kant's ethics. The most daring hypothesis of doing without knowing ever framed, and reversal of the long-held presupposition that knowing and acting must accompany each other if they are to be *morally* effective, Kant's theory of the "possibility"[33] that we can act in independence of the limits of given, phenomenal cognition, and so freed of self-interest in a *merely phenomenal* sense – that possibility without which his own entire *Kritik* might appear instead a mere prison – is one Kant can never deduce logically, illustrate historically, or communicate conclusively, although it clearly subtends his remarks on that other Revolution, in France, whose quality, as self-determining *act*, will remain, Kant states, an ineffaceable "sign of our times" ("Vorzeichen unserer Tage"[34]), regardless of its particular historical outcomes. So the possibility of moral action in Kant remains, as it must, at once absolutely critical and open to question, a non-cognitive

---

33. For a fuller discussion of Kant's own discursive representation of such a "possible" act, see Chap. One, Section One, this study.
34. Kant, *Streit der Fakultäten* A 150 (hereafter *StF*), in *Werkausgabe*, XI: 361.

act, immediately invisible to its agent, precisely because knowledge of it could never be fully provided by the senses. Source and outcome of the abilities and disabilities that compose all of us, both *a priori* and historically, the freedom to act in the mode of thinking Kant called moral, to do without knowing and graphic identity both, is the most remarkable – and unnamed – of Kant's *Einfälle*, and not the subject, in any but a necessarily double or reflected "light," of the poetics of judgment and action presented here. Yet it is the very rigor of Kant's separation of freedom in action from both the representational limits of cognition and discursive mode of judgment that ensures the critical "possibility" of each.

Part I

LINGUISTIC CONDITIONS

Chapter 2

THE "CONDITION" OF JUDGMENT: "COMMON SENSE," OR THE ORIGIN OF LANGUAGE IN KANT'S *THIRD CRITIQUE*

1. "Common Sense" and Signification, or What is Not Tautology

No single statement in Kant's critical philosophy may be met with greater disappointment or disbelief than the assertion made without further conceptualization or explanation in the *Critique of Judgment* (§20), that the "power of judgment" [*Urteilskraft*] – and with it, the entire philosophical project whose coherence and feasibility that power alone ensures – itself relies on the operation of something that Kant both distinguishes from and continues to call "common sense" [*Gemeinsinn*]:

> If judgments of taste (like cognitive judgments) had a definite objective principle, anyone rendering them according to this principle would claim the unconditional necessity of his judgment. If they were without any principle, like those of merely sense-based taste, no one would allow the necessity of them into their thoughts. Thus they must have a subjective principle that determines, only through feeling and not through concepts, but nonetheless generally, what pleases or displeases. Such a principle however can only be seen as a *common sense*, which is essentially different from the common understanding that people sometimes also call common sense (*sensus communis*): for the latter does not judge according to feeling but always according to concepts, even if these are commonly only obscurely represented principles.

> [Wenn Geschmacksurteile (gleich den Erkenntnisurteilen) ein bestimmtes objektives Prinzip hätten, so würde der, welcher sie nach dem letztern fället, auf unbedingte Notwendigkeit seines Urteils Anspruch machen. Wären sie ohne alles Prinzip, wie die des blossen Sinnengeschmacks, so würde man sich gar keine Notwendigkeit derselben in die Gedanken kommen lassen. Also müssen sie ein subjektives Prinzip haben, welches nur durch Gefühl und nicht durch Begriffe, doch aber allgemeingültig bestimme, was gefalle oder misfalle. Ein solches Prinzip aber könnte nur als ein *Gemeinsinn* angesehen werden; welcher

vom gemeinen Verstande, den man bisweilen auch Gemeinsinn (sensus communis) nennt, wesentlich unterschieden ist: indem letzterer nicht nach Gefühl, sondern jederzeit nach Begriffen, wiewohl gemeiniglich nur als nach dunkel vorgestellten Prinzipien, urteilt.³⁵]

Limiting knowledge of things to a coordination of concepts and perceptual representations, and basing his pathbreaking definition of aesthetic judgment *precisely on the opposite*, i.e., on perceptions *shorn of* conceptual and representational content, Kant's critical "revolution"³⁶ in metaphysics makes no concession to and no mention of the rule of "common sense,"³⁷ the collective term for any and all

---

35. Kant, *Kritik der Urteilskraft* (hereafter *KU*) B 65, §20, in *Werkausgabe*, X: 157 (emphasis in text).

36. Kant, *KrV* B XI–XXIII, III: 22–28. On Kant's use of the term "revolution" to describe the reversal in "mode of thinking" at which his *Critique* aims, cf. Chap. One, this study.

37. Kant's inauguration of the term "common sense" [*Gemeinsinn*] in German letters, in distinction from "healthy," "sound," or "common human understanding" [*gesunder* or *gemeiner Menschenverstand*] – popular terms more commonly employed (including, on occasion, by Kant himself) – is underscored in Marina Savi's excellent monograph, *Il concetto di senso comune in Kant* (Milano: Franco Angeli, 1998), to which this analysis will return (see Savi, pp. 12–13). In addition to the already available German terms it does not use, Kant's unprecedented reference to *Gemeinsinn* should also be distinguished from the French notion of "good sense" [*le bon sens*] that, later mentioned in Kant's *Anthropology from a Pragmatic Point of View* (§6, BA 23, XII: XXX), would have been familiar to him within the context of philosophical writing from the well-known opening of Descartes' *Discours de la méthode*: "Le bon sens est la chose la mieux partagée du monde" ("Good sense is the best shared [or distributed] thing in the world.") (René Descartes, *Oeuvres philosophiques* 3 vol., ed. Ferdinand Alquié [Paris: Garnier, 1963, 1967, 1973] I: 568). While the intellectual senses to which they appeal are indeed different – Descartes' "good sense" naming, not without irony, the commonly credited ability to interpret accurately and conduct ourselves rationally on the basis of what we perceive, and Kant's "common sense," explicitly distinguished from exactly such, in his words, "common understanding" in the passage from the Third Critique just cited, bearing with it no such hermeneutic and pragmatic thrust – the link between "common" and "good sense" remains the quality of commonality by which Descartes singly defines the latter as "the best shared [or distributed] thing in the world." Furthermore, although "good sense" in Descartes is a self-crediting practical capacity, its application results from a specifically intellectual act that Descartes, while in a sense very different from Kant's, also calls "judgment" (*Discours*, I: 594), while the "sense" of what Descartes calls "common sense" (*le sens commun*) is, instead, a purely physiological capacity, the name then commonly given a section of the brain credited with "receiving," in common, different "ideas" of physical sensations: "light, sound, odor, taste, heat, and all the other qualities of external objects" (*Discours*, I: 628; see also *Discours*, I: 577). On the history of pseudo-scientific references to such a putative, purely physiological "common sense," see Pavel Gregoric, *Aristotle on the Common Sense* (Oxford: Oxford University Press, 2007), pp. 56–58, 180–82, esp.

intellectual and cultural norms of the circularly self-confirming, ultimately tautological kind (only common sense can define "common sense") that his "Copernican" *Critique* defied.[38] Even as it appears to appeal to the openly platitudinous beliefs Kant directly criticized in the Scottish School of Common Sense philosophy,[39] Kant's introduction of "common sense" remains consistent with

---

38. For Kant's exclusion of "tautological" statements from logic, and equation of what he disparagingly calls the "logic of common reason (*sensus communis*)" ("Logik der gemeinen Vernunft [*sensus communis*])" with "actually no logic, but an anthropological science" ("eigentlich keine Logik, sondern eine anthropologische Wissenschaft"), see Kant, *Logik* A 223, VI: 576, and A 12, VI: 439, respectively.

39. See Scott Philip Segrest, *America and the Philosophy of Common Sense* (Columbia, Mo.: University of Missouri Press, 2010), pp. 25–27, on the distinction and relation between Aristotelian *koine aesthesis* (or "common sensation") and *phronesis* (or "practical wisdom"), the translation of the former as "*sensus communis*" by Aquinas, in the non-Aristotelian sense of a shared capacity for judging among sensations, and the adoption of the latter by Reid's Common Sense philosophy. Focusing on the development of the Common Sense School in Scotland and the U.S., Segrest briefly, somewhat inexplicably suggests that this "commensensical" (or tautological) notion of "common sense" was also fundamental to Kant's critical philosophy, even while linking it to Aristotle's *koine ennoiai*, or "first principles" (26), and quoting at length from Kant's well-known condemnation of Scottish common sense philosophers in the *Prolegomena* (35–36). For the critique of Common Sense philosophy in the *Prolegomena*, see this Chapter, Section Two, n. 68. Far more instructive is Segrest's related discussion of Shaftesbury's and Vico's approximation of "common sense" to "good sense" – including, in Shaftesbury's view, a good sense of humor, or "wit," capable of deflating both popular opinon and philosophical speculation – and of "natural" "social 'affections'" to "a sense of beauty or fitness" issuing in "a kind of aesthetic judgment" and shared "moral sentiment." Segrest's illuminating account of the implantation and dissemination of a prophetic Presbyterianism in eighteenth-century America, most prominently by successive Presidents of Princeton, which based its religious interpretation of knowledge on the same Scottish Common Sense philosophy that Kant was then criticizing as no philosophy at all – i.e., the peddling of that religion's "deepest intuitions about man, God, and the world" as nothing other than "plain common sense" (see 28–33; 56–132) – is both central to his historical account of the propagation of a "belief"-based, "common sense" approach to all discursive philosophy in the United States and sheds an important, contrasting light upon the critical concerns of the current study. On Shaftesbury, and the "difficulties of writing a semantic history of common sense" from Aquinas to its "refutation" by Hegel, see Fritz van Holthoon, "Common Sense and Natural Law: From Thomas Aquinas to Thomas Reid," in *Common Sense*, ed. Fritz van Holthoon and David R. Olson (Laham, MD: University Press of America, 1987), pp. 99–114.

In *Rediscovery of Common Sense Philosophy* (London: Palgrave, 2007), Stephen Boulter makes use of historical and biological evolutionary models of understanding to buttress his case for a general renewal in philosophical discourse of the "common sense" tradition of Aristotle, Reid, and Moore, even while arguing for the nonevolving, conservative juridical

the critical rigor of his own project, or, what is the same, with a supreme lack of traditionally proffered "common sense"[40] on his part. For Kant ends Section 20 of the *Critique of Judgment* by admitting there is nothing whatsoever commonsensical, nothing any one, let alone each of us, can presume to know about the effectivity, existence or basis of the undefined capacity for "common sense" [*Gemeinsinn*] on which his central theory of judgment rests.

Unlike every other "sense," "common sense" in the Third Critique is not an "external" medium through which we experience sensuous objects, but neither is it a hypothetical medium originating solely within the subject. "Common sense" functions instead on the shared or general "presupposition" that it is "given," a "presupposing" importantly defined by Kant, in Section 22, as "really" rather than merely theoretically enacted: "only under the presupposition that there 'is' [or, 'would be:' *gebe**] common sense (by which we do not understand an external sense, but the effect resulting from the free play of our powers of cognition), only, I say, under the presupposition of such a common sense can judgment of taste be rendered;" "[t]his undetermined norm of a common sense is really presupposed by us: our presumed ability to make judgments of taste proves it" ("nur unter der Voraussetzung, dass es einen Gemeinsinn gebe [wodurch wir aber keinen äussern Sinn, sondern die Wirkung aus dem freien Spiel unserer Erkenntniskräfte, verstehen], nur unter Voraussetzung, sage ich, eines solchen Gemeinsinns kann das Geschmacksurteil gefällt werden;" "[d]iese unbestimmte Norm eines Gemeinsinns wird von uns wirklich vorausgesetzt: das beweiset unsere Anmassung, Geschmacksurteile zu fallen").[41]

discourse such a commonsensical approach to philosophy would buttress in turn, without noting any contradiction between the two. Employing the commonsensical argument that it is harder and less reasonable to endeavor to prove a positive negative than a positive or negative, Boulter argues that, by their (positive) "default position" of "healthy" "flexibility," "common sense beliefs" shift the philosophical "burden of proof" to their positive – logical – negation, i.e., the noncommonsensical, purely hypothetical "aporias" that, according to him, have defined the "essence," and resulted in the theoretical excesses, of philosophy from its inception (see pp. 9, 11–12, 18, 25, 36ff., 82, and esp. 100–117 [on "neo-Kantian constructivism"]). While Boulter alludes briefly to Kant's dismissal of Scottish Common Sense philosophy in his "Introduction" (p. xi), he, tellingly, makes no mention at all of the novel, distinctly non-Scottish sense of *"common sense"* ("*Gemeinsinn*") introduced by Kant in the Third Critique, and, consequently, offers no analysis either of its explicitly positive, rather than hypothetical, function, as fulcrum of Kant's entire tripartite project, nor of the significance of its inauguration in the context of the first explicitly *critical* philosophy in history into German letters at large.

40. Albert Einstein memorably analogized the "common sense" "norms" regressively attributable to tradition to the beliefs held by any individual as follows: "Common sense is the collection of prejudices acquired by age eighteen."

41. Kant, *KU*, B 65, 68, X: 157, 159. *Kant's use of the German "first subjective" tense indicative of reported or indirect, rather than first-person or declarative, speech, in describing and referring to "common sense," is also indicative of and consistent with his

As extraordinary as Kant's introduction of "common sense" into critique is his direct self-reference in doing so. Interposed between the preceding clauses concerning, on the one hand, our "presupposition" of an undefined "common sense" "resulting from the free play of our powers of cognition," and, on the other, an ability to judge that both "proves" the "reality" of what we presuppose and depends upon it, is Kant's statement of the origin of these propositions, his own speaking self, "I," the active subject of his "I say" ("sage ich"). As noted (*) in the preceding paragraph, when indicating the presupposed existence of "common sense," Kant employs the mood of the German subjunctive that serves to indicate reported speech and alleged facts ("would be" [*gebe*]), the same verbal tense and grammatical equivalent of quote marks with which he will refer to "common sense" thereafter. Yet, nowhere else in the *Critique* does Kant declare, in direct confirmation of the grammatical function and specifically verbal sense of that tense, the actual fact that he is not hypothesizing, or theorizing, but, quite literally, *saying* this. As if openly enacting the very act of presupposition on which "common sense" and "judgment" are based, Kant verbally indicates the indistinguishability of actually *proposing* that proposition from the presuppositions enabling one to do so by speaking of "common sense" in the first person. Kant, in other words, does what he says as he is saying it, and, in so doing, renders explicit the verbal form his proposal of "common sense" and the common "presupposition" of it share. The logically entailed, temporal or sequential cognitive distinction between proposition and presupposition is eclipsed here by a statement indicating that, like what it proposes, such a proposition is "really" taking place, in a particular speaker's words. Thus Kant's proposition of a fundamental "common sense" defies what we assume common sense to be by declaring itself in fact nothing more nor less than *a fact of speech*, one alleged by a subject ("I") engaged at that moment in the very act of enacting or presupposing it. The difference, in short, between proposing in theory and presupposing in practice the existence and effectivity of what Kant calls "common sense" is limited by Kant to the verbal equivalent of diacriticals: a reporting of speech by a subject himself engaged in the act of presupposition which that speech ("would be" [*gebe*]) describes.

Now, it is fair to say there is not a lot of talking, whether first-hand or cited, in Kant's *Critique*, just as no aspect of its "revolution[ary]," founding hypothesis – that empirical knowledge is not only valid but inevitable when "empirical" is understood not to be empirical but representational and our actions, as subjects of knowledge, are understood to depend less on specific outcomes than our rethinking of how knowledge is composed to begin with – appears to rely on anything resembling "common sense." There is indeed so little talking and so little apparent relation between speech and the theory of how we know and act elaborated throughout the *Critique* that we may overlook the fact that the key hypothetical proof of the

analysis of judgment as a necessarily *verbal* act. For lack of an equivalent verbal tense in English, it is signaled here and throughout this study by diacritical marks inserted in the translations from Kant's text.

"possibility" of – logically undeducible – "freedom" in the Second Critique is based in and decided by a chain not of physical but specifically *verbal* actions, and that these culminate not in an empirical but equally verbal result: the articulation, by a subject, in a causally determined, empirical situation, of a discontinuity between external causality and the determination of any subject's actions. The subject of that situation is a hypothetical "man" who, under "threat" of his own "execution," is "demanded" by "his sovereign" to "bear false witness against an honest man," and its outcome is demonstrated not by way of an "*a priori* synthetic judgment" of the kind Kant's First Critique proposes empirical knowledge is composed, but, instead, a question: "Ask him however, whether, if his prince demanded, under threat of punishment of death, that he bear false witness against an honest man, whether he, no matter how great his love of living may be, would hold the overcoming of [that love of living] for possible" ("Fragt ihn aber, ob, wenn sein Fürst ihm, unter Androhung der ... Todesstrafe, zumutete, ein falsches Zeugnis wider einen ehrlichen Mann ... abzulegen, ob er da, so gross auch seine Liebe zum Leben sein mag, sie wohl zu überwinden für möglich halte ..."[42]).

"*Frag ihn* aber, ob"—"*ask him*, however, whether ..." "he *holds* for possible" that he may *refuse to lie upon demand*: Kant's attempt to deduce the possibility of free, moral actions turns upon actions that are neither empirical nor categorical but *discursive*. "Ask," "threaten," "hold for possible," "refuse," "bear false witness," "demand" – all are acts enabled by speech alone. Verbal of necessity, they lead to a single decisive act whose particular object ("an honest man"), mode ("to bear witness"), and content ("false") depend as much on discourse as does the result for which they are said to provide evidence: that of "confirm[ing]" ("bestätigt ...") the prevalence of the concept of "freedom" in "the order of concepts within us" ("... diese Ordnung der Begriffe in uns"[43]).

Even more importantly, however, what the hypothetical subject of Kant's narrative inherently demonstrates, in finding and affirming it to be "possible" that he might "overcome his love of living" rather than condemn another man through his own lie, is that, as a subject, he identifies his own life – what it is in itself, in absolute distinction from its empirical conditions – with his *relation to the words he says*: with the truth or falsity of the words he employs in relation to any other subject of action whatsoever, rather, again, than to any empirical set of conditions. The absence or presence of a "gallows" "erected" on the spot may indeed prove decisive to a subject's ability to withstand a personal inclination when "object and opportunity present themselves," Kant admits.[44] Yet neither his personal like or

---

42. Kant, *KprV* A 54, VII: 140.
43. *Ibid*.
44. *Ibid*.: "Suppose, that someone pretends his pleasurable inclination would be irresistible if the beloved object and opportunity presented themselves: whether, if a gallows were constructed before the house in which he encounters this opportunity in order to hang him immediately from it after he enjoyed his pleasure, whether he wouldn't overcome his inclination" ("Setzt, dass jemand von seiner wollüstigen Neigung vorgibt, sie sei, wenn ihm der beliebte Gegenstand und die Gelegenheit dazu vorkämen, für ihn ganz unwiderstehlich:

dislike of the "honest man" about whom he is ordered by his sovereign to lie, nor the threat that noncompliance with this order will issue in his own death, may prove similarly decisive to Kant's subject's actions, when these consist of acts committed and expressed to others in language rather than internal calculations of the relative value of any particular pleasure. The fact that such a hypothetical subject cannot "ensure" he "would or would not [bear false witness]" against another "honest" subject, even under sovereign threat, if he does not, of his own demise, means he "must concede" (by yet another verbal act) such a refusal to lie is "possible," and, we, by extension, that he is what Kant calls "free:" "Whether he would do it or not, he will perhaps not trust himself to ensure; that it is, however, possible [he might not], he must concede without doubt" ("Ob er es tun würde, oder nicht, wird er vielleicht sich nicht getrauen zu versichern, dass es ihm aber möglich sei, muss er ohne Bedenken einräumen"[45]).

That such specific discursive acts, and language in general, do not figure prominently, if at all, in the recepton and understanding of Kant's critical project may owe simply to the fact that, like this hypothetical, narrative "confirmation" of "the order of concepts within us," they arise rarely in the interdependent, architectonic account of our *a priori* intellectual powers Kant gives. Yet rarity may itself mean everything in the *Critique*: if talk is cheap, Kant implies, blame it on the cheapness, the meretriciousness or lack of real value of what is said by those who make it appear so, not on the value of language, as a mode of meaning, itself, let alone on its most common modalities: the logically interconnected network of conceptual nominal knowledge all subjects of knowledge use (Kant's own proverbial "phone company"), as well as our ability to ask questions about what we don't know by forming discursive hypotheses, to say nothing of the possibility that any man may decide at any time *not* to lie.

As foundational as is the concept of "freedom," demonstrated solely in acts of speech, to the Second Critique is the noncognitive act of judgment that, separate subject of the Third Critique, is already described in the First Preface to the First Critique as that action whose exercise, in "the mature power of judgment of the time" ("der gereiften *Urteilskraft* des Zeitalters"), defines that time or age as the "Age of Critique."[46] Indeed, even the pivotal paragraph of the Second Critique just cited itself closes with an act of "judging" (rather than knowing, deducing, or concluding), upon which, first, the "recognition" of "freedom" and, second, that of a "moral law" dependent in turn on the recognition of freedom, depend. Of his hypothetical subject, Kant states: "Thus he *judges* that he can do something because he is conscious that he should, and recognizes in himself the freedom without which

---

ob, wenn ein Galgen vor dem Hause, da er diese Gelegenheit trifft, aufgerichtet wäre, um ihn sogliech nach genossener Wollust daran zu knüpfen, er alsdenn nicht seine Neigung bezwingen würde").

45. *Ibid.*

46. Kant, *KrV* A XI–XII, III: 13; see also Kant, *Logik* A 40, VI: 457: "Our age is the Age of *Critique*" ("Unser Zeitalter ist das Zeitalter der *Kritik*").

the moral law would otherwise remain unknown to him" ("Er *urteilet* also, dass er etwas kann, darum, weil er sich bewusst ist, dass er es soll, und erkennt in sich die Freiheit, die ihm sonst ohne das moralische Gesetz unbekannt geblieben wäre"[47]). Yet judgment is also theorized, for the first time in the history of philosophy, to be not only an activity but an *a priori* faculty, indeed, the most critical of all faculties, by Kant. The Third Critique bases the proposition of such an *a priori* faculty, most unusually and for the first time in Kant's philosophy, on what Kant calls, despite his own consistent criticism of anti-philosophical uses of the term, "common sense."

That the pathbreaking ability to bridge the primary analytic division – between theoretical and practical uses of reason and their objects, limited knowledge and free moral action, on which his own *Critique* depends should itself depend on the "presupposed," discursively unanalyzed faculty that Kant, speaking in uncharacteristic *propria persona*, calls "common sense," appears a conspicuous, if not fatal flaw in the "building" [*Gebäude*] of Kant's "system," an exception, as evident as it is inexplicable, to the regularity and autonomy of its logical, "architectonic" exposition.[48] Yet, the analytic weakness unambiguously articulated by Kant's introduction of "common sense" at the close of the First Analytic of the Third Critique, may also be seen to reveal the rigor and integrity of Kant's analytic procedure overall, his refusal either to derive an analytic definition of "common sense" from its commonplace conception or to circumvent the need for analysis

---

47. Kant, *KprV* A 54, VII: 140 (emphasis added).

48. On the "purposive building" and "architectonic construction of knowledge," see Kant, *KU*, B 4, X: 115; *KrV*, B 9, IV: 51; B 503, IV: 449: "Human reason is according to its nature architectonic, that is, it considers all knowledge as belonging to a possible system" ("Die menschliche Vernunft ist ihrer Natur nach architektonisch, d. i., sie betrachtet alle Erkenntnisse als gehörig zu einem möglichen System"); B 860, IV: 695: "Architectonic is the art of systems" ("Architektonik ist der Kunst der Systeme"); "The concept of freedom in us ... constitutes the keystone of the entire building of a system of pure, even of speculative reason" ("Der Begriff der Freiheit ... macht nun den Schlussstein von dem ganzen Gebäude eines Systems der reinen, selbst der spekulativen, Vernunft aus"); B 27, IV: 64: "Transcendental philosophy is the idea of a science, whose whole plan the *Critique of Pure Reason* should sketch architectonically ... from principles ... with full guarantee of the completeness and certainty of all the pieces which compose this building" ("Die Transcendental-Philosophie ist *die* Idee *einer Wissenschaft*, wozu die Kritik der reninen Vernunft den ganzen Plan architektonisch, d. i. aus Prinzipien."); *Logik*, A 143, VI: "In all sciences, but especially in those of reason, the idea of the sciences is the general sketch or outline of it and thus the circumference of all knowledge which belongs to it. Such an idea of the whole ... is architectonic" ("In allen Wissenschaften, vornehmlich denen der Vernunft, ist die Idee der Wissenschaft der allgemeine *Abriss* oder *Umriss* derselben ... Eine solche Idee des Ganzen ... ist *architektonisch*"), et al. Cf. Brodsky, "Architecture and Architectonics: The Art of Reason in Kant's *Critique*," *Canon: The Princeton Journal. Thematic Studies in Architecture* Vol. 3, 1988, pp. 103–118.

in the name of the commonsensical, the assumed rather than articulated presupposition of "Gemeinsinn" first named in the course of that analysis itself.

For in refusing to define "common sense" as "just" "common sense," something beyond, or before, but, in any case, independent of analysis in that it is, simply, given, without relation to anything else, Kant distinguishes the "common sense" of which he speaks from the purely verbal assertion of sense with which it may most easily be confused, tautology.[49] Tautology, verbal truncheon of all pretenders to the mind's supposed "throne,"[50] compels the surrender of reason not to a power greater

---

49. On critical vs. "tautological" statements of "definition," see Kant, *Logik* A 223, VI: 57n6. It was to avoid tautology, as well as its inverse, the infinitely regressive, often ultimately tautological results of a purely "analytic" parsing of statements, that G. E. Moore proposed a philosophy of "Common Sense," i.e., that philosophy concern itself with the non-contradictory combination of "sense-data" and "belief" under which "human beings" operate, rather than a notion of "truth" regarding sensory and mental phenomena that it cannot in fact "analyze." Moore opens his inaugural lecture on common sense: "I wish, for a particular reason, to begin in a particular way. There are, it seems to me, certain views about the nature of the Universe which are held, now-a-days, by almost everybody. They are so universally held that they may, I think, fairly be called the views of Common Sense ... And I wish to begin by describing these views, because it seems to me that what is most amazing and most interesting about the views of many philosophers, is the way they go beyond or positively contradict the views of Common Sense." The basis of "the views of Common Sense," on Moore's account, is a sense-based "belief" in the "existence" of "material objects" and "other human beings" rendering inconsequential the disciplinary distinction between knowledge and "belief" itself ("we believe that we really *know* all these things that I have mentioned"), and substituting the notion of a contradiction-proof "common sense" for that of analytic "truth:" "of the *truth* of these propositions, there seems to be no doubt, but as to what is the correct analysis of them there seems to me to be the gravest doubt." See G. E. Moore, *Some Main Problems in Philosophy* (London: George Allen and Unwin, Ltd., 1953 [based on lectures delivered 1910–11]), p. 2; *Selected Writings*, ed. Thomas Baldwin (London: Routledge, 1993), pp. 118–19, 133. For an excellent analysis of Moore's reliance upon a distinction between "expression" and "analysis," and linguistic "communication" and "content" (or "referent"), see L. Susan Stebbing, *Logical Positivism and Analysis* (London: Oxford University Press, 1933), pp. 7ff, 16–17, esp.; on Wittgenstein's critique of Moore, see Avrum Stroll, *Moore and Wittgenstein on Certainty* (Oxford: Oxford University Press, 1994), pp. 53–54, esp.; on the "intentional solipsism" of Wittgenstein's equation of every individual language with a "private" symbolic system of "verifiable" "meaning," and the "methodological solipsism" of Carnap's theory of content-free, inter-related "propositions" articulated by a "universal" "physicalistic language in the formal mode," see Stebbing, 18–25.

50. Cf. Kant, on the "death of philosophy" at the hands of those who, presenting themselves as "superior" to analytic "discursive" labor, instead incant the words of ancients they "[en]throne" out of their own "incapacity to think," in "Of a Newly Elevated, Superior Tone in Philosophy," ("Von einem neuerdings erhobenen Ton in der Philosophie"), VI: 383, 389–90n (A 309, 412–13).

or essentially different from itself – the unforseeable intellectual event, say, of "a happy notion" ("ein glücklicher Einfall"[51]) or "feeling" ("Gefühl"[52]) – but, rather, to nothing and no power at all but that of stating itself. Equating truth with a willed act of repetition purposed to usurp analysis, and as exactly opposite to the critical clarity of Kant's "discursive thinking"[53] as any single predicative utterance can be, tautology employs the form of predication so as to render any form a redundancy, pretending to include within its limits, and so preclude, not merely all necessary but all possible thought. Just as the age-old advertisment for self-asserting brutality, "might makes right," seeks to supplant all basis for the analyses of right *and* might by dressing the two, disconnected concepts in nearly tautological garb – linking them on no other basis than the pronouncement of a succinct narrative rhyme – so positive logical tautology, an identity statement identifying only itself, represents not self-evidence but the aim to enact, in language, total sovereignty over language, over difference of any kind: the difference between thoughts and things, as between thinking and tautology; the verbal assertion of nothing and destruction of everything but the pure, context-shorn repetition of a word, "itself." Stated so as to abrogate every action of perception, along with the temporality all such acts require, tautological statements are not the result but the *reductio ad absurdum* of "common sense," not its end but its termination. Tautology negates common sense by presuming at once to be, to speak for, and to surpass it, to pass off its own purposeful verbal redundancy as the supposed self-evidence and givenness of reality.

51. Kant, *KrV*, B XI–XII, II: 22. For a full discussion of Kant's logically unsubordinated notion of the "happy notion," see Chap. One, this study.

52. On the origin of acts of judgment in "feeling," see Section Four of this Chapter.

53. See Kant, "Of a Newly Elevated . . .," VI: 380 (A 394). Pertinent to the particularity of Kant's undisclosed concept of "common sense" is its relation, as the basis of judgment, to our capability for "discursive thought." For an opposite view advocating a "*non*-discursive" reliance on common sense "*belief*," see Nicholas Rescher, *Common-Sense: A New Look at an Old Philosophical Tradition* (Milwaukee, WI: Marquette University Press, 2005), p. 32: "A common-sense belief . . . is a nondiscursive and nonreflective belief of which one is certain – and as *reasonably* certain – as one can be of anything." While, according to Rescher, beliefs may be based in inarticulate common sense, it is the "fact" of "linguistic communication" that offers, Rescher also argues, the best evidence of the workings of "common sense:" "The fact that everyday linguistic communication is geared to the ordinary course of things as we generally experience it means that our standard means for verbal communication are intimately geared to our common-sense view of the world and its ways. Linguistic standardism and common-sense thinking are opposite sides of one selfsame coin" (118). While Rescher's argument thus becomes involved in the kind of circular reasoning, assuming "common" "standards of judgment," (93) that Kant's enigmatic reference to "common sense" avoids, his insight into the fundamental interrelation of "prosaic" "communication" and "common sense" also entails one of the most incisive critiques currently available of the philosophical triviality and "disconnected[ness]" of "possible world" and "counterfactual" "methodology[ies]" (see pp. 228–235).

Rather than define "common sense" as itself self-evident, a sense definable by and as tautology, Kant instead relates it, without explicating it, to an analytic definition of judgment, and thus to the very possibility of specifically *critical* (or traditionally anti-"commonsensical") thought. Surprising in that it occurs at all, let alone in the voice of the first person, and describing "common sense" to be as central to the *Critique* as its own demonstration, let alone definition in the terms delimited by the *Critique*, must remain inconclusive, what Kant's reference to "common sense" demonstrates is that "common sense" could never be sufficiently defined as something entitled common sense – another dumb redundancy, dependent, like all tautology, upon its own enforced echo, the appropriation within it, in the guise of merely being "itself," of all that is not it, just as every echo dissembles the Narcissus at its source. For, if stated instead as a tautological "given," "common sense" would preclude all it does not already include as "given," every statement that differs from or refers to something other than its own formal self-mirroring, including, most significantly, the fact of its own essential vacuity.

Like every tautology asserted as a statement referring only and sufficiently to "itself," – a statement, in short, whose predicate "is" its subject – "common sense" defined *as* common sense could do nothing but assert successive assertions of its own success; like every tautology, its truest – most effective and empty – translation is the familiar refrain of all *faits accomplis*, "nothing succeeds like success." Kant's reference to "common sense," by contrast, succeeds in remaking "common sense" – most commonly cited "authority" of anti-intellectual tautology – into a singular object of intellectual inquiry by stating, in unsubordinated addition to it, what that reference does not contain, i.e., an adequate account of what "common sense" is.[54]

---

54. As developed in the present discussion, "common sense" arises in Kant not in reference to itself but in relation to, and as the very "condition" of linguistic utterances that, communicable to and articulable by "everyone," constitute acts of judgment by a subject. Cf. Lynd Forguson's very different view, espoused in *Common Sense* (London: Routledge, 1989), that "common sense realism," predicated on shared "beliefs" and independent of "information" and "opinion," is instead a properly "metaphysical" aspect of mind: "[c]ommon-sense realism deserves to be called a metaphysical view in virtue of the fact that it is an attempt to explain why our conscious experiences are as they are. It deserves to be called a version of realism in virtue of the specific type of explanation it gives: our experiences are as they are because we are related through sense perception and thought to a world which is external to and independent of the experienes we have of it" (15). Following Reid and Moore, Forguson furthermore takes direct issue with Davidson's very different view of a necessary reciprocity between "common-sense beliefs" and "linguistic interpretation" and "concept[s]," one suggestive of the central role of the commonality of language within "common sense" itself: "[a]ccording to Davidson, in order to interpret the utterances of others as meaningful speech, it is necessary to construe those utterances as expressing their beliefs and intentions ... To get the interpretative enterprise off the ground ..., Davidson argues that we must not only assume that they say what they believe, but that most of what they believe actually is true by our own lights" (168); "Davidson's theory of interpretation is essentially a

At the close of the Fourth (and final) Moment of the Analytic of the Beautiful (*Critique of Judgment* §22), Kant acknowledges the failure of his analysis of judgment to account fully for itself, the nonconformity of the formative capability – or, as he calls it, "faculty" ("Vermögen") – of "common sense" with the formality of the analysis that requires it, including the division of our mental abilities into "faculties" themselves. Unlike reason, imagination, and understanding, the principle faculties or capabilities of the mind whose changing relations to each other across the tripartite, architectonic structure of his *Critique* Kant delineates; and unlike the different capacities of experience primarily associated with these, i.e., logic, sensation, and representation, respectively, "common sense" neither has nor could have any clearly defined status or function, and so can be subordinated to neither the "real" and "practical" nor "hypothetical" and "theoretical" conditions, of action and knowledge, respectively, that are analyzed in the *Critique*.[55] Further questioning "whether" such a "constitutive principle of the possibility of experience" as "common sense" even "in fact exists," and "judgments of taste are thus original and natural," or "whether" the "possibility" of "common sense," of a sense ascribed by each to all, is "the idea" of a faculty whose "artificial" "acqui[sition]" and "regulation" of experience is "require[d]" by a "higher principle of reason" instead – in short, whether common sense is "original" or is *a posteriori* to "experience" itself – Kant leaves that fundamental question, and with it, the very credibility of "common sense," undecided. With the negative assertion that he has neither the "ability" nor "desire" to answer it "for now," and positive demurral of any logical need to do so, the last paragraph of Section 22 and the entire series of deductive Moments[56] comprising Kant's Analytic of the Beautiful ends:

theory of *linguistic* interpretation, whereas what I have been arguing is that common sense is (in part) a theory of interpretation of our behavior in general, not just linguistic behavior" (171). While Forguson's view, that we may identify "common-sense realism" in such "languageless creatures" as "prelinguistic infants" and "animals" with whom we share no linguistically formed "concepts," begs the question of how such a necessarily unilateral attribution could be classified as "*common* sense," Davidson's view of linguistically grounded "beliefs" certainly comes closest to Kant's signal grounding of "judgment," *rather than belief*, in linguistically enacted "common sense" (170–71).

 55. See Kant, *KrV*, B XXII–XXV, *Logik*, A 222, VI: 576.
 56. These "moments" employ the four classical analytic "categories" (quality, quantity, relation, and modality), traditional since Aristotle, to describe the beautiful, *pace* Aristotle, as a universally affective dynamic form and event. Kant's categorical analysis thus constructs something that cannot be identified apart from its construction, i.e., the definition of an action whose identity, unlike that of a given object, cannot be separated from the experience-based "feeling" and "presupposed" "condition" of "common sense," necessary condition of the articulate form it takes. Just as the idealist and prescriptive conceptions of neo-Platonic and neo-classical aesthetic theory before Kant included neither subjective "feeling" nor inter-subjective "judgment" in their consideration of the beautiful, so Kant's employment of the kind of classical logical exposition never before related to aesthetic experience aimed

Whether there 'is' [or 'would be:' *gebe*] in fact such a common sense as a constitutive principle of the possibility of experience, or whether a yet higher principle of reason only 'makes' [*mache*] producing a common sense with higher aims into a regulative principle for us; whether taste 'is' [*sei*] an original and natural faculty or only the idea of an artificial one to be acquired, so that a judgment of taste, with its presumption of general determination, 'is' in fact only a demand of reason that such a unanimity in the mode of sense be brought forth; and whether the ought, i.e., the objective necessity of the confluence of the feeling of any one man with the particular one of every other man only 'signifies' the possibility of arriving at this agreement, and judgment of taste only exhibits an example of the application of this principle: this we here neither want nor are able to investigate as of yet, but rather propose now only to break down the faculty of taste into its elements and unite them finally within the idea of a common sense.

[Ob es in der Tat einen solchen Gemeinsinn, als konstitutives Prinzip der Möglichkeit der Erfahrung gebe, oder ein noch höheres Prinzip der Vernunft es uns nur zum regulativen Prinzip mache, allerest einen Gemeinsinn zu höhern Zwecken in uns hervorzubringen; ob also Geschmack ein ursprüngliches und Natürliches, oder nur die Idee von einem noch zu erwerbenden und künstlichen Vermögen sei, so dass ein Geschmacksurteil, mit seiner Zumutung einer allgemeinen Bestimmung, in der Tat nur eine Vernunftforderung sei, eine solch Einhelligkeit der Sinnesart hervorzubringen, und das Sollen, d. i., die objective Notwendigkeit des Zusammenfliessens des Gefühls von jedermann mit jedes Seinem besondern, nur die Möglichkeit, hierin einträchtig zu werden, bedeute, und das Geschmacksurteil nur von Anwendung diese Prinzips ein Beispiel aufstelle: das wollen und können wir hier noch nicht untersuchen, sondern haben vor jetzt nur das Geschmacksvermögen in seine Elemente aufzulösen, und sie zuletzt in der Idee eines Gemeinsinns zu vereinigen.[57]]

The investigation of its own nature signaled as wanting and that lack, as one that Kant himself does not even wish to attempt to repair as of yet, "common sense" names whatever it is that makes judgment a general capacity or faculty, rather than

precisely at excluding non-demonstrable imputations to the workings of what he calls "common sense." Immediately disorienting in effect, Kant's introduction of logical analytic methods into an investigation of subjective experience may be the single most far-reaching theoretical innovation effected in general by the Third Critique. It is fair to say that, without Kant's analytic approach to the subjective experience of the beautiful and the sublime, not only Freud's analysis of the psyche according to the "principles" of "pleasure" and "pain," but the systematic analysis, by Hegel and Marx, of history, society, language, and value – shared experiences of the subject ungrounded and unreferrable in any particular subject or object – appear, in retrospect, unthinkable.

57. See Kant, *KU*, B 68, X: 159–60.

individually contingent operation of taste, disposition or opinion, in Kant. A universal subjective capacity that renders possible the linking of the "pure" "practical reason" of free (or moral) action in the Second Critique with the "practical" and applied nature of "pure (or theoretical] reason" in the First, judgment is not another mode of reason introduced to supplement those between which it mediates. Considered in terms of the modalities of reason Kant describes, judgment neither "legislates" the activity of the mind nor conforms to intellectual "laws," whether these are logical, phenomenal-perceptual and causal, or moral, noumenal and free. Its operation depends instead on an ability whose very normativity renders it immediately at odds with the project of critique.[58] Small wonder, then, that Kant's unadumbrated introduction of "common sense," an appeal unprecedented and unprepared for in the analytic sequence preceding it, has attracted relatively little scrutiny in the separate developments of philosophy and aesthetic theory ever since,[59] and, with one important exception, remains

---

58. In "Kingston, Kant, and Common Sense," *Cambridge Anthropology*, Vol. 18, No. 3 (1995): 40–55, anthropologist of "cosmopolitanism" Huon Wardle instead takes just such a critically productive view of Kant's distinctive identification of common sense as a "faculty," opposing it to the notion of an underlying if "amorphous and sluggishly moving body of 'folk knowledge'" described by such dissimilar theorists as Geertz and Gramsci, and way out of the theoretically tautological "process by which anthropology chases its own tail historiographically" (44, 54). For Wardle, Kant's "common sense" indicates one of "the capabilities individuals display in dealing with an unbounded social context, rather than with an assumed social homogeneity against which individuals are then explained" (42). See also Wardle, "Cosmopolitics and Common Sense," Open Anthropology Cooperative, Working Papers Series No.1, ISSN 2045-57[3 [online] (Oct. 4, 1999), on Kant's "common sense" in relation to the opposing – cosmopolitan and "organistic" – anthropologies of Ulrich Beck and Bruno Latour.

59. See, for example, the passing reference to "common sense" in relation to "judgment" in Susan Meld Shell's exhaustive analysis of epigenetic, organistic, hypochondriacal and other bodily themes in Kant, in *The Embodiment of Reason* (Chicago: University of Chicago Press, 1996), p. 208. See also the brief, initial definition of "common sense" as "a kind of *feeling*, namely the feeling of a certain or, as it were, instinctively correct choice" and its tautological restatement as "a feeling of *sensus communis*" rather than "obscure conceptuality" in Jan Kulenkampff's careful analysis of the relation between aesthetic judgment and rationality, *Kants Logik des aesthetischen Urteils* (Frankfurt a. M.: Klostermann, 1978), p. 99. The obscurity of its conception is the main conclusion of Brent Kalar's discussion of "common sense," in his generally excellent analysis, *The Demands of Taste in Kant's Aesthetics* (London: Continuum, 2006) – "[a]dmittedly, the argument is not as clear and detailed as one might like" (139) – in which the "'effect arising from the free play of the cognitive powers'" (*KU*, Section 20) that Kant identifies with "common sense" is redefined as "none other than pleasure" itself, and Kant's specifically discursive notion of "universal communicability" (Kant, *KU*, B 66, X:158) is replaced by one of "universal validity" (138, 140). Christian Helmut Wenzel's *Introduction to Kant's Aesthetics: Core Concepts and*

overlooked – despite Kant's own unequivocal statement of its "necessity" – by efforts to gain further insight into both the internal conditions and the philosophical ramifications of the *Critique* itself.⁶⁰ Nor, has it been invoked to play any but a negative role in analyses devoted specifically to re-evaluating

Problems (London: Blackwell, 2005) offers a helpful review of philosophical uses of "common sense" before Kant, attempts to distinguish the term from *sensus communis*, and, concludes, like Kalar, by stressing its identity as an "effect of free play," before going on to associate that effect, as it is pointedly not associated by Kant, both with the pseudo-scientific view, inherited from the ancient Greeks (see n. 39, this Section, this Chapter), of "an inner sense or faculty that unites our five senses," and the moral "duty to develop a taste for beauty" (see pp. 80–85 esp.). By contrast, in *Kant and the Claims of Taste* (Cambridge: Cambridge University Press, 1996), Paul Guyer begs the question of what, if anything, the mention of "common sense" is doing in the Third Critique, let alone at its center, concluding, simply, that its "basic meaning...for Kant is...the faculty of taste itself" (405 n.42). For an excellent critique of Guyer's approach to the Third Critique, and Kant in general, as a case of mistaken identity, in which the central "revolution in mode of thought" constituted by Kant's founding "hypothesis" – of a capacity for logically interrelated, exclusively phenomenal cognition based in *a priori* syntheses of empirical experience, and of the newly defined freedoms of *action* enabled by that very delimitation (the "pure" or nonphenomenal practice of "moral" "reason" or "freedom," and the specifically linguistic practice of an aesthetic "power of judgment" by subjects who "feel themselves free" in feeling "pleasure" or "displeasure" before an unknown object) – is instead replaced by the same Humean, empiricist notions of predictability and agreement against which Kant was writing in the first place, see Kalar, pp. 19–36; on Kant's "revolution" in metaphysics see Chapter One, this study.

60. The salient exception to this history of near neglect is Arendt's interpretation of 'common sense' as the basis of Kant's theory of political *sensus communis*, in *Lectures on Kant's Political Philosophy*, ed. Ronald Beiner (Chicago: University of Chicago Press, 1982). While Arendt's recognition of the critical function of "common sense" in Kant speaks to her distinctive ability to read philosophy meaningfully, i.e., with regard to the conditions, practices and consequences defining specifically human activity, her expansive translation of Kant's "common sense" to theory of the *polis* effectively displaces the effectivity of its situation, status, or "standing" within the *Critique* itself. A direct attempt to build upon Arendt by returning Kant's openly incomplete account of "common sense" to its relation to the beautiful is offered in Anthony Cascardi's *Consequences of Enlightenment* (Cambridge: Cambridge University Press, 1999); see esp. pp. 80–86, 161–64. Acknowledging Adorno's skirting of the singularity of "common sense" in Kant (77, 83) as well as Arendt's important "vacillat[ion]" on the "aporia" or logical circle it presents, i.e., the fact that in order to be "communicable" aesthetic judgment must rely on the same "enlarged mentality" that "communicability" is supposed to supply (85), Cascardi refers the unprecedented quality of Kant's "common sense" to our very capability for cognizing precedence, or "memory" (85). Implicitly recalling Plato's theory of the recollection (*anamnesis*) of the Beautiful, Cascardi describes "common sense" as a "lost" "knowledge" that we can "remember," and concludes: "Our participation in judgments that refer to this 'common sense' incites the memory of a

and resuscitating the purport and philosophy of "common sense."[61] By the same token, the questioning of Kant's own judgment, in invoking "common sense" as a first "principle" without demonstrable origin, would demonstrate nothing so much as a failure to understand the critical significance of the act such questions serve to dismiss.[62] Rather than subordinate it to the guiding critical "hypothesis" clearly stated in the Second Preface to the First Critique,[63] Kant raises a series of incontrovertible questions ("whether ... or whether ..." [*ob ... oder*[64]]) regarding the nature of this "common" critical capability – a capability and not a content; a "possibility" ("Möglichkeit") and not a logical necessity or rule – not only refusing thereby to comprehend "common sense" under the rule of any prior, logical or hypothetical "principle" whatsoever, but implying in addition that, whether

knowledge that was itself once conceived as pleasurable" (85–86). While the addition of a formerly "pleasurable" "knowledge" to Kant's theory of our immediate capability for "common sense" effectively mitigates the division between cognition and judgment, otherwise acknowledged by Cascardi (75–79), at the basis of the Third Critique, Cascardi's commentary effectively brings into relief our sense of what is *not* discursively presented to conception in Kant's positively ungrounded reference to "common sense."

61. This includes the full spectrum of positive and negative evaluations of "common sense" philosophies. Contrast, for example, the argument for common sense and against Kant (and "neo-Kantians") in Boulter, *Rediscovery*, (esp. pp. xi, 98–117) with the indictment of both Kant and all appeals to common sense, considered complicit with "disciplinary" stagings of "humiliation," in Paul Saurette, *The Kantian Imperative: Humiliation, Common Sense, Politics* (Toronto: University of Toronto Press, 2005), pp. 12–14 esp. Blurring the strict delimitation of the discussion of "common sense" within the Third Critique as well as the separation underscored within it between the First and Third Critiques, Saurette conflates "common sense" with "common sense recognition," the lattter defined as a "crucial strategy of philosophical persuasion" aimed at convincing us "we all share certain values or claims that we all recognize" without submitting these to "reasoned justification" (pp. 46–47). The persistence of this "subterranean Kantian logic" in contemporary philosophy is evident, Saurette argues, in the implicit recourse to "common sense" made by "Rawls, Habermas, Taylor, and many others" (p. 11, 47–48).

62. See Saurette, *The Kantian Imperative*.

63. Kant, *KrV* B XVI, III: 25: "Till now we assumed that all our knowledge must orient itself in accordance with objects; but all attempts to discern something about them *a priori* through concepts, came through this presupposition to nothing. Let us then try for once the experiment of seeing whether we wouldn't get further in the tasks of metaphysics in assuming objects must orient themselves according to our knowledge ..." ("Bisher nahm man an, alle unsere Erkenntnis müsse sich nach den Gegenständen richten; aber alle Versuche, über sie a priori etwas durch Begriffe auszumachen, wodurch unsere Erkenntnis erweitert würde, gingen unter dieser Voraussetzung zu nichte. Man versuche es daher einmal, ob wir nicht in den Aufgaben der Metaphysik damit besser fortkommen, dass wir annehmen, die Gegenstände müssen sich nach unserem Erkenntnis richten ...").

64. See n. 57, this Chapter.

dismissive, skeptical or simply unquestioning, failures to reflect critically on the significance of "common sense" will obscure the necessity of its effectivity both within the *Critique* and, on its analysis, in ourselves. Still, little is more understandable (if in a distinctly non-Kantian sense) than such acts of distortion or neglect, for the very term, "common sense," contradicts any active, uncommon interest in its regard. It is the very prosaic, unexceptional, indeed, apparently negligible assumption of a common turn of mind with neither known nor even knowable content – of some capacity shared, in the undergoing of a certain kind of experience, by one with all – that has made the capability Kant defined as the most important to judgment, and thus to the whole "building" of the *Critique*, also appear the weakest in his architectonic design: a mere commonplace that, not submitted, like other social conventions (including "taste" itself) to critique, is made to do too much with too little basis or reason. An appeal to "common sense" – verbal last resort and refuge from analysis of epistemological and cultural chauvinists alike – would indeed appear most out of place in Kant, whose powers of analytic scrutiny and comprehensive originality made his multi-faceted *Critique* self-critical like no other philosophical work before it, a theory which every theory of knowledge, aesthetics, or moral action has had to consider since.

Taken alone, in the way it is commonly asserted, "common sense" is indeed a term for what does, or should, "go without saying," an ability unreflectively enacted and relied upon by every practically reasonable mind.[65] It boasts no particular

---

65. This is the aspect of "common sense" emphasized by Sophia Rosenfeld in her own "commonsensical," conspicuously inaccurate summary of Kant's analytic of judgment, in *Common Sense. A Political History* (Cambridge: Harvard University Press, 2011), p. 223: "Though judgments of taste are perforce subjective, they always presuppose and refer to an ideal of universal assent, the possibility, if not the fact, of consensus among all. *Sensus communis* is ultimately the name that Kant gives to this faculty of judgment that leads us, without reflection, to make this comparison or to think from a universal standpoint" (223). Presenting "common sense" in general as both a necessity and evil of political life in a democracy, Rosenfeld's book typifies the circular structure of the "commonsensical" view of "common sense" that it describes (i.e., we agree to agree that we agree . . .), giving short shrift to the problems raised by less opportunistic engagements with the term, and including Arendt alongside Ronald Reagan in its brief concluding compilation of recent examples of its invocation (254–55). Cf. the compelling critique of commonsensical discussions of "common sense," of the very kind Kant similarly critiqued in so-called "Common Sense Philosophy," in Dean Wolfe Manders, *The Hegemony of Common Sense. Wisdom and Mystification in Everyday Life* (New York: Lang, 2006): "Relying on common sense wisdom in everyday life does grave injury to a specific and centrally human chatacteristic: *the potentiality for critical thought.* The hegemony of pragmatic common sense praxis is coextensive with 'anti-intellectual' tendencies that exist, in varying degrees, through the working population. Under the sway of common sense rationality, individuals' ability to entertain general political or social ideas in their own right, outside of their immediate, linear, instrumental context, becomes increasingly difficult, and often undesirable. The

capacities or components but its own, a self-sufficiency that, "knowing" – like a practiced physical motion – what it is about, renders any additional effort of critical analysis or introspection superfluous, if not injurious, to its execution. This would appear true of Kant's provocatively *self-critical* invocation of the term as well, his stated refusal to attempt to answer just such a question, regarding the existence and origin of this particular "faculty," as he directly proposes himself, the pronounced disengagement from further speculation with which his discussion of this "presupposed" faculty comes to an end: "this we neither can nor want to investigate here as of yet" ("das wollen und können wir hier noch nicht untersuchen").[66]

Yet, unlike conventional gestures toward self-evidence, Kant's appeal to a "faculty" he calls "common sense" is part of the final step of a categorical analysis said to have depended, in its every preceding step, upon it. And unlike most appeals to "common sense," Kant's serves rather than impedes the development of a course of critical reflection. Here "common sense" – less defined than it is left undescribed by its broad identification as "effect of the free play of our powers of cognition" – is introduced in response to an exacting formal examination of the felt intangibles of judgment and aesthetic experience in general: acts and experiences that, while unmistakably specific, have defied definition at least since Plato's isolation of truth and beauty, conceived as eternal "Ideas," from the changing manifestations of mimesis. Thus, before dismissing its reference to "common sense" as a retreat from critical reason into banality, it is to the *Analytik* – out of whose positive steps the "necessary" but no less negative "condition" ("notwendige Bedingung") and "undefined norm" ("unbestimmte Norm") of "common sense" are shaped – that we must look if we are to make sense of it rather than read past it, confusing "common sense" with the "hollow" ("schal"), "confident" ("getrost") notion of "common human understanding" Kant criticizes, or mistaking it for the disproof of the entire preceding analytic procedure which it underpins.[67] For if Kant's invocation of

---

intellectual possibilities and powers of critical self and historical reflection atrophy…'what you don't know can't hurt you'" (90–91). Manders also importantly underscores the *linguistic* basis of "common sense," without which any critique of "false consciousness"– of the kind Hegel initiated within philosophy and Marx, Lukács, Lefebvre, and Gramsci brought to bear upon all social forms – would be as unthinkable as judgment would be to Kant (see esp. pp. 177–81). Rather than simply accept as true or dismiss as false the truisms offered by "such common sense phrases as…'time is money,'" "'time and tides wait for no man,'" Manders observes that the "prosaic false consciousness" of "American common sense" contains within its statements the "slumbering seeds of its own transcendence:" that, any "sense" that is "common" is not only, necessarily, a linguistic phenomenon but that, as such, it also provides the basis for its own critical – philosophical, political, and historical – analysis, of the very kind Rosenfeld's incongruously *ipso facto* "political history" does not provide.

66. See n. 57, this Chapter.
67. For Kant's description of his distinctive use of the phrase "Gemeinsinn" as "notwendige Bedingung" ("necessary condition") and "unbestimmte Norm" ("undetermined norm"), see Kant, *KU* B 66, 68, X: 158, 159. For his stark critique in the *Prolegomena* of

"common sense" highlights a banality, it does so consciously, indicating that, just as it participates in judgment, the distinctive noncommonsensical faculty he is here calling "common sense" is an intellectual "effect" in which we all participate, no less than a "condition" of judgment on which, whether or not analytically inclined, we all unconditionally, if inexplicably, rely.[68]

complacent, conventionally "commonsensical" dismissals not of his own *Critique* but, on the contrary, of the radical skepticism of Hume that, on his own account in the *Prolegomena*, occasioned his *Critique,* see the following note.

68. For Kant's explicit distinction between "common sense" and a "common understanding" based instead not in immediate "feeling" but in cognitively predetermined "concepts," see *KU*, B 65, X: 157. For his refutation of the easy assumption of a "common human understanding," in important contrast to his own foundation of judgment on an undemonstrable "common sense," see his *Prolegomena* A 11–12, *Werkausgabe*, VI: 117–18, in which he describes the flawed arguments against Hume of his contemporaries' as follows: "The opponents of the famous man would have had to delve deeply into the nature of reason insofar as it has to do only with pure thinking in order to satisfy their task, which, however, they were unfitted to do. Thus they discovered a more convenient means of doing so without spiting all insight, namely the invocation of *common human understanding*" ("Die Gegner des berühmten Mannes hätten aber, um der Augabe ein Genüge zu tun, sehr tief in die Natur der Vernunft, so fern sie bloss mit reinem Denken beschäftigt ist, hineindringen müssen, welches ihnen ungelegen war. Sie erfanden daher ein bequemeres Mittel, ohne alle Einsicht trotzig zu tun, nämlich, die Berufung auf den *gemeinen Menschenverstand*"). Refusing to take for granted such a "convenient means" of circumventing careful thought, and representing the recourse to "calling upon common human understanding" as nothing more than a "subtle invention of modern times," one deceptively permitting "the hollowest enthusiasts to affiliate confidently with exacting minds," Kant cautions that, "while there is still even a small remainder of insight, one will do well to prevent oneself from grasping at this emergency assistance," whose own "appellation," he concludes, is "nothing other" than a "calling upon the judgment of the herd" ("sich auf den gemeinen Menschenverstand zu berufen, das ist eine von den subtilen Erfindungen neuerer Zeiten, dabei es der schalste Schwätzer mit dem gründlichsten Köpfe getrost aufnehmen… So lange aber noch ein kleiner Rest von Einsicht da ist, wird man sich wohl hüten, diese Nothülfe zu ergreifen…diese Appellation nichts anders, als eine Berufung auf das Urteil der Menge").

2. "Technique"

Instead of attempting to "investigate" directly – as Kant explicitly refuses to do – the nature of that 'faculty' upon which, he no less expressly states, his theory of judgment rests, it may be more useful to consider 'common sense' indirectly, in comparison with another moment in the composition of the *Critique of Judgment* in which Kant carries out just such an investigation with regard to a notion he admits he had employed without sufficient definition in a previous work. Kant's stated negation of his own ability or desire to define the "real" ("wirklich"), "unconditional necessity" of "common sense" to judgment – whether such a shared "sense" is "natural" or "artificial," i.e., owing to "experience" or to "reason" alone – stands in direct contrast with a passage from an early draft of the Third Critique in which Kant notes his own earlier failure to define another, similarly key concept, and, with the assistance of a distinction provided by his theory of judgment, proceeds to remedy that lack. The logical circle that Kant's openly stated analytic reliance upon "common sense" presents – its necessary participation in both the *a priori* principles and active formation of judgment – has its precedent in a similarly difficult logical "ambiguity" ("Zweideutigkeit"[69]) that Kant now not only acknowledges but goes on to clarify by way of an important conceptual distinction extending to his analysis of aesthetic judgment as well.

In the first version of his Introduction to the Third Critique, Kant points to what he calls a logical and semantic "mistake" ("Fehler") committed in his writing on moral action; the lexical conflation therein of the "*pragmatic*" "imperatives" of merely instrumental acts and those of a "pure" or "*really*" "practical reason."[70] According to Kant, the critical distinction he had made, between "really" moral and merely instrumentally "skillful" (or "clever" ["geschickt"]) practices, brought with it a semantic "contradiction" in the general use of the word "practical," one that had been only inadequately resolved, Kant goes on to reflect, by his earlier qualification of the "imperatives" of mere "skillfulness" (or "cleverness" ["Geschicklichkeit"]) as "*problematic*" ("*problematisch*"[71]).

In the course, then, of introducing an analysis not of "free" "moral" action but of the aesthetic "judgment" of "freely delineated" objects, Kant is first able to distinguish what he calls "*technical* imperatives," those of an artfulness employed

---

69. Kant, *KU*, X: 13; the specific writing concerned is the *Grundlegung zur Metaphysik der Sitten*.

70. Kant, *KU*, X: 14 (emphases in text).

71. See n. 75.

toward achieving personal aims, from those whose rules determine their aims to begin with, making the cart (reason's "real, practical aim"), thereby, not so much precede as itself be positively unimaginable without the horse (the possibility of "action" in the "free," "moral sense"). Much like the double – foundational *and* specifically applied – use judgment makes of "common sense," the distinct "imperatives" of moral action and "skill" are both "practical." Yet, since "free," moral actions alone define the end they aim to achieve, the critical difference between them and all other engagements in praxis requires a further division of the general notion of the "practical" into two, distinct and disambiguated terms, itself and another that, contrasting with, refines it. Kant observes:

> Only those [practical principles] which represent the determination of an action directly, i.e., merely through the presentation of their form (according to general laws), without respect to the means through which an object is to be effected, can and must have their proper principles (in the idea of freedom) ... In view of the concern for a certain ambiguity [of terms], all other principles of exercise, to which science may adhere, can be called *technical* instead of practical. For they belong to the *art* of bringing into being whatever it is one wishes there to be, that which can only ever be a mere consequence and no self-sustaining part of any kind of directive in a fully articulated theory. In this way all prescriptions of skillfulness belong to *technique* (or "technology:" "die Technik")* and therewith to the theoretical knowledge of nature as consequence [rather than basis] thereof. From now on, however, we will also use the expression, technique, on the occasions when objects of nature are merely *judged* solely *as if* their possibility were based in art (or "artifice:" "sich auf die Kunst gründe") ....

> [Nur die, welche direkt die Bestimmung einer Handlung, bloss durch die Vorstellung ihrer Form (nach Gesetzen überhaupt), ohne Rücksicht auf die Mittel des dadurch zu bewirkenden Objekts, als notwendig darstellen, können und müssen ihre eigentümliche Prinzipien (in der Idee der Freiheit) haben ... Alle übrige Sätze der Ausübung, an welche Wissenschaft sie sich auch immer anschliessen mögen, können, wenn man etwa Zweideutigkeit besorgt, statt praktischer *technische* Sätze heissen. Denn sie gehören zur Kunst, das zu stande zu bringen, wovon man will, dass es sein soll, die, bei einer vollständigen Theorie, jederzeit eine blosse Folgerung und kein für sich bestehender Teil irgend einer Art von Anweisung ist. Auf solche Weisen gehören alle Vorschriften der Geschicklichkeit zur *Technik** und mithin zur theoretischen Kenntnis der Natur als Folgerung derselben. Wir werden uns aber künftig des Ausdrucks der Technik auch bedienen, wo Gegenstände der Natur bisweilen bloss nur so *beurteilt* werden, *als ob* ihre Möglichkeit sich auf Kunst gründe ...[72]]

As the appearance of the word "art" (or "artifice:" "Kunst") in the second paragraph of this passage indicates, Kant here employs the definitions of "technique"

---

72. Kant, *KU*, X:13–14 (emphasis in text).

and "technical" he now introduces to clarify a formerly "ambiguous" use of the term, "practical," thereby distinguishing moral actions and "principles" ("Sätze") from those defined only by their application of "skill" to "bring into being whatever one wants," in order to make another critical, unambiguous distinction, now in his theory of the aesthetic. For the Third Critique will base acts of "judgment" not on the "technical" "skillfulness" embodied by any particular artistic practice, but on the "free play" of mental powers, and resulting "pleasure," occasioned by the perception of any *either* man-made or natural object. In terms that have remained essentially unchanged in the discourses of art history and criticism ever since, Kant extrapolates from a lexical distinction between "free" and "skillful" "practice" that, by his own account, he had failed to make in attempting to define the basis of moral action, so as clearly to distinguish "aesthetic judgment[s]" from considerations of "objects" "as if their possibility were based on art [or artifice]" alone. Like the skills brought to bear on the execution of a personal aim, "prescriptions" ("Vorschrifte") of "skillfulness" ("Geschicklichkeit") "belong," Kant specifies, *not* to the aesthetic but "to *technology*" ("gehören ... zur *Technik*"), the expedient "means" ("Mittel") of "bringing about" ("bewirk[en]") an "already known" "aim" or goal. Unlike "actions" whose "determination" "present[s] their form" ("Vorstellung ihrer Form") as "hav[ing] its proper principles (in the idea of freedom)," and thus as "necessary" ("nötig") in a critical rather than merely expedient sense, technical acts that work to "bring into being whatever one wishes there should be" find their sole determination in the satisfaction of a personal desire or will. Most significantly for Kant's entire critical system, the failure to distinguish aesthetic from merely technical practices will affect the central mediating role of judgment itself. For those who confuse the aesthetic with the technologically perfected will similarly confuse all aesthetic activities with the achievement of means to an end, "*judg*[*ing*] [such acts] *as if* their possibility were merely based on art" rather than any more fundamental or impersonal aim in which their judgment would also take part.

Thus, while aesthetic judgment may arise in response to objects produced by a skillful application of technology, judgment itself is never based in a recognition of technical ability alone. Were this not the case, judgment would cease to be "universally" *subjective*, which is to say, fully indifferent to the identity of its *objects*, and nature itself would be viewed analogously as the merely technical product of perfected skill. Just as "*technical* imperatives" take as their (tautological) aim the achievement of personally directed, purely technical gains, the equation of the bases of aesthetic judgment in the subject with successful instantiations of *techne* in objects would likewise objectify, and thereby annul, our experience of sublimity, reducing nature itself to the workings of an omnipotent technician whose own causal logic we could explicate, replicate, manipulate and deviate, based on contingent, delimited aims, in turn – with the manifestly disastrous results that the very contradiction, between self-determining natural processes and *techne* developed to abet non-natural, human aims, inevitably entails.

Still, while distinguishing between the aesthetic and the "technical," as between the "technical" and the (real and moral) "practical," Kant concedes that "technical" activities "may" indeed follow "practical rules," just as all acts of "reason" need not be "immediately legislative:" that the elaboration of applied, or "technically practical" rules requires analytic reason as well.⁷³ Yet, aesthetic judgment judges neither the effectiveness of such rules, in their ensemble as a "technology" ("Technik"), nor the specific "technique" required for their skilled application. For, to base judgment upon technical dexterity would be to disable the bases of judgment itself, rendering acts of judgment indiscernible from conceptual cognitions and limiting the objects of judgment to products of perceivable technical artistry or value while willfully ignoring the arbitrary, individual purposes technology may be employed to serve.

Yet, even more pernicious than its limitation of the objects of aesthetic experience would be the expansion of *techne* to the moral realm, our relationship to other subjects. The subordination of the power of judgment to an admiration of skill alone, Kant observes, would inevitably extend the rule of dexterity from the production of inanimate objects to the manipulation of "free human beings" as if they were inanimate objects, just as it would anthropomorphize nonhuman objects into "skilled" subjects, attributing to nature a "technical" "art," rather than causality, of its own.⁷⁴ Finally, the confusion of technical with either moral or aesthetic principles would have the further, logically contradictory effect of placing admiration in contradiction with the moral, or "real." Eradicating all distinction between aesthetic and applied perception as between disinterested and self-interested pleasure, it must, in sum, define freedom and non-freedom to be not in contradiction but identical: intellectually as well as experientially, subjectively and objectively, one and the same.

It is in making, then, this fundamental distinction between a fully "practical" (or moral) use of reason and a merely applied, "technical," skillful, or artful one, that Kant interjects the following note in correction of the "error" he had made in an earlier work:

> *Here is the place to improve upon an error that I committed in the *Foundation of the Metaphysic of Morals*. For, after I said that the imperatives of skillfulness would only command possible, which is to say, *problematic*, aims, so I called the same practical prescriptions problematic imperatives, in which expression a contradiction clearly lay. I should have called them instead the *technical* imperatives of art [or artifice: *Kunst*]. The *pragmatics*, or rules of cleverness, that

---

73. Kant, *KU* B XVII–XVIII, X: 82: "where rules are practical, reason is not thus immediately *legislative*, because [rules] can also be technically practical" ("wo Regeln praktisch sind, ist die Vernunft nicht darum sofort *gesetzgebend*, weil sie auch technisch praktisch sein können").

74. On the manipulation of human subjects as objects, see the citation from Kant immediately following. On the "misconception" of "nature as *art*" ("Natur als *Kunst*") and of a "*technique* of nature" ("*Technik* der Natur") itself "originally arising from judgment" ("ursprünglich aus der Urteilskraft entspringend"), see the first version of the Introduction, *KU*, X: 17.

are subordinate to the conditions of a *real* and thus fully subjective and necessary aim, also stand, of course, among the technical (then what else is cleverness, than the skillful use of free human beings, and even of the natural dispositions and inclinations in them, to one's own ends). The mere fact that the aim, which we prescribe to ourselves and others, namely, personal happiness, does not belong among those aims we merely favor, justifies another special designation of these technical imperatives: for the[ir] task requires not only what is required by [merely] technical [undertakings], i.e., the determination of the manner in which one fulfills an aim, but also the determination of that in which this aim (happiness) consists, which, in the case of general technical imperatives, must [instead] be set forth as already known.

[*Hier ist der Ort, einen Fehler zu verbessern, den ich in der *Grundlagung zur Metaphysik der Sitten* beging. Denn, nachdem ich von den Imperativen der Geschicklichkeit gesagt hatte, dass sie nur bedingterweise und zwar unter der Bedingung bloss möglicher, d.i. *problematischer*, Zwecke geböten, so nannte ich dergleichen praktische Vorschriften problematische Imperativen, in welchem Ausdruck freilich ein Widerspruch liegt. Ich hätte sie technisch, d.i. Imperativen der Kunst nennen sollen. Die *pragmatische*, oder Regeln der Klugheit, welche unter der Bedingung eines *wirklichen* und so gar subjektiv-notwendigen Zweckes gebieten, stehen nun zwar auch unter den technischen (denn was ist die Klugheit anders, als Geschicklichkeit, freie Menschen und unter diesen so gar die Natur-Anlagen und Neigungen in sich selbst, zu seinen Absichten brauchen zu können). Allein dass der Zweck, den wir uns und andern unterlegen, nämlich eigene Glückseligkeit, nicht unter die bloss beliebigen Zwecke gehöret, berechtigt zu einer besondern Benennung dieser technischen Imperativen: weil die Aufgabe nicht bloss, wie bei technischen, die Art der Ausführung eines Zwecks, sondern auch die Bestimmung dessen, was diesen Zweck selbst (die Glückseligkeit) ausmacht, fordert, welches bei allgemeinen technischen Imperativen als bekannt vorausgesetzt werden muss.[75]]

Kant's amended definition of the "imperatives" of "skill" as solely "technical" ("technische Imperativen") attempts to resolve "here," in an Introduction to the Third Critique,[76] the "contradiction" in his initial qualification of such imperatives as

---

75. Kant, *KU* X: 14.

76. The distinction drawn in this first draft of the Introduction between a "merely technical" or "skilled" use of practical reason, and a fully determining, "legislative" or pure "practical reason," is returned to and confirmed in both the A and B editions of the Introduction to the Third Critique as a distinction between those "technical-practical rules ... of art or cleverness in general" (including the "art" of manipulation employed to "exercise influence over men and their will") that, "determined by natural drives," derive solely from "concepts of nature" and those of a "will" which "stands instead under the concept of freedom as well" and whose "laws" "make up the second, namely practical part of [this] philosophy"; see *KU,* B XIII–IV, A XIII–IV, X: 79–80.

"problematic," given that their "foundation" ("Grundlegung") in "artifice," rather than the "things of morality," must contradict the "real"[77] imperative of any, even hypothetical "moral law." The self-contradictory notion of a "problematic imperative" was coined in the *Grundlegung* to distinguish and protect from contradiction the reality and formal (i.e., "pure" *rather than* applied) notion of an imperative capacity for free, moral action itself. While the Third Critique aims to elucidate the bases and function of judgment rather than of self-legislating moral action, just such an explanatory note as that appended "here," to the word, "*technique*," is what is conspicuously missing from its introduction of a problematically imperative – at once self-legislating *and* purposefully applied – "common sense." More than "ambiguous," the conceptual amalgam represented by the Latin, "*sensus communis*," is, by Kant's own admission, one upon which his *Critique* cannot improve. For, in naming a "common" rather than "universal" or "general" (i.e., "transcendental") capability, "common sense" specifically designates not an *a priori* form for perceiving but a kind of shared, *non*-sensory "sense" we either make of, or attribute to perceptions – one whose own basis Kant states he neither "can" nor "wishes to" analyze "now."

Nor will Kant ever commit such an analysis of "common sense" to print. In direct contrast to this explicit attempt "to ameliorate" ("verbessern") an earlier verbal "ambiguity," Kant does not amend the necessary "condition" of judgment he calls "common sense" in later editions of the *Third Critique,* or elsewhere.[78] Choosing neither to revise nor further elucidate its unelaborated assertion, Kant, one might say, declines to engage in precisely the kind of purely "technical" objectification he criticized in the passages just cited, refusing to use "artifice" to produce a concept of "common sense" to fit his aims: "das zu stande zu bringen, wovon man will, das es sein soll"[79] ('so as to bring into being whatever it is one wants there to be"). Rather than make something out of nothing or nothing out of something, thereby displaying nothing so much as personal ambition enabled by a certain limited, self-interested dexterity, we, too, might do better not to follow in the continuing Fichtean tradition of replacing terms Kant purposefully leaves undefined. Like his student's philosophically regressive identification of an unknowable "Ding an sich" with the postulate of an omnipotent ego or *Ich*, and initiation, thereby, of the reversion from critical thinking to subjective idealism that the hypothesis of a speculatively inaccessible "thing in itself" was precisely formulated to impede, the identification of "common sense" with either a sensory *or* formal given would similarly falsify the very dilemma of theoretical knowledge that it designates. Nor should we dismiss instead as merely nonrigorous Kant's

---

77. Kant, *Logik*, A 223, VI: 576.

78. The singularity of the status of "common sense" is underscored by the various, simple and compound uses of the term *Sinn* throughout the *Critique* and elsewhere in Kant. See the excellent comparison of *Gemeinsinn* in the *Third Critique* with the distinct uses of the term in Kant's *Anthropology*, in Savi, *Il concetto di senso comune*, p. 85 n. (See Kant, *Anthropologie in pragmatischer Hinsicht*, § 6, 28, 52.)

79. Kant, *KU*, X: 13.

stated reliance upon an ability of which he can say nothing more than that it alone permits judgment to take place. It may instead prove more fruitful, or at least less vacuous of "sense" – in either Kant's or our "common" sense of the term, if these are not, at first glance, the same – to investigate the constitutive qualities of judgment Kant must and does expose, with unambiguous precision, in his "Analytic" of judgment, if we wish to gain some understanding of the "faculty" of "common sense" on which all enactments of judgment rest.

For, while, unlike the related term, "practical," the "common sense" of Kant's Third Critique "can" neither (in Kant's terms) be disambiguated nor made available to direct analytic definition, it is nonetheless, Kant states, "unconditionally necessary" – which is to say, in no way in "error." And that necessity is all the more "real" in that it derives not from logical analysis, nor from desired objects, but from the analysis of the actual acts of judgment whose practice it enables. Now, starting from an analysis of the activity of judging to arrive at an understanding of the "common sense" upon which that same activity depends may seem as little logical as deducing a premise from its effect. Yet every logical deduction or syllogism might be described as departing, at least in part, from such an unstated logical inversion as well, the assumption of a known quality itself dependent upon some other, prior knowledge (of that quality), a kernel of circular reasoning whose development, pressed against the nominal limits of language, might be explicitly (non-syllogistically) formulated like this: I know that Socrates was a man because he was mortal and I know that all men are mortal because I call "mortal" those beings of limited corporeal life I call "men."

At very least, in considering what, or, indeed, if, "common sense" "may" "really" (in Kant's terms) "be," by way of the qualities in which Kant analyzes acts of judgment to consist, we are already given considerably more to work with than one already known quality alone (mortality), let alone one shared, according to its own logically unsubordinated definition, by every living being imaginable, and so offering no basis for knowledge at all. Whatever constitutes the fundamental "faculty" Kant calls "common sense" – and whatever may be the basis for its founding relationship both to the "power of judgment" and, with judgment, to the possibility of Kant's or any critical project – in attempting to arrive at an understanding of "common sense" by way of an analysis of the power said to depend on it, we can look to what is provided by the logical construction of that analysis: the specific, constitutive and general, rather than circularly defined nominal, qualities it first gives us to consider.

If we wish to try to "make sense" of a "faculty" Kant at once invokes and states he "neither can nor wants to" describe, let alone understand the necessity of the nearly self-contradictory nature of that invocation – one that places 'common sense' squarely at the center of the larger, step-by-step analysis of judgment it concludes, even while acknowledging it cannot be explicated by that rational analysis itself – there is no retrospectively clarifying corrective to which we can refer, no terminological elaboration replacing 'common sense' by a different combination of modifier and noun. Whatever "common sense" is and does, neither of the two terms it combines can be mistaken for the insensible workings or willful applications of technology. Nor can the "undefined norm" and "necessary condition" of "common sense" be equated with the pseudo-imperatives of merely personal "cleverness:" the "effect of our cognitive abilities," "common sense" is neither tautological in principle nor a "skilled" means of achieving a tautological effect, a "technique" that sets the very rules by which it is declared a "success." If we are to deduce the positive "sense" of the analytic lacuna that is "common sense" – deduce rather than elide the significance of that lacuna and foundation of the *Third Critique* itself – we must instead examine Kant's use of traditional logical categories to constitute a new, "critical" definition of judgment.

Like the foundational reference to "common sense" occurring only at its end, the process of consecutive specification preceding "common sense" serves to define the very possibility of a mental power never defined before as such, a "power of judgment" on whose exercise and operation all other intellectual and practical activities depend. Accepting and understanding the necessity of such an inversion in interpretive practice – one whose first condition is stated last in that it is not liable to demonstration itself (or: "mortal" is what I call "men") – may come to prove (or, more accurately, to have proven) a necessary part of the (logically) unprecedented analysis Kant undertakes, one whose own "effect" *upon* the "intellectual faculties" is to extend their interplay, and so put the aesthetic "into play," with respect to any perceptible object.

Most critically, Kant achieves this irreversible "revolution" in the conception of the aesthetic not by objectifying that conception but by analyzing it as an experience and not an object. And the first terms that this first formal analysis of the aesthetic, as the name of a certain kind of *experience in the subject*, must criticize, are its traditional first terms (and misnomers) equating objectifications of "the aesthetic" with "taste."[80] Replacing the notion of a purely "personal" (in the juridical sense of

---

80. In a celebrated footnote to the "Transcendental Aesthetic" of the First Critique (*KrV,* B 36, III: 70n), Kant mocks the peculiarly "German" tendency to conflate the terms, "aesthetic" and "taste," a confusion "grounded," he writes, on the "misplaced hope," first "formulated" by "Baumgarten," that "the critical judgment of the beautiful" can be "br[ought] under the principles of reason," and its "rules" thereby "raise[d]" to the level of a "science." Given that even "the most elegant sources" of these "purported rules" remain "merely empirical" in nature, such "rules or criteria," Kant notes, "can never serve as laws determined *a priori* according to which our judgments of taste must direct themselves." Kant then goes on to suggest that we may "come closer to the language and sense of the ancients, whose separation of knowledge into αιϲθητα και νοητα is well known" ("näher treten würde, bei denen die Einteilung der Erkenntnis in αιϲθητα και νοητα ist berühmt") by "taking" the "aesthetic" sometimes in a "transcendental, sometimes in a psychological sense" ("teils in transzendentalen Sinne, teils in psychologischer Bedeutung zu nehmen"). The preceding portion of the note criticizing the German use of the term, "aesthetic," begins: "Germans are the only ones who now use the word 'aesthetics' to designate that which other critique calls taste. The ground of this is the failed hope, conceived by the excellent analyst Baumgarten, of bringing the judgment of the beautiful under the principles of reason and raising the rules of these to the status of a

corporeal) passive experience mistakenly modeled on inarticulate, physiological sensation, with an active, express "power" of judgment at once subjective and general in its form and meaning, Kant initiates a series of reversals that redefine not only the aesthetic but the relation of the aesthetic to moral practice (or "pure reason") as well. Just as he "hypothesize[d]" that the path of metaphysics might cease to circle upon itself if it "dare[d]" to reverse, and so discover, its own proper starting point and end – departing from *how* it is we know things, rather than *what* "things" are, without our knowing them, "in themselves"[81] – Kant redefines aesthetic theory by reversing the order of its investigation, starting with how it is we experience objects aesthetically, rather than speculating on what inherently aesthetic objects or transcendental Ideas of the Beautiful must be in themselves. By starting from a general experience of the subject, rather than a theory of Ideas or prescriptive specification of objects, Kant is instead able to analyze *that experience* "in itself." In so doing, he initiates a logical cascade of reversals and substitutions of investigative objects in turn: the replacement of individual, culturally specific rules for the appreciation of the aesthetic, with a general, subjective "feeling" of "freedom;" of freedom from all necessity, with the necessity of its own "communication;" of communication of a subjective feeling, with acts of impersonal denomination; and of action, with its own, logically unfounded "faculty" and "foundation," "common sense."[82]

science. The effort, however, is in vain. For intellectual rules or criteria, are, according to their most *distinguished* sources, not empirical, and thus can never serve toward *determined a priori* rules according to which our judgment of taste must direct itself..." ("*Die Deutschen sind die einzigen, welche sich jetzt des Worts *Ästhetik* bedienen, um dadurch das zu bezeichnen, was andre Kritik des Geschmacks heissen. Es liegt hier eine verfehlte Hoffnung zum Grunde, die der vortreffliche Analyst Baumgarten fasste, die kritische Beurteilung des Schönen unter Vernunftprinzipien zu bringen, und die Regeln derselben zur Wissenschaft zu erheben. Allein diese Bemühung ist vergeblich. Denn gedachte Regeln, oder Kriterien, sind ihren *vornehmsten* Quellen nach bloss empirisch, und können also niemals zu *bestimmten* Gesetzen a priori dienen, wonach sich unser Geschmacksurteil richten müsste...").

81. See Chapter One, n. 6, this study. Again, this – to use Kant's terms – unprecedented "happy notion" is the "critical" "revolution" in philosophical thinking and point of departure of Kant's entire *Critique* that Guyer, even while making Kant his subject, either fails to grasp or chooses to ignore, basing his "measure[ment]" of Kant's "failures" on Humean-empirical rather than critical and logical criteria for (inevitably unattainable) success. Were one to assess the mimetic "success" or "failure" of a fully abstract, non-pictorial language, the category mistake involved both in procedure and result would be no less severe than Guyer's *a priori* exclusion of the stated hypothetical foundation of the *Critique* from his own philosophically anachronistic, revisionist account of a "Kant" before or without Kant.

82. By contrast, see Noah Lemos, *Common Sense* (Cambridge: Cambridge University Press, 2004), p. 8, on the opposition of Scottish common sense philosophy to the view "that there is a 'faculty of common sense' or that one's considered judgments are known *via* such a faculty."

3. "Free"

The defining "quality" of judgment, on Kant's analysis, is an absence of "interest" in the objects it perceives. Thus, the "First Moment" of the "Analytic of the Beautiful" ascribes to specifically *aesthetic* judgments the impartiality of mind traditionally reserved for ethical judgments before (and after) Kant's *Critique*. Effectively rewriting conventional conceptions of the aesthetic, Kant extends that impartiality to moral purposes as well: no less than personal appetites and "purposes" ("Zweck"), the general capacity to "judge" Kant defines is subject to no impersonal moral interest or stake. Nor is it subject to socially promoted interests or "tastes." The "disinterest" of the "power of judgment" even in the "existence" of the object judged suspends not only the *a priori*, representational and causal formation of cognitions, but the *a posteriori* – historical-social, whether instrumental or cultural – utilization of these we call "ideological" as well.[83]

As if to underscore the universality and impersonality of this first categorical aspect of judgment, and with it, of the entire Analytic to follow, Kant admonishes imitators of the contemporary theorist he himself most admires when excluding potential conflations of political and moral considerations with the experience and judgment of the aesthetic he describes. The first proper noun to arise in the Analytic of the Beautiful is "Rousseau," the philosopher to whose universal theory of "human rights" Kant, by his own positive acknowledgement, owed the "righting" of the selective bias toward "cultivation" of his own pre-critical moral thought (his stated debt to Hume, Rousseau's erstwhile host, described by Kant to be, rather, of the negative kind.[84]) It is not the obvious example of a monarchist, who would, in all likelihood, commend them, but the unlikely example of a "Rousseau-ist"

---

83. Kant, *KU* B 5, X: 116.

84. On Kant's early and unwavering acknowledgement of Rousseau as the moral philosopher who first "taught [him]" and "set [him] to rights, that the cultivation of knowledge does not constitute the honor" and "rights of mankind" ("Roussau hat mich zurecht gebracht ... [und] gelehrt, dass die Kultivierung ... unserer Erkenntnis nicht die Ehre [und Rechte] der Menschheit ausmacht"), see Klaus Reich's classic monograph, *Rousseau und Kant* (Tübingen: J. C. B. Mohr, 1936), reprinted in *Rousseau und die Folgen*, Hrsg. R. Bubner, K. Cramer, R. Wiehl [Göttingen: Vandenhoeck & Ruprecht, 1989]), pp. 80–96. See his *Prolegomena*, for Kant's "free admission" ("Ich gestehe frei") that he was "first" "awoken" from "many years" of "dogmatic slumber" by Hume's attack on causality, whose effectivity Hume deemed, in Kant's inimitable description, "a mere bastard of imagination impregnated by experience" "falsely considered by reason to be its own child" ("dass die

populist who would condemn them, that Kant employs to critique accounts of taste determined by social and cultural "interests," including personal interest and pleasure taken in the "existence" of aesthetic objects operating as indices of accumulated power and wealth. Directly preceding the naming of Rousseau at the opening of the First Analytic are the imagined comments of a self-styled rustic who has attempted to model himself, incongruously, on a (purely hypothetical) "original," or literally pre-historical, "homme sauvage," Rousseau's stated theoretical fiction of a pre-human human, lacking language, social relations, or relationships of any kind, made famous by his *Discours sur l'origine et les fondements de l'inégalité parmi les hommes*.[85] The views of a wholly unacculturated subject, no less than

---

Vernunft... [den Begriff der Kausalität] fälschlich für ihr eigen Kind halte, da er doch nichts anders als ein Bastard der Einbildungskraft sei") (Kant, *Prolegomena zu jeder künftigen* A 13, *Ibid.*, VI: 116). The crucial distinction *and* conflict between Hume's conception of mere "habit," made to "arise" ("entsprungenen") in the guise of "subjective necessity" by a so-called or pseudo "law of association" extrapolated from events (in direct contradiction with the formal basis of all law for Kant) and Kant's discussion of the intellectual "origin" ("Ursprung") of causality as a "concept," "arisen from pure understanding" rather than "arrived at by way of experience as apprehended by Hume" ("nicht, wie Hume besorgt hatte, von der Erfahrung abgeleitet, sondern aus dem reinen Verstande entsprungen"), describe the two sides of the problem of defining the origin or basis of language that Kant articulates across the tripartite composition of the *Critique* (Kant, *Prolegomena* A 9, 11, 14, *ibid.*, VI: 116–117, 119).

85. See Jean-Jacques Rousseau, *Discours sur les sciences et les arts; Discours sur l'origine, et les fondements de l'inégalité parmi les hommes* (Paris: Flammarion, 1992 [Paris: Plissot, 1751; Geneva, 1755]). For an excellent discussion of Rousseau's specifically temporal rather than historical and causal conception of "nature," "natural man," and, consequently, of "revolution" (the latter shared by Kant), see Dick Howard, *The Politics of Critique* (Minneapolis: University of Minnesota, 1988), pp. 162–63 esp.: "Rousseau broke through the classificatory image of nature as an immediately real presence; the originary state of nature arises only once society is already constituted ... The point is not to integrate a history into the General Will, promising to complete its quest for dialectical synthesis or transparency. Rousseau's fundamental insight makes evident the originary leap which institutes temporality. This leap, for which no logic or causality can account, institutes at the same time the state of nature... constantly instituted as orginary at the same time that its originary structure can never be made permanent. This defines its temporal structure. In this sense, Rousseau formulates a theory of revolution. The political reflection which institutes nature as temporal is not susceptible to reduction to a theory of history. Revolution is the rupture with history, the advent of the new, which can never be predicted but only made." On Kant's view of revolution as the necessary moral antithesis to natural or historical development, see esp. pp. 5–7: "Kant opposed revolution and supported the French Revolution. He apparently could not *think* this leap, and yet recognized it as an instance of the very causality of freedom on which his ethics (and ultimately his entire system) had to rest [...] the causality of freedom which would permit one to think of a revolution as something not merely necessitated by the phenomenal order of world development."

those of the cultural elite that made of Rosseau's "wild man" a fashionable ideal, are proffered by Kant so as to be *excluded* from the entirely disinterested, wholly nonconceptual (and thus noncultural) perception of objects at which his account of judgment aims:

> The pleasure which we combine with the presentation of the existence of an object is called interest. Such interest is thus always related to the faculty of desire, either as the determining ground of the same or as necessarily connected to its grounds of determination. When we ask if something is beautiful, however, we do not want to know whether we or anyone else is or could be partial to the existence of a thing, but, rather, how we judge it in the mere act of observation (perception or reflection). If someone asks me whether I find the palace that I see before me beautiful, so may I well say, I don't like the kind of thing that is made only to be gawked at; or, in the manner of that Iroquois Sachem, that nothing in Paris is more to his liking than the cooking shops; even more may I vilify, in good *Rousseau-ese*, the vanity of the great who waste the sweat of the people on such superfluous things; finally, I can easily persuade myself that, were I to find myself on an uninhabited island without hope of ever coming upon other men, and were able to conjure up such a majestic edifice merely by wishing, I would not even bother to take the trouble to do so if only I already had a hut that were comfortable enough for me. That is all well and good; *only it is not what we are talking about now [nur davon ist jetzt nicht die Rede]*. We only wish to know if the mere perception of an object is accompanied within me by pleasure, no matter how indifferent[86] I may be in view of the existence of the object of this perception. One can easily see that what is involved in my being able to say [of an object] that it is *beautiful*, and that I have taste, *is that which I make out of this external perception within myself, and not that which I depend upon in the existence of the object*... We must not be occupied whatsoever with the existence of things, but, rather, completely indifferent in that regard, in order to play the judge in things of taste.

> [Interesse wird das Wohlgefallen genannt, *was* wir mit der Vorstellung der Existenz eines Gegenstandes verbinden. Ein solches hat daher immer zugleich Beziehung auf das Begehrungsvermögen, entweder als Bestimmungsgrund desselben, oder doch als mit dem Bestimmungsgründe desselben notwendig zusammenhängenden. Nun will man aber, wenn die Frage ist, ob etwas schön sei, nicht wissen, ob uns, oder irgend jemand, an der Existenz der Sache irgend etwas gelegen sei, oder auch nur gelegen sein könne; sondern, wie wir sie in der blossen Betrachtung (Anschauung oder Reflexion) beurteilen. Wenn mich jemand fragt, ob ich den Palast, den ich vor mir sehe, schön finde: so mag ich zwar sagen: ich

---

86. Kant interprets the very appearance (or "Phänomen") of "indifference" ("Gleichgültigkeit") to be the initial, outward manifestation of judgment on which the possibility of a *critical* philosophy depends. See Kant, first draft of "Vorrede" to the first edition of the *First Critique*, X: A XI–XII.

liebe dergleichen Dinge nicht, die bloss für das Angaffen gemacht sind, oder, wie jener irokesische Sachem, ihm gefalle in Paris nichts besser als die Garküchen; ich kann noch überdem auf die Eitelkeit der Grossen auf gut *Rousseauisch* schmälen, welche den Schweiss des Volks auf so entbehrliche Dinge verwenden; ich kann mich endlich gar leicht überzeugen, dass, wenn ich mich auf einem unbewohnten Eilande, ohne Hoffnung, jemals wieder zu Menschen zu kommen, befände, und ich, durch meinen blossen Wunsche, ein solches Prachtgebäude hinzaubern könnte, ich mir auch nicht einmal diese Mühe darum geben würde, wenn ich schon eine Hütte hätte, die mir bequem genug wäre. Man kann mir alles dieses einräumen und gutheissen; nur davon ist jetzt nicht die Rede. Man will nur wissen, ob die blosse Vorstellung des Gegenstandes in mir mit Wohlgefallen begleitet sei, so gleichgültig ich auch immer in Ansehung der Existenz des Gegenstandes dieser Vorstellung sein mag. Man sieht leicht, *dass es auf dem, was ich aus dieser Vorstellung in mir selbst mache, nicht auf dem, worin ich von der Existenz des Gegenstandes abhänge, ankomme*, um zu sagen, *es sei schön*, und zu beweisen, ich habe Geschmack ... Man muss nicht im mindesten für die Existenz der Sache eingenommen, sondern in diesem Betracht ganz gleichgültig sein, um in Sachen des Geschmacks den Richter zu spielen.[87]]

The first condition of the power to judge an object – an absence of "interest in... its existence" – entails the negation of any practical attachment to that object in either a cognitive or moral sense, the interests of reason described by the First and the Second Critique respectively.[88] In every sense we can imagine, the object of judgment is neither a recognizable "object" ("Gegenstand"), nor, at one remove from objective existence, the recognizable indication of such existence, its non-objective yet meaningfully extant sign. Only by lacking all notion of what a perceived object either signifies or is "good for" (whether in Kant's larger moral or "merely technical" sense), indeed, by lacking any conception of what it is at all, can the subject of the specifically aesthetic experience of a sensuous object "judge" it – or, as Kant puts it, in the passage just cited, "play the judge."[89] Like "the free play of

87. Kant, *KU*, B 5–7, X: 116–17 (emphasis added).
88. For Kant's description of "interest" as either cognitive, i.e., based in a formal representation of an object of perception; or moral, based in a concept of the good believed to be promoted by a perceptual object; or "affective," based in the "excitement" of "desire" for "the existence of the object," and the negation of each of these in relation to judgment, see esp. Kant, *KU*, B 9–14, X: 118–123.
89. What Kant writes in the *Logik* of cognitive "errors" in "understanding," or intellectual "judgment," he may as well have written of errors in the "common understanding" *of* aesthetic judgment here. In the former case, the "sole basis for the arisal" of "all such error" is "to be sought," he states, "*in the unremarked influence of the sensory upon the understanding*, or more precisely stated, upon judgment" ("[d]er Entstehungsgrund alles Irrtums wird daher einzig und allein in dem *unvermerkten Einfluss der Sinnlichkeit auf den Verstand*, oder, genauer geredet, auf das Urteil, gesucht werden müssen" [Kant, *Logik* A 76–77, VI: 480–81]). In the case

understanding and imagination" – the nonconceptual relation that Kant goes on to define as the sole "communicable" content of judgment[90] – the subject who judges "plays the judge" *not* because judgment is a frivolous rather than fundamental activity, but because, in relation to the purposes of the two Critiques it alone can mediate, the exercise of judgment must be both impartial and without consequence, which is to say, as disinterested in, as it is unproductive of conceptual, empirical or moral objectives or aims.

Serving no purpose other than mediating the strictly divided realms of pure and practical reason hypothesized by the *Critique*, the act of judgment is, thus, "free," in Kant's terms, in every way an act can be: the absence of any and all "interest" in an object on the part of its freely perceiving subject itself reflects the "freedom" of the form delineated in the object so perceived.[91] Alternately derided and admired as either an aesthetic "formalist" or groundbeaking advocate of abstraction in art, Kant specifies that the forms perceived in aesthetic experiences, whether of pictures or picture frames, poems, draperies, or pepper plants planted in rows (to recall just a few of the improbably equivalent "objects" Kant names[92]), must not only be perceived to be free of recognizable cognitive content, but must be indeterminant or "free" in themselves, objects, whether natural or artificial in basis, that Kant gathers together under their single shared quality of offering to perception "free[ly]" "delineat[ed]" forms. His first description of that which pleases in any object we "find" "beautiful" states:

> In order to find anything to be good, I must always know what kind of thing this object is, that is, I must have a concept of it. In order to find beauty in such a thing, I need have no concept of it at all. Flowers, free delineations, linear tracings [or traits] intertwined with one another without purpose under the name of foliage, mean nothing, depend on no determined concept, yet please.
>
> [Um etwas gut zu finden, muss ich jederzeit wissen, was der Gegenstand für ein Ding sein soll, d.i. einen Begriff von demselben haben. Um Schönheit woran zu finden, habe ich das nicht nötig. Blumen, freie Zeichnungen, ohne Absicht in einander geschlungenen Züge, unter dem Namen des Laubwerks, bedeuten nichts, hängen von keinem bestimmten Begriffe ab, und gefallen doch.[93]]

of "judgment" no longer identifiable with "understanding" except insofar as the latter remains in free play with imagination or conflict with reason, i.e., in specifically aesthetic experience, it is, by contrast, not the sensory itself but "interest" in the sensory "existence" *of an object* that would compel us to mistake distinct objective qualities for the properly subjective bases of aesthetic judgment, and individual interest for the distinctive power of judgment itself.

90. Kant, *KU*, B 29, X: 132.
91. *KU*, B 11–13, X: 120–21; B 49, X: 146.
92. For these and other heterogeneous occasions for the exercise of judgment mentioned by Kant, see Kant, *KU* B 209, 43–44, 215, 211, 72, X: 261–62, 142, 265, 262,163.
93. Kant, *KU*, B 11–12, X: 120.

Whether two-dimensional in origin or in outline, a "delineation" is a sensible yet *non*phenomenal appearance, which is to say, it is the appearance of appearing "free" from "meaning" or "representing" any "thing." In this way, the "subject" it renders perceptible to the senses is nothing other than the internal state of the subject capable of perceiving it – for Kant, any subject who, suspending practical knowledge of the identity and use of an object, instead feels pleasure (or displeasure) in the conceptually unsubordinated appearance of "traits" whose dynamic "intertwining" the senses actively record and trace. In the act of judging such a "delineation," something sensible and yet "free" of objectification, that "represents nothing, no object determined by a definite concept" ("sie stellen nichts vor, kein Objekt unter einem bestimmten Begriffe"), the subject of judgment, as if taking the place of that indeterminable object, similarly "feels him or herself fully *free*" ("sich ... völlig *frei* fühlt"[94]).

To be of the sensory world but make no use of it – to derive no knowledge or practical value but solely a different, impractical sense of one's own ability to be engaged by an experience that is "free" of either representational, cognitive or consumable, or nonrepresentational, inconsumable moral content – is to be a subject who, shorn of "interest," instead "makes [something] out of an external perception inside [himself]."[95] The subject who "makes something out of" perception that is not identical with perception, who makes something unknown "inside [himself]" while attending to something unknown outside himself, thus "feels," like the dynamic form of such an object, "free." *Here aesthetic judgment offers, by way of an unknown perceptual object, a new mode of being in the subject.* The judging subject "feels," in the mode of aesthetic experience, what Kant states is the "real" purpose of his "negative," critical project: to render not only knowledge but actual agency, or action "free" of delimited perceptual-phenomenal conditions, possible.[96] Disentangling experience in general from "positive" – idealist or skeptical – philosophy of experience and moral theory alike, Kant, in the *Critique of Pure Reason,* first limits (and thus ensures) its epistemological content. Separating epistemological and conceptual from aesthetic experience, or cognition from judgment, he then does precisely the inverse, analyzing judgment as a "power" based in a freedom from limited application, a "feeling free" arising with a sensory delineation of freedom perceived.

The "freedom" of which we have no "cognition" but which we *"can think"* takes the non-cognitive form, in the Second Critique, not of judgment but of a certain kind of unconditioned law. Unlike cognition and judgment, this is a law in which empirical experience can play no part, "[f]or," Kant reasons good humoredly:

> everyone's will does not have one and the same object at every moment; rather everyone has his own object (his own pleasure), which, even if it could be made

---

94. Kant, *KU*, B 49, X: 146; B18, X: 124 (emphasis in text).
95. See this Chapter, this Section, n. 87.
96. Kant, *KrV* BXXIX, III–32.

to agree with the guiding aims of others, is far from sufficient for the making of a law, because the exceptions that one will have to make to it from time to time are endless and could never be determinately included in one general rule. The kind of harmony to come out of this resembles that of a certain satirical poem, in which the soulful agreement of a married couple set on each other's destruction is represented: *O wonderful harmony, what he wishes, she wishes, too*, etc.; or what is recounted of the pledge King Franz the First made to Emperor Carl the Fifth: what my brother Carl wants (Milan), I want to have, too. Empirical grounds of determination do not suffice for any general external legislation, but also just as little for an internal one; for everyone bases his inclination on one subject, and everyone else on another, and in every individual subject one inclination exerts most influence at one moment, and another, at another moment. To make a law sufficient to rule under the condition of agreement with it on all sides is completely impossible.

[Denn der Wille aller hat alsdenn nicht ein und dasselbe Objekt, sondern ein jeder hat das seinige (sein eigenes Wohlbefinden), welches sich zwar, zufälligerweise, auch mit anderer ihren Absichten, die sie gleichfalls auf sich selbst richten, vertragen kann, aber lange nicht zum Gesetze hinreichend ist, weil die Ausnahmen, die man gelegentlich zu machen befugt ist, endlos sind, und gar nicht bestimmt in eine allgemeine Regel befasst werden können. Es kommt auf diese Art eine Harmonie heraus, die derjenigen ähnlich ist, welche ein gewisses Spottgedicht auf die Seeleneintracht zweier sich zu Grunde richtenden Eheleute schildert: *O wundervolle Harmonie, was er will, will auch sie* etc., oder was von der Anheischigmachung König Franz des Ersten gegen Kaiser Karl den Fünften erzählt wird: was mein Brüder Karl haben will (Mailand), das will ich auch haben. Empirische Bestimmungsgründe taugen zu keiner allgemeinen äusseren Gesetzgebung, aber auch eben so wenig zur innern; denn jeder legt sein Subjekt, ein anderer aber ein anderes Subjekt der Neigung zum Grunde, und in jedem Subjekt selber ist bald die, bald eine andere im Vorzuge des Einflusses. Ein Gesetz ausfindig zu machen, das sie insgesamt unter dieser Bedingung, nämlich mit allseitiger Einstimmung, regierte, ist schlechterdings unmöglich.[97]]

A "law" that is "legislative" at every moment for all must be independent of all "empirical grounds of determination." Its "condition" can be neither an external object, nor any "agreement," or metaphorically ascribed, metaphysical "harmony," among subjects: neither the "union of souls" wonderfully satirized by Kant in a married couple mutually desirous of each other's destruction, nor of siblings, who, as king and emperor, both covet the same territory. All, even allied subjects are not only distinct in their positive and negative objects of desire, but are internally at odds with themselves, subject, *as* subjects, to changes in desire over time, "now this, now that inclination takes preferential influence" ("bald die [Neigung], bald eine

---

97. Kant, *KprV* A 51, VII: 137.

andere im Vorzuge des Einflusses"). The single sufficient, or defining condition of a law thus lies not in experiential circumstance but in the degree of "freedom" from circumstance enacted in its own form: "Given, that only the mere legislative form of maxims is the sufficient ground of determination of a will, ... so must such a will be thought as entirely independent from the law of nature of phenomena, namely, the law of causality... Such an independence ... is called *freedom* in the strictest, i.e., transcendental understanding ..." ("Vorausgesetzt, dass die blosse gesetzgebende Form der Maximen allein der zureichende Bestimmungsgrund eines Willens sei ... so muss ein solcher Wille als gänzlich unabhängig von dem Naturgesetz der Erscheinung, nämlich das Gesetz der Kausalität ... gedacht werden. Eine solche Unabhängigkeit aber heisst *Freiheit* im strengsten, d.i. transzendentalen Verstande").[98]

The Second Critique names that independent, self-legislating form, and sole "law" of a "free will," the "moral law:" the only law one is truly free – from all particular, positive conditions – to make for one's self, rather than constrained, by personal inclinations and phenomenal conditions, either to follow or to break.[99] The Third Critique calls what we "*make out of* ... external perception within [ourselves]," without interest in "the *existence* of the object," judgment. While both moral action and judgment are "ma[d]e" within the subject, on the basis of "power[s]" inhering in every subject, they are fundamentally different in a critical aspect. Judging is what we do not when we *act* as free, or self-legislating, agents, but when we "*feel ourselves free*" to exercise the non-legislating "power of judgment," "to play the judge." And judgment of aesthetic experience does not rule or make law regarding experience of any sort; its "making" depends instead on a "feeling" of freedom arising within subjects in the absence of a cognitive object. The condition of judgment is not that we act in accordance with a law we have given ourselves but that we "feel" *and* articulate something "made within [ourselves]" "out of ... external perception," something that was not "there" – neither "inside" nor "outside" us – before, but comes about with our "feeling free" of our own or any particular "interest" in the "existence of the object." To judge in the Third Critique is, in a new and profoundly meaningful sense, to act as a subject compelled by the "feeling" of "freedom" to speak.

98. *Ibid.*, A 52, VII: 138 (emphasis in text).
99. *Ibid.*, A 53, VII: 139 *et passim*.

4. "Feeling"

How can an experience of "freedom" in sensory perception be related to a "faculty" so little admitting of freedom as "common sense"? What experience could possibly be "free" enough, both from a (hypothetical) cognitive ability to form heterogeneous, conceptual-experiential representations *a priori*, and an overriding ability to act as "free" (moral) agents in disregard of such representations, so as truly to be able to mediate between them? What does a subject "free" of the forms of knowledge, of moral action, and even of "constructive" rather than hypothetical modes of thinking do?[100]

Kant calls such an experience "feeling," and little in the First and Second Critique prepares us for the introduction of the term. Associated before and after Kant with the turn from philosophy toward the cultivation of personal "sensibility" elaborated by, among others, Hutcheson, Shaftesbury, Burke, and Hume, accounts of subjectivity that focus on the role of feeling in experience typically supplant theoretical inquiry with empiricist, often theatrical descriptions of the private emotions experiences arouse. The credited ability of "sensibility" to invest perception with moral content, to be as inviolable in its personally felt "sense" of things as is the inarticulate, nonmoral and private experience of "feeling" itself, sustains precisely the kind of intellectual complacency – epistemological no less than ethical and political – that Kant's *Critique* aimed foremost to counteract.

The precedent for Kant's inclusion of "feeling" *within* philosophy, not as aberration but as basis of the coherence of his own *Critique*, lies not with either spiritual or empirical theories of sentiment and sensibility but with the nonpositivist epistemology of Rousseau, the thinker whose heterodox linkage of feeling *with* cognition rendered him permanently ineligible for election to the ranks of sentimentalists, aesthetes and "sensible souls" professing the guidance of "feeling" alone. For, identifying the role of "feeling" in the progress, regress and revolutions of civil society – from the creation and inevitable increase of social inequality and brutality to a contracted state of equality constituting by universal convention the rule of all by all – Rousseau, recalling the ancient stoics, critiqued its active cultivation as cause and sign of societal decay. Yet, unlike the stoics, Rousseau considered "feeling" not in antipathy to but as a basis of reason itself. The first modern theorist to analyze emotion as an inherently social rather than individually subjective phenomenon, Rousseau performed his own, historically misinterpreted revolution in philosophical thinking by recognizing in "feeling" a motive force whose occurrence

---

100. Kant, *KrV*, B XI, III: 22.

and effects must be considered in distinction from cultural and empirical givens if the nature and history of human reason and experience are to be understood.

More than any other philosopher, it was the purportedly pure rationalist, Kant, who grasped the full scope of, and faithfully integrated within his own systematic thinking, the larger philosophical role of "feeling" in Rousseau. For, rather than define a supposed "state of nature" to which Rousseau supposedly wished all mankind to return, the experience of feeling first distinguished from purely physical urges by his *Discours* marks the passage and "change"[101] from a retrospectively "hypothesized"[102] "natural man" – imagined, for comparative analytic purposes, to possess the same corporal needs but none of the intellectual attributes and passions of men – to actual men and women as they know each other and themselves historically, i.e., on the basis of their social – differential, comparative and contractual rather than empirical-positive – relation. It is *because* "natural man" does *not* "feel" (or reason, or remember, or imagine, or even desire or do anything beyond that which will sate his immediate physical needs) that he is proffered only hypothetically by Rousseau, not as an ideal of nonsocial man but to oppose the supposed naturalness of unequal and enslaving social relations. "Rousseau-ists" (to use Kant's phrase) who instead equate "feeling" with innocence, present as distorted a caricature of the critical role "feeling" plays in the speculative epistemology, anti-theological social theory, and anti-naturalist "social contract" of Rousseau, as histories of the Enlightenment typically offer of the biographical Rousseau, that of a social "savage" (noble or not) in conflict with the rationalism of the age, philosopher who decried the intellect and praised the heart.[103]

---

101. See J.-J. Rousseau, *Discours sur l'origine* ..., pp. 177, 227, 256, *et passim*. On the significance of Rousseau's ethical and political theory for Kant's, see Reich, *Rousseau und Kant*; Irving Petscher, "Jean Jacques Rousseau. Ethik und Politik," in *Rousseau und die Folgen*, pp. 1–23, and Otto Vossler, *Rousseaus Freiheitslehre* (Göttingen: Vandenhoeck & Ruprecht, 1962).

102. Cf. Chapter One, n. 16, this study, for Kant's introduction of the scientific mode of hypothetical reasoning into discursive philosophy; see n. 104, this Chapter, for the full quotation from Rousseau regarding the necessity of "dispensing with the [supposed historical] facts" that his theory of inequality will prove mere fictions, and of replacing them with "hypothetical, conditional" reasoning instead.

103. Extending, improbably, from Voltaire to Derrida, a long series of critics have condemned (or, in the case of Starobinski, commended) the idealization or ideology of nature Rousseau's theory supposedly promotes, just as his literary production, along with that of a host of central eighteenth-century authors – Goethe, Diderot, Goldsmith, Richardson, Hölderlin, and early Wordsworth, among them – has been viewed to presage romanticism by making of "feeling" a secular religion. That Rousseau, as influential a novelist as theorist, may have placed "feeling" and "nature" at the center of his work not to advance anti-intellectual biases, whether reactionary, naïve, or ideological in basis, but to designate (in advance of Kant) the rational limits of rational analysis, has not figured in his own typical characterization as anti-enlightenment scourge.

While "feeling" is as central to Kant's critical "hypothesis" as it is to Rousseau's,[104] the non-narrative, architectonic form of Kant's *Critique*, in direct contrast to Rousseau's "hypothetical" theoretical fiction, makes the introduction of feeling at its very center appear less like evidence of a naturalist ideology than an insignificant misstep or logical weakness: a failed "moment" in the analytic rather than narrative sense. And, indeed, whether "feeling" of any kind can successfully fulfill the central

A contrasting analysis of Rousseau's position within a tradition of theoretical and fictional writing "beyond feeling" is offered in the final chapter of Brodsky, *Words' Worth: What the Poet Does* (New York and London: Bloomsbury, 2020). Rei Terada's *Feeling in Theory. Emotion after the "Death of the Subject"* (Cambridge: Harvard University Press, 2001) deftly renews and extends Rousseau's introduction of feeling into theory by identifying its presence within the analysis of his writing by Derrida and de Man in particular. No less than in the theoretical writings of Kant, Rousseau and Wordsworth, analyzed here, the intervention of feeling has played a pivotal critical role in eighteenth-century literary texts in particular, one that underscores, rather than excludes, the larger theoretical, moral and epistemological import of their fictions. I have attempted to analyze some of these in, "Narrative Representation and Criticism: 'Crossing the Rubicon' in *Clarissa*," in *Reading Narrative: Form, Ethics, Ideology*, ed. James Phelan (Columbus: Ohio State University Press, 1989), pp. 207–219; "Whatever Moves You: 'Experimental Philosophy' and the Literature of Experience in Diderot and Kleist," in *The Tradition of Experiment from the Enlightenment to the Present. Essays in Honor of Peter Demetz*. ed. Nancy Kaiser and David E. Wellbery (Ann Arbor: University of Michigan Press, 1992), pp. 17–43, and "Beyond the Pleasure of the Principle of Death: Goethe's *Werther* and Goldsmith's *Vicar of Wakefield*," in *Einsamkeit und Geselligkeit um 1800*, ed. S. Schmid and R. Emig (Hamburg: Carl Winter Verlag, 2008), pp. 29–40.

104. See Rousseau, *Discours sur les origine et les fondements* . . ., para. 6, p. 169: "Let's begin by clearing away all facts, for they don't touch upon the question. We must not take the research into which one can enter on this subject for historical truth but only as hypothetical and conditional reasoning more appropriate to elucidating the nature of things than to showing their true origin" ("Commençons donc par écarter tous les faits, car ils ne touchent point à la question. Il ne faut pas prendre les recherches, dans lesquelles on peut entrer sur ce sujet, pour des vérités historiques, mais seulement pour des raisonnements hypothétiques et conditionnels; plus propres à éclaircir la nature des choses qu'à en montrer la véritable origine"), and Kant, *KrV*, B XXIII, III: 28n: "So the central laws of the movements of the heavenly bodies granted confirmed certainty to that which Copernicus only assumed at first as an hypothesis, and proved at the same time the invisible power that connects the universe (Newtonian attraction), which would have remained forever undiscovered if Copernicus had not dared, in a counter-sensical but true way, to look for the observed movements not in the objects of heaven, but in their viewer. In analogy with that hypothesis, I present in this Preface the transformation in mode of thinking brought forward in this Critique only as an hypothesis . . ." ("So verschafften die Zentralgesetze der Bewegungen der Himmelskörper dem, was Kopernikus anfänglich nur als Hypothese annahm, ausgemachte Gewissheit, und bewiesen zugleich die unsichtbare den Weltbau verbindende Kraft (der Newtonische Anziehung), welche auf immer unentdeckt geblieben wäre, wenn die erstere es

role Kant accords it in the *Critique* remains, of necessity, an open question. For, in order to conform to Kant's hypothetical division of our powers into "faculties," the function of feeling within the mediating faculty of judgment must itself be two-sided; like any "bridge" or "overpass" ("Übergang"[105]), this one, so-called by Kant, must have one foot in each of the two Critiques whose "unoverseeable chasm" ("unübersehbare Kluft"[106]) of separation it spans. Thus, unlike Rousseau, for whom the passions color cognition, and thus moral action in turn,[107] Kant logically divides 'feeling" and the aesthetic experience it accompanies into two, apparently contradictory feelings: those of "pleasure" [*Lust*] in the beautiful and "displeasure" or "pain" [*Unlust*] in the sublime.

The opposition of positive "pleasure" to its negation in "displeasure" that Kant makes central to the specifically non-narrative, architectonic exposition of his *Critique* will provide the nonrational basis for diachronic – dialectical and/or differential – models of experience articulated in literature, philosophy and theory of experience after Kant. For the early and late romantics, Goethe, Schiller, Hölderlin, Kleist, Keats, Wordsworth, and P.B. Shelley, as for the great authors of "modern life," Baudelaire, Mallarmé, Rilke, Kafka, Proust and Celan, no less than those of modern theoretical reflection, from Hegel and Feuerbach to Marx, Freud, Husserl, Heidegger, Horkheimer, Adorno, Marcuse, Benjamin, Lévi-Strauss, and their ongoing descendants, Kant's identification and division of the equally noncognitive experiences of positive and negative "feeling" – experiences of excess at work within and alongside rationally structured relations – prove productive in a distinctly "historical" or narrative sense, providing the structure for dynamic conceptions of individual development, of social, political and cultural formation, and of history itself. While Kant famously refuses to investigate the structure of time, hypothesizing it to be an *a priori* "form" of perceptual experience instead, it is his introduction of two immediately opposed poles within the single nonconceptual realm of "feeling" that will offer others a basis for delimiting and integrating individual oppositional events diachronically. For, considered in its

---

nicht gewagt hätte, auf eine widersinnliche, aber doch wahre Art, die beobachteten Bewegungen nicht in den Gegenständen des Himmels, sondern in ihrem Zuschauer zu suchen. Ich stelle in dieser Vorrede die in der Kritik vertragene, jener Hypothese analogische, Umänderung der Denkart auch nur als Hypothese auf...").

On the key role played by "feeling" in the Third Critique, and by his theory of judgment in the development both of Kant's ethics and his Rousseau-inspired, political theory of self-legislation, see Howard, *The Politics of Critique*, pp. 10–12, 184: "Republican law is not like the causal laws of nature; it is structured like the judgment of beauty's 'lawfulness without law' which is justified through a public process of interaction ... the 'freedom to make public use of one's reason at every point.'"

105. Kant, *KU*, B XIX, X: 83.
106. *Ibid.*
107. See Section Six, this Chapter.

necessary internal tension rather than systematic external function, Kant's "bridge" allows for the ascription to experience of a certain generative logic, a development endowing lived time with, if not a coherent, then at least a temporally "extensive," articulable and representable, "shape."

No such configuration of diachrony is laid out in Kant's *Critique*. On the one hand, time, that "schema" distinguished as entirely "internal" in origin and perceptible only *a posteriori*, in the comparative perception of physical change, is a wholly indemonstrable, purely hypothetical "form," whose "art," "monogram of the pure imagination *a priori*," remains "hidden in the depths of the human soul."[108] On the other hand, precisely because its "art" enables diachronic experience in the first place, time appears practically irrelevant to the immediate, nonrepresentational and nonconceptual "feeling," of "pleasure" or "displeasure," produced within us at any moment we engage, as subjects, in specifically aesthetic perceptions of sensory objects. Such perceptions issue not in the formation of stories, but of judgments, and within the "playful" activity of judging, the schematic role played by time in cognition is neither assumed nor put into question. Its integral formalizing function is instead experienced – if it can be said to be experienced at all – as cancelled or suspended. For, if "free play" means anything, it is the absence of all schematization, whether that of experience by temporal perception or, in Kant's terms, of time as an *a priori* "schema" in itself.

Yet the act of judging, if it is to be recognized as such and so made available to analysis in the first place, must present itself in some external or expressive, and not merely hypothetical theoretical form. That form and expression of the "feeling" of "pleasure" or "displeasure" is not temporally predicated in Kant, but it is, no less for that, articulated. What articulate form, then, does "feeling," in Kant, take?

---

108. Kant, *KrV* B 181, X: 190. Cf. the discussion of the schema in Chapter Two, Section Nine, and Chapter Three, this study.

5. Speech Act and "Communicability"

The expression by the power of judgment of the experience of "feeling" – central mediating activity of the *Critique* as a whole – consists in the statements, "It is beautiful," "It is sublime."[109] In direct contradiction of the commonplace view of Kant as inattentive to the nonrational properties and potential of language explored by such contemporary and later "anti-Enlightenment" thinkers as Hamann, Nietzsche, Heidegger and Wittgenstein (or, earlier, by Pascal, Vico, Hobbes, Condillac, Rousseau and Diderot), the medium of the power of judging in the Third Critique, unlike that of any other purported "faculty" or "capacity," is not only specifically described but described specifically to be that of speech. Already in his attribution of the feeling of freedom to the apperception of a subject who judges ("the person who judges feels himself fully *free*"[110]) and of "generality" ("Allgemeinheit") to the feeling of pleasure judged ("he [who judges] must believe he has reason to attribute a similar pleasure to everyone"[111]), Kant states that it is only in the act of "speaking" that this combined experience of freedom and generality of feeling at once articulates and constitutes itself, makes itself and makes itself known. Judgment *speaks* and what it says does not name but qualifies, describing an unknown nominative subject ("it") by a simple predicative complement ("is beautiful;" "is sublime"). It is because the "subject" of judgment can find no "personal," as "he"[112] can find no "objective" basis for the

---

109. Cascardi comes closest to acknowledging the entirely technical, verbal definition of judgment Kant constructs, before noting the formal resemblance of these sole utterances of judgment to cognitive or constative statements: "The claims, 'It is beautiful' and 'It is sublime' (which are quite remarkably, the only two examples Kant offers of claims of taste), may, as we have said, take the same form as assertions of epistemological facts" (Cascardi, *Consequences of Enlightenment*, p. 81).

110. See n. 113, this Section, this Chapter, for full citation.

111. Kant, *KU*, B 18, X: 124–25.

112. The awkwardness, peculiar to English, of having either to choose between or to double all pronominal and adjectival references ("he or she;" "his or her") to a single, implied general subject, is both exacerbated and eradicated by Kant's use of the term, "subject," to redefine the concerns of philosophy itself. For, in Kant, that common noun serves both to designate, in traditional logical terms, the placeholder of a purely grammatical function, and to name the new, central focus of a necessarily "impure," and thus "critical" philosophy, the distinctly human "manifold" of mutually complementary *and* contradictory "faculties" that it is, or should be, the task of philosophy to analyze.

"feeling" that "he" speaks in the first place, and it is *as speech*, the mode of manifestation shared by all, that judgment indicates its general, nonprivative nature:

> Since [judgment] does not base itself on any inclination of the subject (nor on any other dominating interest), but rather *because* the judging subject [der Urteilender] feels himself fully *free* in view of the pleasure he attributes to the object, so can he discover the grounds of this pleasure in no personal conditions that would depend upon his subject alone, and thus must regard it as grounded in that which he can presuppose of *everyone else*; consequently he must believe he has reason to attribute a similar pleasure to everyone. He will thus so *speak of the beautiful, as if* beauty were a quality of the object and judgment, logical (constituting a cognition of the object through concepts) ... For [aesthetic judgment] has this similarity with logical judgments, that we can suppose its validity *for everyone*.
>
> [Denn da es sich nicht auf irgend eine Neigung des Subjekts (noch auf irgend ein anderes überlegtes Interesse) gründet sondern *da* der Urteilende sich in Ansehung des Wohlgefallens, welches er dem Gegenstande widmet, völlig *frei* fühlt; so kann er keine Privatbedingungen als Gründe des Wohlgefallens auffinden, an diese sich sein Subjekt allein hinge, und muss es daher als in demjenigen begründet ansehen, was er auch bei jedem andern voraussetzen kann; folglich muss er glauben Grund zu haben, *jedermann* ein ähnliches Wohlgefallen zuzumuten. Er wird daher *vom Schönen so sprechen, als ob* Schönheit eine Beschaffenheit des Gegenstandes und das Urteil logisch (durch

The Third Critique further complicates this double, technical and philosophical usage by rendering explicit, and splitting, the single, grammatical and analytic "subject" implied in the First and Second Critiques. The "subject" who judges commits a definitively grammatical act – an act of speech – but does so not *in propria*, nor indeed in any, *persona*, but, rather, impersonally to begin with: the first word and subject of the discourse uttered by the "subject" who judges is not "I" but an undefined "it."

Finally, that personal qualities, including those typically assigned to genders, do not define Kant's "subject" – whose hypothesized, limited and unlimited abilities are themselves the new, philosophically "heterogeneous" subject of his *Critique* – is underscored by Kant's critical doubling of that subject by the qualifier, "transcendental," to signify *not* some purely immaterial subject somehow divorced from all experience but one whose capacities *for* both experience *and* action are not conditioned upon any particular experience. Defined only by the ability to produce the logical syntax for connecting, and so to understand formally delimited experience, and to act, both in intellectual and "moral matters," in "freedom" from those very forms of perceptual cognition, the "transcendental subject" – which, for Kant, means any and all subjects – is as undefined by conventional marks of "identity," whether personal or cultural, chosen or imposed, as by the empirical givens or *accidens* of birth.

Begriffe vom Objekte eine Erkenntnis desselben *ausmache*) wäre ... darum, weil es doch mit dem logischen die Ähnlichkeit hat, dass man die Gültigkeit desselben *für jedermann* daran vorasussetzen kann.[113]]

The assumption of the general validity of judgment is reflected in the fact of its verbal articulation. It is the specifically *verbal* mode, and not "mode of thought," ("Denkungsart"[114]) of judgment, its enactment in an utterance understood to be comprehensible and attributable to all, that lends it the "logical" quality "constituting" the constative form of "cognition," even while what it says says nothing about either that assumption or the subject's personal "inclination" with regard to the object that occasions it, but is instead limited to "speak[ing]" merely "as if" speaking of a "quality of the object" itself. The relationship of judgment to logic implied by its exclusive realization in verbal form, the very form whose grammatical and syntactic rules of comprehension are similarly required for the exercise of logic generally, remains one of implication rather than identity, causing judgment to appear at once universal and immediately particular in origin, its "real,"[115] rather than merely phenomenal meaning both self-evident and covert, "objective" and "subjective" – a speech act, in short, whose "ground," like that of every speech act, is and can be nothing but the "subjective condition" of "the general capacity for communication," rather than any "sensation" as such:

> If pleasure in a given object preceded, and only general communicability were acknowledged in judgments of taste, there would be a contradiction. For such pleasure would be nothing other than the mere pleasantness of a sensation and thus, by its nature, could have only private validity, because immediately dependent solely upon the internal presentation by which an object *is given*.
>
> *Thus it is the general capacity to communicate* [or general communicability] of an internal state that *must constitute the ground of a judgment of taste as its subjective condition*.
>
> [Ginge die Lust an dem gegebenen Gegenstande vorher, und nur die allgemeine Mitteilbarkeit desselben sollte im Geschmacksurteile der Vorstellung des Gegenstandes anerkannt werden, so würde ein solches Verfahren mit sich selbst im Widerspruche stehen. Denn dergleichen Lust würde keine andere, als die blosse Annehmlichkeit in der Sinnenempfindung sein, und daher ihrer Natur nach nur Privatgültigkeit haben können, weil sie von der Vorstellung, wodurch der Gegenstand *geben wird*, unmittelbar abhinge.

---

113. Kant, *KU*, B 18, X: 124 (emphases in part my own).
114. See next note, for the specifically "theoretical" and "practical" "modes of thought" belonging, by contrast, to the realms of cognition and action, respectively.
115. On the "practical," both "moral" and verbal bases of the "real," see n. 55, Chapter Two, Section One, this study.

Also ist es die allgemeine Mitteilungsfähigkeit des Gemützustandes in der gegebenen Vorstellung, *welche, als subjektive Bedingung des Geschmacksurteils, demselben zum Grunde liegen*....[116]]

The expression of a feeling (of pleasure or displeasure) in words that *do not express that feeling*, the "immediate" experience of a subject, but something else instead, a "capacity to communicate" that states of something *not* itself, "it is beautiful," "it is sublime," and nothing more, appears both sufficiently empty of particularity to resemble statements that are logical "for everyone," i.e., statements constating logical "knowledge" of "objects through concepts" and nothing more, *and* "free" of the cognitive content given shape by conceptual, logical statements, and thus logical – if one can say so much – only *in part*.[117]
The confusion of logic with "feeling" that his analysis of the specifically verbal mode of judgment describes is one Kant neither advances nor avoids, and if it seems as unsuited to the rigor of his distinctions among, and definitions of, the "faculties of reason" as does his undefined (necessarily overtly ungrounded, i.e., *neither* strictly *a priori nor a posteriori* referential) denomination of the "condition" upon which judgment depends "common sense," a less conventional – or, in Kant's terms more critical – inspection of them reveals the grounds of that confusion to

---

116. Kant, *KU* B 28, X: 131 (some emphases added).
117. See David W. Crawford, *Kant's Aesthetic Theory* (Madison: University of Winsconsin Press, 1974), pp. 16–17, for a perceptive analysis of the "discrepancy" between logical and grammatical form in the verbal articulation of judgment Kant defines. In criticizing Kant's "imprecis[ion]," in this and other aspects of his Analytic (including its failure to conform to the Aristotelian table of categories presented in the First Critique), Crawford brings to the fore the distinctions between both judgment and logic-based statements, and judgment and the grammatical representation of the experience in which judgment is based, when imprecisely observing himself that while judgment "affirms" "a feeling of pleasure" in the "person making the judgment" (in fact it does no such thing), "the grammatical subject of the judgment is," instead, "the object" in whose perception the pleasure is felt (16). Most significantly, Crawford emphasizes the critical distinction between the "mere sensation" of "pleasure" had in "simply sensing an object" and "condition" of "common sense" that Kant states "underlies the faculty of judgment." What he does not recognize, and this work argues, is that what distinguishes "common sense" from any individual "sensation" is its own necessarily *verbal* basis and realization: "[i]f the judgment of taste were made simply and directly on the basis of a pleasure in having a given sensation (simply sensing the object), it could make no claim to universal validity. The pleasures of mere sensation (that is smell, taste, texture, sound, or sight is pleasing to me) are completely subjective, in Kant's view; they vary from individual to individual.... By relating the pleasure in the beautiful to the faculty of judgment, however, Kant claims to have shown how it is possible for judgments of taste to make this claim for universal validity. He maintains that the principle which underlies the faculty of judgment (*sensus communis*) is a condition for any experience whatsoever" (27–28).

be those that determine the rigor of Kant's analysis itself. For in describing judgment as a "feeling" in a subject (i.e., an I who feels pleasure or displeasure) articulated in the "communicable" verbal form of a logical, universally valid statement about an object (i.e., "It is beautiful;" "It is sublime"), Kant describes – and must describe – an experience that is *neither theoretical nor practical but expressible*: a "feeling" that produces neither knowledge nor action but *words*, a statement, uttered by someone who could be anyone, "logically" constating *not that feeling* but a quality of something, of any undefined thing, outside ourselves. The subject who, in judging, "speaks of the beautiful as if beauty were a quality of the object and judgment were logical" neither knows anything nor acts in any physical or moral sense, *but says*; and, consistent with saying the speech act it speaks – sole act the "power of judgment" effects – the specifically verbal production of judgment must owe to an experience neither cognitive nor moral "reason" can define, one unencompassed by their separate, "object" "realms"[118] of sensory objects and the Good respectively. Rather than representing or enacting any object, any subject who, in the experience of "feeling," "feels himself free," is free to speak of something *in the place of feeling itself*. Judgment speaks "as if" what it says "were *constitutive* of a cognition of the object through concepts" even while employing no such concepts and constituting no such cognition. Rather than expressing a

---

118. See Kant, *KU*, B XVIII–XXII, X: 82–85: "Our complete faculties of knowledge have two realms, that of the concepts of nature and that of the concept of freedom ... two different realms which ... continuously restrict each other in their effects in the sensory world ... Thus there must be a ground of the unity of the supersensory, which lies at the ground of nature, with that, which the concept of freedom practically contains, whose concept, while neither theoretically or practically attaining to a cognition, thus makes possible the transition [or bridge] from the mode of thinking according to its principles of the one to that according to its principles of the other ... This is *the power of judgment*, about which one has cause to guess by analogy, that it too may contain its own principle; which, even when no field of objects stands as its realm, can have some [or any] ground [or floor]" ("Unser gesamtes Erkenntnis vermögen hat zwei Gebiete, das der Naturbegriffe, und das des Freiheitsbegriffe ... zwei verschieden[e] Gebiete, die sich ... in ihren Wirkungen in der Sinnenwelt unaufhörlich einschränken ... Also muss es doch einen Grund der *Einheit* des Übersinnlichen, welches der Natur zur Grunde liegt, mit dem, was der Freiheitsbegriff praktisch enthält, geben, wovon der Begriff, wenn er gleich weder theoretisch noch praktisch zu einem Erkenntnisse desselben gelangt, mithin kein eigentümliches Gebiet hat, dennoch den Übergang von der Denkungsart nach den Prinzipien der einen, zu der nach Principien der anderen, möglich macht ... Dieses ist die *Urteilskraft*, von welcher man Ursache hat, nach der Analogie zu vermuten, dass sie eben wohl ... doch ein ihr eigenes Prinzip ... in sich enthalten dürfte: welches, wenn ihm gleich kein Feld der Gegenstände als sein Gebiet zustände, doch irgend einen Boden haben kann"). On this particular discussion of the lack of a defined "realm" of the objects of aesthetic judgment, and consequent extension of the grounds, or territory, of its "power" anywhere at all, cf. Chapter Three, Section One, this study.

personal sense or feeling of a subject, judgment is spoken as a *general* statement about an unnamed but *specific object* ("it"), and it is in expressing itself in the form of the definition, *rather than subjective judgment,* of an object it does not know that judgment effectively passes for something else, a constative statement that "possesses this resemblance to the logical, that we can presuppose its validity for everyone.,"[119]

The deductive circle described here by Kant's identification of judgment with its pronouncement, the empirical indistinguishability of the subjective experience of feeling from the general verbal, or "speech" act in which judgment consists, is as irresolvable as it is plain. For, rather than committing a mere "mis"-translation from (a) subject to (an) object, the act of "judgment" translates nothing – neither subject nor object – to begin with; indeed, if ever a verbal action put the fatally conventional epistemology of concepts of translation into question – their recursive evasion, by temporary displacement, of the problems and powers each and every language presents – it is that of "judgment," the singularly verbal, and single pivotal, critical "faculty." Rather than expressing an inevitable conceptual error or conditional, individual aberrancy, the speech act that is judgment speaks with the universal "validity" of logic, a disinterested illocution performable by anyone, just as its constative, logical form, in speaking of an "it" rather than for an "I," makes judgment that particular kind of speech act ascribable to everyone else. Part of discourse or part of action; piece of the language of "merely nominal" conceptual logic or of the "real being" and "first basis of the possibility" of things: in theorizing the particular power of judgment Kant renders that very opposition – organizing principle of his entire critical project and strict methodological division drawn between "nominal" and "real definitions" in his *Logik*[120] – a distinction itself merely nominal in scope, dependent only on the end of the reversible definition of judgment, i.e., as enactable only in speaking and as speech act, at which one chooses to begin.

As in his refusal to speculate on the bases of "common sense," Kant makes no attempt here to resolve the rational puzzle of the identity of the mental capability he proposes, to disentangle the premises from the consequences of its circular

---

119. *Ibid.*

120. See Kant, *Logik* A 221–22, VI: 576: "Objects of experience allow merely nominal explanations. – Logical nominal definitions of given concepts of the understanding are taken from an attribute; real definitions, by contrast, out the being of the thing, out of the first basis of its possibility. These last thus contain that which always pertains to the thing, the real being of the same" ("Erfahrungsgegenstände erlauben bloss Nominalerklärungen. – Logische Nominal-Definitionen gegebener Verstandesbegriffe sind von einem Attribut hergenommen; Real-Definitionen hingegen aus dem Wesen der Sache, dem ersten Grunde der Möglichkeit. Die letztern enthalten also das, was jederzeit der Sache zukommt, das Realwesen derselben.") For an analysis of the centrality of Kant's redefinition of the distinction between "real" from "nominal" definitions in his *Logik* to his *Critique,* see Brodsky, *The Imposition of Form, Studies in Narrative Representation and Knowledge.* Princeton, NJ: Princeton University Press, 1987, pp. 36–52 esp.

definition, even to decide which is which, premise *or* consequence, so as to order them into a logically consecutive, deductive chain. The "moments" of Kant's *Analytik* – like the organizational categories they employ – are descriptive, not hypothetical or speculative. Refusing equally to arrive at a single, "real" or "nominal," origin of judgment by playing Solomon to his own formulation, he chooses instead to emphasize that, while judgments "resemble" logical procedures in their constitutive "validity" for – which is to say, their utterability by – all *subjects*, that validity and that resemblance rest on no conceptions of the sensory, and so no logical constitution and cognition of *objects* at all.

The particular descriptive speech act, "it is beautiful," can and will only be uttered when understood to be valid of an object in view, as it were, of the "feeling" of any subject. Yet because judgment consists of no knowledge of an object, either *de facto* or *de jure* (a logical distinction effectively effaced by the activity of judgment itself), it remains, despite the *form* of logical, constative language it takes, an *act* of speech and nothing more: nothing more, that is, than speech standing for the feeling common to every subject by designating instead a "quality constitutive of an object," a substitution of object for subject, and of a referential copular statement for the report of an action ("feeling"), spoken without any personal "interest" in performing that speech act at all.

Kant's description of an internal power of judgment whose universality stems from being externally identifiable with speech reminds us that, like speech acts themselves, language as a whole depends on concepts but not concepts alone. The language that enables logical procedures also enables the replacement, in the act of articulation, of inarticulate "feeling," and the confusion of the two, logic and the mere appearance thereof, may prove as critically productive as it is misleading. The fact that any single judgment no less than the singular qualities that define all acts of judgment are both made available to us only through speech, indicates that, just as a truly "private language" is not a language but an oxymoron – a notion of "language" invented by a subject who himself could never remember it because, entirely internal or unexpressed, it cannot be received or recalled as extant by anyone – so without speech there would be no judgment, insofar as we can understand and imagine it.

The question, however, which the reversible structure of the foundation of judgment raises as its result, is *whether without judgment, there could be speech*: whether language, repository of all discursive concepts, definitions, logical conceptual relations, and, thus, of all knowledge in Kant, originates with the noncognitive faculty of aesthetic judgment itself, an inarticulate "feeling" *disguised in being articulated* as a constative statement, the, strictly speaking, illogical birth of language and of logic that makes the movement or "transition" within the *Critique* – as within every subject – between the limits of logical, phenomenal cognition and the "practical" realization rather than merely "technical" imitation of "free" action possible.[121] Like the *a priori* forms of time and space, the conceptual

---

121. See Kant, *KU*, B XIX-XX, X: 83–84.

content of language appears fully formed within the *Critique*, just as the linguistic basis of all possible epistemology is given by its founding "hypothesis." Yet in the Third Critique language is instead the unique modality of a noncognitive ascription to an object. What is ascribed to that object, to any object, perceived as if for the first time – which is to say, as a "free" form or even "not-form,"[122] something apparent but without content, severed from any pre-existing knowledge of or interest in it on our part – is a quality predicative not of its conceptualization but of its nonconceptual and thus unstated experience: the experience, free even from the fundamental operations of schematism, of how that perception makes the subject "feel."

"It is beautiful" – which is to say, I feel pleasure in the mere perception of it, in the "free play of imagination and understanding" that it occasions in me – is the speech act that does not speak for itself, but for "it," and for "it" as it is perceived, without constitutive knowledge, not by an "I" but by "everyone" ("jedermann"). The perception that occasions feeling and the feeling that occasions judgment first occur as judgment in a speech act, a specifically noncognitive use of speech. Thus it is that this particular origin of judgment, in a feeling so impersonal or general that only language can express it, indicates at the same time the unique generality attributable to language, any language, itself. That power which is "merely contemplative," which is "indifferent as regards the existence of an object," which is "not directed to concepts," not "*based* on concepts, nor has concepts as its purpose," may in turn share not only the generality of language with regard to its own formal expressive mode, but indicate how such an inherently disinterested, general form of expression could have been formed to begin with.

For, how could language, which includes the possibility of speech acts, i.e., inherently "generally communicable" ("allgemein mitteilen lassen"[123]) acts taken in independence of the cognitive and persuasive measures of speech that language provides, ever "free" itself from such limited, "technical" aims so as to act with the distinterest of a *techne*? Or, by the same token, we may ask, in what merely contemplative experience – the experience by a subject of an unknown object, "it" – can "the general communicability" ("allgemeine Mitteilbarkeit"[124]) of language, repository of knowledge, instrument for the formulation and pursuit of interests, *and* expression of merely contemplative experience alike, disengage itself from the captive language we use and so allow a disinterested power, that of judgment, to articulate itself in the first place? But this is as much as to ask how language as mode of action, rather than means of appropriation or even known intention, originates.

---

122. *Ibid.*, B XLIX, X: 103.
123. Kant, *KU*, B 66, X:158.
124. *Ibid.*

6. Rousseau's Nouns

The notion that judgment, in being spoken, by any perceiving subject, "as if"[125] of an object, has something to do with what makes language language – a system of delimitation of unlimited complexity and effectivity, rather than a limited means to an end – is comparable with another, very different description of language similarly enacted *in lieu of* cognition, the account of the "origin of languages" hypothesized by Rousseau. If the predicate of Kant's *dictum*, "our age is the Age of Critique," merely signified a delimited period within a specific historical chronology, the birthdate of that "age" might be fixed at 1750, the year Rousseau responded to the public question posed by the Académie de Dijon: "do the arts and sciences improve morals?" Enacting in word and in deed its own openly allegorical first sentence, Rousseau's prize-winning First Discourse appeared on the international scene of letters as if "from nothing."[126] By one of the most celebrated

---

125. See this Chapter, Section Five, n. 113.

126. In the first words of Rousseau's first speculative publication, there may be no "greater" – more vivid and comprehensive – "spectacle" in Western letters than that staged in the introductory sentence of the First Discourse itself, in which Rousseau manages to represent the entire trajectory of mankind's active development "out of nothingness" in the simplest of allegorical scenes, first iteration of a life's work of remarkable sentences articulating the practical poetics defining all human history: "It is a great and beautiful spectacle to see man depart in some way from nothing by his own efforts; to dissipate by the lights of his reason the shadows in which nature had enveloped him. . . ." ("C'est un grand et beau spectacle de voir l'homme sortir en quelque manière du néant par ses propres efforts; dissiper, par les lumières de sa raison les ténèbres dans lesquelles la nature l'avait enveloppé . . ." [*Discours sur les sciences et les arts; Discours sur l'origine* . . ., p. 30]). In the recursive arc of the human "departure from nothing" into subjecthood that the progress of the complete sentence proceeds to describe, enlightenment, romanticism, and further, oppositely oriented enlightenment follow alternately upon each other, proceeding *past* the (Nietzschean) narrative summit of the subject's surplus striving "to elevate himself above himself" ("s'élever au-dessus de lui-même"), to the "still greater and more difficult" feat of his "returning inside himself to study man and come to know his nature" ("ce qui est encore plus grand et plus difficile, rentrer en soi pour y étudier l'homme et connaître sa nature . . ." [*Ibid.*]). For an excellent account of the interdependent political and cultural formations that the "spectacle" of man's "departure from nothing" into history narrated in the (spectacular) first sentence of the First Discourse entails, see Zev Trachtenberg, *Making Citizens: Rousseau's Political Theory of Culture* (NY: Routledge, 1993).

ironies of history, its critique of the inevitable corruption of private and public morals by artful replacements of the "appearance" of virtue for virtue, and of deceptively accumulated might for right – artifice used to garner personal power at the cost of others' physical and intellectual "enslavement" – won for its author the very kind of "celebrity" that the *Discours* so effectively, famously demystified.[127]

Unlike Kant's Analytic, Rousseau's account of linguistic articulation takes the quasi-fictional form of a story, in which the emergence, first, of language, and, secondly, of cognition, are consequences of an immediate experience of ignorance: of knowing that one does not know what one perceives and thereby "knowing" – if such a knowledge were possible – negation alone. Where Kant's *Critique*, when describing the ability to communicate a noncognitive perception, says "judgment" – one of several powers, if the uniquely pivotal one, articulated within its architectonic organization of our mental capabilities – Rousseau's cognitive allegory says "origin of language," the articulation, as if for the first time, of a specifically verbal form in response to a perceptual experience itself occurring as if for the first time, which is to say, without our already "knowing" it as such (or, in Kant's formal terms, cognizing it *a priori*). Still, both Analytic and narrative at once allow and obligate their authors to consider language in distinction from any conceptual knowledge or frame: to understand it as a systematic means of articulating signification, through predication and symbolization, whose defining norms and rules, or grammar, share the generality of logic even while remaining in themselves independent, or, in Kant's terms, "free," of the cognitive conclusions to which the exercise of logic leads.[128]

---

127. The irony of the fact that the work which granted Rousseau immediate international fame took aim at the attainment of precisely just such "celebrity" was far from lost on Rousseau. The first sentence of the 1751 "advertisement" to the publication of the *Discours* states: "Qu'est ce que la célébrité? Voici le malheureux ouvrage à qui je dois la mienne" [What is celebrity? Here is the unfortunate work to which I owe my own], J.-J. Rousseau, "Avertissement," *Discours sur les sciences et les arts*, p. 25). See also the fine Introduction to the *Discours* by Jacques Rogier, whose opening echoes Rousseau's words: "The celebrity of Rousseau dates from the *Discours sur les sciences et les arts*..." (pp. 5–22 [5]).

128. The constitutional differences and overlappings between logic and language, as these bear directly upon the verbal acts of judgment enabled by what Kant calls "common sense," are discussed in the preceding Section Five; for Kant's discussion of the overlap between statements of judgment and logical statements, see esp. n. 113.

A stunning re-evaluation of Rousseau by Fredric Jameson in *Valences of the Dialectic* (New York and London: Verso, 2009) goes precisely to this point. Distinguishing Rousseau's "reasoning" from received notions of "Enlightenment Reason," much as this study describes Kant's invocation of a verbally operative "common sense" whose unknown derivation Kant asserts he neither "wants" to nor "can research now," Jameson defines the apparently paradoxical outcomes and lacunae of Rousseau's "truly ... historically original" "reasoning" not as failings but, on the contrary, as "the "reconstruction of history in thought." Indeed, the

In his *Discours sur l'origine, et les fondements de l'inégalité parmi les hommes* (1755), Rousseau next describes the very proposition of an "origin" of language as presenting an inherent analytical problem, since, logically speaking, "there would have had to have been words to establish the use of words," i.e., an articulation of thought of the very kind language alone provides, as well as an agreed means of being in "common agreement" on the conventional forms of that articulation, forms whose universal usage define the existence of a "language" in the first place.[129] The complete subject of this Second Discourse, however – the "origin, or foundations of inequality" – suggests a plurality of sources for distinctions of status drawn among its users that language specifically does not make. Rather than presenting the logical paradox of a single origin dependent upon its own earlier establishment, and so, infinitely receding from view – a one which is not one, but also not zero or two – the question of the "origin and foundations" of "inequality" refers by name to a condition of non-universality, a non-linguistic condition whose causes differ from each other. Whereas language is an integrated, purely conventional system for symbolic and communicative action that, like all fully systematic, or "arbitrary," conventions, must be performed in order to "be" "itself" (and vice versa), "inequality," on Rousseau's analysis, has two separate sources qualitatively distinct from each other in mode and effect: the natural, or empirical-physical, and the social, or man-made.

fact that that "reasoning" leads Rousseau to an "unprecedented" recognition of logical-historical "contradiction," as demonstrated in his discussion of the origin of language in the Second Discourse in particular, makes him, Jameson concludes, "the impossible founder" "not only . . . of structuralism" but "of the dialectic itself" (see "Rousseau and Contradiction," *Valences*, pp. 303–314). Jameson helpfully identifies the historical contradictions articulated by Rousseau's specifically historical "reasoning" (what this study calls his hypothetical "narrative"—in contrast to Kant's "architectonic"—logic) as analogous, both in structure and significance, to "one of Kant's great discoveries:" that Kant, "for whom the reading of Jean-Jacques was fully as decisive," reformulated Rousseau's demonstration of the "impossibility of thinking about origins" in his deduction of the fundamental "antinomy" at work in all possible thinking about time. As discussed in this study, it is precisely that antinomy, and the temporal dependence of "internality" upon "externality" in which it results, that Kant describes as the basis for "being in time" ("Dasein in der Zeit"), the question of whose occurrence ("How?" ["Wie?"]), like that of "change" itself, he utterly frankly and logically concludes, "we cannot answer" (on the Second Preface, see this Chapter, Section Ten, n. 256; see also Chapter One, n. 9). On Rousseau and Marx, see also Robert Wokler, *Rousseau, The Age of Enlightenment, and Their Legacies* (Princeton: Princeton University Press, 2012), esp. pp. 214–232; Lucio Colletti, *Ideologia e società* (Bari: Universale Laterza, 1975).

129. J.-J. Rousseau, *Discours sur l'origine . . .*, pp. 205–209. On the differing, interrelated theories of the origin of the language presented in the *Discours sur l'origine . . .*, on the one hand, and the *Essai sur l'origine des langues,* on the other, see Mira Morgenstern, *Rousseau and the Politics of Ambiguity* (University Park, Pa.: The Pennsylvania State University, 1996), pp. 12–13, 17–20.

The habitual confusion of the two "foundations," by which social definitions are taken to reflect natural givens, requires Rousseau to investigate how social inequality came about. Rousseau calls this second kind of "inequality" "moral or political" (rather than "natural or physical") "because it depends on a sort of convention" rather than proceeds from empirical givens, and, instead of confirming distinctions of natural accident and context, institutes arbitrary ones artificially.[130] In this, its solely conventional basis, then, the condition of social inequality resembles that of language, whereas qualities of "natural" inequality – say, of size, or strength, or shape, or location – resemble neither linguistic nor social distinctions in that they are based exclusively in empirical, measurable givens.

The difference, then, between kinds of "foundations" of inequality is not incremental but categorical, and it is in response to the absolute distinction between them that Rousseau hypothesizes a kind of "man" absolutely distinct from man as we know him: a "savage" or "natural man" theoretically defined as a being existing without a concept of men. Not recognizing others or himself *as* men and so lacking all basis and desire for forming either social, comparative cognitive-conceptual, imaginative, or even emotional – indeed, any other than merely immediate, physical – relations, the "natural man" perceives neither similarity nor difference between objects or within individual objects over time: a thing is the thing it is at each moment it appears, and the mental life of "savage man," had he one, would be doomed to the mental violence of death by tautology.

Deprived of all knowledge," such a man "can only feel the passions" "nature" fleetingly imposes upon him.[131] His "heart asks for nothing" since "no imagination

---

130. J.-J. Rousseau, *Discours sur l'origine* . . ., p. 167. See Sally Howard Campbell, *Rousseau and the Paradox of Alienation* (Plymouth, UK: Lexington Books, 2012), pp. 13–41 esp., for a clear description of and contrast between the "social isolation of natural man" and artificial alienation of man from man by "property" in civil society.

131. "The passions derive their origin for their part from our needs, and their progress from our knowledge, for one can only desire or fear things either insofar as one has ideas of them, or by the simple impulse of nature; and the savage man, deprived of all enlightenment, only experiences the passions of this last kind; his desires do not exceed his physical needs; the only goods that he knows in the universe are food, a mate, and rest; the only evils that he fears are pain and hunger. I say pain and not death, for no animal will ever know what death is, and knowledge of death, and of its terrors, is one of the first acquisitions man would have made in distancing himself from the condition of animals" ("Les passions, à leur tour, tirent leur origine de nos besoins, et leur progrès de nos connaissances; car on ne peut désirer ou craindre les choses que sur les idées qu'on en peut avoir, ou par la simple impulsion de la nature; et l'homme sauvage, privé de toute sorte de lumières, n'éprouve que les passions de cette dernière espèce; ses désirs ne passent pas ses besoins physiques; les seuls biens, qu'il connaisse dans l'univers sont la nourriture, une femelle et le repos; les seuls maux qu'il craigne sont la douleur et la faim; je dis la douleur et non la mort; car jamais l'animal ne saura ce que c'est que mourir, et la connaissance de la mort, et de ses terreurs, est une des premières acquisitions que l'homme ait faites, en s'éloignant de la condition animale" [*Ibid.*, pp. 195–96]).

speaks to it," and that figurative, or catachrestic silence – the absence of speech and all power of reflection within one in whom they had never existed – renders even the external "spectacle of nature" "indifferent" to his eye.[132] A being who need never imagine or speak, in that he is, "so to speak, always wholly with himself" ("pour ainsi dire, toujours tout entier avec soi"[133]), and, so we might equally and literally say, does not know what he is missing, is someone who indeed can only be said to have been in a "hypothetical" sense, in that, existing only and wholly "with himself" and "the sole feeling of his present existence," he has as little "idea" of anything beyond the immediate reach of his senses as he does "of the future." Just as the "natural man" can imagine no present different from this one, he engages in no activity capable of exceeding perceived identities in the present by producing a mediating and replicable – inherently historical – sign. A being lacking any "idea" of himself, as a subject of experience, or of the objects of his or any experience, can leave no memorializing record of either behind.

Rousseau's hypothetical "savage" or "natural man," a being that can solely be defined speculatively to resemble man in the first place, is, then, no one either Rousseau or anyone else can have known, let alone can or should aspire to resemble or become, not because in order to be this not-quite man one would have to "turn back the clock," but because, however and wherever this "man" is, there is no clock, just as there is neither empirical nor internal experience of self or others to speak of. "Natural man," Rousseau's name for the negation of all relations *and* temporally extensive identities, is a fiction allowing him in turn to negate or disallow the supposed naturalness of the unequal social relations and identities of "the men before our eyes."[134] It is these, social and historical men who, "with the help of communication," "invent" "ideas," "knowledge," "curiosity," "foresight," and, with them, the possibility of "progress," along with the accumulations of power that accompany the invention of conventional "inequality" itself.[135]

The one invention upon which all these last depend, Rousseau declares, is language, and the "immense space" Rousseau states man had to have "traversed," and the "infinite time" it must have "cost," for language to have "first been invented," are phenomenal and experiential metaphors for the categorical distinction he has already hypothetically drawn, between men, "in a pure state of nature," whose corporeal unequalness, given by nature, would be entirely empirical in origin, and men "in need of languages," whose "inequality" they themselves author.[136] Summoning those who would reflect on these second, conventional or "moral" foundations of social inequality to "consider how many ideas we owe to the use of words," Rousseau asks his reader's "permi[ssion] to consider for a moment the predicament of the origin of languages" ("l'embarras de l'origine des langues").[137]

132. *Ibid.*, pp. 204, 196, 216–217, 181.
133. *Ibid.*, p. 175.
134. *Ibid.*, p.180.
135. *Ibid.*, pp. 198–209.
136. *Ibid.*, pp. 204, 198
137. *Ibid.*, p. 183–85.

Analogous to his notion of a pre-historical, "natural" or "savage man" conceived, by "hypothetical and conditional reasoning,"[138] for the sole purpose of providing a comparative vantage point[139] from which to analyze the socially enacted inequality we mistake for natural, Rousseau begins his discussion by attributing a similar, hypothetically natural origin to language, too, equating "the first language" with "cries of nature" and naturally expressive "gestures" before swiftly proving the insufficiency of these to do what only a non-natural "language" of "signs" "substitut[ed]" for immediate, physical "actions" can do:

> ... but since gesture barely indicates objects that are present, or easy to describe, and visible actions; since it is not of universal usage, because darkness, or the interposition of a body render it useless, and since gesture demands attention rather than excites it, one thought to oneself, finally, to substitute for gesture the articulations of the voice, which, without having the same relationship with certain ideas, are more appropriate for representing them all, as instituted signs; substitution which can only be made by common consent, and in a manner rather difficult to practice for men whose rough organs had not yet had any exercise, and even more difficult to conceive in itself, since this unanimous agreement must have been motivated, and the word seems to have been absolutely necessary in order to establish the use of the word...
>
> [... mais comme le geste n'indique guère que les objets présents, ou faciles à décrire, et les actions visibles; qu'il n'est pas d'un usage universel, puisque l'obscurité,

---

138. *Ibid.*, p. 156.

139. Rousseau repeatedly defines the "savage man" he has hypothesized both as a being "possessing nothing" (neither "particular" personal properties nor artificially appropriated property) in that his actions aim only to satisfy immediate, physical needs, and as the being whose state of "natural" "equality" consists precisely in that of "being nothing." See *Ibid.*, p. 220; the first sentence of First Discourse (see n. 126, this Section, this Chapter); and Second Discourse, *Ibid.* p. 254 in which Rousseau describes the "revolution" that inevitably "closes the circle" described by our "departure" from the natural state: "Here is the last term of inequality, and the extreme point which closes the circle and touches the point from which we departed. Here all particulars become equal again because they are nothing" ("C'est ici le dernier terme de l'inégalité, et le point extrême qui ferme le cercle et touche au point d'où nous sommes parties. C'est ici que tous les particuliers redeviennent égaux parce qu'ils ne sont rien"). See also the admonition to the reader to beware that "founder of civil society" who claims and stakes out property as his own: "Beware of listening to this imposter; you are lost if you forget that fruits are everyone's and the land belongs to no one" ("Gardez-vous d'écouter cet imposteur; vous êtes perdus, si vous oubliez que les fruits sont à tous, et que la terre n'est à personne"). Kant's view of the earth's surface is exactly the same: "The earthly ground [*Boden*] belongs to no one," *Metaphysik der Sitten* §12, XIII: 372; cf. C. Brodsky, *In the Place of Language. Literature and the Architecture of the Referent* (NY: Fordham University Press, 2009), pp. 13–14.

ou l'interposition d'un corps, le rendent inutile, et qu'il exige l'attention plutôt qu'il ne l'excite, on s'avisa enfin de lui substituer les articulations de la voix, qui, sans avoir le même rapport avec certaines idées, sont plus propres à les représenter toutes, comme signes institués; substitution qui ne peut se faire que d'un commun consentement, et d'une manière assez difficile à pratiquer pour des hommes dont les organes grossiers n'aviaent encore aucun exercice, et plus difficile encore à concevoir en elle-même, puisque cet accord unanime dut être motive, et que la parole paraît avoir été fort nécessaire, pour établir l'usage de la parole ...[140]]

Similar to false genealogies deriving words from supposedly more originary, natural gestures, is their attribution to a domestic source that begs the very question of origins it pretends to answer. Neither view, which merely displaces what it does not know, can describe the 'origin of language' without describing a circle as well:

[T]o say that the mother dictates to the child the words that he must use to ask her for one thing or the other shows well how one teaches languages that are already formed, but does not teach us how they are formed ... [Here is a] new difficulty even worse than the preceding one; for if men needed words in order to learn to think, they needed to know how to think even more to find the art of the word ...

[(D)e dire que la mère dicte à l'enfant les mots dont il devra se servir pour lui demander telle ou telle chose, cela montre bien comment on enseigne des langues déjà formées, mais cela n'apprend point comment elles se forment ... Nouvelle difficulté pire encore que la précédente; car si les hommes ont eu besoin de la parole pour apprendre à penser, ils ont eu bien plus besoin encore de savoir penser pour trouver l'art de la parole.[141]]

Even if we were to "cross for a moment the immense space that must have existed between the pure state of nature and the need for languages" ("franchissons pour un moment l'espace immense qui dut se trouver entre le pur état de nature et le besoin des langues"[142]), Rousseau reasons further, it would remain impossible to conceive how "much time and how many circumstances were necessary" for "the easiest part of language," "solely physical substantives," to be "invent[ed]," to say nothing of "purely abstract" "general ideas," such as "number, abstract words, aorists ... verbal tenses, verbs, particles, syntax, propositions, and reasonings," and the innumerable other grammatical and analytical forms that themselves "form the logic of discourse."[143] Describing himself as "frightened by these multiplying difficulties," Rousseau offers to "leave the discussion of this difficult problem to whomever else wants to undertake it," and, explicitly abandoning the question he cannot answer of "[w]hatever these origins may be" ("[q]uoi qu'il en soit de ces

140. *Ibid.*, p. 205.
141. *Ibid.*, pp. 203–4.
142. *Ibid.*, p. 204.
143. *Ibid.*, pp. 206–208.

origines"[144]), he returns to those of inequality in society, whose institution, through acts of appropriation combining verbal designation ("'This is mine'" ["Ceci est à moi"]) with physical delineation (the "enclosure of a terrain" ["ayant enclos un terrain"]), itself depends upon a prior institution of language.[145] Thus, even as it itself proves unavailable to definition, the origin of language defines the passage in Rousseau's social theory from "natural," equally indifferent, or nonsocial "man," to the unnatural "institution [of] inequality"[146] among social men: from the necessary fiction of an imaginary man without language, to men, as they know and interact with each other, with language. Yet, while a *story* originating with a "savage" or prelinguistic man may be "hypothesized" for the sake of an account of social man based on "reasoning,"[147] rather than blinkered cultural assumptions or retroactive justifications, the *moment* in which those hypothetical, untraceable beginnings become a future and present state of inequity – how and when a posited fiction of universal neutrality is negated by a positively negative reality – cannot be attributed properly to either side of the natural/social-historical divide. For it is that very division – between unconscious existence and conscious experience, physical compulsion and comparative, analytic knowledge, and all the human relations and endeavors that stem from this last – that the formation of language, the substitution of signs for sensuous immediacy and subsequent social occlusion of such (hypothetical) immediacy, would have to bridge.

Of note here is Rousseau's openly figural spatialization, in the preceding passage and elsewhere,[148] of what would conventionally be represented as a *temporal* development or course of events. Rather than limiting his speculations to the passage

---

144. *Ibid.*, p. 209.

145. *Discours sur l'origine,* p. 222. I have discussed the necessary involvement of language in the artificial invention of property adduced in the Second Part of the Second Discourse in, *In the Place of Language,* pp. 9–16. For a lucid discussion of the "prerequisite" of "equality" both for international "peace" and social "stability," comparing Rousseau's theory of history with Marx's in the *Eighteenth Brumaire,* see Christine Jane Carter, *Rousseau and the Problem of War* (New York: Garland, 1987), pp. 212–13.

146. *Discours sur l'origine* . . ., p. 219.

147. *Ibid.,* p. 169.

148. *Ibid.,* p. 197: "The more one thinks about this subject, the more the distance from pure sensations to the simplest cognitions increases in our view; and it is impossible to conceive how a man would have been able, by his own sole strengths, without the assistance of communication and the spur of necessity, to cross such a great interval" ("Plus on médite sur ce sujet, plus la distance des pures sensations aux plus simples connaissances s'agrandit à nos regards; et il est impossible de concevoir comment un homme aurait pu par ses seules forces, sans le secours de la communication, et sans l'aiguillon de la nécessité, franchir un si grand intervalle"). Cf. *Ibid.,* pp. 198, 204 and *Discours sur les sciences et les arts,* p. 54, for similar descriptions of the immeasurable – because categorically transformative and unprecedented – change that "is" the "origin" of language and inequality as an incalculable "space" or "distance," or "infinite time."

of time required for language to emerge, Rousseau refers instead to the "immense space" that man would have had to "traverse" to proceed from the "pure state of nature to that of the need for languages." A similar spatialization marks the origin of Rousseau's own entrance into public letters as well. The opening sentence of his prize-winning *Discours sur les sciences et les arts*[149] represents all of human progress as a visual scene – "un grand et beau spectacle"– occurring both *in* space and *by* spatial means: "It is a grand and beautiful spectacle to see man depart, by his own efforts, out of nothingness ..., to cross with giant steps the vast expanse of the universe."[150]

Such explicitly spatially figural or scenographic language is especially striking in Rousseau. Keenly aware of the illusion of knowledge that metaphoric speech effects, Rousseau announces he will compose his theoretical work in the unadorned, direct language of prose: "my subject concerning man in general, I will strive to use a language which suits all nations."[151] Consistent with his critical insight into the logical "conundrum" any attempt to identify the "origin" of language outside of language presents, Rousseau's decision to "use a language" of "general" hypothetical, rather than empirically specific reasoning to present his unconventional theses indeed "suit[ed]" his writings not only to "all nations" but all times: whatever opinion one may hold of Rousseau's argument, and wherever and whenever those opinions obtain, the prose style in which Rousseau argues *against mistaking convention for nature* defies the temporality of social conventions themselves, and so has remained among the most communicative and authoritative in French prose.

For the same reasons, Rousseau's use here of a distinctly unsuited, externalizing metaphor to describe the complete "change"[152] within man that the "establishment" of language entails, is so conspicuous as to indicate no accident but, rather, an equally conscious choice, that of staging change itself as an unmistakably fictive appearance, spectacle or scene. In writing about the formation of language in spatial, visual terms, Rousseau purposefully avoids the greater conceptual error conventionally committed in its regard: that of misrepresenting the *temporality* of that formation – whether in gradual, progressive and developmental, or unmediated and disruptive terms – as a representable presence, a series of objects co-present with themselves at identifiable moments in time. Rousseau's "discourse" figures the origin of language in metaphoric

149. See n. 126, this Section, this Chapter.

150. *Ibid.*

151. *Discours sur l'origine* ..., p. 169: "Mon sujet intéressant l'homme en général, je tâcherai de prendre un langage qui convienne à toutes les nations." Wordsworth describes the "prosaic" language "really used by men" of his poetic project in nearly identical terms; see this Chapter, Section Eleven, and *Words' Worth*, pp. 3–56 esp.

152. "[T]he use of the word established itself and perfected itself insensibly in the breast of each family, and one can go on to conjecture how diverse particular causes could expand language and accelerate its progress by rendering it more necessary ... Everything begins to change how it seems" ("l'usage de la parole s'établit ou se perfectionne insensiblement dans le sein de chaque famille, et l'on peut conjecturer encore comment diverses causes particulières purent étendre le langage, et en accélérer le progrès en le rendant plus nécéssaire ... Tout commence à changer de face" (*Discours sur l'origine* ..., p. 227).

spatial terms, as the fictive *mise en scène* of an enormous space somehow crossed, so as not to *misrepresent* it in apparently logical, causal narrative form.

Unlike the story of a "natural man" whose hypothesized, prior existence provides a critical lever for understanding social man at present, no story of the origin at the center of that story – that of an origin of language already determined logically to be unknowable – is committed by Rousseau to print. The origin of language, unlike that of social man from "natural man," cannot be the subject of a story-line in the *Discours* exactly because, unlike the openly fictive hypothesis of a "natural" subject, the natural capability for fiction – for understanding and action engendered by artifice, by convention – that made (and makes) language "language," and not a subject available to diachronic mimesis to begin with, was "then" and remains "now" real and ongoing, did and does exist.

The exception to Rousseau's refusal to narrate language formation is his "Essai sur l'origine des langues où il est parlé de la mélodie et de l'imitation musicale" (written 174?; 175?; 176?; posth. pub. 1781). Never published by Rousseau, even its exceptional status remains equivocal, in that this story is one its author did not want circulated and read.[153] The *Essai*, one could say, is the exception that Rousseau himself refused to externalize, to let take its "place" in history by appearing as one chapter in the author's bibliographical chronology.[154] Its specific date of composition unknown, the facts surrounding the "origin" of the *Essai* itself remain, appropriately enough, uncertain.[155] For, while Rousseau does indeed literally "attempt" to describe

---

153. The excellent annotations to the first publication of the *Essai* from an unpublished 1761 manuscript edited by Charles Porset (*Essai sur l'origine des langues, où il est parlé de la mélodie et de l'imitation* musicale, ed. Charles Porset [Paris: Nizet, 1969]) include an exchange of letters with Malherbes (also dating from 1761) in which Rousseau states his "resolution to suppress" the work. While Malherbes, Rousseau's only correspondent to have written of having been sent the work, asserts Rousseau would "be wrong" to "deprive the public of it," Rousseau deems his "dissertating on languages" "unworthy of public attention" (pp. 9–10).

154. It is no coincidence that, when finally published in a modern standard edition, the *Essai* proved both the original meeting ground and grounds for critical disagreement (regarding the *Essai* and Rousseau in general) between otherwise similarly minded critical theorists: Jacques Derrida and Paul de Man. See Derrida, *De la grammatologie* (Paris: Editions de Minuit, 1967), pp. 235–378; De Man, *Blindness and Insight* (Minneapolis: University of Minnesota Press, 1983 [reprint of orig pub. 1971]), pp. 102–41.

155. While noting the strong divergence in the analyses of the origin of language presented in the *Essai* and the *Discours* of 1754, Porset nonetheless concludes "without equivocation" that the former must have "originated" with the latter (*Essai*, p. 12). Yet Porset's reconstruction of the probable origin of the *Essai* demonstrates nothing so much as Rousseau's success in making the hypothetical dating of that origin co-extensive with history itself. Citing Lanson's contrary view, published in 1911, that, while the "*Essay* is certainly in contradiction with the *Discourse on Inequality*," it could not have been written later than 1750, he also references Masson's speculation, "one year later," that the *Essai* was first written as a "note" to the 1754 *Discours*, but then reworked separately by Rousseau, who called it a "fragment," until (at least) 1761 (*Essai*, pp. 16–24).

the origin of language by way of a visualizable scene in his "essai," that scene is represented only insofar as it is seen by one of its actors, and "what" that actor sees, and, subsequently, does, are explicitly attributed, by the narrator of the scene, to an exclusively internal act, the unknowing production of a mental fiction. In Rousseau's narrated scene of the origin of language, what is "seen" is not what is visible but a metaphoric appearance of what is not visible, and the man who sees and acts upon that metaphor in fact views "other" men without knowing he is doing so. Instead, the object he contemplates is a metaphor of his own involuntary making, one that, moreover, includes him in its purview and operation. While avoiding the problem of postulating a human community of any kind before the communicative basis for such a community exists,[156] the individual experience this narrative version of the origin of language recounts is both singular ("a savage man . . .") and doubled by the very external circumstance that triggers it (". . . in meeting others will at first be afraid"). For, in seeing, for the first time, "other" beings who appear to pose no immediate relation or resemblance to himself, this individual subject of language experiences a feeling – in Rousseau's terms, a "passion" – resulting in a visual misperception of what he sees. The experience of an internal "passion" in an act of external perception produces something unlike either – a linguistic utterance – and the first word articulated in this doubly experiential origin of language is what Rousseau calls a "trope." In Chapter III of Rousseau's *Essai*, entitled, "That the first language must have been figural" ("Que le premier langage dût être figuré"), the particular trope in which the visual scene of a man first seeing other men results is "giants" ("Géants"), a misnomer indicating more about the non-natural, subjective basis of language than the given object it names.

Like Descartes and Locke before him, Rousseau sharply distinguishes animal from human language, arguing in Chapter I of the *Essai* that, while animals which "live and work together" "have a natural language to communicate among themselves," "the animals that speak them have them at birth," making such "natural languages" "everywhere the same."[157] Just as animal language is

---

156. This is the particular circular dilemma to which Condillac's account of the origin of languages, according to Rousseau, falls prey; see the critique of Condillac's *Essai sur l'origine des connaissances humaines* (1746) in the *Discours sur l'origine . . .*, pp. 199–204.

157. See *Essai*, p. 39: "beavers, ants, bees have some natural language to communicate among themselves, I do not doubt. There is even grounds to believe that the language of beavers and that of ants are in gesture and speak only to the eyes. Whatever may be the case, precisely because all these languages are natural, they are not acquired; the animals that speak them were born with them, they all have them, and they are everywhere the same: they do not change, and do not make the least progress. The language of convention only belongs to man. That is why man makes progress in the good as well as the bad and why animals do not. This single distinction seems to be far-reaching; one can explain it, or so one says, by the difference between [human and animal] organs. I would be curious to see that explanation" ("les castors, les fourmis, les abeilles ont quelque langue naturelle pour s'entre-communiquer, je n'en fais aucun doute. Il y a même lieu de croire que la langue des castors

predetermined by nature and "cannot change,"[158] the language that, based instead in "convention,"[159] is determined solely by men, takes its origin, in the *Essai*, in the "specific distinction of man" defined by Rousseau in the Second Discourse: "his quality," unique among sentient beings, "of being" and "act[ing] as" "a free

et celle des fourmis sont dans le geste et parlent seulment aux yeux. Quoiqu'il en soit, par cela même que les unes et les autres de ces langues sont naturelles, elles ne sont pas acquises; les animaux qui les parlent les ont en naissant, ils les ont tous, et partout la même: ils n'en changent point, ils n'y font pas le moindre progrès. La langue de convention n'appartient qu'à l'homme. Voilà pourquoi l'homme fait des progrès soit en bien soit en mal, et pourquoi les animaux n'en font point. Cette seule distinction paroit mener loin: on l'explique, dit-on, par la différence des organes. Je serois curieux de voir cette explication"). See also *Discours sur l'origine*..., p. 225.

158. Cf. Descartes' discussion of "automates" and animals, *Discours de la méthode*, Pt. 5, in *Oeuvres philosophiques,* I: 628: "if there were such machines that had the organs and the appearance of a monkey, or some other animal without reason, we would have no way of recognizing that they weren't just the same nature as animals; whereas, if they had a resemblance with our bodies and imitated as many of our actions as was morally possible, we would always have two very certain ways of recognizing that they were not true men. The first of these is that they could never use words, nor other signs in composing them as we do to declare to others our thoughts. For one can well imagine that a machine would be so made that it proffers words ... but not that it arrange them diversely to respond to the meaning of anything that is said in its presence, as even the wildest men can do ..." ("s'il y avait de telles machines, qui eussent les organes et la figure d'un singe, ou de quelque autre animal sans raison, nous n'aurions aucun moyen pour reconnaître qu'elles ne seraient pas en tout de même nature que ces animaux; au lieu que, s'il y en avait qui eussent la ressemblance de nos corps et imitassent autant nos actions que moralement il serait possible, nous aurions toujours deux moyens très certains pour reconnaître qu'elles ne seraient point pour cela des vrais hommes. Dont le premier est que jamais elles ne pourraient user de paroles, ni d'autres signes en les composant, comme nous faisons pour déclarer aux autres nos pensées. Car on peut bien concevoir qu'une machine soit tellement faite qu'elle profère des paroles ... mais non pas qu'elle les arrange diversement, pour répondre au sens de tout ce qui se dira en sa présence, ainsi que les hommes les plus hébétés le font"). See also Locke, "Of Words or Language in General," in *An Essay Concerning Human Understanding* (London: Viking Penguin, 2004), p. 361 (emphasis in text): "Man ... had by nature his organs so fashioned, as to be *fit to frame articulate sounds*, which we may call words. But this was not enough to produce language; for parrots, and several other birds, will be taught to make articulate sounds distinct enough, which yet, by no means, are capable of language. Besides articulate sounds therefore, it was further necessary, that he should be *able to use these sounds, as signs of internal conception*; and to make them stand as marks for the ideas within his own mind, whereby they might be made known to others, and the thoughts of men's minds be conveyed from one to another."

159. Rousseau, *Essai*, p. 39.

agent."¹⁶⁰ Dormancy of the human attribute of "freedom" – the ability, definitive no less of human agency than of *agency* itself as a uniquely human quality, to act in independence from natural determination – is what defines the theoretically posited, pre- or nonhistorical state of Rousseau's hypothetical "savage man," just as its temporary forgetting or full "renunciation" define for Rousseau the socially instituted mechanisms of master-slave relations.¹⁶¹ It is this internal quality of being a "free agent" capable of "resisting" the "commands" of "nature" that distinguishes man from animals similarly capable of "understanding" but not resisting those commands, Rousseau observes:

> Every animal has ideas because he has senses, he even combines his ideas up to a certain point, and man only differs to a greater or lesser degree from the animal in this regard. Some philosophers have even purported that there is more difference between one man and another than between a man and an animal; yet it is not so much understanding that specifically distinguishes man among the animals as his quality of being a free agent. Nature orders every animal and the beast obeys. Man undergoes the same [natural] impression but recognizes himself as able to acquiesce to or resist it. And it is above all in the consciousness of this freedom that the spirituality of the soul of man shows itself: for physical qualities explain in some way the mechanism of the senses and formation of ideas, but in the power to will, or, rather, to choose, and in the feeling of this power one only finds purely spiritual acts, about which one can explain nothing by mechanical laws.
>
> [Tout animal a des idées puisqu'il a des sens, il combine même ses idées jusqu'à un certain point, et l'homme ne diffère à cet égard de la bête que du plus au moins. Quelques philosophes ont même avancé qu'il y a plus de différence de tel homme à tel homme que de tel homme à telle bête; ce n'est donc pas tant l'entendement qui fait parmi les animaux la distinction spécifique de

---

160. Rousseau, *Discours sur l'origine*..., pp. 182–83, *et passim*.
161. Beginning with its famously dichotomous first sentence, man's innate capacity for, and enslaving "renunciation" of "freedom" form the double subject of Rousseau's landmark *Social Contract*: "Man is born free, and everywhere he is in chains. Whoever believes himself the master of others is no less a slave than they" ("L'homme est né libre, et partout il est dans les fers. Tel se croit le maître des autres, qui ne laisse pas d'être plus esclave qu'eux" [*Du contrat social* (Paris: Garnier Flammarion, 1966 [orig. pub. 1762]), p. 42]; "[For any man] [t]o renounce his freedom is to renounce his quality of being a man, the rights of humanity, even his own duties. There is no possible compensation for anyone who renounces everything. Such a renunciation is incompatible with the nature of man, and to remove all freedom from his will is to remove all morality from his actions" ("Renoncer à sa liberté c'est renoncer à sa qualité d'homme, aux droits de l'humanité, même à ses devoirs. Il n'y a aucun dédommagement possible pour quiconque renonce à tout. Une telle renonciation est incompatible avec la nature de l'homme, et c'est ôter tout moralité à ses actions que d'ôter toute liberté à sa volonté" [*Ibid.*, p.46]).

l'homme que sa qualité d'agent libre. La nature commande à tout animal, et la bête obéit. L'homme éprouve la même impression, mais il se reconnaît libre d'acquiescer, ou de résister; et c'est surtout dans la conscience de cette liberté que se montre la spiritualité de son âme: car la physique explique en quelque manière le mécanisme des sens et la formation des idées; mais dans la puissance de vouloir ou plutôt de choisir, et dans le sentiment de cette puissance on ne trouve que des actes purement spirituels, dont on n'explique rien par les lois de la mécanique.[162]]

The quality of "free agen[cy]" defined to distinguish man in the *Discours* is linked to distinctively human language in the *Essai* by Rousseau's conception of the 'passions,' feelings arising as independently of reason as of physical sensations and sensory needs. In the story of the origin of human language that Chapter III of the *Essai* narrates, the origin of man and of the word, "man," are one, and men and human language are first enacted in freedom not only from nonhuman nature but from recognizably human reflection alike. Language, on this account, no more resembles "natural" sounds or gestures or any other mimetic reduction of language to an extension of the senses, than it represents memories or associations deriving from known conceptions. Rather than in any (imagined) dominance of the sensory *or* the conceptual, human language originates in the experience of a conflict between the two: between the immediacy and ignorance of the senses and the experiential limits of cognition; between seeing something one has never seen and confusing habit with knowledge and past experience with present. The inability of immediate sensation and applied reason to overcome the chasm between them issues in a violent feeling – a heightened awareness of internal incapacity – whose most accurate representation must thus also be empirically inaccurate, a "trope." Occasioned by an object whose misapprehension it at once extends and belies, the "first language" must be just as incapable of naming its own mistaken basis, of recognizing itself as a "figural" purveyor of fiction rather than of "proper" terms and definitions. For, a "*first* language" cannot, by definition, judge itself against norms defined by any other already given, articulate form.

On the one hand, then, as Rousseau's stories imply and all his writings demonstrate, language is our primary and undying means of critiquing such perceptual-conceptual fictions. On the other hand, as those same stories imply and his Second Discourse and *Essai* demonstrate, language must be incapable of

---

162. Rousseau, *Discours sur l'origine*..., p. 183. Todorov's subscription to the mistaken, if conventional view of Rousseau "as a partisan of the state of nature ... contemptuous of man in society" is belied not only by this passage, positively distinguishing man's "consciousness" of his ability (or "moral" "freedom") "to resist" the "mechanical" "commands" of "nature" in comparison with every "animal['s]" "obe[dience]" to them, but the entirety of the Second Discourse. See Tzvetan Todorov, *Frail Happiness*, trans. John T. Scott and Robert D. Zaretsky (University Park, PA: Pennsylvania State University Press, 2001 [orig. French pub. 1985]).

critiquing itself if it is to originate at all. A self-critical language could not come into being. And, yet, it is because language, unlike purely logical or functional systems, cannot "be" itself before becoming itself, it is also "free," like human "agency" and Rousseau's own hypothetical narratives, to originate, to occur rather than merely occupy yet another link in a predetermined causal chain: to emerge from a penumbra of habitual, empirical and internal givens *as* language, an involuntary invention independent of all of these. Since there "is" no language (or, for that matter, "non-language") in or with which to compare and analyze it, the "first language" of Rousseau's account can continue to develop alongside the "experiences" whose very terms it (mis)names, adjusting itself in view of past empirical events and shaping expectations of experience to come. Just as misconceptions extended in time by linguistic expression can only be corrected in hindsight, so language can only be oriented toward the future by foresight. Neither forward nor backward looking by definition, however, a "first language," or language without language, must instead be blind to itself – to why it names and what it names – in order to be born.

With the birth of human language, "history"[163] – as concept and as content – is born as well. Like the ungrounded origin of Kant's critical "revolution" in a "notion" or "Einfall,"[164] and Kant's declared refusal to "research" the basis of the "ground" of judgment, in the "condition" he calls "common sense," in the Third Critique, Rousseau's origin of language can only be "hypothetical" in that, in the absence of any prior language, such an event cannot have left any intelligible signs of itself. Unavailable to historical research of any kind or method, the "first language" is not a picture, extension, or inscription of something a subject either "knows" or doesn't need to know (in that it is already given), but a word attributed by one man to others before he knows himself or them to be men, a name given to objects whose first, noncognitive perception he *experiences* by "feel[ing] fear:"

> A savage man, in meeting others, will first of all feel fear. His fear will have made him see these men bigger and stronger than himself; he will have given them the name 'Giants.' After much experience he will have recognized that these pretended Giants, being neither bigger nor stronger than him, do not agree in stature with the idea that he had first attached to the word "Giant."

163. The fact that, like his literary and autobiographical works, Rousseau's conceptual writings, too, employ narrative form, reflects neither an analytic deficit nor penchant for story-telling on Rousseau's part, but a rigorous adherence to the theoretical insight into representation undertaken in any sphere of action that he and Kant share, or, in Kant's terms, their "common sense": the recognition that reflection of any kind relies on representation, and that representation requires language, which, like all speculative and fictive representation is not empirically but actively constituted, and thus "historical," i.e., narrative, receptive and productive, memorializing and anticipatory, repetitive and differentiating, mirroring and distortive, and, in all events, temporal in nature.

164. See n. 8, n. 51, Chapter One, this study.

[Un homme sauvage en rencontrant d'autres se sera d'abord effrayé. Sa frayeur lui aura fait voir ces hommes plus grands et plus forts que lui-même; il leur aura donné le nom de Géants. Après beaucoup d'expériences il aura reconnu que ces prétendus Géants n'étant ni plus grands ni plus forts que lui, leur stature ne convenoit point à l'idée qu'il avoit d'abord attachée au mot de Géant.[165]]

Rousseau defines the first word as the expression of an error of perception, the name or trope for that which mistakenly appears bigger, more powerful than me. Employing a euphemism for what might well be called "all of human history," Rousseau blandly states without further commentary that, "after many experiences" ("après beacoup d'expériences") – occurrences of no defined quality, number or content, whose stated posterity ("after") follows the event of naming contiguously, without any distinct causal link back to that "origin" itself – the subject in whom language originates comes to see the error of his ways, or, what is the same, of his language's names. "After many experiences" whose sole precedent – a feeling of "fear" surpassing and so unconstrained by real evidence – ensures their likewise violent, if not murderous character, the inventor of language recognizes that the "others" his "fear" had presented to him as larger and stronger than him are in fact just like him, and invents the proper term "man" to designate two beings, self and other, in one.

The delay in the invention of the proper term or common noun, its secondary status as an after-thought, or, more accurately, an after-feeling and first-thought, appears, in retrospect, to make as good narrative as it does logically indemonstrable sense. For, before that corrective, general appellation, and before the "many experiences," as unentailed as they are undefined, that follow upon his encounter with a "giant" of his own, perceptual and linguistic making, "man" had neither name for nor knowledge of himself. The "man" who learns, only secondarily, that he is one "man" among many, sets the primary term and trope "giant" aside, reserving it for the literal designation of all beings he *will* perceive – either at future moments of impassioned ignorance *or* in their revisionist aftermath, "after many experiences" have taught him to see properly – as "larger and stronger" than himself. As to whether the former trope, reborn as a proper term, will turn, as if by magic, into a trope again – misnomer and displacement of an unrecognized passion, rather than nominal end term of a dispassionate, comparative analysis – no one, least of all its originally deluded speaker, can rightly say.

Nor is such clairvoyance available to Rousseau's reader. For, the "objective" difference between impassioned perception and empirically accurate cognition, no less than the temporal experience required for their proper distinction, prove as

---

165. Rousseau, *Essai*, p. 47. Of special note here is Rousseau's omission from this narrated "scene," of language originating at once within and outside of man, of any copular attachment to "these men" of the qualities ("larger and stronger") falsely attributed to them. Rousseau's faithful recounting of an act of seeing occurring in complete ignorance of its "object" refuses to represent, as if objectively, the states, mental impressions, and acts it narrates, recounting, hypothetically and indirectly, instead: "will have made him see them," "will have given them," "will have recognized that . . .".

elusive to the subject of Rousseau's story as to its telling, a shadow cast, or "immense distance crossed," by the coupling of perception with feelings that Kant calls "the power of imagination" (*Einbildungskraft*). Recalling Kant we may say that the same difference that allows for nonconceptual *aesthetic* experience and the "disinterested," or "free," speech act of "judgment" in the Third Critique, issues in figural conceptualization and its correction – the language of epistemology – in Rousseau.

Like the subject who judges in Kant, the being in whom language originates in Rousseau does not speak in the first person, for, of, and about himself. Both the subject whose judgment, originating in a "feeling" brought about by the perception of an unidentified object, can only be rendered on the basis of a universal, yet logically ungrounded faculty called "common sense," and "a natural man" who, encountering "others" like him for the first time, experiences a powerful feeling or "passion" in which a (mistaken) designation originates, act at once verbally and in freedom – from causality, knowledge, or interest – by "speaking" or "saying" something about something ("it is beautiful") or someone else ("giant") in a general sense. Instead of stating the "passion" he feels, the speaker who first becomes a subject in the act of speaking speaks impersonally, "as if" in the third person. Similarly, rather than present himself as party or partial to what he says, he who "plays" at judging "speaks" – to recall Kant's observation on the identity of judgment with speech (Third Critique, B 18) – "as if beauty were a quality of the object" and not a term standing for the "relationship" of that "object to a subject," a relationship the subject does not cognize but "feels."[166]

166. Consistent with this analysis, the companion "passion" to the "fear" felt before the unknown other in Rousseau is "love," whose accompanying, objectifying trope might just as well be "the beautiful," another instance of mistaken identity – or, for that matter, mistaken difference – occurring in the dynamic, noncognitive perception of an object. See Rousseau, *Discours sur l'origine ...*, p. 200, and *Essai*, Chapter IX, "La formation des langues méridionales," p. 123, on encounters between young women and men at the well: "Young girls came to look for water for housekeeping, young men came to water their herds. Their eyes, accustomed to the same objects from infancy, began to see other sweeter ones. The heart moved itself toward these new objects, an unknown attraction rendered it less savage, it felt the pleasure of not being alone. Water became insensibly more necessary, the animals were thirsty more frequently; one arrived in haste and one departed with regret. In this happy age where nothing marked the hours, nothing obliged one to count them; time had no other measure than amusement and boredom ... There was the true cradle of peoples, and from the pure crystal of fountains departed the first fires of love" ("Les jeunes filles venoient chercher de l'eau pour le ménage, les jeunes hommes venoient abreuver leurs troupeaux. Là des yeux accoutumés aux mêmes objets dès l'enfance commencèrent d'en voir de plus doux. Le coeur s'émut à ces nouveaux objets, un attrait inconnu le rendit moins sauvage, il sentit le plaisir de n'être plus seul. L'eau devint insensiblement plus necessaire, le bétail eut soif plus souvent; on arrivoit en hâte et l'on partoit à regret. Dans cet âge heureux où rien ne marquoit les heures, rien n'obligeoit à les compter; les termes n'avoit d'autre mesure que l'amusement et l'ennui ... Là fut enfin le vrai berceau des peuples, et du pur cristal des fontaines sortirent les premiers feux de l'amour").

This occlusion of the self by the judging subject gives its language the character of language – of general comprehensibility that language alone articulates and allows – in that what Kant's speaking subject of judgment says qualifies an object already understood to be properly described by the language being employed. By contrast, what appears proper to the speaker turns out to be improper in Rousseau, a "trope" that hides the disproportionate "passion" behind it, and general language arises only narratively, "after many experiences," as the correction of an initial perceptual error. Rousseau never reveals whether that passion itself is named, whether the subject who, subjecting himself to "fear," ever recognizes that subjection as such, even *"after"* having recognized he had misjudged his object. Rousseau's hypothetical narrative names the "fear" at its origin; Rousseau's hypothetical "man" – either before or after recognizing "other men" – does not. Proceeding systematically rather than narratively, Kant's analysis of judgment rules out all personal articulation of "feeling" in the first place, stating no one would be so "ridiculous" as to "justify" the "pride he takes" in his individual "taste" by articulating, even to himself alone, the thought, "this object ... is beautiful *for me.*"[167] For, to judge an "object" "beautiful" is at once to decouple it from the temporary, contingent disposition of any personal, speaking subject. Or, as Rousseau might state, without the sense of universal assent attached to such appellations as "giant" – or "master," or "slave," or "citizen," for that matter – neither tyranny, nor submission, nor social contract, could come into existence, let alone prevail.

In Kant's Analytic as in Rousseau's story, then, an originary statement about something or someone else carries with it a sense of generality – the sense that what is said, while standing in for a "feeling," is "objective" rather than "subjective" in quality – but in one case that quality is articulated as an adjective, in the other, as a noun. Both terms are part of the nomenclature of discursive language systems yet the epistemologies that stem from them contrast sharply. Extending from abstract and general concepts to objects, nouns, like "giant" or "man," name identities in which qualities of any or no number are assumed to be contained. Grammatically independent of any specific qualitative conditions, their function is nominal and logical above all – thus the perfectly grammatical designation, "the married bachelor," whose nonsensical combination of qualities has come to name the very possibility of logical paradox itself. Conversely, adjectives, like "beautiful," designate free-standing, differential qualities attributable to any number of nouns

167. Kant, *KU*, B 20, X: 126: "Es wäre ... lächerlich, wenn jemand, der sich auf seinen Geschmack etwas einbildete, sich damit zu rechtfertigen gedächte: dieser Gegenstand (das Gebäude, was wir sehen, das Kleid, was jener trägt, das Konzert, was wir hören, das Gedicht, welches zur Beurteilung aufgestellt ist), ist *für mich* schön. Denn er muss es nicht *schön* nennen, wenn es bloss ihm gefällt." [It would be ridiculous if someone who prided himself on his taste thought to justify himself to himself: this object (the building that we see, the dress that that one is wearing, the concert that we hear, the poem that is present for our judgment), is beautiful *for me*. For he must not name (something) *beautiful* when it only pleases him].

and dependent upon none; their meaning unsubordinated to the controlling grammatical rules of predication, they are of purely descriptive, applied or comparative, and absolutely no logical use.

In Kant's and Rousseau's theoretical derivations of language from "feeling," the objects that a speaking subject either qualifies by an adjective or designates by a noun are both unknown. The speech act of judgment, in replacing everyday nominal knowledge with a declaration of "a quality of an object," frees otherwise architectonically delimited faculties to "play" or come into conflict, with no prospect of either (cognitive) conceptual resolution or (aesthetic) transcendental synthesis in sight. By contrast, nominal cognition, while also originating in a speech act, replaces an immediate misperception colored by "passion" with its singularly linguistic objectification in a "trope." Just as "judgment" arising not from concepts but from "feeling" must be enacted linguistically, in speech acts grounded in the *a priori* sense of "general communicability" that constitutes "common sense," so Rousseau's story of language first formed "when passion fascinates the eyes" ("lorsque la passion fascine les yeux"[168]) ensues from a kind of judgment as well, but one that misjudges both its object and itself, "masquerading," even to the consciousness of its speaker, as a constative utterance[169] instead.

The perceptual error of Rousseau's first speaker mistakes the effects of feeling for empirical facts. His larger categorical error is to mistake (mis-)judgment for cognition. True to Rousseau's theoretical narration of the purely conventional nature of social relations, that error informs both the origin of language, first among all conventions, and of all human, or language-based, history, to come: the mistaking of conventional social relations for natural conditions, and of grammatical relations for empirical evidence. For, just as the universal applicability of grammar first makes a social contract among subjects possible, redefining these as citizens possessing equal powers and rights, so grammar, too, offers the model for conventional rather than physical subordination, the founding and "civil" institutionalization of (mis-)appropriation that, mistaking human for natural or

---

168. "This is how the figural word was born before the proper word, when passion fascinates the eyes and the first idea that it offers us is not that of the truth" ("Voilà comment le mot figuré naît avant le mot propre, lorsque la passion nous fascine les yeux et que la première idée qu'elle nous offre n'est pas celle de la vérité" [Rousseau, *Essai, op. cit.*, p. 47].)

169. See J. L. Austin, *How to Do Things with Words* (Cambridge, Mass: Harvard University Press, 1962), pp. 3–6: "Not all true or false statements are descriptions, and for this reason I prefer to use the word 'Constative' ... The type of utterance we are to consider here is not, of course, in general a type of nonsense; though misuse of it can, as we shall see, engender rather special varieties of 'nonsense.' Rather, it is one of our second class – the masqueraders" that "quite commonly" "masquerade as a statement of fact, descriptive or constative ... and that, oddly enough, when it assumes its most explicit form. Grammarians have not, I believe, seen through this 'disguise,' and philosophers at best incidentally ... I propose to call it a *performative sentence* or a performative utterance."

divine attribution and cause for effect, originated in the ungrounded "first" predicative trope, "'this is mine.'"¹⁷⁰

Acts of judgment, by contrast, prohibit acts of appropriation by expressly articulating a quality of an object generally or impartially: "it is beautiful," "it is sublime" take no part in the institution of inequality to which the origin of language in acts of misconception lead inexorably in Rousseau. In this way Kant's articulate act of judgment already provides the model for contemporary analytic approaches to language which, stymied by or blind to the general problem of nominalism, have come to consider the adjective the essential discursive form, or at least have tentatively concluded as much from the demonstrable incapacity of logic to define any noun linguistically without definitional regression or recursivity.¹⁷¹ In the context, however, of hypothetical analyses of the necessarily *non*logical origin of language – of the mismatch between logic and sensory experience designated by any noun made to speak for a specific subject rather than a purely grammatical function – Kant's predecessor in granting linguistic priority to perceivable qualities, and, thus, to experiential adjectives rather than originally tropological nominal concepts, is Rousseau's personal interlocutor and contemporary origin of language theorist, Diderot.

---

170. Like the origin of languages, the origin of property hypothesized by Rousseau in the Second Discourse takes the form of a general narrative allegory, the only mode capable of illustrating in retrospect such an empirically and logically inexplicable event. I have offered a fuller discussion of the founding acts of predication and spatial demarcation that, grounded in nothing but each other, constitute the equally figurative objectification of referent by reference at the (fictive) origin of "property" and "civil society" according to Rousseau, in *In the Place of Language*, pp. 9–16.

171. A turning point in the assessment by analytic philosophy of the capacity of logic to define and derive implications from language is Saul Kripke's review of the uncertainty of the conceptual content of any noun, from "common" nouns through proper names, in *Naming and Necessity* (Cambridge, Mass: Harvard University Press, 1972). In this analytic philosophy has followed Wittgenstein in questioning the association of language with logic *per se*, regarding language instead as regulated by context-specific rules and norms, and any practice *as* linguistic that conforms to a "private" or, in a larger sense, internal logic based in rules its own practice defines. See also Kripke, S. *Wittgenstein on Rules and Private Language* (Cambridge, MA: Harvard University Press, 1984).

7. Diderot's Adjectives

Rather than hypothesize an historic error in the perception of an object arising whenever a blinding "passion" ("fear") "fascinates the eye," Diderot's theory of the origin of language starts with the more radical premise that all sensory perception is and must be unreliable, in that it routinely includes a wide range of blindspots inhering in the conditional nature of our experience of sensible objects itself. The variability of objects and sensation, of the relation of sensation to consciousness, and of the attentiveness and operations of consciousness itself, all ensure, Diderot reasons, that perception will tell us both more and less than we can know with accuracy about anything occurring outside *or* within us, not exceptionally but as a matter of course. Not only unprecedented but commonplace perceptions are limited, extended, heightened, and mitigated by the unpredictable sharpness or dullness, absence or "presence of mind," which is to say, by both the conscious and unconscious effectivity and ineffectivity with which our senses relay them to the mind. For the very same reason (of their own unavailability to reason), the changing external stimulation and internal operation of the senses can provide no basis, *a posteriori*, for a "general" or "common sense" definition of the "condition" enabling linguistic action, according to Diderot.

Thus it is that, by a turn of logic rarely dared within the parameters of rational thought, Diderot proposes we instead follow a radically counter-intuitive method for determining how language comes about. The most effective, if not the only way to investigate language "before" language – to understand how language is formed before language forms the basis for the understanding required for language – must rather reverse the supposed causal relation of physical sensation to articulate speech, Diderot contends. By impeding, completely or partially, the unspeaking sensory component of experience, we may first observe how the mind, operating without the fleeting and variable nature of sensation, invents its own, linguistically conditioned "experience:" what it "sees" when it cannot see, how it "speaks" when it can neither hear nor speak, procuring evidence by producing a language designed to deliver it when sensory and empirical givens don't obtain. Just as subjects naturally furnished with a full complement of senses are regularly "blind" and "deaf" to language – failing to disassociate the "mute" data of sensations from the complex construction, sense and source of the necessarily systematically articulated language that they, as subjects, freely use – so subjects for whom such disassociation is itself instead given, cannot, for that very reason, mistake a fully fabricated system of conventions – both symbolic and grammatical – for the effects of natural sensations. Paradoxically dependent either, on the one hand, on still prior conventions and thus a descent into logical regression, or, on the other, on a single, hypothetical individual's initial, impassioned error of perception, and "later," comparatively engendered self-correction – an historic change itself externalized in the conscious splitting of a single, unconsciously duplicitous "trope" into two "literal" designations eventually rendered social and conventional, i.e., "common" rather than "proper nouns" – the rationally elusive nature of the origin of those conventions makes it indeed logical and not fantastical to suggest that the only real, rather than circular, retrospective or hypothetical evidence of the origin of language from experience may be most readily found in the languages made and practiced by subjects for whom language is in fact necessarily *known, by way of (the* a priori *absence of) experience,* to be an explicitly artificial producer of sense. These are the languages investigated in Diderot's extraordinary "Letter(s) on the "Blind" and "Deaf and Mute," "as used by those who see" and "hear and speak."[172]

To understand the real origin of language – to conceive what any language (and only language) both is and does, without basing that conception on (linguistically enabled) cognitive conventions – Diderot turns to sign systems whose own self-evident, material immediacy he knows he cannot just as immediately understand. Explicitly entitled for the "use" they make of their subjects, Diderot's semi-speculative "Letter(s)" imitate the necessary pragmatism of the sensorily deprived, making subjects who cannot either see or hear stand for those who do, just as those subjects make a present sense stand in for an absent one. These invented means of replacing *de facto* physical absence with fabricated presence are languages. Rendered conspicuous – *by* the sensorily deprived, *to* the hearing and sighted – as conveyors of sense *by other means*, such compensatory languages are primarily, unmistakably substitutional, "metaphoric" or "symbolic," in that they are invented by subjects naturally incapable of mistaking language for nature, those for whom confusing linguistic sense with sensation, and sensation with symbolization is impossible *per force.*

---

172. "Lettre sur les aveugles à l'usage de ceux qui voient' (1749), "Lettre sur les sourds et muets à l'usage de ceux qui entendent et qui parlent" (1751), in Diderot, OC, IV: 15–107, 109–228. On both the Letters, see Franco Venturi's seminal study, *Jeunesse de Diderot (de 1713 à 1753)* trans. Juliette Bertrand (Paris: Albert Skira Editeur, 1939), pp. 142–67, 237–82.

Forced to make do with experience that experience tells them is limited,[173] subjects "deprived of one sense"[174] are not freed, by a sense-based illusion of freedom from all experiential and communicative constraint, to speculate at will about the nature or content of the sensory phenomena they are missing. If they wish to make themselves, including their sensorily independent thoughts,[175] generally communicable in any way, they must instead *use* the sensations supplied by one sense to form a language designed to "speak" for another. Detaching sensation from its immediate sensory context and attaching it to a necessarily conceptual one, the sensorily deprived naturally doubly denaturalize experience, replacing its mute immediacy with a coin of significance forged of a fusion of catachresis with chiasmus – a two-sided currency each of whose "faces" requires the "blind" backing of the other to appear to mean at all. Crossing present with absent sensation so as to endow absence itself with a separate sensible presence, the languages of subjects unblinded by illusions of sensory self-sufficiency expose, *in extremis*, the "real," or fully constructed, nature of all languages, as the former is critically defined by Kant: their replacement of purely empirical, infinitely varied and undependable sense perceptions with perceptible and systematically repeatable symbols. In speaking for and in the place of *inexistent* perceptions, languages invented by subjects deprived of a part of sensory experience are thus definitively *linguistic* (rather than gestural or otherwise mimetic) to begin with:

173. In this regard, Diderot's sensorily deprived subjects experience, as a matter of course, the principle of universal skepticism regarding any sense-based certainty proposed – necessarily hypothetically – in Hume's contemporaneous *Enquiry Concerning Human Understanding* (1739–40): the theoretical proposition that knowledge gained on the basis of sense perceptions is always partial at best. Similarly, it was to Hume's demonstration of the unavailability of an exhaustive sense-based epistemology that Kant attributed his own "critical" "revolution in the mode of thought" of philosophy, i.e., his practical limitation of epistemology to the phenomenal field of "representations" of "objects" that the *a priori* forms and logical structures accompanying our perception provide. To such "phenomenal" knowledge Kant opposed the "real" – unlimited because nonexperiential – knowledge of "things" as they may be "in themselves" that he attributed only to the sensorily unlimited: subjects engaged in "free," i.e., phenomenally and causally undetermined, moral action; cognitions of the "real things" of mathematics; and "God," or "immortality." To the degree that, like Kant's self-critical subject, they know what they do not know, and are forced to translate, materially and consciously, from a state of sense-based ignorance to knowledge by constructing a formal language to represent to them what they do not experience, Diderot's sensorily deprived – knowing practitioners of the linguistic condition of their own phenomenal experience – would stand somewhere between Kant's "man" and "God."
174. Diderot, *OC*, IV: 34.
175. In rendering in palpable sensory form that which they do not and know they cannot sense in the world, Diderot's sensorily deprived directly recall Kant's mysterious first geometer ("Thales, or whatever-his-name"), whose external "representation" of the pathbreaking "figure" of the equilateral triangle was not drawn from sensory experience but "constructed *a priori*" from "concepts" alone. See Kant, *KrV*, XI–XII, III: 22 and this study, Chapter One.

inherently symbolic means for signifying a conventional sense unfounded in any immediately antecedent sensation. The invention, not of a new, pseudo-natural mode of sensation, but of a semantic mode that abstracts from specific sensory givens to represent a general "idea" unhinged from sensation, the origin of language in Diderot's "Letter(s)" binds absence to presence symbolically, or in part.

In the first "Letter," Diderot calls this intellectual act of origination, by which a part or partial sense of a whole is abstracted and transferred elsewhere, "metaphorical," but, unlike the figural distortion to which the passions submit an unknown perceptual object at the origin of language in Rousseau, this act compensating for an absent perception represents its object accurately, just in necessarily non-identical, artificially composed form.[176] Writing in response to the query of an unnamed (and possibly entirely fabricated[177]) addressee, Diderot uses the purported interest of his interlocutor in the cognitive abilities of subjects whose sight has been restored as a pretext for demonstrating the unique ability of the blind to illuminate the intellectual operations we all perform. Summing up the separation of "symbol" from sensation on which his entire theory of language, as of dramatic acting and dramatic and novelistic writing, draws, Diderot asserts categorically: "Madame, one has to be lacking a sense in order to know the advantages of the symbols destined for the senses that remain" ("Madame, il faut manquer d'un sens pour connaître les avantages des symboles destinés à ceux qui restent"[178]).

Like his friend and intellectual confrère Rousseau, whose later interest in natural morphology will extend and reflect Diderot's own early "experimental philosophy,"[179] Diderot recognizes that any investigation into the origin of language must devolve into a vicious circle unless a subject outside that circle – a necessarily hypothetical subject in whom reason and language are not yet indistinguishable – can be imagined to undergo an experience in which the invention of linguistic "symbols" is compelled. Pointing, for the first time, to a felt cognitive lack, such an experience would require the absence of phenomenal self-evidence. Its subject may be, like Diderot's addressee, a fiction *in toto* or in part, but not so the "symbols" – artificial, material, and technical, rather than either feigning naturalness, or fictive, in nature – that must originate at once inside and outside the subject's mind.[180] This is the invention of a language of "symbols" belonging to

176. Diderot, *OC*, IV: 41.
177. See Yvon Belaval, "Introduction," in Diderot, *OC*, IV: 3.
178. Diderot, *OC*, IV: 34.
179. On the theory and practice of what he named "experimental philosophy" in all Diderot's works, from the early *Pensées philosophiques*, scandalous *Bijoux indiscrets* and "Lettre[s]," through the *Encyclopédie*, *Salons*, *Religieuse* and *Paradoxe sur le comédien*, see Brodsky, "Whatever Moves You", pp. 17–44.
180. This is how Kant (and, later, Husserl) describes the "origin of geometry:" a "pathbreaking" ("bahnbrechend") act of simultaneous mental and external construction on Kant's account, the founding of geometry originates anew with every written transmission and internalization of its principles according to Husserl. See: Kant, *KrV*, XI-XII, III: 22; Husserl, "Die Frage nach dem Ursprung . . ." (for full citation, see n. 12, Chapter One, this study).

no individual subject, proper to no individual object, and so of 'use' and available to all, and of language itself as the inherently active constitution of meaning-bearing, or communicative, relations, which is to say, with Diderot, as constitutively "metaphorical." "Trope" or "metaphor," psychical or physical, impassioned or empirical in origin: language occurs in both Rousseau and Diderot when psyche and physiology are experienced as split. Just as he "uses" the blind to get a better, necessarily "metaphoric" view of the whole of nature, whose infinite, constantly changing forms can never be seen, let alone pictured, whole,[181] so Diderot will turn to the deaf and mute to discover what no speaking subject can say: how "symbols" designating "doubl[y]" meaning-bearing, "metaphorical" relations themselves attain relative positions of significance within the regular – grammatical and syntactic – construction of language chains.

Diderot bases his account of language in the "Letter on the Blind" on the actual experience and achievements of Nicholas Saunderson, a contemporary professor of mathematics at Oxford and author of *The Elements of Algebra* (Cambridge, 1740). Forced by the absence of sight to "invent" a language of "symbols" standing for objects that are not and will never be evident, "Saunderson," on Diderot's account, is at once a real historical person and his author's symbolic invention. Since the conventional symbols of mathematics – numbers, letters, lines, operational signs, and figures – stand for phenomenally independent entities identified in function of equations and other reciprocal and combinatory relations in much the same way, Saunderson may have indeed been the perfect subject to invent a symbolic system which must signify identities in a "double," "metaphorical" manner, substituting meaningful relations for inherent sensory limitations.[182] Yet, just as his anti-theological deathbed speech – "translated," Diderot states, "from the fragments that remain of it" – is in fact entirely of Diderot's own making, Diderot's blind "Saunderson" must be "seen" in a "double light" as well, as actual inventor of an extant language and the "Letter"'s ventriloquized vehicle of the theory of language it describes, a talking symbolization of the necessary origin of language in

---

181. Diderot, *OC*, IV: 50–51. Its proto-Darwinian description of the infinite material permutations of nature, including such finite, "malformed" and "monstrous productions" as its blind speaker, "Saunderson," himself, landed the author of the "Lettre sur les aveugles" in jail shortly after its publication: Diderot was imprisoned at Vincennes from July 29 to November 3, 1749. On Diderot's own "concrete" discursive "style" as manifestation of the interdependence between language and materialism his writings variously theorize and represent, see J. p. Séguin, *Diderot. Le Discours et les choses* (Paris: Librairie Klincksieck, 1978): "In an obsession with things, Diderot finds paradoxically the primacy of language: to move toward the concrete is finally to be attentive to the creation of the real which is nothing other than all linguistic systems, seized in language and in speech" (17). On the interdependence of the transformation of forms and liberty itself in Diderot's theory of the poetics of nature, see Jacques Chouillet's classic study, *Diderot: poète de l'énergie* (Paris: Presses Universitaires de France, 1984 [orig. pub. 1964]).

182. Diderot, *OC*, IV: 34, 41.

symbolization. In that language is, by definition, discontinuous with immediate physical experience, every language must originate as Diderot's "Saunderson's" does, articulating what the senses are incapable of conveying, either of experience or its absence. Even (the historical) Saunderson's everyday discourse reflected this independence from sensation, Diderot reports. Just as phenomenal perception can never be mistaken for linguistically communicated sense in his case, so Saunderson used his native language in a manner no less essentially "symbolic" than the mathematical language he invented. As if every quotidian experience brought with it a renewed occasion to articulate the relational basis of language expressed *per force* in its origin, Saunderson's conversational speech was also unusually "fertile with happy expressions" ("fécund en expressions heureuses"), Diderot notes, constructions that, like Kant's geometer's "happy notion" ("glückliche[r] Einfall"[183]) of the arithmetically translatable triangle, are "proper to one sense, to touch, for example, ... and metaphoric at the same time to another sense, such as the eyes, from which results a double light for him to whom one talks, the true and direct light of expression and the reflected light of metaphor" ("celles qui sont propres à un sens, au toucher, par exemple, et qui sont métaphoriques en même temps à un autre sens, comme aux yeux; d'où il résulte une double lumière pour celui à qui on parle, la lumière vraie et directe de l'expression, et la lumière réfléchie de la métaphore."[184])

Describing the origin of language as an internally executed transfer of sense,[185] the "Letter on the Blind" does not stipulate what kind of word Saunderson's "doubly reflected," "proper" and "metaphoric" language employs to that end. Impeded from immediately perceiving the objects named by words, the historical Saunderson created a tactile mathematical "language" whose corporal elements – a rectilinear "table" divided into small squares defined by holes at their corners and center, in which pins bearing either "large" or "small" heads are situated – allowed him both to symbolize numerical values by manipulating the variables of the pins' size and

183. See n. 8, n. 51, Chapter One, this study.
184. Diderot, *OC*, IV: 41; 34: "It is quicker to use symbols that are fully invented than to be the inventor of them, as one is forced to be by deprivation" ("il faut manquer d'un sens pour connaître les avantages des symboles destinés à ceux qui restent ... Il est bien plus court d'user de symboles tout inventés que d'en être inventeur, comme on y est forcé, lorsqu'on est pris au dépourvu").
185. Diderot's theory of the innate capacity of all subjects, demonstrated of necessity by the sensorily deprived, to transfer the information received by one sense "metaphorically" to another either empirically impaired or absent, is in fact the actual working basis of such state-of-the-art "sensory-substitution devices" as those currently enabling blind subjects to "see" (via body-worn micro-video cameras delivering digital information in the form of electronic impulses to their tongues) and deaf subjects to "hear" (via worn microphones attached to speech processors delivering digitally coded impulses to electrodes implanted in an otherwise sensorially impaired inner ear). (See Nicola Twilley's descriptive account of such technologies in, "Sight Unseen," *The New Yorker,* May 15, 2017.) While sensory deprivation renders the blind cognizant of the transfers they teach themselves to make,

position (each possible combination signifying a different single digit), and to construct geometrical figures by "fix[ing] lines of "strings of silk" around them.[186] Providing a physical solution to the problem of combining algebra with geometry already resolved "on paper" by Descartes' *Discourse on Method* and *Geometry*, whose historic use of "letters" or *chiffres* to symbolize unknowns (including the subject of thinking, "I") allowed immeasurable quantities, like irrational numbers, to be integrated into equations for the first time, the "happy expressions" of Saunderson's calculating "machine" are the felicitous arrangements of the tactile system he has devised, combinations of pins sometimes "name[d]" by "letters of the alphabet," to symbolize, in their size and configuration, numbers and lines:

> In supposing that Saunderson only employed pins with large heads to designate the limits of his figures, he could dispose of pins with small heads around them in nine different ways, all of which were familiar to him. Thus he hardly encountered difficulties except in the cases where the large number of angular points that he was obliged to name in his demonstration forced him to have recourse to the letters of the alphabet. We have not been told how he employed them.

subjects endowed with a full complement of senses are more likely to be "blind" to the fully conventionalized metaphors upon which prosaic and conceptual discourse rests. Landmark accounts of this tendency, in everyday speech no less than in philosophy, include: Hobbes, *Leviathan* (London: Viking Penguin, 1985 [orig. pub. 1651]), Part I: "Of Man," Chap. 2, "Of Imagination," Chap. 3, "Of Words," Chap. 4 "Of Speech," esp.; Locke, *Essay Concerning Human Understanding* (*London: VikingPenguin 2004* [orig. pub. 1689]), Bk III: "Of Words;" Hume, *A Treatise of Human Nature* (Oxford: Oxford University Press, 1978 [orig. pub. 1739–40]), Bk. I: "Of the Understanding," Pt. III: "Of Knowledge and Probability," Section VI, "Of the Inference from the Impression to the Idea," Bk. III: "Of Morals," Section I–III, esp.; Baudelaire, "La fausse monnaie," *Oeuvres complètes* (Paris: Editions du Seuil, 1968), pp. 168–69 [orig. pub. 1864]; Nietzsche, "Über Wahrheit und Lüge im aussermoralischen Sinne" ("On Truth and Lie in the Extra-Moral Sense") (Stuttgart: Reclam, 2015 [orig. pub. 1896]); Heidegger, *Identität und Differenz* (Frankfurt: Klostermann, 1957); Derrida, *La mythologie blanche* (Paris: Editions du Seuil,1971); Paul de Man, "The Epistemology of Metaphor," *Critical Inquiry*, Vol. 5, No. 1 (1978), pp. 13–30.

186. Diderot, *OC*, IV: 39. Consistent with the transfer of sense Saunderson's symbolizing "machine" enacts, Diderot supplements his own discursive explanation of its functioning with illustrations reproducing in two dimensions some examples of the combinations of size and location that transform physical pins into representations of numbers and figures (see *OC*, IV: 37, 40). In so doing he returns Saunderson's tactile invention to the very visual field it was created to replace. While Diderot probably accepted this regressive development as an inevitable, if ironic, aspect of his efforts to educate the sighted, that irony is itself effectively mitigated by the change his inserted *planches* wreak upon the visual: having already been given shape by (Diderot's descriptions of) Saunderson's "language," the visual now appears a poor derivative, rather than a primary auxiliary, of mathematics.

[En supposant que Saunderson n'employât que des épingles à grosse tête, pour designer les limites de ses figures, il pouvait disposer autour d'elles des épingles à petite tête de neuf façons différentes, qui toutes lui étaient familières. Ainsi il n'était guère embarrassé, que dans les cas où le grand nombre de points angulaires qu'il était obligé de nommer dans sa démonstration le forçait de recourir aux lettres de l'alphabet. On ne nous apprend point comment il les employait.[187]]

Now, number is itself a value or quality, independent of objects as such, just as geometrical figures are not visual but mathematical in basis. Diderot's ostensible purpose in the semi-fictional "Letter on the Blind" was to take a position on the then contentious philosophical and scientific question, first posed of Locke by the British scientist, William Molyneux, of whether a subject "born blind," whose "sight" is "restituted" (by the removal of cataracts), would be able to "distinguish" a "sphere" from a "cube" "immediately" upon sight.[188] Not only in his dismissal of "the Molyneux problem" as ungrounded in the actual experience of any seeing eye, but in his account of the "light" shed upon all language formation by the necessarily "metaphoric" languages of the blind, Diderot describes the origin of language as the

187. Diderot, *OC*, IV: 39–40. I have investigated Descartes' algebraization of geometry in *Lines of Thought. Discourse, Architectonics, and the Origin of Modern Philosophy* (Durham, N.C.: Duke University Press, 1996). See also Diderot's description of the enhanced ability of someone who cannot see "to make the passage from physics to geometry" by proceeding in the sense the sighted would consider backwards, that of calculating, based on phenomenal forms he can feel, geometrical "suppositions" concerning physical phenomena he cannot otherwise perceive: "The blind man thus takes suppositions for [or supposes them to be] that which is given to him: a ray of light is taken for a thin, elastic string, or for a sequence of little bodies that strike at our eyes with an incredible speed, and he calculates accordingly. The passage from physics to geometry is made, and the question becomes purely mathematical" ("L'aveugle prend donc les suppositions pour ce qu'on les lui donne: un rayon de lumière pour un fil élastique et mince, ou pour une suite de petits corps qui viennent frapper nos yeux avec une vitesse incroyable, et il calcule en conséquence. Le passage de la physique à la géométrie est franchi, et la question devient purement mathématique") (*OC*, IV: 42–43).

188. Diderot, *OC*, IV: 54ff. Along with Locke, the cataracts surgeon, William Cheselden, and, surprisingly, Berkeley, while in opposition to Condillac (see *OC*, IV: 56–61), Diderot's response to the larger question underlying the Molyneux problem, of whether nominal promotes real knowledge, is a decided no: "Here is my opinion on the ... preceding questions: I think that the first time the eyes of someone blind from birth open to the light, he won't perceive anything at all; that some time would be required for his eye to experiment upon itself ("Voici maintenant mon opinion sur ... les questions précédentes: Je pense que la première fois que les yeux de l'aveugle-né s'ouvriront à la lumière, il n'appercevra rien de tout; qu'il faudra quelque temps à son oeil pour s'expérimenter" [IV: 66–67]; "However I do not think in any way that the eye cannot teach itself, or, if it is permitted to speak thus, experiment upon itself" ("Cependant je ne pense nullement que l'oeil ne puisse s'instruire, ou, s'il est permis de parler ainsi, s'expérimenter de lui-même" [IV: 62])).

act of abstracting a quality or condition from the innumerable – or, what amounts to the same, physically imperceptible – qualities of objects as such. The "separation," rather than elimination, of sensory qualities by which Diderot defines "abstraction" in the "Letter on the Blind" – "abstraction consists only in separating by thought the sensory qualities of bodies, either from each other, or from the body that serves as their base" ("l'abstraction ne consiste qu'à séparer par la pensée les qualités sensibles des corps, ou les unes des autres, ou du corps même qui leur sert de base") – "results" in the logical corollary that "someone born blind perceives things in a much more abstract way than we do, and, in questions of a purely speculative nature, is probably less subject to making mistakes" ("il s'ensuit que l'aveugle-né aperçoit les choses d'une manière beaucoup plus abstraite que nous; et que dans les questions de pure spéculation, il est peut-être moins sujet à se tromper").[189]

As in his definition of "abstraction" as an act of highlighting or foregrounding rather than excluding "sensory qualities," such that perception is made apperception – an experience of the *act* of aesthesis, rather than action erased as it transpires – so Diderot's own "abstract" consideration of how language originates never "separates" sensory qualities from each other nor abstraction itself from sensuous experience except by the experimental speculations of "thought." For the same reason, Diderot considers common nouns to be purely artificial abstractions purposefully divorced from any real, negative or positive, experiential basis or value. *An invention of logic rather than language*, common nouns tell us nothing, Diderot contends, about the things they denote, reflecting them not in a "double light" but no light at all. Just as "tree," in designating a general unqualified concept intended to subsume an infinite number of organic objects, must fail to describe the particular sensory qualities of any tree we may experience, so common nouns could not have derived directly, in an at once immediate and comprehensive exercise of "abstraction," *from* experience. It is instead, Diderot reasons, in the "separation" of sensory qualities from the individual "bodies" that are their "base" that subjects of experience, *aided* "by thought," must have abstracted striking individual qualities from experience to form their first words. For Diderot, language, originating, as it does for Rousseau, alongside acts of perception, proceeds not from a singular experience of "passion" concealed as it is displaced into "trope" – the figural expression for a first, false impression whose correction and replacement by common nouns follow only "after" ample comparative "experience" – but, rather, with the already inherently comparative term for a quality common to any number of experiences, the adjective.

This is the conclusion of Diderot's second "Letter" on the partially sensorily deprived, those compelled by the absence of hearing, the most immediate language-bearing sense, to identify objects not by repeating the arbitrary name others have assigned to them and that they cannot hear, but by naming the specific sensory qualities they themselves non-auditorily perceive. For Diderot, in other words, orality and oral mimicry (or onomatopoeia) have nothing to do with either the formation or sensory and intellectual function of language at all. As "the Molyneux problem" of the uncertain relation between intellectual conception and

---

189. Diderot, *OC*, IV: 32.

sense perception posed the occasion for the "Letter on the Blind," the "Letter on the Deaf and Mute as Used by Those who Hear and Speak" (1751) begins by addressing another issue regarding the foundation and founding functional purpose of language of vital importance at the time, namely, the logical problem posed by those linguistic "inversions" of adjective and noun sequences that reverse a syntactic order believed to have once had historical – as it now has logical – priority. At stake was the central thesis of the Port-Royal grammarians that grammatical form and logical form are entirely homologous, such that the "art of speaking" reflects the "art of thinking" that itself reflects the power of "reason" endowed by "nature" in man.[190] According to this view, French grammar embodied the best linguistic model for logical, analytic thought in that it placed nouns – the conceptual prerequisite of any definitional logic – before verbs, adjectives, and complements. The fact that reversals of this purportedly natural order, or "inversions," occurred not only in other languages, including and especially ancient ones, but in contemporary French as well, raised the question of the empirical validity of the Port-Royal thesis and, with it, the possibility that logic was not the governing force behind language formation and use to begin with. In a chapter devoted to "Inversions" in his *Essai sur l'origine des connaissances humaines*, Condillac had argued against Port-Royal that analytic and inverted orders are "equally natural," depending on "the relationship of the ideas" involved; that French, which generally excludes inversions, is "less lively" than Latin; and that "preference" for one language or the other is not a logical but a personal matter, whose determination depends on the "mind" of the "individual."[191]

Diderot, on the other hand, approaches the problem of inversions (as one might guess) by inverting it. First, he inverts the temporal terms of the controversy itself. Rather than representing irregular, contemporary deviations from traditional syntactic order, "inversions" were a regular feature of ancient oratory, Diderot asserts. Even such basic semantic elements as declension "endings," so his argument goes, were subject to "transposition" within the full grammatical and syntactic construction of ancient periodic sentences. Citing Cicero's *Oratio* for Marcellus, he comments:

> What I have just said about the inversion of the beginning of the Oration for Marcellus is applicable to all inversions. In general, in Latin and Greek periodic sentences, no matter their length, one perceives from the beginning that the author having had a reason to employ one ending instead of another did not

---

190. See A. Arnauld and P. Nicole, *La Logique ou L'Art de penser*, revised edition, ed. p. Clair and F. Girbal (Paris: Librairie Philosophique J. Vrin, 1981 [orig. pub. 1662]), pp. 38, 103–4, esp.

191. Etienne Bonnot de Condillac, *Essai sur l'origine des connaissances humaines, ouvrage où l'on réduit à un seul principe tout ce qui concerne l'entendement humain*, ed. C. Porset, intro. J. Derrida (Paris: Editions Galilée, 1973 [orig. pub. 1746]), pp. 247–52. Thorough discussion of Condillac's *Essai* and its direct influence on Diderot and others is offered in Hans Aarsleff, *From Locke to Saussure: Essays on the Study of Language and Intellectual History* (Minneapolis: University of Minnesota Press, 1982), pp. 146–224.

have in his ideas the inversion that rules in his terms. In effect, in the preceding period, what else determined Cicero to write *diuturni silentii* in the genitive, *quo* in the ablative, *eram* in the imperfect, and so on, but a pre-existing order in his spirit that was entirely contrary to that of expressions; an order to which he conformed without knowing it, subjugated by a long habit of transposing? And why wouldn't Cicero have transposed without perceiving he was doing so, since this is what happens to ourselves when we believe we have formed our language according to the natural sequence of ideas?

[Ce que je viens de dire de l'inversion du commencement de l'oraison pour Marcellus, est applicable à toute autre inversion. En général, dans une période grecque ou latine, quelque longue qu'elle soit, on s'aperçoit, dès le commencement, que, l'auteur ayant eu une raison d'employer telle ou telle terminaison plutôt que toute autre, il n'a avait point dans ses idées l'inversion qui règne dans ses termes. En effet, dans la période précédente, qu'est-ce qui déterminait Cicéron à écrire *diuturni silentii* au génitive, *quo* à l'ablatif, *eram* à l'imparfait, et ainsi du reste, qu'un ordre d'idées préexistant dans son esprit, tout contraire à celui des expressions: ordre auquel il se conformait sans s'en apercevoir, subjugué par la longue habitude de transposer? Et pourquoi Cicéron n'aurait-il pas transposé sans s'en apercevoir, puisque la chose nous arrive à nous-mêmes, à nous qui croyons avoir formé notre langue sur la suite naturelle des idées?[192]]

Pitting modern against traditional usage, the mistaken historicization of inversions as stemming from an historically determined decline, "rather than the long habit of transposing" already effective in ancient texts, demonstrates nothing so much as the irrelevance of the debate it has framed to its object, the significance of linguistic order itself, except insofar as it reveals a profound misunderstanding of the basis of the rules by which language makes sense. Partly refuting the moderate position of Condillac, whose combined account of the formation and availability of varying word orders in any language he, in large measure, follows, Diderot again overturns rationalist presuppositions regarding the source and content of linguistic practices, arguing that what his contemporaries consider "inversions" were once considered straightforward, and that the analytic order is in fact the inversion of the order of language of its origin:

I wouldn't want to assert generally and without distinction that the Latins do not invert and that we do. I would only say that if, instead of comparing our sentence to the didactic order of ideas, one compares it to the order of the invention of words, to the language of gestures for which oratory language was gradually substituted, it appears that we invert, and that of all the peoples on earth there is none that has as many inversions as we have.

[Je ne voudrais donc pas avancer généralement et sans distinction que les Latins ne renversent point, et que c'est nous qui renversons. Je dirais seulement qu'au

---

192. Diderot, *OC*, IV: 154–55.

lieu de comparer notre phrase à l'ordre didactique des idées, si on la compare à l'ordre d'invention des mots, au langage des gestes auquel le langage oratoire a été substitué par degré, il paraît que nous renversons, et que de tous les peuples de la terre il n'y en a point qui ait autant d'inversions que nous.[193]]

This ultimate inversion of the grammatical principle of inversions questions the significance of that principle itself, suggesting that, rather than judging linguistic usage according to a "didactic order of ideas," we consider instead the order of experience reflected in the "order of the invention of words." The distinction Diderot draws here, between schematized and reflective orders of language, re-introduces the factor of temporality that grammatical-logical rules of language exclude, considering the use of language as a constitutive part of our intellectual interaction with sensory experience, rather than a mechanically applied, experientially independent, grammatical and morphological code for coordinating and concatenating specific cognitive contents – as Port Royal would have it – "logically." Just as the question posed by "the Molyneux problem" excluded time as a factor in the ability of the eye to "recognize" what it sees, anticipating, instead, either an immediate or no linkage between "restored" vision and "stored" "ideas,"[194] so the "didactic order of ideas" excludes the temporally dependent relation of sensation and reflection required for "ideas," or content, to be formed in the first place. It is these latter that require, in turn, the heterogeneous formation of language itself, and Diderot's first question in the second "Letter" concerns not the properly logical ordering of words, but, how, to begin with, "languages were formed:"

> In order to treat the matter of inversions well, I believe it appropriate to examine how languages were formed. Sensory objects were the first to strike the senses, and those that reunited several sensory qualities at the same time were the first named; these are the different individual things that compose the universe. Sensory qualities were then distinguished from each other and given names; these account for the majority of adjectives. Finally, having abstracted from these sensory qualities, one found or believed one found something in common among these individual things, such as impenetrability, extension, color, figure, etc, and one formed metaphysical and general names and almost all substantives.
>
> [Pour bien traiter la matière des inversions, je crois qu'il est à propos d'examiner comment les langues se sont formées. Les objets sensibles ont les premiers frappé les sens, et ceux qui réunissent plusieurs qualités sensibles à la fois ont été les premiers nommés; ce sont les différents individus qui composent cet univers. On a ensuite distingué les qualités sensibles, on a trouvé ou cru trouver quelque chose de commun dans tous ces individus, comme l'impénétrabilité, l'étendue, la couleur, la figure etc. et l'on a formé les noms métaphysiques et généraux, et presque tous les substantifs.[195]]

193. Diderot, *OC*, IV: 164.
194. Diderot, *OC*, IV: 163, on the "storehouse" ("magasin") of "ideas" kept in our minds.
195. Diderot, *OC*, IV: 135.

As Diderot's account of language formation concludes, the conceptualization of sensory qualities "found or believed to be found" to be "common" to "individual" objects (qualities such as "impenetrability, extension, ... etc.") led to the creation of the "nouns" of "metaphysics and nearly all substantives," with the chiastic result that the objects of actual sensory experience came to be eclipsed by the nouns used to name them, and, "little by little, one got used to believing that these nouns represented real beings" ("[p]eu à peu on s'est accoutumé à croire que ces noms représentaient des êtres réels"), thereby exchanging nominal existences for real.[196] The multiple "sensory qualities" that originally caused objects to be noticed came to be considered "simple accidents" ("de simples accidents") instead, and the "adjectives" that name them, as less essential to language than "substantives," even though, in articulating and representing the continually changing, objective and affective nature of experience – for Diderot, the only, if always inadequate, uses of language that matter – "the substantive is properly nothing, and *the adjective is everything*" ("quoique le substantif ne soit proprement rien, et que *l'adjectif soit tout*"[197]).

The philosophical controversy regarding inversions inverted "the natural order of ideas," according to Diderot, in "imagining that the adjective was really subordinate to the substantive" ("l'on s'est imaginé que l'adjectif était réellement subordonné au substantif"[198]), and this is the second way in which he uses a controversy he considers without validity or epistemological interest to introduce an understanding of the relation between language and experience that, like temporality, had not been considered before. For "ideas," Diderot proposes, are not the erasure but the signature of experience, whose "natural order" reflects discrete acts of perception rather than the deductive hierarchy of a nominalist logic: "Asked what a body is, you will answer that it is *an extended, impenetrable, shaped, colored and mobile substance*. But remove all the adjectives from this definition and what will remain of this imaginary being you call *substance*?"[199] For Diderot, the answer to that question is nothing – nothing, that is, but the insubstantiality of defining one common noun by another.

The hypothesis, that "different [sensory] qualities" made manifest in parts or "portions" of material things would have "affected . . . a man see[ing] a body for the first time," does not translate, however, into a theory of language conflating words with sensations for Diderot. On the contrary, it leads him to the opposing "idea" that, in order to understand the organization of language, one would have instead to "decompose, so to speak, a man, and to consider what he has from each of the senses he possesses" ("[m]on idée serait donc de décomposer pour ainsi dire un homme, et de considérer ce qu'il tient de chacun des sens qu'il possède"[200]). The many partial sensations we experience at any moment are followed just as instantly by others, Diderot suggests, such that the very act of their perception requires the

196. *Ibid.*
197. *Ibid.* (emphasis in text).
198. Diderot, *OC*, IV: 135, 137.
199. Diderot, *OC*, IV: 136.
200. Diderot, *OC*, IV: 140; see also 158, 162.

exercise of "successive and detailed attention" in time, just as "the state of the "soul," "indivisible" in itself, can only be made "manifest" by the countervailing "force" of "analysis" originating in our intellect:

> The state of the soul in an indivisible instant was represented by a crowd of terms demanded by the precision of language which distributed a total impression into parts: and because these terms were pronounced successively, and were only heard and understood insofar as they were pronounced, one was led to believe that the affections of the soul that they represented had the same succession, when nothing could be further from the case. One thing is the state of our soul; another thing is the account that we give of it, whether to ourselves or to others; one thing is the total and instantaneous sensation of this state; another thing, *the successive and detailed attention that we are forced to give it in order to analyze it, to make it manifest, and to make ourselves heard and understood. Our soul is a moving tableau after which we paint without cease*: we employ a lot of time to render it with fidelity but it exists in its entirety and at the same time: the spirit does not proceed step by step like expression.
>
> [L'état de l'âme dans un instant indivisible fut représenté par une foule de termes que la précision du langage exigea, et qui distribuèrent une impression totale en parties: et parce que ces termes se prononçaient successivement, et ne s'entendaient qu'à mesure qu'ils se prononçaient, on fut porté à croire que les affections de l'âme qu'il représentaient avaient la même succession; mais il n'en est rien. Autre chose est l'état de notre âme; autre chose le compte que nous en rendons soit à nous-mêmes, soit aux autres: autre chose la sensation totale et instantanée de cet état; *autre chose l'attention successive et détaillée que nous sommes forces d'y donner pour l'analyser, la manifester et nous faire entendre. Notre âme est un tableau mouvant d'après lequel nous peignons sans cesse*: nous employons bien du temps à le rendre avec fidélité; mais il existe en entier et tout à la fois: l'esprit ne va pas à pas comptés comme l'expression.[201]]

It is on the basis of their own empirical condition – of partial sensory "decompos[ition]" -- that the modes of "speech" necessarily invented by the unhearing and unspeaking put the temporal "transpositions"[202] of sensory experience into articulation into relief. Unable to rely on vision, the naturally "decomposed" forge a material mode of symbolization that, necessarily "abstracted" from the "instantaneous" complexity of sensory experience, renders the "metaphoric" nature of language a tactile reality perceptible to sighted and unseeing alike.[203] Furthermore, in basing his *understanding* of the composition of language on both

---

201. Diderot, *OC*, IV: 161 (emphasis added).
202. Diderot, *OC*, IV: 154–55.
203. For a fuller examination of the ongoing separation of sensation from knowledge in Diderot's *Letters*, see the complementary study to this one, *Words' Worth*, Part Three, Chapter 11.

observable and hypothetical "states" of "decompos[ition]," Diderot underscores the absence of any natural correlation between language and actual sensation. Like his "Saunderson," the real or contrived basis of that absence makes no difference: it is its connection to the act of symbolization that matters. And just as apparently natural conditions cannot explain *a posteriori* the linguistic condition exposed by the "decomposed," so can no ready-made language linking sensory and nonsensory experience to articulation disguise it, in that what these ongoing acts of articulation and representation, "our ceaseless paint[ing] after," continuously compose, is a "language" formed *because* it does not – indeed, cannot – represent something one otherwise already knows. Language here *acts* as a kind of counter-spirit both to the "state" of constant change, "composition" and "destruction" equated by both Diderot and his "Saunderson" with "nature,"[204] and the equally dynamic "total[ity]" that is the "state of the spirit [or "soul": âme"). "Successive," "step-by-step," and "analytic," it "decomposes" the distinct sensory qualities that transpire in the "spirit" "all at once," "transposing" fleeting sensations into articulate forms of communication "metaphorically" permitting internal experience to be "seen," "heard and understood" for the "first" time, rather than "sink," forever unrepresented (in Keats' immortal words), "to nothingness."

The ignorance to which language responds in Rousseau, by contrast, is not of objects of which, for either real or hypothetical physiological reasons, the subject experiences no direct sensation, nor of the incessantly "moving *tableau* of the soul" that, by definition, no subject can directly sense and know. Neither purely objective nor subjective in basis, language is instead formed in Rousseau in the context of the unprecedented perception of an other just like him whom the perceiving subject cannot recognize to resemble himself, not least because his "own" self is misperceived by him as his alone, and the origin of language resulting from that experience names not the feeling, "fear," that such a complex misperception inspires – a "passion" with the power "to fascinate the eye" in the stead of any visible object – but rather an object of imagined dimensions *rationally* commensurate with that (inherently irrational) *feeling*, i.e., a terrifyingly oversized, *physically* incommensurate other, or "Giant."

On Diderot's view, the incommensurability of "simultaneity" and difference at work at every moment of perception impedes all subjects from "seeing" *without* the uniquely symbolic and successive mode of language. Language allows subjects to "express" a complex experience not through its impassioned misprision and projection in "figural language," or "trope" ("Giant"), but the direct converse, a series of grammatically "analytic" acts distinguishing and "attach[ing] many ideas" to "a single expression":

> *I would willingly eat this here* are only modes of a single sensation. *I* marks the person who feels it; *would eat*, the desire and the nature of the felt sensation; *willingly*, its intensity or its force; *this here*, the presence of the desired object; but

---

204. Cf. Chapter One, n.18, this study.

the sensation does not have in the soul this successive development; and if it could command with twenty mouths, each mouth saying its word, all the preceding ideas would be rendered simultaneously... But, lacking many mouths, this is what one has done: one attached many ideas to a single expression.

[*Je mangerais volontiers celui* ne sont que des modes d'une seule sensation. *Je* marque la personne qui l'éprouve; *mangerais*, le désir et la nature de la sensation éprouvée; *volontiers*, son intensité ou sa force; *celui*, la présence de l'objet désiré; mais la sensation n'a point dans l'âme ce développement successif du discours; et si elle pouvait commander à vingt bouches, chaque bouche disant son mot, toutes les idées précédentes seraient rendues à la fois ... Mais au défaut de plusieurs bouches, voici ce qu'on a fait: on a attaché plusieurs idées à une seule expression.[205]]

A "single," "discurs[ive]ly develop[ed]" "expression" gives single "successive" voice to the cacophony of "many mouths" by "decomposing" so as to recompose it into the symbolic diachrony that is language. Perception, judgment, and feeling occur together within the "state of the soul" – "*to see* an object, *to judge* it beautiful, *to feel* a pleasurable sensation, *to desire* possession, is the state of the soul in a single instant" ("*voir* un objet, le *juger* beau, *éprouver* une sensation agréable, *désirer* la possession, c'est l'état de l'âme dans un même instant") – but whereas "Greek and Latin," Diderot asserts, "render" that "state" semantically, through "a single word" in whose "pronounce[ment] all is said, all is understood" ("que le grec et le latin rendent par un seul mot. Ce mot prononcé, tout est dit, tout est entendu"[206]), modern languages render it grammatically, through a logical category of word defined to designate a single property common to multiple "ideas," as described above, "the adjective."[207] In the relation of perception, judgment, and feeling related within a "single expression" just cited, adjectives distinguish an unnamed object ("it") by naming neither its true nor tropological identity ("man," or "Giant") but its quality ("beautiful," "pleasurable"), and the transitive verbs of which those qualities are the complements, "to judge" and "to feel," may only be grammatically predicated by adjectives. Here – in the peculiar cases of judging and (nonsensory) feeling – grammar reveals, rather than rules out, a semantic oddity: transitive verbs that attach primarily not to objects but to qualities. Attached to a feeling rather than a cognition, and unattached to any specific subject, object or context that would prevent its being *generally* "pronounce[able]" and "underst[andable]") (or in Kant's terms *generally* "communicable") in the first place, language originates, in Diderot's second "Letter," to "decompose" into discrete, grammatically sequenced, verbal acts a multitude of sensations experienced at once.

In Kant, that simultaneous multiplicity or copresence of "many mouths" does not occur within a single subject, but among subjects. In addition to the "play" or "conflict" of cotemporaneous feelings of pleasure and pain, judgment, in order to

---

205. Diderot, *OC*, IV: 158.
206. Diderot, *OC*, IV: 162.
207. Cf. Chap. One, n. 26, this Section, this Chapter, n. 199, n. 200, n. 201.

be judgment, i.e., a generally pronounceable act of speech, must originate "as if" in all possible speaking subjects at once, on Kant's account, just as it must join distinct parts of speech into a single spoken "synthesis" of subject and adjectival predicate, a sentence. No less than the synthetic judgments *a priori* composing Kants critical theory of cognition, aesthetic judgments in Kant's *Critique of Judgment* reveal the active intellectual sense of the sentence to an extent matched in philosophy before Kant only by Descartes' *cogito*.[208]

208. Refusing to constate an idea of "I" antecedent to its employment in a predicative action, and basing the "I"'s existence only on its repetitive (self-)constitution as a bridge (*ergo*) across actions (*cogito, sum*), the fundamentally discursive sense of Descartes' *cogito* may be closest to Kant's (common) sense of judgment. Cf. Béatrice Longuenesse, *I, Me, Mine: Back to Kant, and Back Again* (Oxford: Oxford University Press, 2017), pp. 81-82, for a similar view of the shared discursive ("propositional") basis of Descartes' "I think" and Kant's. That the *cogito* expresses neither "innate ideas" nor an assumed authority of "the subject," but rather *predicates one statement upon another employing the same grammatical subject*, does not figure in Chomsky's important assessment of Descartes' view of language, as unique "instrument for the free expression of thought and appropriate response to new situations" undetermined by "stimulus control," "animal" "passions," or any other "mechanical explanation" (see *Cartesian Linguistics* [Cambridge, MA: MIT Press, 1966] pp. 5-13, 87, esp.). Yet it is no coincidence that the *cogito*, first modern account of independent intellectual action and first stated enactment (outside *Genesis*) of existence through verbal predication, offers the central philosophical touchstone for Chomsky's own groundbreaking theory of language as contextually independent, infinitely productive "system of generative rules" or "deep grammar" of predication (see also Chomsky, *Language and Mind* [NY: Harcourt Brace Javonovich, 1968], pp. 4-23, esp.). In a related discussion in *From Locke to Saussure,* pp. 107-112, 170-176 esp.), Aarsleff takes issue with Chomsky for failing to include Condillac in his consideration of 18th-century language theorists, while, in his own translation of Condillac's *Essai*, he mistakenly condemns Descartes for failing to do what he did best, i.e., understand, use, and represent language as an instrument of "action" (see Etienne Bonnot de Condillac, *Essay on the Origin of Human Knowledge*, trans. and ed. and with an Introduction by Hans Aarsleff [Cambridge: Cambridge University Press, 2001], esp. pp. xiii-xvii). Rightly praising the importance of language in Locke's *Essay,* Aarsleff thus inaccurately opposes what he (ironically accurately) calls "the Cartesian discourse of the mind" to Locke's "open admission that words often have an active role in thought" (Condillac, *Essay,* tr. Aarsleff, xvi; "discourse of the mind," interestingly, is not Descartes' phrase but Hobbes'; see *Leviathan,* Bk I, Chapter 3, p. 96). From the entirely and necessarily discursive statement of the *cogito* to the deduction and discussions of the primarily creative capacity of language that directly precede it in the *Discours,* nothing is more central to Descartes' reinvention of philosophy (or even its retrospectively characterized "rationalism") than his understanding of the fundamental, active role of language in thought. (Locke's rejection of all "syllogistic" reasoning is likewise misattributed by Aarsleff to the influence of [Cartesian] "rationalism," while Descartes' own rejection of syllogism was in fact explicitly specifically based on the sophistic use [and abuse] of the form by the Scholastics [xiv]).

8. Kant's Predicates: "Synthetic Judgments *A Priori*" and "A General Voice"

Judgment in Kant entails the feeling of freedom in addition to that of pleasure or pain, and to "feel oneself fully *free*" is to free oneself simultaneously from one's personal or partial point of view.[209] This feeling of freedom gives "the judging subject" "reason to believe" that the "pleasure" he or she[210] is experiencing is distinct from any other that can be felt by a "private individual" in that it is grounded not in a sensorily determined, corporeally delimited but, rather, an "undetermined" "*common* sense," in Kant's social and semantic rather than commonplace sensory meaning of the term: a productive "faculty" – for externally articulating and so communicating any experience – "attributable" to "everyone" else. Rather than identifying either an object (noun) or a quality (adjective), the sentences of *judgment* combine unnamed objects with the names for fundamentally abstract qualities; speech acts in the first place, judgments depart from the logical circle described by accounts of language that attempt to derive its essentially social and conventional basis from the constative utterances of single individuals. The analogous logical difficulty involved in according "the faculty" of "common sense" and fundamental "ground" of "judgment" either *a priori* and formal, or *a posteriori*, experiential status in the Third Critique – a dilemma inhering in the necessarily heterogeneous nature of the universal "sense" of aesthetic experience Kant proposes – finds its resolution in a "free" action of "communication" committed by an individual subject that redefines subjective "free[dom]" as independence from "private" conditions, a "feeling free" in "one's self" which, unlike traditional, philosophical and cultural oppositions between "self" and "other," simultaneously "presupposes" the feeling of such freedom, occasioned by an unknown, conceptually undetermined object of perception, in *all*.[211] The speaker

---

209. Kant, *KU* B 18, X: 123.

210. The use of masculine and/or feminine pronouns and possessive adjectives, here and elsewhere throughout this book, reflects the particular difficulty of expressing in English a general, non-gendered subject (in the singular nominative or any other case) as well as the impossibility of coordinating the genders of possessive adjectives with those of things possessed (rather than of their possessors), as German does as a rule. In colloquial English there is no accurate, grammatically regular mode that, without resorting to periphrasis, can represent any single subject speaking judgment in the "general voice."

211. The only precedent to Kant's description of the "free" enactment of a simultaneous communicability of self with alterity occurs, uncoincidentally, in Rousseau's necessarily philosophical *and* political account of human beings acting in their unique capacity as "free

who "feels himself or herself... fully free" expresses this not by saying so, or indeed saying anything regarding him or herself, *but in saying of the object whose perception occasioned that feeling,* "it is beautiful." In so doing the judging subject employs both the distinct parts of speech described by Rousseau and Diderot to mark the differing cognitive origins of language, and, *in combining these,* effectively makes their referential field, like their individual speaker, general in scope. For, instead of a "trope" ("*Giant*") proffered in the place of a subject's unstated feeling ("fear") with regard to his or her own person, the noun designating an unknown object of perception in Kant is a fully impersonal pronoun ("it"), itself as "free" from all specific knowledge, feelings, and interests as the subject "feels himself" in speaking it. Similarly, the adjective that Kant's judging subject employs to qualify that undefined pronoun describes no particular sensible aspect of it (size, shape, sound, texture, or color) but rather a general quality ("beautiful," "sublime") serving as a placeholder "abstracted" from all particular qualities, one "it" shares or, more precisely, is experienced to hold equally in "common" with our "sense" of other particular, while equally unknown, sensuous objects: the quality not only of appearing, but of moving us to use the – externally undetermined – word "beautiful" with regard to them.

Most importantly, however, Kant's aesthetic judgment does not simply add an abstract adjective to a noun; like any speech act, the specifically verbal nature of aesthetic as of any "judgment" in Kant requires that it be articulated in a general,

agent[s]," i.e., subjects "free" to form, communicate with and govern each other via universally binding agreements or conventions. In signing over their own naturally limited ability to realize "private" "individual" interests, whether capricious, acquisitive, or compulsive in nature, "free agents" achieve the artificial standing or status, and acquire and experience the "sovereign" rights of "citizens" first defined by the formal convention of a "social contract." See *Du contrat social*, esp. Chap. VI, "Du pacte social" and Chap. VII, "Du souverain," for Rousseau's accounts of the "act" by which the "particular person of each contracting subject," "giving himself to everyone and to no one," joins the "moral" and "political body" of a contractual society (pp. 51–52). See also *Discours sur l'origine* ... esp. pp. 182–83, on man as a "free agent." Like the capacity for "free agency" equally definitive of, even when still latent in, "natural" *and* "social man" in Rousseau's accounts of human history, the "alienation" of private wishes by a "general will" first originating in freely contracting subjects is not only clearly critical for Kant's later historical and political writings on the centrality of "theory" to "practice" – including the requirement, for the constitution of any contractual state, of universal literacy and free, social "communication" of thought beyond any individual mind through its uncensored "publication" – but his own critically pivotal, pathbreaking "bridge," among individuals no less than individual human "capacities" or "faculties," constituted of a theory of aesthetic judgment as "free" action spoken in a "general voice." For a contrary comparison of Rousseau's concept of the "general will," not with the general communicability definitive of any language but, on the contrary, with the particularity of an "aesthetic object," see C. N. Dugan and Tracey B. Strong, "Music, Politics, Theater and Representation in Rousseau," in *Cambridge Companion to Rousseau*, ed. Patrick Riley (Cambridge: Cambridge University Press, 2001), pp. 329–64 [323–33]).

predicative sentence. *"Free" aesthetic judgments are "synthetic judgments a priori"* of the very kind Kant defines as the main philosophical "principle" and "revolution in mode of thinking" enacted by his *Critique* – an essential formal fact whose forgetting underlies, to a large extent, the controversy and misconceptions that continue to trail his Third Critique. For, the main "question" and "task" the entire tripartite *Critique* poses of itself, and on which, Kant states, the entire "building" of its "architectonic plan" and "system of principles of pure reason" rests, is whether *synthetic* predicative statements, or "synthetic judgments *a priori*, are possible."[212] In Section IV of the Introduction to the *Critique of Pure Reason*, "On the Difference between Analytic and Synthetic Judgments," Kant compares statements whose predicates can be shown by analysis to be identical to the cognitive concept we hold of their subjects – statements, in other words, whose predicates are indistinguishable from the definition of their subjects – with those whose predicates are instead *judged* as "necessarily belonging"[213] to their subjects *synthetically*. Like aesthetic judgments, "synthetic judgments" are based not in definitional conceptual knowledge but "experience:"

> In all judgments, in which the relationship of a subject to a predicate is thought . . ., this relationship is possible in two ways. Either the predicate B belongs to the subject A as something that is contained (in a concealed way) in this concept A; or B lies completely outside concept A, even though it stands in conjunction with it. In the first case I call this judgment *analytic*, in the other case, *synthetic*. Analytic judgments (that are positive) are thus those in which the conjunction of the predicate with the subject through identity is thought, while the other kind, in which the conjunction is thought without identity, should be called synthetic judgments. . . . For example, when I say: all bodies are extended, so this is an analytic judgment. For I need not depart *from the concept* that I join to [the word] "body" in order to find "extension" conjoined to it, but rather only analyze the concept, i.e., become conscious of the manifold of qualities which I at any time think in it, in order to find its predicate within it; it is thus an analytic judgment. By contrast, if I say: all bodies are heavy, that predicate is something completely different from that which I think within the mere concept of a body generally. The addition of such a predicate therefore produces a synthetic judgment.
>
> *Judgments of experience, as such, are altogether synthetic. For it would make no sense for an analytic judgment to be grounded upon experience . . .*
>
> [In allen Urteilen, worinnen das Verhältnis eines Subjekts zum Prädikat gedacht wird . . ., ist dieses Verhältnis auf zweierlei Art möglich. Entweder das Prädikat B gehört zum Subjekt A als etwas was in diesem Begriff A (versteckter Weise)

---

212. Kant, *KrV* B 27, B 18, III: 64, 58–59: "The actual task of pure reason is precisely contained in the question: "*How are synthetic judgments a priori possible?*" ("Die eigentliche Aufgabe der reinen Vernunft ist nun in der Frage enthalten: *Wie sind synthetische Urteile a priori möglich?*").
213. Kant, *KrV* B 13, III: 54.

enthalten ist; oder B liegt ganz ausser dem Begriff A, ob es zwar mit demselben in Verknüpfung steht. Im resten Fall nenne ich das Urteil *analytisch,* in dem andern *synthetisch.* Analytische Urteile (die bejahende) sind also diejenige, in welchen die Verknüpfung des Prädikats mit dem Subjekt durch Identität, diejenige aber, in denen diese Verknüpfung ohne Identität gedacht wird, sollen synthetische Urteile heissen ... Z. B. wenn ich sage: alle Körper sind ausgedehnt, so ist dies ein analytisch Urteil. Denn ich darf nicht *über den Begriff,* den ich mit dem Körper verbinde, hinausgehen, um die Ausdehnung, als mit demselben verknüpft, zu finden, sondern jenen Begriff nur zergliedern, d.i. des Mannigfaltigen, welches ich jederzeit in ihm denke, mir nur bewusst werden, um dieses Prädikat darin anzutreffen; es ist also ein analytisches Urteil. Dagegen, wenn ich sage: alle Körper sind schwer, so ist das Prädikat etwas ganz anderes, als das, was ich in dem blossen Begriff eines Körpers überhaupt denke. Die Hinzufügen eines solchen Prädikats gibt also ein synthetisch Urteil.

Erfahrungsurteile, als solche, sind insgesamt synthetisch. Denn es wäre ungereimt, ein analytisches Urteil auf Erfahrung zu gründen....[214]]

The judgment, "it is beautiful" (or "sublime"), is just such a synthetic predication. Based on the experience of an unknown sensory object whose material form (or formlessness) gives rise to feelings of pleasure (or pain) and freedom in the subject who perceives it, judgments, spoken by subjects, predicate those objects generally, yet in a way that neither defines nor relies on conceptual knowledge of them in the first place. In the predicating judgment, "it is beautiful," the unnamed object turned subject, "it," only "is" a subject insofar as "is" is predicated on the quality, "beautiful," and "beautiful" is said to be a quality of "it" only insofar as it is experienced *and* articulated as such. In order for that synthesis of subject and predicate to be enacted in speech, the individual experience of the world on which it is based must be as independent of individual proclivities as its language must be unburdened of traditional and contextual connotations, freedom of "feeling" and of speech conjoining an unknown object to a general quality *originating together* here in the formation of "synthetic judgment" itself.

No less than in his proposition of its formalization in a universal "moral law" in the Second Critique, freedom in the *Critique of Judgment* is no private matter for Kant. Following the larger mediating, "communicating" function by which he introduces aesthetic judgment as the necessary "bridge" between the mutually exclusive realms of "phenomenal" (conceptual) cognition and "noumenal" (moral) action, no subject can "feel ... fully *free*" without supposing rather than opposing such feeling in others. Indeed any purely individual "freedom" *limited* to merely "private" – changing and contingent – circumstances constitutes not "freedom" for Kant, but, rather, a contradiction in terms. This feeling, whose "presuppos[ition]" in every other subject is inseparable from its experience by any individual subject, is described as arising within each subject on the basis of a characteristically Kantian

---

214. Kant, *KrV* B 11–12, III: 52–53.

"*as if*" ("als ob"[215]). Like Diderot's notion of language necessarily formed in a "double" – "direct" and "reflected – light," the meaning of the "free" expression of aesthetic pleasure (or pain) via the predication of an object by a speaking subject – its significance *as* a judgment rather than a unilateral statement of fact – is itself predicated upon its correlation with the capacity of other subjects to so judge, to express themselves (and other selves) *as subjects* rather than "private" individuals whose perceptions and judgments, much like those of Diderot's fully sensing subjects, are, ironically, impeded by the blindspots of "positive," "private" circumstance, the shortsighted view, of putatively "full" presence, mistakenly credited by the sighted.

Yet, in the case of aesthetic judgment, unlike that of any other general "faculty" analyzed across Kant's *Critique*, the speculative hypothesis of an internal "presuppos[ition]" is the basis of an action undertaken exclusively and materially in language, a perceptible speech act that, *as speech*, cannot, by definition, originate in a single individual alone. And unlike the "concept of freedom" that Kant calls a "fact of pure reason"[216] whose uniquely non-causal, noumenal basis he attempts – and, by his own critical criteria, must fail – to deduce in the Second Critique (filling that inevitable logical lacuna with the conditional narrative of "possible" action discussed at the opening of this study), the "feeling" of "free[dom]" attributed to judgment in the Third Critique is not and cannot be the object of a rational deduction *to begin with*, in that it is experiential and practical, rather than conceptual and cognitive, in basis – its occurrence constituting what we might call a "fact"[217] of judgment derived from its linguistic rather than logical identity. An ability dependent upon no individual agent or enactment, nor upon either logical or contingent conditions, *it is language, the necessary condition and medium of its enactment, that allows judgment to be "free" in the first place*. As described in the passage from the Third Critique, §6, already cited in full,[218] the "subject" who

---

215. See Hans Vahinger's seminal study of the hypothetical basis of Kant's representational epistemology, *Die Philosophie des Als Ob* (Leipzig: Felix Meiner Verlag, 1911). The present study seeks to underscore the equally important hypothesis of others' freedom on the part of any individual who "feels himself fully *free*," a defining *experience* of freedom, issuing in aesthetic judgment, that contrasts with the "idea" of "freedom," or "fact of reason," articulated formally in Kant's hypothetical "moral law." I have analyzed Kant's logical inability to deduce, and resulting narrative production of "freedom" in *The Imposition of Form*, pp. 68–86.

216. Kant, *KprV*, A 57, VII: 142.

217. Initially designated as one of the three noumenal "ideas" of theoretical reason in the First Critique, then as a "concept" of practical reason in the Second Critique, which, after proving undeducible, is ultimately designated a practical "fact of [pure practical] reason" (*Faktum der Vernunft*) itself identifiable with the very "form" of "the moral law," "freedom" must be understood in strict separation from specific phenomenal manifestations of any kind across the framework of Kant's *Critique*. Similarly, a "fact" of judgment would consist of nothing more nor less than its linguistic performance, and is therefore neither "phenomenal" nor "real" in the strict Kantian sense. On the "real" (mathematical and moral) and "nominal" (phenomenal) see n. 120, Section Five, this Chapter.

218. See n. 113, Section Five, this Chapter.

feels himself fully *free* ... can discover as grounds for this pleasure no private conditions that would depend on the subject alone, and thus must view it as grounded in that which he can also presuppose in everyone else ... He will thus *speak of the beautiful as if* beauty were characteristic of the object and the judgment were logical ... because it has this resemblance to the logical, that it can presuppose its validity for everyone.

[sich ... völlig *frei* fühlt; so kann er keine Privatbedingungen als Gründe des Wohlgefallens auffinden, an diese sich sein Subjekt allein hinge, und muss es daher als in demjenigen begründet ansehen, was er auch bei jedem andern voraussetzen kann; folglich muss er glauben Grund zu haben, jedermann ein ähnliches Wohlgefallen zuzumuten. Er wird daher *vom Schönen so sprechen*, als *ob* Schönheit eine Beschaffenheit des Gegenstandes und das Urteil logisch ... wäre ... darum, weil es doch mit dem logischen die Ähnlichkeit hat, dass man die Gültigkeit desselben für jedermann daran vorasussetzen kann.[219]]

Finding no "grounds" for this feeling that could "depend solely" on "his own subject" – the "private conditions" impinging upon each of us at any time – he or she who "judges" *what* he or she "feels," experiences an object in a way no conditions other than those of a disinterested aesthetic experience allows. For the "pleasure" felt in the purely sensory perception of any object is a personal event, and to "feel" pleasure on the basis of sensation is not to be "free" but dependent for one's pleasure on that sensation – free, indeed, of cognitive or moral aims, but never "in [one's] self." Sensory pleasure as such depends on the sensory experience of the object that provides it, making a purely sense-based distinction between such states as love and addiction difficult to draw, in that both signify a subject "bound," "made over," or "sentenced to" (*ad-dire*) to another corporeal existence, a bondage to, rather than "free[ing]" of the subject from the sensation on which a privative pleasure depends.[220] Just as any thing of any purpose and content can provide the occasion for sensory pleasure, pleasure itself is of little interest to Kant except insofar as it is accompanied by the "feel[ing]" of "freedom" that aesthetic experience occasions within the "self." It is that feeling of freedom *as* a subject that allows the subject to "judge" rather than require the source of its pleasure, which is to say, to speak of it in the impersonal, third person ("It is beautiful"), expressing thereby the abstract, common and communicable sense of the "presupposed validity" of that judgment "for everyone."[221]

219. Kant, *KU*, B 18, X:124 (emphasis added in part).

220. Beginning with its literal Latin meaning, the Oxford English Dictionary details the equally appropriate technical, personally, and literarily descriptive uses of "addict," from Roman law through the New Testament to English political history and Shakespeare; see *OED*, Two-Volume Edition, 1971, I: 25.

221. That presupposition may "resemble logic" but, unlike logic, involves the sensory manifestation of a form perceived, and the pleasure or pain felt in that perception. The always partly perceptual and dependent, partly universal and independent, heterogeneous

By contrast with pleasure arising from being bound over, subjected to an object of sensation, the pleasure (or pain) a subject who *judges* feels depends on the "dynamic form"[222] of the object he perceives, *but not on that object alone*; and it depends on the "freedom" he "feels" in himself, *but not on himself, as subject, alone*. Only on the double basis of both can feelings of "pleasure" (in the object) and "freedom" (in the subject) coincide: pleasure in the beautiful (or displeasure in the sublime) that the mere perception, rather than any motivating "interest" in the object perceived, provides; and freedom "in [one's] self" (rather than *from* something external to the self) which that mere perception, in the felt absence of any interest, *telos* or purpose within the self, provides. Neither a cognitive nor a consequential act, aesthetic judgment, defined in the Introduction to the *Critique of Judgment* as the "bridge" ("Übergang") over the "chasm" ("Kluft") between them, performs the additional function few if any material bridges do, of preventing both sides from falling headlong into that abyss.[223] What judgment does cannot alter the categorical difference between the "realms" of the First and Second Critiques (or of the "concepts of nature" and the "concept of freedom"[224]), the "chasm" of kind between limited and unlimited, representational and nonrepresentational "realms" that no judgment can transform, fill, or transcend. Employing the phenomenality of the objects of one and the freedom of the mode of the other, what the heterogeneous faculty of judgment does do is communicate across the incommunicability that at once divides knowledge and moral action and enables them, without either "depending" on or constituting a fully independent, or alternative, "realm" of its own.[225] (In Kant's "architectonics," unlike either Heidegger's "dwelling" or Habermas' public sphere and square, a "bridge" is a passage between mutually exclusive realms of action *a priori*, not a domain or home for either "Being" or practical, "communicatve action" itself.[226])

---

and thus undeducible basis of that presupposition is what Kant calls, in no less hybrid terms, the both "grounding" and "undetermined norm of common sense" (Kant, *KU*, B 68, X: 159).

222. Kant, *KU*, B XLIX, 49–50, 79–82 X: 103, 146–47, 168–170.

223. *Ibid.*, B XX, X: 83.

224. *Ibid.*

225. *Ibid.*, B XVIII, X: 82.

226. Cf. Paul de Man, "The Temptation of Permanence" (1955), reprinted in de Man, *Critical Essays, 1953-1978*, trans. Dan Latimer, ed. Lindsay Waters (Minneapolis: University of Minnesota, 1989 [orig. French pub. *Monde Nouveau*, Oct. 1955]), esp. pp.30-40, on Heidegger's equivocal uses of such architectural terms as "build," "ground plan," "dwell," and "bridge" to "unite," rather than maintain the division between incommensurables represented by "'earth and sky, divine and moral'" in Hölderlin's poetry, and to make "dwelling" itself thus seem to "indicate two kinds of" (equally incommensurable) "acts," those of residing, as if in a home, and the radical departure from any such home in "poetic action." See Jürgen Habermas, *The Theory of Communicative Action*, 2 Vol., Trans. Thomas McCarthy (Boston: Beacon, 1984 [orig. pub. 1981]), esp. Chap. 1 – 5, I: 1–273, II: 1–111.

The combined feeling of freedom and pleasure experienced in view of an object is communicated in a predicative statement by its subject, but in words that neither state those feelings nor say anything about the particular subject nor object of perception at all. Instead, the "synthetic judgment" in which the "free" experience of "pleasure" in perception results "resembles" statements "sprung from logic" in that, like logic, it "presupposes" its (*a priori*) "validity" for "everyone."[227] The universal "validity" "presupposed" in and by the speech act of aesthetic judgment is void of specific (either nominal or qualitative) content. No "concepts" are articulated by judgment (not even those of beauty or sublimity themselves), just as no object is named by it, "for from concepts there is no passage to the feeling of pleasure or displeasure" ("[d]enn von Begriffen gibt es keinen Übergang zum Gefühle der Lust oder Unlust"[228]), which is to say, no "passage" and passage alone of the kind provided by aesthetic judgment alone: a "synthetic judgment" with no other content than the general predicative quality the judgment itself provides. By extension, the "claim" of judgment to interpersonal "validity" stems not from any sense of "generality" ("Allgemenheit") "placed in objects" themselves, but is instead "bound to a claim to subjective generality itself" ("es muss damit ein Anspruch auf subjektive Allgemeinheit verbunden sein").[229]

Albena Azmanova returns the Kantian core of Habermas's social theory from "communicative action" to the communicability underlying acts of judgment specifically, in *The Scandal of Reason. A Critical Theory of Political Judgment* (New York: Columbia University Press, 2012). Seeking to mediate the "paradox" of theories of "judgment" torn between "moral" or "ideal theory" and "political realism," Azmanova proposes "a 'critical consensus model' of normative validity" and "preference transformation" achieved by way of "communication that allows normative consensus and social criticism to coexist" on the basis of "collective reasoning" (4). Like aesthetic judgment in Kant, such a "model of judgment," she states, "develops neither as a stipulation of criteria and conditions of normative justification nor as an empirical account of political decision making" (5). While Azmanova offers lucid summations of the reliance of Habermasian social theory, Rawls' theory of justice, and Arendt's political theory on Kant's Second, First, and Third Critiques, respectively, and provides thoughtful commentary on the limitations of each, her welcome recognition of the "normative force of linguistic forms" in Kant neither distinguishes between such a specifically "social" "form" and the ungrounded "norm" of "common sense" on which Kant bases judgment in particular, nor considers the specifically linguistic basis of the "communicability" on which her own theory of "social hermeneutics" depends (see pp. 30–42; 65–135). The "communicability" of speech defining any act of judgment in Kant is instead oddly equated in her analysis with the absence of language, a "meaningful silence" or (paradoxically) "tacit articulation of what is critically relevant," where "[t]he 'relevant'" provides the "starting point of judgment as 'making-sense-in-common,'" i.e., the changing, empirical *rather than* "necessary," linguistic "condition" of what is in Kant, by contrast, a *foundational* "common sense" (128–29).

227. *Ibid.*, B 19, X: 125.
228. *Ibid.*
229. *Ibid.*

As if to indicate how far from Kant's critical sense of a "subjective generality" "ground[ed]" in "common sense" our own thinking about the aesthetic has come, we now call such "synthetic" "subjective" "judgments" "objective," even though they replace the identity of the object with a single abstract quality ("It is beautiful;" "it is sublime"). For Kant, they are, instead, "subjective" in a specifically "general" sense precisely because, while necessarily and explicitly verbal, they leave, along with the object, the subject of speech out of the picture: "judgments" would not be "general" but rather "laughable," Kant states, if they referred their predications to the individual identity and contingent opinions of the subject who speaks them. Defining such statements as "self-justifications" based merely on "pleasant" sensations, whose sole, sophistical "principle" – "everyone has his *own* taste (of the senses)" – runs directly contrary to the critical theory of judgment (and thus the very possibility of judging, rather than opining or reporting) he describes here, Kant writes:

> In the case of the beautiful things are entirely different. Indeed, it would, on the contrary, be laughable, if someone who was somewhat proud of his taste thought to justify himself in saying: this object (the building, that we see, the dress that one is wearing, the concert that we are hearing, the poem that is posited for judging), is beautiful *for me*. For he must not name it *beautiful* when it pleases merely him;... but when pronouncing something beautiful so must he attribute to others just the same pleasure: he judges not only for himself, but for everyone, and thus speaks of beauty as if it were a quality of things. He says, the *thing* is beautiful; and does not thereby more or less count on the agreement of others in his judgment of this pleasure, because he found them frequently in agreement with his, but *demands* it from them.
>
> [Mit dem Schönen ist es ganz anders bewandt. Es wäre (gerade umgekehrt) lächerlich, wenn jemand, der sich auf seinen Geschmack etwa einbildete, sich damit zu rechtfertigen gedächte: dieser Gegenstand (das Gebäude, was wir sehen, das Kleid, was jener trägt, das Konzert, was wir hören, das Gedicht, welches zur Beurteilung aufgestellt ist) ist *für mich* schön. Denn er muss es nicht *schön* nennen, wenn es bloss ihm gefällt ...; wenn er aber etwas für schön ausgibt, so mutet er andern eben dasselbe Wohlgefallen zu: er urteilt nicht bloss für sich, sondern für jedermann, und spricht alsdann von der Schönheit, als wäre sie eine Eigenschaft der Dinge. Er sagt daher, die *Sache* ist schön; und rechnet nicht etwa darum auf anderer Einstimmung in sein Urteil des Wohlgefallens, weil er sie mehrmalen mit dem seinigen einstimmig befunden hat, sondern *fordert* es von ihnen.[230]]

What kind of voice speaks neither of the "feelings" of a subject nor bases what it says on the spoken "agreement" of "other subjects" ("anderer Einstimmung") with its words, no matter how "frequently" ("mehrmalen") such individually

---

230. *Ibid.*, B 20, X: 126 (emphases in text).

voiced agreements may be "found" ("befunden")? What kind of voice speaks so "objectively" as to say nothing about a particular object that *could* be subject to disagreement because what it says "depends" neither on the object spoken of nor on the subjects who speak it? What kind of voice, in short, can never say "I"?

This "voice" ("Stimme"), as Kant calls it, gives voice not to "rules" that can either override or generate our and others' experience of "feeling," nor does it articulate "reasons and propositions of reason" capable of persuading individuals to a similar experience, or name the particular "sensations" ("Empfindungen") on which still other individuals may believe their "pleasure depends." Those voices belong only to so many individual "I"'s, whose stated views can never coincide (or, as the German language would put it – but Kant, importantly, does not – *übereinstimmen*) because they misconstrue aesthetic experience as "subjective" (in the noncritical sense), i.e., a matter of private proclivity or conviction, and their complement as external approval and validation, confusing thereby the "general" enactment of "judgment" with the personal cultivation of "taste." Such individual "I"s require and legitimize overriding authorities whose voices serve, at a second remove, to "judge" their own: arbiters and regulators of "good" taste; rationalists of the pleasure afforded by "having" taste; and those who conflate "taste" with the physical sensation for which it is falsely named. Just as judgment in Kant does not rely on, indeed excludes "concepts" of its object, it speaks with a voice independent of any of the individual voices from which these various conceptions of it emerge:

> When we judge objects merely according to concepts, so all perception of beauty is lost. Thus there can also be no rule according to which someone can be compelled to acknowledge something as beautiful. Whether a dress, a house, a flower would be ("sei") beautiful: no one lets his judgment be cajoled by reasons and principles of reason to that conclusion. One wants to submit the object to one's own eyes, just as if one's pleasure depended on the sensation; and nevertheless, when one names an object beautiful, one believes one has a general voice, and makes claim to the accession of everyone, since otherwise every private sensation would decide only for him and his pleasure alone.
>
> Here we can now see that in the judgment of taste nothing is postulated other than such a *general voice*. . . .

> [Wenn man Objekte bloss nach Begriffen beurteilt, so geht alle Vorstellung der Schönheit verloren. Also kann es auch keine Regel geben, nach der jemand genötigt werden sollte, etwas für schön anzuerkennen. Ob ein Kleid, ein Haus, eine Blume schön sei: dazu lässt man sich sein Urteil durch keine Gründe oder Grundsätze beschwatzen. Man will das Objekt seinen eigenen Augen unterwerfen, gleich als ob sein Wohlgefallen von der Empfindung abhinge; und dennoch wenn man den Gegenstand alsdann schön nennt, glaubt man eine allgemeine Stimme für sich zu haben, und macht Anspruch auf den Beitritt von jedermann, da hingegen jede Privatempfindung nur für ihn allein und sein Wohlgefallen entscheiden würde.

Hier ist nun zu sehen, dass in dem Urteile des Geschmacks nichts postuliert wird, als eine solche *allgemeine Stimme*....²³¹]

In this important initial formulation of "a general voice" of judgment, the later problem of "common sense" already comes into view. In "naming" an "object" "beautiful," "one believes one has a general voice" – that is, one believes the utterance of that speech act does not speak for one's self alone – and, in naming this belief, Kant proceeds to judge or generalize from it, redefining "such a general voice" as the sole "postulate" of the act of judgment itself. The (not quite) formal act of postulating from a "general" instance of language rather than causal logic – "Here is now to be seen, that in judgment nothing is postulated but such a *general voice*" – is echoed in the introduction and reformulations of the notions of "common sense" already cited at the opening of this analysis:

> Such a principle (that determines [or, "would determine:" *bestimme*], only through feeling and not through concepts, but nonetheless generally, what pleases and displeases [or "would please:" "*gefalle;*" "would displease:" "*misfalle*"]) can only be regarded as a *common sense*, which is essentially different from the common understanding that one sometimes also names common sense (*sensus communis*)...
>
> Thus only under the presupposition that there "is" [or, "would be:" *gebe*] common sense (by which we do not understand an external sense, but the effect resulting from the free play of our powers of cognition), only, I say, under the presupposition of such a common sense can judgment of taste be rendered... This undetermined norm of a common sense is really presupposed by us: our presumed ability to make judgments of taste proves it. Whether in fact such a common sense... "exists" [or "would exist:" *gebe*]....
>
> [Ein solches Prinzip (welches nur durch Gefühl und nicht durch Begriffe, doch aber allgemeingültig bestimme, was gefalle oder misfalle) aber könnte nur als ein *Gemeinsinn* angesehen werden; welcher vom gemeinen Verstande, den man bisweilen auch Gemeinsinn (sensus communis) nennt, wesentlich unterschieden ist...
>
> Also nur unter der Voraussetzung, dass es einen Gemeinsinn gebe (wodurch wir aber keinen äussern Sinn, sondern die Wirkung aus dem freien Spiel unserer Erkenntniskräfte, verstehen), nur unter Voraussetzung, sage ich, eines solchen Gemeinsinns kann das Geschmacksurteil gefällt werden... Diese unbestimmte Norm eines Gemeinsinns wird von uns wirklich vorausgesetzt: das beweiset unsere Anmassung, Geschmacksurteile Zu fallen. Ob in der Tat einen solchen Gemeinsinn... gebe....²³²]

231. *Ibid.*, B 26, X: 130 (emphasis in text).
232. *Ibid.*, B 65, 68, X: 157, 159. On Kant's employment of the "first subjunctive" rather than indicative tense when describing the referent and use of the term, "common sense," now redefined in his "Analytic of Judgment" as the "necessary" linguistic "condition" of its enactment in a "general voice," see this Chapter, Section One, n. 41.

The "common sense" which may or may not in fact "exist" and on which the execution of judgment depends, speaks in the "general voice" and single "postulate" of the theory of judgment itself. "A general voice," sole voice that never says "I," must speak to and for every subject by speaking, instead, *of* an unnamed object. The voice of every subject states, in speech qualifying an object, something "generally communicable" among subjects. That quality has no "objective" content, nor does it contain or represent in any semiotic sense the experience of a subject. Contingent, transitory, and formally unpredictable by definition, "feeling," the individual experience of an individual subject *in the absence of a sign*, is as little "communicable" in itself to the subject in whom it occurs – whether Rousseau's first impassioned subject of speech, Diderot's inventive subjects of sensory deprivation, or any other, more conventionally conceived linguistic subjects – as it is to other subjects, other selves. *Any subject who feels, and speaks of "his" or "her" feeling, says "I."* Whether speaking or silent, feeling speaks for a self. *The exact opposite takes place in Kant* (in Rousseau, and in Diderot). The subject who "feels" "pleasure" on Kant's analysis of judgment, also "feels himself," at the same time, "fully free," which is to say, freed from the contingent limits of "private conditions" to translate, in the "general voice" of judgment, "his" or "her" "feeling" into general language about an object that makes that object – rather than any individual subject of experience – into the subject of a "generally communicable" predicate. Every individual subject is subject to "his" or "her" changing experience and interests, but the subject of *judgment*, speaking subject of "a general voice" that says of an object, "it is beautiful," "it is sublime," speaks of something whose particular name and identity, like his or her own, he or she no longer represents alone.[233] In judging, he or she speaks the principle of speech, "general communicability," with every (perceptual) transposition from subject to object, (felt) transposition from object to subject and (spoken) transposition from subject to subject that he or she makes, without each of which "communicability" could never be "general," and what we call "language" would not be language at all.

The "general voice" is language spoken in response to a "feeling" by a subject that simultaneously "feels [it]self free" to speak without identifying its experience with an empirical "I" or object. "General communicability," independent of any particular experience, is the formal content of the speech the "general voice" of judgment articulates. Judgment, in others words, speaks the principle of speakability. In this, "such a general voice" expresses, in external and thus perceptible linguistic form, the mysterious "internal form" underpinning all perception in general that Kant calls "the schema."

---

233. This is why, no matter the particular empirical object or aesthetic form experienced by Kant's judging subject, Kant's will always be a (if not *the*) "modern" theory of aesthetic experience and, conversely, of any "modern art." In that Kant's theory of aesthetic "judgment" and "pleasure" excludes no phenomenal object or perceiving subject, it will always include the future of art – "new" subjects and objects of aesthetic experience, and "old" subjects and objects renewed – within its purview.

9. "The Schema," or Language Inside

For good or for ill, *understanding* requires a *form* of communication. The "schema" is the invented medium of understanding hypothesized by Kant's *Critique*. Described in the Second Preface to the First Critique as an "experiment" in metaphysics, that hypothesis takes for its model the "revolution[s]" in "mode of thinking" that "change[d]," as they ensured the development of mathematics and the pure sciences,[234] an investigation by the mind of its own capabilities resembling Copernicus's turn from empirical to rational-*theoretical* reasoning in the investigation of the external world. The theoretical "analogy"[235] Kant proposes between the practices of mathematics and natural science, on the one hand, and moral action, judgment and epistemology (or science of mind), on the other, includes within itself, however, this salient difference, that while theoretical science of the natural world must alternate between formal reasoning and empirical data, even while refusing to limit the former to the latter, metaphysics must join the two in order to produce its objects of study in the first place, making the empirical inseparable from the formally delimited way in which we question and understand ourselves and the world. While that external world, and not the "world" of the mind, is the final concern of theoretical science that turns from the sensory evidence of physical interactions toward the dispositive logic of reason so as to understand the laws governing external phenomena in the first place, the *bases* of such understanding, as of all conceptual, moral, imaginative, and material action, comprise the first and last – *a priori* and *a posteriori* – theoretical concern of metaphysics.

---

234. Kant, KrV B XVI, III: 25: "I should think that the examples of mathematics and natural science, which became what they are now through a revolution suddenly brought about, would be remarkable enough to contemplate the essential pieces of the change in the mode of thinking that has become so advantageous to them and, at least, in so far as their analogy as rational cognitions with metaphysics allows, to make the experiment of imitating them. Until now one assumed that all our knowledge must conform to objects ..." ("Ich sollte meinen, die Beispiele der Mathematik und Naturwissenschaft, die durch eine auf einmal zu Stande gebrachte Revolution das geworden sind, was sie jetzt sind, wäre merkwürdig genug, um den wesentlichen Stücke der Umänderung der Denkart, die ihnen so vorteilhaftig geworden ist, nachzusinnen, und ihnen, so viel ihre Analogie, als Vernunfterkenntnisse nachzuahmen. Bisher nahm man an alle unsere Erkenntnis müsse sich nach den Gegenständen richten ...").

235. *Ibid*.

For this reason Kant recognizes that his own formal hypothesis requires a content specific to itself, a specifically formal content or *form for making content* that would not be adaptive but applicable overall, a "technique" or "art" both originating in and binding upon the mind if it is to apprehend the world at all.[236] When the object of the mind is theory "of mind" in every sense, it can rely on no external information to describe the myriad actions composing the mind "itself," i.e., the amalgam of sensation, association, comparison and reflection, knowing or recognizing, remembering, projecting, imagining and inventing, thinking, forgetting, positing and negating, each distinguished from and joined to the other by no determining procedure or method the mind possesses, without thereby *failing to distinguish those actions from effects (of perception)*, and thus confusing universally subjective with particular empirical givens.[237] Yet neither can any theoretical reflection on specifically human activity fail to substantiate what it hypothesizes without risking logical regress. In this respect, the difference between theories of metaphysics and of mathematics and science resembles the difference between geometry and mathematics in general: between theory whose hypotheses can be concretely represented (in figures, objects, and contexts) and theories that invent specifically nonrepresentational (or "symbolic") languages to elaborate autonomous conceptual and computational logics.

Like a critical metaphysics, geometry does not logically deduce or symbolically calculate but, instead, graphically and physically "constructs" its objects. "The first person who demonstrated" the necessity of the equilateral triangle, Kant writes in the First Critique, "found"

> that he must bring forth not that which he either saw in the figure or deduced from mere concepts and, so to speak, forgot about its qualities, but through that which he thought into it himself, according to concepts *a priori*, and represented (through construction) . . .
>
> [nicht dem, was er in der Figur sahe, oder auch dem blossen Begriffen derselben nachspüren und gleichsam davon ihre Eigenschaften ablernen, sondern durch

---

236. Cf. n.72, Section Two, this Chapter.

237. Such subject-object confusions characterize the brief life of every "new," "spectral" or "speculative," "materialism" or "ontology," historically recurrent projections of subjective "life" onto objects *by subjects* that, whether reveling in an infantile regression into Disney-like fantasiae of object-animation, or adopting an ultra-Humean skeptical stance precluding any and all mental action to precisely the same effect, seek so to mystify as to render not only science but any social or historical formation unthinkable. They demonstrate nothing so much as the necessity of Kant's entire critical project, like Rosseau's social epistemology, and Galilean and Copernican natural science to base themselves on predicating "hypotheses," and that the singular desire for identity and contempt for the difference every act of predication instantiates is tantamount not only to an enforced evacuation of all conceptual relations, but a hatred of philosophy itself.

das, was er nach Begriffen selbst a priori hineindachte und darstellte (durch Konstruktion) hervorbringen müsse....²³⁸]

The inseparability of an external body from its conceptualization in an act of representation conjoined to the thinking that goes "into" it ("not what he saw in the figure but ... that which he *a priori* thought into it and represented [through construction]") is the condition upon which, as Kant describes it, his own demonstration of the experimental hypothesis of synthetic *a priori* cognitions – like that of the "pure geometrical concept" of a circle represented, *a priori*, in a circular material object – must depend:

> In all subsumptions of an object under a conception, the representation of the object must be *homogeneous* with the conception; in other words, the conception must contain that which is represented in the object to be subsumed under it ... So the empirical concept of a *dish* is homogeneous with the pure geometrical concept of a *circle*, in that the rounding, which is thought in the first, can be seen in the second.
>
> Now, pure conceptions of the understanding, when compared with empirical perceptions, or even with sensuous perceptions in general, are quite dissimilar or heterogeneous, and never can be found in any perception. How then is the *subsumption* of the latter under the former, and consequently the *application* of the categories to phenomena, possible?
>
> [In allen Subsumtionen eines Gegenstandes unter einen Begriff muss die Vorstellung des ersteren mit der letzern *gleichartig* sein, d. i. der Begriff muss dasjenige enthalten, was in dem darunter zu subsumierenden Gegenstande vorgestellt wird ... So hat der empirische Begriff eines *Tellers* mit dem reinen geometrischen eines *Zirkels* Gleichartigkeit, indem die Rundung, die in dem erstern gedacht wird, sich eim letzteren anschauen lässt.
>
> Nun sind aber reine Verstandsbegriffe, in Vergleichung mit empirischen (ja überhaupt sinnlichen) Anschauungen, ganz ungleichartig, und können niemals in irgend einer Anschauung angetroffen werden. Wie ist nun die *Subsumption* der letzteren unter die erste mithin die *Anwendung* der Kategorie auf Erscheinungen möglich ...?²³⁹]

In this key passage on the "heterogeneous" orders of concepts and objects, Kant himself raises and faces the central question of the *practical* feasibility of his own *Critique*. For, as an "experiment" in thinking, Kant's fundamental hypothesis requires no logical demonstration. Yet, in that its purview is conceived as precisely *not* "pure" of, but rather as applied to the empirical world, such a critical hypothesis, unlike purely speculative ones, does require an accompanying account of how that "application" ("Anwendung") can be carried out. "How," in short (or, in Kant's

---

238. Kant, *KrV*, B XI–XII, III: 22. See Kant's account of the simultaneous, external and internal "construction" of the equilateral triangle, Chapter One, n. 8, this study.
239. *Ibid.*

immediate terms, "How now" ["Wie nun"]) can we "subsume" the *a posteriori* stuff of cognition to *a priori* forms of cognition, given that the latter, by definition, can only be conceived of hypothetically in the first place? Put in equivalent, perhaps more readily available terms: we may well hypothesize the analytic necessity of a singular unity, "one," but by what means do we apply it, as an *a priori* "form" or "category," to the infinitely divisible things of the world, let alone to itself whenever we construct a new, inherently synthetic unity, "two" (and so forth)? How, based on the hypothesis, "one," are either empirical identification or arithmetic operations possible?

The significance of such a question is not "merely" hypothetical, however, but, commensurate with any *critical* hypothesis, real and practical for Kant, and in raising it he addresses the problem of "method" never resolved, at least with regard to cognition and judgment of the empirical world, by Descartes. Appropriately, Kant's answer responds to the question of feasibility essential to any practice: that of "how" an action is to proceed, rather than "what" is to be done. Instead of simply deferring the problem by inventing a higher faculty capable of governing and taking precedence over the heterogeneous faculties of conceptual understanding and sensory perception whose coordination with each other produces the "representations" we know, Kant introduces the inherently practical notion of an "*art*" inhering in the mind, a (non-reproductive) "*technique*"[240] for rendering the heterogeneous homogeneous he calls the "schema."[241]

A conception without precedent, no single notion in Kant's *Critique* may more sharply distinguish its theory of *a priori* representational knowledge from the idealist and empiricist epistemologies preceding it – all of which, since antiquity, have described empirical knowledge to one degree or another as a necessary *development*, whether natural or cultivated, from sense perception – no less than the many sensualist and aestheticist marginalizations of knowledge, including false equations of "knowledge" with sensation, that have succeeded it. Locke's historic debunking of the notion of "innate ideas" propounded in the place of experience by idealizing neo-Cartesians repeats a classical, still lively conflict regarding the "sources" of knowledge to which Kant directly, and distinctively, responds.[242] Arguing against Platonic notions of "innate" "states of knowledge" in favor of the mechanical procedural approach to cognition institutionalized by the Scholastics after him, Aristotle narrates, in the *Posterior Analytics*, "animal"

---

240. Cf. n. 72, Section Two, this Chapter.

241. The ancient Greek "schema" (σκημα), signifying physical form or figure, maintained its meaning in early modern English; Kant's use of it to mean an internal *techne* for the "production" of knowledge is unique in both the German and English philosophical and linguistic traditions, and is noted as such in the standard English history of the term. See *OED*, Oxford University Press (1971 ed.), p. 2,663.

242. On the double "sources" ("Quellen") of our knowledge, see Kant, *KrV* B 1, 33, III: 45, 69, *et passim*.

"development[s]" of the cognitive "capacity" for "sense-perceptions," through their "persistence in the soul," eventual "systematization," and final "stabilization" as "knowledge," as follows:

> all animals ... possess a congenital discriminative capacity which is called sense-perception. But though sense-perception is innate in all animals, in some the sense-impression comes to persist, in others it does not. So animals in which this persistence does not come to be have either no knowledge at all outside the act of perceiving, or no knowledge of objects of which no impression persists; animals in which it does come into being ... can continue to retain the sense-impression in the soul: and when such persistence is frequently repeated a further distinction ... arises between those which out of the persistence of such sense-impressions develop a power of systematizing them ... So out of sense-perception comes to be what we call memory, and out of frequently repeated memories ... develops experience. From experience again – i.e., from the universal now stabilized ... within the soul ... originate the skill of the craftsman and the knowledge of the man of science ...
>
> We conclude that these states of knowledge are neither innate ... nor developed from other high states of knowledge, but from sense perception.[243]

Kant's "schema" is, precisely, *not* "animal"-"developmental" and so subject to neither varying degrees of impressionability nor frequency of repetition, and, with these, external manipulation over time. Yet no more is it an applied mechanics or ideational capability of the mind. Whereas Aristotle furnishes analytic logic with the useful tool of the "category" and Plato's Socrates creates the logic of speculative discourse by opposing "representations" to "Ideas" – intellectually rather than experientially practical conceptions whose utility to thinking Kant's *Critique* maintains – Kant introduces the new notion of a noncontingent or "transcendental," "pure" or *a priori* "schema" on the same basis that, he stipulated, necessitated his hypothesis of a "transcendental theory of judgment" in the first place, that of the need for a "third" and "mediating" mode of intellectual action, this time within and enabling cognition itself. Kant answers his own question of "how" perceptions can be "subsumed" "under" concepts as follows:

---

243. Aristotle, *Posterior Analytics* 99b25–100a10, *The Basic Works of Aristotle*, Ed. Richard McKeon, (New York: Random House, 1941), pp. 184–85. The nearly perfect replication of Aristotle's naturalist account of the "develop[ment]" of "science" by present-day behavioral "sciences"—and the opposition of what, by dint of the most primitive binary logic, they likewise dub "innate" *because* they can neither physically observe nor control it, to that which, because, it appears to them something they *can* externally observe and control, they conversely dub external "sense perception"—should give pause to anyone seeking to elevate the mechanics of Aristotle's so-called "materialist ontology" above the basest methods of behavioral conditioning.

Now it is clear, that there would have to be some kind of third thing, which, on the one side, is homogeneous with the category, and homogeneous with the phenomenon, on the other, and so makes the application of the former to the latter possible. This mediating representation must be pure (without anything empirical about it) and so, on the one side, *intellectual*, while on the other side, *sensory*. Such a representation is the *transcendental schema*.

[Nun ist klar, dass es ein Drittes geben müsse, was einerseits mit der Kategorie, andererseits mit der Erscheinung in Gleichartigkeit stehen muss, und die Anwendung der ersteren auf die letzte möglich macht. Diese vermittelnde Vorstellung muss rein (ohne alles Empirische) und doch einerseits *intellektuell*, andererseits *sinnlich* sein. Eine solche ist das *transzendentale Schema*.[244]]

As the *formal* "representation" of Kant's hypothesis that all knowledge of "sensory" "phenomena" is representational, i.e., already mediated *by* formative, intellectual operations of delimitation and coordination, the schema is "necessitated" but not contained by that hypothesis. It is itself, in other words, unmediated, and yet not itself its own first cause. Just as "no [single] image of a triangle could ever be adequate to the concept of a triangle," so "sensory conceptions" must have "schemata" rather than "images of objects" "at their foundation."[245] And just as the hybrid conception – of "an image" for "a concept" – that Kant "name[s] the schema" is itself the "representation of a general procedure of imagination,"[246] so the formation of the schema, medium of this hybridity, must precede the production of specific images in Kant, and it is in this context that Kant describes an originary power to image unattached to any particular sensory experience, a "pure imagination *a priori*," which is to say, an imagination by definition unimaginable, whose identifying mark is the "schema," its own imageless, "so to speak, monogram:" an at once abstract and concrete insignia, sign, or initialing script. Of the identity of the origin of the schema, Kant states critically:

We can only say this much: as the *image* is the product of the empirical faculty for productive imagination, the *schema* of sensory concepts ... [is] the product and, so to speak, a monogram of the pure imagination *a priori*, through and according to [or after] which images first become possible, and which only become linked to concepts by way of the schema that designates them.

[So viel können wir nur sagen: das *Bild* ist ein Produkt des empirischen Vermögens der produktiven Einbildungskraft, das *Schema* sinnlicher Begriffe ...

---

244. Kant, *KrV* B 177–78, III: 187–88.
245. *Ibid.*, B 179, III: 189.
246. *Ibid.*, B 180, III: 189: "Diese Vorstellung nun von einem allgemeinen Verfahren der Einbildungskraft, einem Begriff sein Bild zu verschaffen, nenne ich das Schema zu diesem Begriffe" ("This representation of a general procedure of imagination providing a concept with its image I call the schema to this concept").

ein Produkt und gleichsam ein Monogramm der reinen Einbildungskraft a priori, wodurch und wonach die Bilder allererst möglich werden, wie aber mit dem Begriffe nur immer vermittelst das Schema, welches sie bezeichnen, verknüpft werden müssen.[247]]

According to its provocative definition here by Kant, "the schema" not only "mediates" – it, "so to speak" ("gleichsam"), speaks, "designating" ("bezeichnet") the very "concepts" ("Begriffe") it "links" ("verknüpft") to "images." Analogous to the "images" "produced" by our "empirical faculty of imagination," the schema, Kant states, is "produced" by an imagination "pure" of experience, "through and according to [or after] which" all "image" production "first" "becomes possible." Impure or "empirical" imagination mediates between the logical "categories" of reason and the contingency of "phenomena[l]" experience to produce the *a posteriori* "images" linked to our cognitive representations. In the case of the imageless schema, however, rather than mediate between the "heterogeneous" powers of reason and perception, a "pure" power of imagination is "said" both to "produce" *and* to leave behind in the mind its own calling card, the signature or temporally transmissible sign of the "means by which" ("vermittelst") imagination is routinely empirically "appli[ed]" ("Anwendung"). Preceding and independent of sensation and conceptualization alike, the schema mediates not by imaging but by "join[ing] "concepts" and "images" in an act of "designat[ion]," the signing and assigning of a specifically linguistic "bond" ("verknüpft").

What Kant "names" "the schema" "mediates" in that it, too, "names," and "language," intellectual and applicable through and through, may be its other, more common *pseudonym*. For, "monogram" of the "pure imagination *a priori*," the schema is both the mode of communication between the intellect and the senses *and* the source of the designations that, in its capacity as a single, "homogeneous" medium, it communicates. The schema, in other words, allows us to make "communicable," or "common" "sense," on the "inside," of the "sensory" objects we experience on the "outside," to *bring into communication the "sense" of a concept* it "*designates*" *with the speechless*, unknown, indeed, strictly speaking, un-experienced *sensations of the "senses."* Without this "monogram" of a "pure," or nonimitative, imaging power – "product" ("Produkt") in the form of an abstract sign or signature, of a power *to signify rather than* image – even the images we produce, let alone the sensory experiences we undergo, would remain fundamentally incommunicable with concepts, and thus to ourselves as well.

Yet, the same may be said of the *nonconceptual* sensory experience Kant calls "aesthetic." The "monogram" and "product" of an independent power of imagination, whose own unique power to "designate" ("bezeichnet") "joins" ("verknüpft") experience with concepts, *the schema functions in the perceiving subject as "common sense" does in the act of aesthetic judgment*, speaking for and thus communicating, across spatial, temporal and individual differentiation, sensations that, in its

---

247. *Ibid.*, B 181, III: 190 (emphasis in text).

absence, would leave no trace of their individual occurrences, just as the "common," inherently "communicable" "sense" grounding *and* spoken in judgment, rather than reporting the speaker's feeling,[248] qualifies an unknown object "for everyone" or not at all. Like the schema – the *Critique*'s own necessary, *a priori* "construction" not of a perfectly rational geometric figure brought into being by "thought," but of a "monogram" scripted by imagination alone to "designate" and, in so doing, "join" external manifestations to our power to form – aesthetic judgment designates an internal experience articulable by anyone. The schema, Kant's "transcendental" "representation" of the internal power to "designate," speaks no less powerfully in the verbal practice of judgment. As the cognizing schema "binds" understanding to perception in the definitively communicable medium of conceptual designations, so aesthetic judgment, in "say[ing]" something of an unknown sensory object, "it," qualifies that object "for everyone:" regardless of whether spoken in a private or public context, *the "general voice" of judgment abolishes, in the act of its expression, the distinction between private and public spheres.* And like the schema, judgment, too, "joins" "heterogeneous" orders of experience *a priori*, binding the discursively continuous, yet epistemologically discontinuous, qualitative and nominal components it designates so as to "construct," like a geometer "think[ing]" without reference to subjective experience, the predicative statement and "communicable" judgment it "brings forth:" "it is beautiful," "it is sublime."

The "common sense" in which, Kant states, aesthetic judgment is "ground[ed]," and whose own basis he asserts he has neither the ability nor wish to "investigate," is no more commonsensical a notion than that of a "monogram" "sa[id]" ("so much

248. The complex relation of language and feeling in the Third Critique, the former articulated "in response" to, even while supplanting the latter, substituting speech about an unknown object for the inarticulate passions of an individual subject, resembles Rousseau's account of the origin of language in its suggestion that no feeling can both be experienced and speak its name at the same time, and differs from it in that, instead of displacing and occluding a subjective feeling ("fear") in the objective form of a nominal figurative utterance ("Giant"), Kant's account of speech qualifies an unidentified object, using an abstract adjective ("beautiful") to forge a kind of middle ground between subject and object. For, no matter how much they appear to indicate "a part of" objects themselves, adjectives are the part of speech most indicative, as Diderot described, of our *experience* of objects: unlike a feeling of fear that, occluding an experience of ignorance by "fascinating the eye," is in turn occluded by an appellation falsely constating an "objective" state of things based on a metalepsis (because I feel "fear" of this unknown other [of an unknown me], he must be or have been objectively bigger than me), the predicative complements, "beautiful" and "sublime," are qualities possessing precisely no objectifiable, constatable basis in Kant, or indeed, in any theory of the aesthetic since antiquity. The, by turns, dependent and mutually exclusive relation of language to feeling described in theory and literature during and after Kant's "Age of Critique" is discussed in ""The Real Horizon," the concluding Part of *Words' Worth*, complementary study to this work.

can we only say..." ["so viel können wir nur sagen"[249]]) to be inscribed, *a priori* and indelibly, in the mind, the – at once internal and external[250] – identifying mark or signature of a power of imagination, antecedent to any particular experience, whose "product" it is. Just as the First Critique demonstrates the practical validity of a hypothetical theory of universal phenomenal or limited knowledge, and the Third Critique analyzes the "transcendental" or universal faculty of judgment it itself proposes we all possess – a specifically non-conceptual "power" that "speaks" impersonally, or "for everyone" – the schema required to make knowledge "possible" has its *a priori* counterpart in Kant's theory of judgment in "common sense." One produces the language that the other must employ.

249. Cf. n. 247, this Chapter, this Section.

250. Kant's description of the "schema" as the "monogram" or marking carried within the mind of an imagination "pure" of, or previous to, and thus capable of forming experience relates directly to the interaction between language and external, earth-bound markings required for the production of history. I have described that interaction in a study of the heterogeneous composition of referentiality, and reference-based, demarcating history (*In the Place of Language* ... [2009]), which argues that the acts, events and presences of the past that we understand to constitute history are dependent for their persistence and perception as such on the mutual supplementation of external, material markings in space with systematically significant, linguistic or other communicative signs. This study argues the complementary view that any (by definition, nonhistorical) "origin of language" would have to be, by contrast, simultaneously internal and external to begin with, and that Kant's mysterious "schema" performs the redoubtable discursive task of representing and so "fulfilling" just such a need. For, a "monogram" or signature of an imagination whose power remains independent of experiential (external and historical) limitations must be at once indivisible from the medium in which it is engraved and superficial or external enough to be externally legible and identifiable as such. As his theory of judgment bases its own possibility on a "common" rather than individually contingent "sense," Kant's theory of knowledge requires a "schema" in which the distinction between external and internal, rather than corporeally and spatially defined, is produced as it is traversed by a "pure" power of "imagination" operative within the mind. As discussed in the complementary study to this book, on Wordsworth's directly related theory and practice of "common language" poetry, such an "imagination" makes its own representational appearance, both as imaged "power" and purely linguistic referent or name, in Book VI of Wordsworth's *Prelude*. See *Words' Worth*, Part II, Chapter Nine, "Imagination," pp. 79–95 in particular.

10. What is Articulation?

Initialing "monogram" of a "pure *a priori* imagination" capable of "joining" "sensory" experience with "concepts," and the *Critique's* own "representation" ("Vorstellung") of a necessary "third" ("ein Drittes") "mediat[ing]" capability ("vermittelst") that, "intellectual on the one hand" ("einerseits intellektuel"), and "sensuous on the other" ("einerseits sinnlich"), is nonetheless "pure" ("rein"), or fully non-"empirical" ("ohne alles Empirische") in basis, Kant's "schema" offers a no less necessary "representation" of the formation of language at its "origin." That "origin" must remain between diacriticals, or "so-called," because, just as it is neither contingent upon nor defined by any specific moment, cause or content, but, rather, is enactable at any moment in any context, or *a priori*, to define it as an "origin *a priori*" (or without origin) is a contradiction in terms. For the same reason, its representation is no more image-able than it is derivable from any empirical thing. For, while it first makes the "production" of any "image" "possible," the "schema," Kant emphatically states, is anything but an "image" itself.[251] Calling card of an "imagination" – and, Kant underscores, "at all times only of the imagination" – that does not image, but initials, the "art" or *techne* of the "schema" cannot be referred back to sensory experience but rather remains "hidden," Kant famously figures, "in the depths of the human soul," and the only proper content of what Kant calls "this" (his) proposed (critical, non-Aristotelian) "schematism of understanding" (rather than things) is thus our own undeducible "internal sense," not of any sensuous thing but of "time" as we experience it: "schemata are nothing but *a priori determinations of time*."[252]

---

251. Kant, *KrV*, B 181–82, III: 190. In one of the sublimely prosaic moments of the First Critique, of a piece with the description of "seeing as the poets see" in the Third, Kant describes the critical difference between his new, "transcendental" use of the term "schema" and any conception we may hold of an "image," stating that it matters little whether the "image" made be of a "triangle" or a "dog," let alone of such a co-existing "multitude" or "mass" of individual identities as contained within the numerical designation, "one thousand," no single image can "reach," but rather each must stem from "the generality of the concept" ("triangle," "dog," "one thousand") to begin with, generality to whose "schematic" combination with the sensory in general no particular "image" could ever be "adequate" (*KrV*, B 180, III: 189). Absent the internal "art" of the schema, in other words, one imaged "dog" would either have to be all dogs, in a kind of *day* when all cows are black (to upend Hegel's famous phrase), or no dog would be a "dog," nor would there, finally, be such a thing as "images" (or "representation," or memory), only present, and indistinguishable, sensuous masses as such.

252. Kant, *KrV*, B 184–185, III: 192–193 (emphasis in text).

Similarly, the "three analogies of experience" Kant introduces into the "Transcendental Analytic" soon after the notion of a necessarily "mediating" "schema," *must* be analogical, rather than directly empirical or logical in origin, in that they conceive experience with regard not to any (*a priori* temporal) objects themselves, nor "to time itself" ("der Zeit sich selbst"), but to the basic modes of temporal differentiation ("permanence," "successivity" and "simultaneity") ("Beharrlichkeit, Folge, und Zugleichsein") first made distinguishable (and "time" thus conceivable) by a means of "interconnection" ("Verknüpfung") permitting us to "perceive" "the existence of objects in time" ("Existenz der Objekte in der Zeit"). That interconnected, and thus inherently comparative or "analogical," temporally differentiating mode of perception allows Kant to conclude, in radical divergence from all philosophy before him (and convergence with all literary representation at any time), that experience "itself" is a product of syntax: "so is experience only possible through a notion of the necessary interconnection of perceptions" ("Erfahrung ist nur durch die Vorstellung einer notwendigen Verknüpfung der Wahrnehmungen möglich"[253]). By analogy, we, too, may conclude that, whatever an unimaginable power of "pure imagination *a priori*" may be, and whatever, if any, may be its own identifiable origin and script, the schema that is its "product" is also its specifically temporal offspring, or text. The nonfinite capability of the "art" of the schema, like that of language, to join the radically different orders of conception and sense perception into representations which the same schematically mediating "understanding" can in turn "interconnect," is fundamentally linked, then, if necessarily by "analogy," to the experience of "time itself." Within the operations of the "schema," language and temporality are at all times coeval.

For, uniquely comparable to linguistic forms, the so-called "sensory concepts" ("sinnliche Begriffe") that Kant's "schematic" "determinations of time" produce work both ways: they are *sensory* (externally sensible) instantiations of (internally produced) concepts and *conceptions* of the sensory whose single "pure" – because, paradoxically, necessarily hybrid – content may be critically called not "time itself" (whatever that may be) but its experiential product, temporality. And unlike both idealist and empirical-materialist conceptions of the sensory, they are thus also neither internal nor external in basis, but must be both, which is to say, communicable or *social*. In addition to introducing time into perception, Kant's conception of a "schema" capable of mediating internality and externality "in time"[254] effectively squares the permanent, analytic circle of how properly social, rather than mechanically, physically determined, relations come about in the first place: how what the author of the revolutionary *Social Contract* dispassionately called the necessity of "convention" can be produced without relying on prior social conventions – in short, how social conventions, which is to say conventions and social formations of any kind, can begin to begin with. Unlike false accounts of the "natural" basis of the willful imposition and unwilled suffering of creaturely, physical force whose mythologizing "histories" Rousseau was first to criticize, Part One of his

---

253. Kant, *KrV*, B 219–220ff., III: 216–217ff.
254. Kant, *KrV*, B 183ff, III: 191ff.

Second Discourse demonstrates the inalienable operation across time of a physically undetermined, definitively human capacity for forming society *by mutual agreement or convention*, itself demonstrated *rather than* disproven by the logical impossibility of identifying a "first," or *non*-regressive, "origin" of all conventions, or language. That irresoluble paradox, of a first convention both requiring and preceding the conventional or agreed upon means for convening or agreeing in the first place, irrefutably exposed by Rousseau in Part One, is then abruptly replaced by Rousseau *in toto*, and without further commentary, with a mechanical etiology of nonsignifying, purely circumstantial "languages" and "societies" conditioned no less than purely physical compulsion on mere force of proximity in the Second Discourse, Part Two. As described in Section Six of this Chapter, that logically recursive, textually occluded problem of an at once temporally and semantically paradoxical "original convention" is accounted for in Rousseau's "Essay on the Origin of Languages" by a hypothetical narrative relating a disfiguring "fear" of human alterity and equality to ignorance. Whether represented as a circular logical conundrum or as a linear narrative of impassioned error and belated correction, social relations and linguistic relations are and remain equally coterminous in both cases. For the Rousseau of the undateable "Essay" (that he, or the alter-ego Rousseau himself called the "juge de Jean-Jacques,"[255] refused to publish in his lifetime), the problem of constructing a logical chronology of language is misconstrued to begin with, in that any first word would have had to have been born of excess, not ratio, in order to depart from an as yet unarticulated norm. Just as the first word would originate in a blinding passion it occludes by misconceiving and misnaming an other in its stead, inventing a "trope," "Giant," for what the other is not, so the recognition of an always latent sameness of self and other that, first acquired "after much" comparative "experience," can only be established rationally through a belated invention of the common noun, "man." In tandem with temporality, Rousseau, like Kant, suggests that sociability – whether viewed as universally "natural" or in the eye of the beholder; as conceptual fiction, or expendable convention – is as dependent upon linguistic articulation, a signifying act of some kind, as is any form of human communication and relation, from doubt to acknowledgement, mistrust to "selfless" (or "moral") action, confusion regarding "truth" to "commitment" to a ("moral") "cause," and from the designation of bodily co-existence in space to nonlocal equality of "rights" "under law."

---

255. Rousseau completed the three dialogues comprising *Rousseau, juge de Jean-Jacques* in 1776. One of his final works, like his similarly self-representing, autobiographical-autofictional *Confessions* and *Rêveries d'un promeneur solitaire*, it was also only published in 1782, after the death of its authorial subject (1778), making the identification of "which" Rousseau we are to take at "his" word- the representing and reflecting subject *or* represented subject-as-object – or as Rousseau famously calls the latter in the opening lines of the *Confessions*, the "me" ("moi") he "will be ("et cet homme, ce sera moi") once portrayed "in all the truth of his nature" ("dans toute la verité de sa nature), not as his (unrepresented) self, but as "a man" ("un homme"). See Rousseau, *Rousseau, juge de Jean-Jacques*, ed. A. C. Fusil (Paris: Plon, 1923).

But this is as much as to say that, in order for objects to be related to each other and to us *as* objects, and for subjects to relate to other subjects *as* subjects, rather than objects, the heterogeneous combination of sensory impressions and conception produced by the schema must also be universally communicable. Their internal production must be externalized, made as "common," or extracted from personal properties as any abstract, common noun, by articulate forms of which the simple grapheme of the "monogram" – recognizable yet lacking demonstrable referent – is an especially fitting, because entirely "imaginati[ve]" "representation." Deduced and defined by Kant at the opening of the "Transcendental Doctrine of Judgment" of the First Critique as "a [necessary] third" capacity for formal "mediation" between sensation and conception, the operation of the schema within understanding resembles the "mediating," "third" "power" of "judgment" within his critical philosophy, a "power" or capability likewise inseparable from its "own" external communication in third-person declarative statements ("it is beautiful ..."). Just as an object in the world provides its occasion, aesthetic judgment requires articulation within the world. In this respect, not only the essential communicating function of the Third Critique within Kant's overarching "architectonic" project," but the "mediations" individually internal to the First and Third Critiques relate to each other as each other's "inside" and "outside," or, in the terms of the Second Preface, within the necessarily reciprocal relation of "internal" to "external" that is the only possible basis for our experience of change, and temporal existence or "Dasein" in general.[256] In the essentially hybrid, so-called "sensory concepts" of the schema and speech acts of judgment, a similar, internal-external, or necessarily translateral temporalization of experience is effected, with the difference that the source of temporal "determinab[ility]" ("bestimmbar[keit]"[257]) occasioned by the schema lies in the temporally hybrid

---

256. Kant, *KrV* B xl–xli, III: 38–9 (emphasis in text): "I am solely conscious of my being in time [*Dasein in der Zeit*] (and of the determinability of the former in the latter) through internal experience, and this is more than merely being conscious of my representation of myself to myself, but is rather the same as the *empirical consciousness of my being in time*, which is only determinable through a relation to something that, bound to my existence, *is outside me*. This consciousness of my being in time is thus bound identically with the consciousness of a relationship to something outside me, and thus it is experience and not an invention (or fabrication [*Edrichtung*], sense and not imagination, which inseparably links that which is external to me with my internal sense" ("*Allein ich bin mir meines Daseins in der Zeit* (folglich auch der Bestimmbarkeit desselben in dieser) durch innere Erfahrung bewusst, und dieses ist mehr, als bloss mich meiner Vorstellung bewusst zu sein, doch aber einerlei mit dem *empirischen Bewusstsein meines Daseins,* welches nur durch Beziehung auf etwas, was, mit meiner Existenz verbunden, *ausser mir ist,* bestimmbar ist. *Dieses Bewusstsein meines Daseins in der Zeit* ist also mit dem Bewusstsein eines Verhältnisse zu etwas ausser mir identisch verbunden, und es ist also Erfahrung und nicht Erdichtung, Sinn und nicht Einbildungsdraft, welches das Aussere mit meinem inneren Sinn unzertrennlich verknüpft ...").

257. *Ibid.*

nature of articulation itself. For, necessarily available *a priori*, the schema makes knowledge possible, while, just as necessarily acting only *a posteriori*, i.e., *upon* experience, its own temporal hybridity makes it impossible for the "heterogeneous" cognitions (unlike those of geometric constructions) the schema produces necessarily to prevail in time.[258] In suspending knowledge, by contrast, the noncognizing power of judgment would have the counter-effect of separating temporality from any possible chronology, making an *a posteriori* power of articulation the "first" moment or "origin" of an experience "free" of just such schematic cognitions, and the "determinations of time" produced with them.

Like two sides of a single page, the "inside" and "outside" of any dividing demarcation are not merely formal, but substantive, and the demarcations between Kant's individual Critiques are indeed substantive in a specifically *critical* sense. For, unlike equally tautological statements of subjective opinion or subjectively supposed, empirical "givens," critical analyses understand the *substance of experience* to be the product of formal or impersonal relations, whether the "experience" involved results in knowledge, feeling, a state of being, or condition, and whether the "substance" in question appears as "real" or "self-determining" as history, or as "nominal" and apparently unrelated to the "real" as fiction. While any "system" of knowledge depends on the internal coherence of its formation, in order for a systematic epistemology to be "critical" (rather than purely symbolic or self-referential), it cannot be fully autonomous, which is to say, incommunicative with the other intellectual activities whose rational, representational, and imaginative means it shares, just as those activities tied by their common means to knowledge – "moral" and scientific "reasoning," theoretical hypothesis and empirical experimentation, historiographic, literary and aesthetic representation and interpretation – must engage with issues of cognition even while not explicitly epistemological in aim, contributing to and so altering any viable theory of how we know. By the same token, while the formation of a philosophical – or indeed of any non-natural – "system" requires its own defining, operational closure, Kant's "critical" "system" includes within it the opening and "passage" ("Übergang"[259]) from one intellectual activity to another that, delimited by the partial commonality of elements and faculties composing these activities, also borders upon disrupting

---

258. Graphically put, or "looked at" from the other end, as it were, of the telescope, the consequences of temporally correlating acts of imagination with *knowledge* are as enormous as, or co-extensive with, the external acts and internal consciousness of experience composing all human (as opposed to natural) history. Wordsworth suggests the same in stating, in his "Preface to Lyrical Ballads," that any attempt to "account for the present state of the public taste" would have not only to "point out the manner in which language and the human mind act and re-act upon each other" but "retrace the revolutions, not of literature alone, but likewise of society itself." See William Wordsworth, "Preface to *Lyrical Ballads*," in *The Prose Works*, ed. W. J. B. Owen and Jane Worthington Smyser, 2 vols. (Oxford: Clarendon Press, 1974), I: 121, and *Words' Worth*, p. 9, n. 5.

259. Kant, *KU* B XX, X: 83, et passim.

the effective operation of each. The consideration of relations obtaining before, within, and in negation of identity, developed into the central modality of philosophy by Hegel's temporal delineation of the dialectic and Heidegger's unreservedly differential description of "Being," finds its unlikely precedent in a synchronic, systematic description of distinct intellectual activities the internal coherence of which depends in turn upon the differentiation of each from the other, yet whose asymmetrical overlap ensures that they will remain open and in relation. Like the "schema" that, as if "join[ing]" individual lines into a single meaning-bearing "monogram," relates, *a priori* and inextricably, the divided, "intellectual" and "sensory" capabilities of the mind, the "passage" between *a priori* cognitive consistency and "free" acts and "feelings," whose shared field of reference is the external world, is the articulate activity Kant calls "judgment."

The relation between the synthetic speech acts of judgment and the synthesis of sensory experience and intellect into "sensory concepts" by the schema also points, by way of and with Kant, to a larger truth about language and what it does, by way of and with each subject. Language is not only the universal "third" means of "mediation" "(Vermittelung") and "communication" ("Mitteilung") between subjects – two words sharing the common term for means, mean and middle ("mit") in German. It is the means with which we distinguish and define ourselves in relation to a temporal world, not as either impervious or subordinate but, precisely, as "subject" to it, inherently *capable* of being affected rather than determined by natural forces. Neither "master" nor "slave," in Goethe's Faust's or Milton's Satan's consumingly unilateral understandings of those terms, the subject instead meets the world, so to speak, halfway, "joining," however *non*-synthetically, one external form – discourse – to another – objects.

For, in basis and in general, the articulation of language binds "internal" experience – an otherwise nonexistent content – to "external" form. To call such externalization "fiction" is surely to miss its point, the extraordinary, utterly ordinary service it performs as "bridge" not only between a subject defined as the repository of certain common powers and all that is or appears extraneous to such a subject, but across the chasm, between delimited substance and unlimited powers, operative within (and only within) every subject. For nature is nature, as Spinoza axiomatically describes, because in it the infinite power and necessary substance of God wholly determine, contain, and derive from each other.[260] The defining powers of the subject described by Kant, by contrast, determine and derive from an external form of containment, an extra externality they produce themselves. As the "pure imagination *a priori*" "produc[es]" "the schema" – its own signature, calling card, or "monogram," whose recognizable form constitutes a kind of *externality*, ungrounded in previous experience, *within* the mind, defying thereby all vestiges of naturalized "space" in our understanding of the mind's productions – so the articulation of language, any language, delimits otherwise

---

260. See esp. Part One, Propositions 7–16, of the *Ethics*, in Spinoza, *The Ethics and Selected Letters*, trans. Samuel Shirley (New York: Hackett, 1982 [orig. pub. 1677]), pp. 34–62.

unmediated and thus unknowable experience by "containing" it in the recognizable external forms it first composes, representing and defining – speaking of – experience as if the systematic, logical and nominal limits of language were as substantial as those of the empirical world.

Within Kant's "architectonic" "building" of reason, "judgment" is indeed the "middle realm" between (applied, cognitive) theory and (pure, moral) practice: an applied practice of speech. This is speech that, without moral or cognitive posture, speaks "for everyone," not as willed or knowingly designated representative of all other subjects, but by working definition of "judgment" itself. For, as in every other constitutive activity of the subject analyzed in Kant's *Critique*, here, too, "theory" analyzes an already active "practice." In the case of judgment, however, practice specifically and explicitly requires an intermediary, articulation. The language in which it is spoken is itself the "middle realm" of judgment in Kant, the necessary, articulate form in which both theory and practice of judgment *and* all subjects of judgment meet – their "*common* sense" in the abstract sense that the schema is the signature conjoining form and sensation, making all "experience," in Kant's words, "cognitive," which is to say, sensory and conceptual at once. In Kant its "origin" lies in neither "end" of a circular chain of deduction, nor in any one subject, but in a "power to judge" that, activated by a feeling arising from the perception of an unknown object, first articulates and apportions (*Ur-teil*) in external forms a statement in which that object is predicated by being identified, not by name, but with a quality.

Just as Kant hypothesizes the necessity of a schema ("so there has to be a third thing…"[261]) that, in direct contrast to the "image[s]" of "the empirical…imagination," is instead a legible, external sign or "monogram" of the "pure imagination,"[262] so, in its capacity as articulation, rather than empirical conceptualization, *language is externalization*. By this is meant neither the projection nor imaging, displacement nor transmission or translation, from "inside" to "outside," or from one subject to others, of a meaning any subject already knows, but rather the act of articulation upon which the indirection we call meaning – the necessary nonidentity of any meaning with its means – depends. Signs, markings, symbols, characters, emblems, images, icons, words all externalize, make indirectly perceivable, thoughts and relations of every order, kind and description – from "empirical" observations to categorical definitions, from acts of speech to the analytic discourse we call "philosophy," and theoretical speculation to fiction – that, without them, would have no "known" or even imagined, let alone communicable, existence at all.[263]

Yet language "is" externalization in another, less technical sense as well. In containing what it includes, each act and instance of articulation excludes what it

---

261. Kant, *KrV* B 181, III: 190. See Section Nine, n. 244, this Chapter.

262. See n. 247, Section Nine, this Chapter.

263. The most familiar, unequivocal realization of this fact is perhaps the least understood as such. In order to produce, by purposefully faulty employment of syllogistic means, the new, indirect *meaning* of "I think" – "therefore I am" – the circular or illogical sentence we now call Descartes' "cogito" had first to be stated, articulated. Cf. n. 208, Section Seven, this Chapter.

does not contain, constituting, thereby, an "outside" to its every "inside." Specifically verbal articulations, however, endow externality with the additional quality of commonality: an abstracted, or entirely inorganic "second skin" operating independently of the spatial and temporal constraints of purely physical articulations and inarticulate experience alike. Arising like a kind of gloss or scrim between each subject and the external world, even while they tear the veil of apparent phenomenal impenetrability between subjects, bringing invisible "internal" lives into communication with each other in entirely unforeseeable ways, verbal articulations make the perceptibly "external" or "other" into another, separate subject brought into "contact" with other subjects by way of the discursive surfaces they share. Neither tactile nor phenomenal in any sense, these are the surfaces we ourselves externalize when we partake and join in discourse – surfaces so definitive of our own existence that it is them alone we mean when pronouncing, without the slightest hint or consciousness of irony, we'll "be in touch."

Verbal articulation, then, makes containment into an externally uncontained realm of contact, a "third," middle ground between inside and outside, subject and other (as well as subject *as* other). But this is as much as to say, in positive rather than negative terms, that, in excluding what it does not contain, the act of articulation also includes the externality – the common, wholly nonphenomenal "ground" – it creates. Unlike the representational knowledge we make of our delimited perceptions of a phenomenal, external world, articulation *produces* the particular – common rather than empirical – externality in which it itself is based. In this, it not only comprehends the necessarily mutually exclusive realms, of the perceptible or phenomenal and ideational or noumenal, that Kant's "faculty" of judgment "bridges" or "mediates," but the generative basis of Hegel's dialectic. And in this, the composition of externalization that is articulation contains "within it" every predictably circular rehearsal (disguised, in un-self-conscious, "post"-Hegelian fashion, as discovery) of whether externality *or* consciousness, negation *or* sublation, matter *or* idea, subject *or* predicate, the resistant particular *or* form of thought is bound to emerge the victor of an ongoing process that specifically requires their opposition. For the discontinuous movement of the dialectic itself requires its "own" "second skin" of articulation, too.

11. World Without Words: Wordsworth

There may exist no more effective representation in English of Kant's articulate theory of judgment – its realization, in acts of speech, of an otherwise ungrounded, nonprivative or "common sense" – than the common language poetry and poetic theory of Wordsworth. As *Words' Worth,* the complementary case study to this investigation of the linguistic condition of judgment and agency in general, lays out in detail, Wordsworth's express rejection, in the "Preface to *Lyrical Ballads,*" of the cluttered landscape of vacuously extravagant figures then passing for "poetic diction," was the theoretical expression, unrestricted to any historical moment, of the poet's attempt to represent in "real language" the experience of an external world not only unadorned of worn tokens of poeticism, but directly at odds with the framing or delimitation of experience required for its phenomenal representation. In order to effect that positive, "material"[264] *and* conceptual change – both in poetic practice and in our understanding of the interrelationship between language and any "subject"'s "perception"[265] of the empirical – Wordsworth must first replace the phenomenal externality of the world, within which subjects move, with a *nonphenomenal externality* that, like language, is an externality we construct rather than represent, and what the poet discovers each time he does so is a world of "things" that, *rather* than remain external, "enter unawares into [the] mind" of the subject subjected to *them.*[266]

---

264. William Wordsworth, "Preface to *Lyrical Ballads,*" in *The Prose Works*, ed. W. J. B. Owen and Jane Worthington Smyser, 2 vols. (Oxford: Clarendon Press, 1974), I: 140.

265. In the unfinished manuscript posthumously entitled, "The Sublime and the Beautiful," Wordsworth describes any verbal conceptualization ("talk") of a "sublime" "object" as dependent upon the interaction of that object with *a subject who perceives it* in nonprivative terms identical to Kant's: "to talk of an object as being sublime or beautiful in itself, without references to some subject by whom that sublimity or beauty is perceived, is absurd." See Wordsworth, *Prose Works*, Appendix III to *A Guide Through the District of the Lakes*, II: 357. While Wordsworth denied having read Kant's Third Critique – the work of aesthetic theory most admired by his close friend and collaborator, Coleridge – perhaps no theorist or critic better (or more inherently) demonstrated and explained the active bases of Wordsworth's poetics than Kant.

266. William Wordsworth, *The Fourteen-Book Prelude,* ed. W. J. B. Owen. Ithaca: Cornell University Press, 1985 [orig. pub. 1805, 1850], Bk. V: 385.

Like Kant's theory of an ability to judge based on *not* knowing the "objects" we speak of, Wordsworth's poetics of "real language" suspend all perceptual-conceptual *conflations* of language *with* the world, revealing the "real" of his heterodox concept of "real language" to be an actively differentiating, nonphenomenal capacity for perceiving, experiencing and representing the world not as we know, but rather immediately undergo it. As narrated in his poetry, the resulting experience for the subject is an immediate loss of external orientation, a sense of nothing – no external thing – so much as of feeling "lost."[267] Like the "delineations" and "dynamic forms" that, emptied of the cognitive content of schematic combinations of sensation with a concept, arouse a "feeling" of "freedom" articulated in the verbal act of judgment instead, the "regular," ongoing movement of dynamic syntactic delineation *across* evenly measured but often enjambed, grammatically regular, yet unpredictably predicated blank verse lines, and the estrangingly active "objects," or objects acting like subjects, whose dynamic, external perception Wordsworth's "real language" poetry represents, combine stark graphic simplicity with mimetic contents turned alien, if not altogether unrecognizable. As the poet describes the "undetermined sense" and "blank desertion" of "thoughts" that his own experiential transgressions of cognitive limits put to "work" – specifically, the work of negation – within his "brain:" "[n]o familiar shapes/Remained, no pleasant images of trees,/Of sea or sky . . .".[268] More remarkable still, the usurpation of recognizable phenomenality that his own external actions in the phenomenal world bring about extends to the most elemental, "familiar" "sense" of the language used to describe common phenomena themselves, or, as the poet proceeds to state, consecutively articulating and stripping words of their meaning: ". . . or sky, no colours of green fields."[269]

Wordsworth's articulations of cognition *negated* sets into relief the experience of a subject deprived not only of the gravitational and directional orientation in and delimitation of space we call "place," but of the *signposts* for shaping one's way in the world provided by referential-conceptual language itself. Each "familiar" object we either sense directly or internally "envision" we conceive as something of some extension somewhere, an object in space, and that conceiving is representational, denominational, linguistic. When objects appear instead as "things" shorn of names, comparative qualities, and all other formal means of determination, the subjects who perceive them lose in turn the ability to conceive them. The "undetermined sense" of an autonomous, nonphenomenal world in which "scenes" of movement, enacted by a subject so as to transgress the very bounds of their staging, result, is a world of "unknown modes of being" and "huge and mighty forms, that do not live/Like living men:"[270] a world without language, and thus without subjects as well.

---

267. Wordsworth, *The Prelude* (1850), VI: 596; (1805), VI: 529.
268. Wordsworth, *The Prelude* (1850), I: 391–397; (1805), I: 419–424.
269. Wordsworth, *The Prelude* (1850), I: 397; (1805), I: 424.
270. Wordsworth, *The Prelude* (1850), I: 392–98; (1805) I: 419–25.

Language – any language – *is* the formative, *always two-sided* boundary that we make: the architectonic line at once dividing and conjoining "inside" and "outside," here and there, this and that, and any subject and a world including other subjects of which she or he is a no less material part, and it had to be made, externalized, to be that line. Without language, without its external forms and the fact and experience *of* externality delimited by those forms, the virtual line of articulation dividing external from internal and enabling the external mode of the activity we call *thinking*, would vanish, not only in time, but in the present as well. In that *they are not objects*, not cognitive phenomena of any sort, the otherwise "meaningless" things of language are as indivisible from the production of thinking, and of meaning, as is the reproducible, and thus materially and temporally resistant interface between any subject and any other subjects they provide, all otherwise objectively subjected to the organic corporal limits of space and time. As if in demonstration of that very real, i.e., nonphenomenal linguistic condition of any subject's temporal existence, the dying Keats, even while deeming his own "name" "writ in water,"[271] wrote other "things" to the last, giving nonorganic, transtemporal external form to both his thought *and* corporeal experience as long as (indeed, according to his post-mortem, far longer than) the increasing limitations of his consumptive, not yet quarter-century "old" body allowed. And it is those articulated, linguistic things that make their readers not only reference their author's name, but dispute that referent's prophecy of its own erasure from the writings of history, false fruit of the mental myopia that all consciously transitory, bodily existence may entail.

By contrast, recalling the inarticulate "concourse wild/Of jocund din" provoked by "mimic hootings" "bl[own]," willfully and incongruously, to "silent owls," Wordsworth's poetry makes the redoubtable attempt to represent, *in language rather than artificially mimicked animal sounds*, "echoes" of his efforts to extinguish the line between inside and outside, and so to experience, by purposefully staged *external* means, externality without language. This is no dream of a "pure" yet somehow *not* purely physical materialism (let alone of a somehow tangible, discoursible, yet "pure" – neither conceptual nor physical – "space"), whether personified by us as "mute" and thus pathetically available to our own anthropomorphizing ventriloquism, or personally provoked into "long halloos" perceived as deafening, non-cognizable menace or, for that matter, as "true," because "animal" merriment occurring somewhere "beyond" all ethical reflection. Nor is it the lie of somehow *speaking* from a position of self-appointed omnipotence able to espy all these suppositions from an "outside" that, according to those suppositions, does not exist, in that their very conception as such aims precisely to erase the articulate delineation of outside and inside allowing for their external perception, and any accompanying – definitively

---

271. The memorial stone inscription Keats wrote for himself was, famously paradoxically, "Here lies one whose name was writ in water." His wishes ignored, and a stone covered in sentimental phrases and symbols (broken lyres, etc.) placed at his grave at the Protestant Cemetery in Rome instead, a small footstone with the epitaph he did desire was later placed there by friends. See Robert Gittings' excellent *John Keats, a biography* (NY: Little Brown, 1968) for a clear, understatedly gripping, while never sentimental account of the poet's short life.

nonomnipotent – experience of "feeling," in the first place. Wordsworth's is instead the un-self-deceiving desire to write poetry undefined by *either* intentionally "poetic" signatures *or* any "natural" experience the subject can recognize. Yet, even to experience oneself become the passage of an "other" as terrifying as Rousseau's "Giant" to his unselfknowing subject – to first recognize the self *negatively,* as "other" to itself, its senses immediately subjected to a "scene" of "dim and undetermined sense," its archival "mind," expropriated of all "familiar images" and "colours" by "huge and mighty forms" that "move through"[272] it instead – is not to erase but to undergo delimitation and difference in the profoundest sense.

Such is the basis of the explicit assertion of the necessary conjunction of perceptible material limits and language made in the opening words of the "Essay on Epitaphs:" "[i]t needs scarcely be said, that an Epitaph presupposes a Monument, upon which it is to be engraven."[273] As the material "external sign" serving specifically to "point out the place where [the] Dead are interred," the monument replaces the "body" there "mouldering" with the inorganic marker of a locus presently delimited in space – referential sign of a past organic life necessarily delimited in time.[274] Conversely, the universally intelligible, verbal "epitaph" "engraven" upon the monument is a "[w]riting" "exposed to all," its "conjunction" of our object-independent "faculty of reason" with specifically interactive, "*social* feelings," producing "an intimation or assurance within us, that some part of our nature is imperishable."[275] The "co-existent and twin birth of Reason" with "the sense of Immortality" consisting of "nothing less than infinity" requires "a receptacle without bounds or dimensions," and such a receptacle is the mind through which unknown forms "move" in *The Prelude*.[276] What the combination of the epitaphic word and spatially delimiting monument represent is the combination of the boundless and delimited that defines each individual subject's nonfinite experience, i.e., *not* the flow but, importantly, the "*overflow*"[277] that makes experience itself an always partial representation of the infinite.

272. Wordsworth, *The Prelude* (1850), I; 396–97; (18050, I;423–242
273. "Essay on Epitaphs" (1810), Owen and Smyser, I: 49.
274. "Essay on Epitaphs," I: 58. I have developed a theory of referentiality conjoining "place" with the potentially marking materiality (or, in Wordsworth's terms here, "engraven" "external signs") of language, in *In the Place of Language*.
275. "Essay on Epitaphs," II: 50 (emphasis in text).
276. "Essay on Epitaphs," II: 51. See this Section, this Chapter, n. 274.
277. Wordsworth's most often repeated description of poetry – "All poetry is the spontaneous overflow of powerful feeling" – is itself only the first part of the very extensive sentence and definitional paragraph in which it appears, whose further development directly contradicts it: "... powerful feeling: but though this be true, Poems to which any value can be attached, were never produced on any variety of subjects but by a man who being possessed of more than usual organic sensibility had also thought long and deeply. For our continued influxes of feeling are modified and directed by our thoughts, which are indeed the representatives of all our past feelings ...", *Ibid.,* I: 126. For a detailed analysis of this extraordinarily extended, purposefully self-contradictory, explicitly temporally delineated definition of poetry on Wordsworth's part, see *Words' Worth,* Part One, Section Four.

In Kant such delimitation, and the sense of self as agent of otherness that it enables, is instead invented as it is articulated in verbal acts called "judgment:" statements predicating an unknown object with a quality undefined by sensory particulars, its meaning "undetermined" except by the act of stating "it" ("... is beautiful;" "... is sublime") as if one were "any and every other" ("jedermann"). In the place of a purely internal, and thus necessarily inarticulate sensation, and in the place of the "I" who speaks only of his or her own pleasure or displeasure, judgment, in speaking of an undefined "it" *outside* the speaker, becomes the linguistic scene of speech sayable by all: medium of the "mighty forms" of material articulation never identifiable with but underlying all possible phenomenality, both "familiar images" *and* their estrangement, or phenomenality dialectically conceived (as it will be, not by the unknowing, because theoretically and practically *mediating* "power to judge" necessarily defined as such within the overarching *co-extant* structure of Kant's "architectonic" system, but by the developmental history of "consciousness" shaping the equally necessarily *temporal* "phenomenology of spirit" in Hegel).

Finally, "judgment" is itself "free," on Kant's analysis, of being *either* phenomenal and thus necessarily "nominal" *or* moral or mathematical and thus "real," precisely *because it is an act of speech*: neither a definition of an apparent object nor pure construction of a thing but a statement doing something in saying something only manifestable in language – a nonparticular, neither deducible nor demonstrable predication, "it is beautiful" – *instead of* constating something else. That speech act takes the form of a noncognitive statement generally qualifying an object on the basis of the feeling its experience provokes within the subject. It is an act articulating an outside that, since ungrounded in knowledge, cannot be said to exist without it. The language of judgment – language to begin with, before nominal definitions and substitutions obtain – turns the subject outward, is the subject's outside, the second skin of communication we express into the world in order to "have" externality of mind. At the same time it is the external form not of one but all subjects, the form of making sense – of making externality perceptible as such – of which language first avails us, and, by the very definition of language, everyone, regardless of personal "sensibility" or means of access to sensation, shares: in Kant's terms, a necessary, and necessarily "*un*determined norm" or otherwise indeterminable "*common* sense." On the other side of Wordsworth's ability to "see," in Kant's words, "as the poets do,"[278] i.e., to see *linguistically*, rather than conceptually, a world without words whose nonphenomenal reality most resembles that of language itself, is Kant's world of necessarily verbally externalized aesthetic judgment, referential acts of predication that define neither a finite subject nor object but articulate, the way poets do, the quality of the relation of subject and object and dynamic form to perception that any subject can experience between the two.

Judgment requires imagination but what we cannot imagine may be just such an invention as Kant is compelled to call, in a radically literal sense, common sense, as

---

278. See Chapter Three, Section Three, n. 366, this study.

indeed it may be the only means by which particularly accessed sensation is entirely replaced by singularly commonly accessible signification: the internal "revolution" replacing sensory contingency with thinking, and the unthinkable particularity of any and all discrete empirical experience with an articulation of the "freedom" to think in words spoken in a singularly "general voice." Active, relational and differential, *a priori* (rather than "commensensical" by always latterday, which is to say, *a posteriori*, tautological consensus,), Kant's "general voice" designates the mode of "self"-expression in which any subject who judges speaks. The "sense" of its articulations proper to all who perform it, the purely verbal "forms" (as Saussure defined the actively constitutive "signs" of any "language"[279]) of which the speech acts of judgement are composed all enact the nonparticular differentiations of meaning that we, in using them in differing *a posteriori* contexts, already all agree to convene. No less than "Rerum virusque cano," "the world lay all before them," "Was it for this . . .," and "I was born . . .," "it is beautiful" is the matter-of-fact statement of a verbally indicated world. The speech act that is judgment, acting so as to predicate an unknown object in a "general voice," represents no "thing" but the internal as well as externally conventional, representational, imagined, and historical world of words Wordsworth would do without while subjecting himself to the "other," unimagined side coincident within it, employing verbal signposts so as to take them, in the act of doing so, to their "prosaic" limit.

Perhaps less imaginable still, however, Kant's "power of judgment" is also the "bridge," "Übergang" or "passage" from ourselves to a "world" within which we must be "lost:"[280] an externality, no less *within us*, of which, like Diderot's "Saunderson," we know ourselves blind, in that, permanently unavailable to visible or imagined spatialization, its temporal existence as materiality ("Dasein in der Zeit") can never be perceived schematically, nor, thus, "experience[d]" by "analogy." Like a noncommonsensical "common sense," the content of the unique "inner sense" of the schema, "pure product of the imagination *a priori*" whose "form" is "time,"[281] is not sensation but articulation, the inherently social capacity for marking – and so remarking, delimiting and therein differentiating one from another, internal from external, then from now – and thus for experiencing *any* difference, anything "outside" *or* "within" ourselves, which is to say, with Kant, "change" of any kind at all. Without the faculty for externalization of experience, of "feeling," through a "common" or shared "sense" not of any cognitive representation, let alone thoroughly acculturated *or* purely schematic "sensory conception"[282] of

---

279. Saussure, *Cours, de linguistique générale*, ed. C. Bally, A. Sechehaye et A Riedlinger (Paris : Payot, 1971 [1916]), Pt. II, Chap. IV §4, "Le signe dans sa totalité," p. 169.

280. William Wordsworth, *The Prelude* (1850), VI: 596.

281. Kant, *KrV* A 182, III: 190: "the schema is a transcendental product of the power of imagination . . . according to the condition of its form (of time) . . ." ("das Schema . . . ist ein transzendentales Produkt der Einbildungskraft . . . nach Bedingung [seiner] Form (der Zeit) . . .".

282. Cf. n. 247, Sections Nine, this Chapter.

an object, but of any object's formative relation to any subject *a priori*, or predication – the "transcendental," i.e. "general" "capacity" to enact articulation that Kant calls "judgment" – not only would all our other capacities for action, indeed action itself, be inconceivable, let alone practicable, but our cognizing, moral, and "feeling" selves, such as they are or can be, could never even be dreamed of, let alone experienced, enacted, or thought. And, rather than produce an internal "form" "of time" codependent upon our ability to experience the external world, without the power to articulate, to externalize the experience of anything external to us, we, even while "living," would simply occupy another piece of space within it, no more capable, in Wordsworth's words, of "feel[ing] the touch of earthly years" or, for that matter, becoming "lost," than "rocks and stones" "rolled round in earth's diurnal course."[283]

---

283. William Wordsworth, "A Slumber did my Spirit Seal," ll.3–4, 7–8.

Part II

MISSING SENSES AND POETICS

Chapter 3

"JUDGMENT" AND THE GENESIS OF WHAT WE LACK: "POETRY," "SCHEMA," AND THE "MONOGRAM OF IMAGINATION" IN KANT

1. "Judgment" in the "Age of Critique"

Part One of this study identified in Kant's "Analytic of Judgment" an account of the enactment of judgment that is at once a description of the "origin of language:" of speech that, originating in the "feeling" experienced by an individual subject before an unknown object, both "frees" the speaker (from his or her personal interests) to "speak for everyone" and requires, as its common "ground," something Kant calls the "faculty" of "common sense." The content-free commonality or "communicability" of "sense" hypothesized, for the first and last time, by Kant at the conclusion of the final "Fourth Moment" of the "Analytic" (in which Kant defines the "modality" of aesthetic judgments – last analytic category he employs to describe the capacity for judging – as that of being "necessarily" available to any subject at any time), in no way resembles the platitudinous "common sense philosophy" or received ideas of "common human understanding" explicitly dismissed by Kant in the First Critique, and later *Prolegomena*, as a tissue of banalities masking, and so postponing acknowledgement of, the fundamental need for a critique of their baseless complacency.[284] Rather than general notions circularly asserted, accepted and perpetuated by unstated reflexive convention, Kant's "common sense" consists in internal *acts* of "judgment" necessarily externalized in being *spoken* in a "general voice," verbal articulations whose sense is not "pre-dict-able" or conventional but produced as inherently "communicable" to begin with, and whose (hypothetical) *a priori* or (experiential) *a posteriori* basis Kant states he neither "can" nor "wishes to" "research."[285]

To a degree unmatched in any philosophical endeavor before or since, the "power" Kant calls "judgment" is made central to the actual and future development

---

284. Kant, *KrV* B XXXIII, III: 34; See also Chapter Two, n. 37, this study.
285. See n. 57, Chapter Two, Section One, this study.

of theoretical reflection, i.e., the "revolution" in "mode of thinking" that his critical philosophy performs.[286] Both the pivotal analyses of the Second and the Third Critiques – the former demonstrating the "possibility" that each subject may "indeed" act in "freedom" from his or her own (phenomenally limited) "self-interest," thereby "confirm[ing]" not the probability but "fact" (or "deed," *Tat*) of a "moral law;" the latter describing an inherently "communicable," declarative speech act that, qualifying the unknown object of an experience of "feeling," "speaks for every" subject who "feels himself free," from personal inclination and interest, in so speaking – result in acts of judgment in which judgment and language coincide. Thus it is no coincidence that, along with a wave of necessarily hypothetical speculations on how language could have originated, "judgment" itself emerged as a way of thinking about the capacities or "power[s]" of human experience in general during a time of fundamental inquiry that we, designating and delimiting such activity as an historical period even as history alternately buries and re-enacts it, call "*the* Enlightenment," and Kant, who instead described "enlightenment" as the "right" and "inclination" of "humanity" at *any* historical moment "to think," called "the Age of Critique."[287] Since to think about the twin activities of "enlightenment" and "judgment" involved in any "critical" "revolution in mode of thinking" is, in Kant's view, neither to arrive at the accurate judgment of any specific object or experience nor to clarify any subject or answer any question definitively, but rather to reflect upon what the "fact" of noncontingent thinking enables us to do, so any examination of the genesis of judgment in Kant's own thinking must acknowledge frankly that, analogous to the impossibility of arriving at an archeological "origin" of language, it can rely on no given, empirical or contextual conditions to determine what the gratuitous or "free" "power" to speak called "judgment" in Kant's *Critique* is.

As discussed in Part One of this study, the "power of judgment" is the "mediating link" ("Mittelglied") connecting the otherwise incommunicable "realms" ("Gebiete") of cognitive or theoretical and noncognitive or moral reason in Kant's architectonic system.[288] Like the undelimited "time" of "enlightenment" itself, it can never be sufficiently recalled that, by submitting cognition of the world, on the one hand, and action in the world, on the other, to what he called "critique," Kant reversed the conventional definitions of these as, respectively, pure and practical. Pure reason, once submitted to the *a priori* formal limits of representational knowledge hypothesized in the First Critique, is, in practice, in Kant, impure – not independent of experience and so free to speculate at will, but instead exercised, in an involuntary fashion, only insofar as it is applied to experience, the sensory and

286. See n. 1, Chapter One, this study.
287. See Note 2, A XI, Preface to First Edition, First Critique, Kant, *KrV*, III: 13; see "Beantwortung der Frage: Was ist Aufklärung?" ("Answer to the Question: What is Enlightenment?"), Kant, XI: 53–61 (58, 61).
288. Kant, *KU*, B XIX–XXII, X:83–85.

formal "perception" of objects named by concepts and linked by logical categories (chief among these, causality).[289] Theoretical – so-called "pure" – reason is thus *not* pure but rather "practical" in the *Critique,* a "heterogeneous"[290] (because both sense-based *and* formal) rather than autonomous exercise of the mind. Such a hybridized formation of knowledge, incapable by definition of "knowing" things as they may really be, or "in themselves" ("an sich"), is limited in its purview to the "phenomenal" objects we perceive, which is to say, the cognitive representations we form, *a priori,* of the empirical objects we experience.

An analogous reversal of terms holds reciprocally for so-called "practical" reason. Once submitted to the analysis of the Second Critique, practical reason – the reason of moral action – will prove itself to be "pure," in that it alone acts, by definition, in complete freedom from the formal limitations ascribed to phenomenal perception in the First Critique. "Practical" or "applied" reason, then, turns out to be pure because, unlike reputedly "pure," "theoretical" reason, it is truly self-determining,

---

289. No single lexical translation may be more responsible for the ongoing distortion of his critical theory than that of Kant's distinctly perceptual use of the term, "Anschauung" (similarly used soon after by Hegel as synonym for sensory perception), by its near semantic opposite, the spiritual and theological term, "intuition." (For an early instance of Kant's use of "Anschauung" to signify decidedly "sensory perception" ("sinnliche Anschauung"), see Kant, *KU,* X: 35; for full quotation, see n. 344, this Chapter, Section Three.) Still, perhaps more than that of any other common noun he adopts, Kant's specifically *non*intuitional use of "Anschauung" may be seen to stand *in nuce* for the irreversibility of the impact of his *Critique* upon all areas of philosophical inquiry to come, the obstacle rather than invitation to reprises of idealist or sensationalist metaphysics in every field from language and aesthetic theory, theory of history, and moral philosophy, to philosophy of mathematics, logic and cognition. In employing the term in its concretely literal sense of "an-schauen" – "to look at" or "upon" (as in the related term, "Schauspiel," a drama or "play" staged for the "looking") – Kant's "Anschauung" combines perception with the noncontingent ability to structure perception formally (in space and time) and "discursively" ("diskursiv") (by way of logically related concepts and "*a priori*" "categories," including causality). As opposed to the conventional use of "intuition" to designate an entirely internal notion or idea, "Anschauung" in Kant is "heterogeneous" ("heterogen") *because applied* ("angewandt") *a priori,* or to begin with, its "double" ("zweierlei"), contingent and noncontingent, empirical and intellectual composition closer to a practicable framework for the enactment of "representations" of the material world ("Darstellungen" or "Vorstellungen," similarly used for theatrical showings and presentations in German) than it can ever be to the notion of a purely self-emanating "idea." In this, Kant's "Anschauung" – a purely formal act of perception, or "looking at" – enacts upon the notion of an "innate" "intuition" employed by skeptical and idealist philosophies alike the same "revolution" ("Revolution") that his Critique's essentially hybrid "hypothesis" ("Hypothese"), of "applied" or impure, yet *a priori* knowledge "dared" ("gewagt") "introduce" into metaphysics in their stead (see *KrV* B XI – 176, III: 22, 23, 25, 26, 28, 28n, 31, 109, 187, et.al.).

290. Kant, *KrV* B 176–77, III:187.

free of the causal reasoning and representational knowledge that would limit the actions of a fully independent, noncontingent will, and defined by no formative, or *a priori,* conceptual condition other than the "concept" or "idea" of freedom itself. The theater of action of practical reason is the same, delimited sensory world of our perceptions, but the guiding *metteur en scène,* both of its origination and ultimate purpose or orientation, is "the unconditioned" ("das Unbedingte"), supersensory ("übersinnliche") "realm" ("Gebiet") of "ideas" ("Ideen"), and, chief among these, that of "freedom" itself, the single "idea" we "must be able at least to *think*" ("wenigstens müssen denken können"), "without contradicting [ourselves]" ("wenn ich mir nur nicht selbst widerspreche"), by dividing "thinking" from "cognition" and limiting the purview of the latter to empirical givens.[291] Precisely because "thinking" represents no particular cognitive content to the mind, it is free to accompany, without elaboration or contradiction, every delimited action described in Kant's *Critique.* Similarly, in that thinking, as Kant describes it, is an action producing *nothing we can know*, Kant can state "freely," or without contradiction, on behalf of every subject: "I can *think* what I want [or what I will]" ("*denken* kann ich was ich will"), in which "will" ("want") names no mere wish but the "freedom" to act in independence from purely personal wishes, in which what any "I want[s]" is not limited to its individual, phenomenal self-interest.[292]

Still, between the fully defined and divided realms of the impure, or applied, reason of our knowledge of the natural world, and the practically pure or self-determining reason of "free" or "moral" action in that world, Kant posed, *not*

---

291. Kant, *KrV*, B XXVII, III: 31. That the nonreferential notion of "freedom" is (along with that of God and immortality) one of three "ideas" we "can think" (but not know) makes it, in structural terms, the "positive" complement to the "negative" or "critical" "hypothesis" limiting knowledge to the representation of phenomenal objects in the First Critique (see in particular the Preface to the 2nd Edition [*KrV* B XXIV-XXIX, III: 29-33]). To prove that "freedom" follows from the very project of epistemological critique, i.e., that even while outside the limits Kant sets for "all empirical conditions" ("aller empirischen Bedingungen"), it is nonetheless demonstrable by strictly logical deduction, is the purpose of the Second Critique, in which the attempt to derive and unravel a specific "concept of freedom" ("Freiheitsbegriff") from its inextricable "entanglement in inconceivables" ("in Unbegreiflichkeiten verwickelt") inevitably proves infeasible and Kant is instead compelled to acknowledge the "imposition" of the "form" of that "concept" upon "us," an illogical act of force to whose "confirmation by experience" ("auch die Erfahrung bestätigt") he then appeals so as to demonstrate *a posteriori* - i.e., in strictly pre- and *non*-critical fashion - the actual existence of "this ordering of the concepts in us" ("diese Ordnung der Begriffe in uns"). See *KpV* A 53-54, VII: 139-40. Its "imposition" once noted, the "idea" of "freedom" is subsequently referred to as "the concept of freedom" throughout the Second and Third Critiques (see, for example, *KU*, B XX, cited n. 292, this Chapter). For an early analysis of Kant's explicit logical impasse here, and extraordinary interjection of an "imposition" of the "form" of "freedom" upon the unfailing architectonic logic of the *Critique* that produces it, see Brodsky, *Imposition*, Part One, Chapter 2, pp. 21-87).

292. Kant, *KrV*, B XXVII, III: 31 (emphasis in text).

another "*reason*," but a "*power*," that of "judging." While it is conventional to equate Kant's – and, by association, any – rationally elaborated philosophy with a sterile determinism, it is the thoroughly nonmechanical *power* of judging, positioned as the central action of the internally divided *Critique*, that just as actively and powerfully disrupts any such equation. For, Kant submits the power to judge to criticism, too. The Introduction to the *Critique of Judgment* states unequivocally that a "power" uniquely capable of providing the "passageway" between the "modes of thought," and "ground of unity" between the "different worlds," of "freedom" and of "nature" must for the same reason possess no "proper realm" of its "own:"

> Now even if an unoverseeable gulf is fixed between the realm of the concept of nature, as the sensory, and the realm of the concept of freedom, as the supersensory, so that no transition is possible from the first to the second (that is by way of the theoretical use of reason), just as if these two were so many different worlds, the first of which can have no influence on the second; so *should* the second of these have an influence on the first, namely, the concept of freedom *should* make real in the sensory world the purpose given to it by its laws; and nature must consequently also be able to be so thought, that the lawfulness or regularity of its form may at least determine itself together with the possibility of those purposes to be effected following the laws of freedom. – Thus there must be a *ground* of the *unity* of the supersensory which lies at the basis of nature, with that which the concept of freedom practically contains; a ground whose concept, while attaining neither theoretically nor practically to its cognition, and, by the same token, *possesses no proper or particular realm*, still makes possible the transition from the mode of thinking, according to principles, of the one, to the mode of thinking, according to principles, of the other.

> [Ob nun zwar eine unübersehbare Kluft zwischen dem Gebiete des Naturbegriffs, als dem Sinnlichen, und dem Gebiete des Freiheitsbegriff, als dem Übersinnlichen, befestigt ist, so dass von dem ersteren zum anderen (also vermittelst des theoretischen Gebrauchs der Vernunft) kein Übergang möglich ist, gleich als ob es so viel verschiedene Welten wären, deren erste auf die zweite keinen Einfluss haben kann: so *soll* doch diese auf jene einen Einfluss haben, nämlich der Freiheitsbegriff *soll* den durch seine Gesetze aufgegebenen Zweck in der Sinnenwelt wirklich machen; und die Natur muss folglich auch so gedacht werden können, dass die Gesetzmässigkeit ihrer Form wenigstens zur Möglichkeit der in ihr zu bewirkenden Zwecke nach Freiheitsgesetzen zusammenstimme.– Also muss es doch einen Grund der *Einheit* des Übersinnlichen, welches der Natur zum Grunde liegt, mit dem, was der Freiheitsbegriff praktisch enthält, geben, wovon der Begriff, wenn er gleich wieder theoretisch noch praktisch zu einem Erkenntnisse desselben gelangt, *mithin kein eigentümliches Gebiet hat,* dennoch den Übergang von der Denkungsart nach den Prinzipien der einen, zu der nach Prinzipien der anderen, möglich macht.[293]]

---

293. Kant, *KU,* B XX, XXI: 83–84 (emphasis added in part); cf. Chapter Two, Section Four, n. 105, this study.

The "ground of the unity" of sensory nature and freedom that Kant is about to describe is no ground, in the sense of an independent reason or basis, but rather a conduit operating as a communicative or syntactic medium – "bridge" or "passage" or "overpass" ("Übergang") – between two independent intellectual capacities or "realms," that of "theoretical" reason applied to phenomena in the hybrid form of "understanding," and that of a "pure" "practical reason" itself constitutive of "free" moral action. Each of these realms is delimited as much by what it excludes as what it includes – "things in themselves" and "freedom," on the one hand, and the *a priori* limits and "categories" of cognition on the other – and each is formally defined by the hypothetical rules and laws that govern its constitution: the rule of representation and causal relations defining the sensory realm of phenomenal cognition, and the self-legislating law of freedom *from* phenomenal interest as well as contingency defining the supersensory realm of moral action. What additionally, significantly distinguishes the "ground" of a connective "power" that provides a "bridge" between realms rather than "possesses" a "realm of its own," is that, in addition to possessing no particular or proper content, *it is ruled and constituted by no "law."* Kant continues:

> Still, in the family of high cognitive faculties, there is yet a middle term between understanding and reason. This is the *power of judgment*, and one has cause to suppose by analogy that this power, even when it may not contain its own legislation, may still well contain its own principle, which may be sought according to laws, although this principle is merely *a priori* subjective; a principle which, even if it presents no field of objects as its own realm, still may have some territory having a certain characteristic for which this principle may be valid.
>
> [Allein in der Familie der oberen Erkenntnisvermögen gibt es doch noch ein Mittelglied zwischen dem Verstande und der Vernunft. Dieses ist die *Urteilskraft*, von welcher man Ursache hat, nach der Analogie zu vermuten, dass sie eben sowohl, wenn gleich nicht eine eigene Gesetzgebung, doch ein ihr eigenes Prinzip, nach Gesetzen zu suchen, allenfalls ein bloss subjektives a priori, in sich enthalten dürfte: welches, wenn ihm gleich kein Feld der Gegenstände als sein Gebiet zuständle, doch irgend einen Boden haben kann, und eine gewisse Beschaffenheit desselben, wofür gerade nur dieses Prinzip geltend sein möchte.[294]]

The power of judgment mediates between two "realms" of reason, the phenomenal and nonphenomenal or noumenal, whose distinct laws of operation and opposing objects delimit the critical, "unoverseeable gulf" between them. That power may have "its own principle," Kant states, but is ruled by no inherent laws; and, instead of "its own realm" or "domain" ("eigentümliches Gebiet"), it has what he loosely calls "any old territory" ("irgend einen Boden") or "field" at its disposal.

---

294. Kant, *KU*, B XXII–XXIII, X: 85 (emphasis in text).

Kant's atypical substitution here for "ground" ("Grund") – the figuratively conceptual term he had used to designate the unifying function of judgment within the tripartite structure of the *Critique* – by the distinctly physical terms, "field" ("Feld") and "territory" (literally: "floor" ["Boden"]), to designate the indefinite bounds of the purview of "judgment" in the world, already indicates the prosaic nature of the "objects" ("Gegenstände") to which its "power" may extend. "Any old" ("irgend einen") "field" indeed: for, as the wildly disparate occasions for the exercise of judgment elaborated by Kant make evident, the unpredictable – undelimited and unregulated – "territory" of aesthetic experience, as Kant now defines it, may be encountered anywhere and consist in anything, if only that thing is encountered freely, i.e., without either *a priori* causal and cognitive conceptions, or *a posteriori* conceptual prejudices. Wherever and whenever we experience the subjective power of judgment – a feeling of pleasure or displeasure, experienced in the noncognitive perception of an object, "communicated" in being replaced by an impersonal predicative statement formally reminiscent of logic – "there," in the communicable act of the third-person copular that first refers to it, the otherwise undefined "territory" of "the power of judgment" takes place. In that judgment requires the particular perceptual experience Kant calls "aesthetic," even as they are "free" of both conceptual knowledge and personal psychology, acts of judgment are not in themselves "self-legislating," free of any object "outside" them. Linguistic in its enactment, the "power of judgment" qualifies (rather than logically defines) an object. On whatever objective basis the subjective faculties of imagination and understanding engage each other in pleasurable "free play," or, in perceiving an objective absence of form, reason and imagination instead conflict "violently," "there" another outcropping of the "field" of judgment appears. *Inherently transitional, rather than appropriative or territorial*, that "field," "ground" or "floor" that is really a "bridge" is the "passage" or "middle ground" we call "the aesthetic."[295]

Viewed, then, from the perspective of the power of judging, a way of perceiving that all sensuous perception carries with it as the arresting of cognition, a kind of outline or shifting shadow of all cognitive objects, the "unoverseeable gulf" between theoretical and practical reason – yawning abyss of potentially unbridgeable dualism – appears instead as a playground of unlimited dimensions, one whose furthest bound similarly cannot be seen. If anything defines this open field of pleasurable forms or painful "nonform" ("Unform"), it is certainly not a known, predetermined content: whether terrifying or pleasurable in effect, Kant's aesthetic "territory" is definitely not a theme park.[296] Exactly "because no definite concept limits them to a special rule of cognition" ("weil kein bestimmter Begriff sie auf eine besondere Erkenntnisregel einschränkt"), both the "free play" and violent conflict of the faculties brought about by the power of judgment occur on the most diverse, indeed conceptually contrary "ground[s]:" "irregular," "wasteful nature" no less than geometric pyramids; pyramids designed and built by man or amassed by nature

---

295. Kant, *KU*, B 29, X:132.
296. Kant, *KU*, B XLIX, X:103.

from heaps of ice; the ocean at rest, the ocean roiled in storm, as well as the individual seashells it turns up; the massive built interior of St. Peter's, the natural external shapes of individual birds and flowers no less than the repetitive delineation of the latter on decorative "wallpaper" ("Papiertapeten").[297] The undefined "realm" of judgment that extends to all these equally is and remains genuinely unknown "territory," a veritable wilderness in which the singular and the commonplace, imposing and gratuitous, "purposive" and "formless" all appear to the mind very much as they do in Kant's unprecedented analysis: unanticipated, logically and hierarchically unsubordinated, neither "high," nor "low," but side by side.[298] When it comes to the pleasurable "free play" (or painful "conflict") of judgment, in other words, you can't tell the players by the scorecard. There *are* players – understanding, imagination, and reason – but no scorecard: no rules predetermine the play of the mind, no concept designates knowledge of an object the mind affords. Instead of these there is something Kant calls "universal communicability" ("allgemeine Mitteilbarkeit"), simply, the "communicability" "of a feeling" ("eines Gefühls") that one senses is not proper to one's self alone.[299] Personal taste and preferences are well and good, Kant suggests: *chacun à son goût* he would be the first to agree. Yet it is precisely one's personal predilection, approbation, or "taste," what one might "wish" or not wish for oneself, that is *not* at issue in judgment as he defines it and which he distinguishes plainly from such individual views as follows: "If someone asks me whether I find the palace which I see before me beautiful, so may I very well say: I don't like that kind of thing that is made merely for the sake of ostentation ... One can grant me all this and endorse it; only it just so happens that this is not what we are talking about now" ("nur davon ist jetzt nicht die Rede").[300] Independently of whether one or any one of us "like[s] that kind of thing," the "universal communicability" that alone defines the power that is judgment is based on what Kant calls "common sense" ("Gemeinsinn"), a notion whose prominent, indeed controversial role in recent reception of the *Critique of Judgment* belies the understated, entirely heterodox basis of its self-evidence for Kant.[301] For, given the

297. Kant, *KU*, B 29, X: 132; B 72, X: 163; B 88–89, X: 174; B 95, X: 179, B 119, X: 196; B 49, X: 146.

298. Kant, *KU*, B 133, X: 208.

299. Kant, *KU*, *B* 66, X: 158.

300. Kant, *KU*, B 6–7, X: 116–117.

301. Along with Schiller's pivotal translation of Kantian aesthetic "play" into political life, no other notion is as central to Habermas's post-Kantian formulation of "communicative action" in liberal society, which makes the linguistic "communicability" of "sense" in a commonly shared public sphere (a concept literalized in early modern English-language communities by the delineation of a central "village, "town" or "city commons") its guiding theoretical principle. Nor may any notion be more objectionable to social and aesthetic theorists whose avowed political aim takes exception to the notion of the unexceptional (as reflective of a *status quo* that any participation in "communicative activity" is supposed to reify). As analyzed in *Words' Worth*, the complementary study to this exposition of Kant's

universality of the only possible mode of cognition theorized in his First Critique, that of representations of sensory perceptions linked *a priori* by the formal syntax of logical categories and delimited by the *a priori* synthetic forms of time and space, the "power to judge" defined in the Third as arising with the perception of a sensory but nonrepresentational, noncognitive form, or even *Unform* or nonform, would, by extension, be no less impersonal, commonplace or general. Indeed, logically rather than ideologically speaking, the kind of power constituted by a "common sense" *not of sensation but articulation* – and with articulation, of its own "communicability" – would be no less "common," by necessity, than the very abilities "to imagine and to understand" whose "free play" compose the act of judging (the "beautiful") in the first place.[302] For by "judgment" Kant means not the ability to produce a specific content or meaning capable of subordinating imagination to understanding, but, precisely, *to imagine at the same time one perceives,* and so to "feel" something in view of some unknown thing that brings these two activities into semantic suspension, whether in violent, cognitively irresolvable conflicts of the kind experienced in perceiving objects we judge "sublime," or in the pleasurably unresolving, noncognitive "free play of intellectual faculties" ("freies Spiel der Erkenntnisvermögen"[303]) defining our experience of objects we judge "beautiful."

It is here, in the context of "common sense," that Kant's talk of "wallpaper"[304] – in itself a perfectly apt and perfectly inconsequential example of an occasion for judgment to come into play – instead appears, when compared with another sensory form it resembles, especially theoretically telling. For, if it is generally true that genuinely philosophical inquiry finds no object or circumstance unworthy of reflection, Kant alone may possess the lack of philosophical prejudice necessary to make the experience of inherently superfluous wall coverings critically reflective

---

poetics of judgment, the exclusive "use" of the "common" and "prosaic" "language really used by men" that Wordsworth identifies with any poetry "worthy of the name," in also aligning language with history by identifying it as, rather than opposing it to action, comes closer to Kant's inherently modern theory of judgment not as consensus-driven but "grounded" *a priori* on a distinctly social "condition" than either its Habermasian or anti-Habermasian progeny. See Jürgen Habermas, *Theorie des kommunikativen Handelns* 2 Bde. (Frankfurt: Suhrkamp, 1981), in which Habermas's inaugural opposition of a communicative "lifeworld" to the objectification of life by rational functionalism anticipates his focus, in *Der philosophische Diskurs der Moderne* (Frankfurt: Sukrhamp, 1985; see pp. 294–367, esp.), on "subject-centered reason" over "systems-rationality" and the "possibility of a consensus" in the "the making of meaning" reached through "processes of mutual understanding" carried out in "public" and "private" "everyday life." See also Habermas's trenchant critique of Luhmann's "prelinguistic" definition of "meaning" as "identical significations" made "present" "autocatalytically," i.e. without need for verbal communication let alone interpretation, within both "psychic" and "emergent social systems" (*Diskurs*, pp. 369–385).

302. Kant, *KU,* B 29, X: 132
303. Ibid.
304. Ibid., B 49, X: 146.

of the pivotal power of a philosophical system. Without implicitly commending a holistic *Bauhaus* aesthetic, nor, for that matter, the purposefully capricious aesthetics of Dada (even if, in historical fact, he may have presaged them both), Kant indicates by way of this banal example not a human propensity for the *heimlich* and all forms of home decoration but the indispensable and undelimitable bases of a defining and positively *unheimlich* capacity for moral action. For Kant considers the free pattern of decorative wallpaper as yet another "territory" to which judgment extends, but excludes from the "realm" of judgment just such a pattern when it adorns a covering of another object and kind, one whose very existence, while just as sensuous and even pleasurable, is not decorative but instead vitally necessary to the "subject" – in both senses of the word – of the *Critique* itself. Kant denies that the free, dynamic forms delineated on wall coverings may similarly be judged beautiful when rendered inextricable from the merest phenomenal appearance of the agency whose freedom from phenomenality it is the central aim of *Critique* to constate: when engraved, that is, in human skin. The curving shapes of "tattoos" could be judged just as beautiful as decorative wallpaper, Kant goes on to state, if only the canvas used for their delineation "were not a human being" ("wenn es nur nicht ein Mensch wäre").[305] And it is here that Kant's singularly iconoclastic analysis of specifically aesthetic judgment recalls another analysis of judgment – not of the aesthetic but of actions – considered immoral in its day for the very reason that, instead of confusing judgment either with cognition or with moral prescriptions, it based itself instead in the analytic terms of Kant's Third Critique.

---

305. Kant, *KU,* B 50, X: 147.

2. Judgment and "Indifference:" the "Common Sense" of Imagination in Arendt and Kant

In *Eichmann in Jerusalem. A Report on the Banality of Evil* (published first in installments in the *The New Yorker*, then in book form in 1963), Hannah Arendt characterized Adolf Eichmann as a man who lacked all imagination. In her report on Eichmann's testimony she termed the "evil" resulting from that lack "banal," thus consigning herself along with her subject to a codetermining reputation for infamy (the more in excess of the imaginable the actions of the one, the more in default of the morally acceptable, the attribution of these acts to an absence of imagination, on the part of the other). Yet, while the consequences of Eichmann's actions at every level and in every realm of human activity – empirical and intellectual, individual and social, political and jurisprudential, scientific and cultural, historical, actual, and potential, to name some of the most obvious – were and remain ultimately inestimable in their ongoing effects, it is not their incalculable outcome but their immediate basis that Arendt describes. While widely rejected in favor of the more reassuring view of Eichmann as an exceptionally and inexplicably evil individual, and all condemnation of his actions as unexceptionably good, such views, Arendt's analysis implies, might themselves be more, rather than less in agreement with the exceptionally programmatic nature of those actions, in that such a program relies, in the first place, on the negation of an unexceptional, or commonsensical, sense of humanity. Rather than a "'monster,'" Eichmann, she states, is a "clown," an undistinguished person in every way whose lack of even basic commonsensical intelligence impeded him from completing either a secondary or elementary trade school course of education; whose combination of baseless, apparently compensatory vanity with a self-evident sense of personal deficiency exhibited publicly in an insistently "bragging" "clownishness," testified above all to his fear of being considered a nobody, and feeling, not only of no regret for manufacturing the mass death of entire international populations – according to transnational categories his own self-appointed group identified or "selected" for extinction *within* nations – but that he himself (unself-ironically) could not "live without being a member of something or other."[306] While boasting of an intelligence he did not possess, Eichmann, for Arendt, demonstrated most obviously the glaring absence of any at all by lacking the elementary "common sense" required to recognize the nonsensical nature of

---

306. Hannah Arendt, *Eichmann in Jerusalem. A Report on the Banality of Evil* (NY: Viking, 1963), p. 55.

any "objective" policy of genocide, i.e., one whose aim and object, in "peacetime" as in "wartime," is the negation by people of "a" people among people – i.e., a policy of abysmal self-contradiction that must destroy *all* it touches.

Just as Arendt views Eichmann's platitudinous testimony as the stuff of banality, for there to be moral action, rather than universalist platitudes regarding particular "moral problems" ("the Jewish problem," the problems of "deviancy" and "Bolshevism" then; the problems of "the poor," "'alien'" and "'undocumented'" now) we *must at least* (in Kant's terms) "*be able to think*" and, *in thinking*, understand that what Eichmann was unable to imagine was itself in no way extraordinary. For Eichmann, in order not to be nobody, there had to be nobody that was not Eichmann, or, just the same, nobody defined as not to belong, by its own definition, to the group to which he, Eichmann, was only too pleased to belong, and thus genocide was merely the attainment of a positive object so defined. The "solution" to a so-called "problem" – that of non-identity within identity of any kind – objectified, anthropomorphized, and classified as such, necessitated not only its own purely physical objectification and thus relentlessly *spatial* modes of "finalization" (external labeling, first of garments, then of human bodies themselves; spatial tracking, corporal removal and public "round-ups" of human beings for the purpose of segregating, ghetto-izing, shipping and spatially "concentrating" their bodies within spaces created for their on-site extermination, cremation and ejection into space itself), but an evacuation of every mental action other than identification itself based on the identification of identity with space (viz. "Lebensraum"). As much as the achievement of an *ad hoc* material or ideological benefit of any practical kind, the annihilation of whatever was defined as the outside that this identification required aimed equally to annihilate, through purely physical, corporal means, perhaps the most *commonsensical* of all metaphysical principles: that of the impossibility of fully identifying – and so spatially conflating – the particular and the general.

For the same reason that his "clownish" inflation of identity included "no room" within it for the most commonsensical conception of the general, Eichmann's "evil" was so "banal" as to lack all common sense of violence, of a commonality, in the literal sense of common to all, *not* based in the unrelenting production of exclusion and death. For the realm to which Eichmann's understanding did not extend was, for all beings endowed with understanding *and* imagination, the most ordinary, indeed, the most commonsensical: that of the perception by human beings of other human beings among them. Incapable of imagining another like him who, at the same time, is not him, which is to say, incapable of "think[ing] from the standpoint of somebody else," Eichmann, while fully conscious of his actions, was not only fully unperturbed by, indeed proud of what he did, conceived, and ordered to have done to others: he demonstrated himself just as unable to reflect on those actions as to understand and so judge them, and himself, in the very sense that understanding requires imagination for judgment.[307] Arendt never questioned the judging of Eichmann. Indeed, she issues an unequivocal critique, unequalled among philosophical assessments of judgment and undiminished in contemporary significance, of the failure to judge

307. *Ibid.*, p. 49.

individuals as a failure to judge whatsoever. She criticizes the German Protestant Church for publicly identifying the basis of its own retrospective admission of "guilt" as a failure of "mercy" piously granted *in exchange for evil*, rather than of morally acknowledging, let alone seeking "justice" *for the innocent*, and mocks the popular "public opinion" that only groups and not individuals may be judged, precisely for the reason that "an indictment of all Christianity" or, for that matter, as so often self-defeatingly asserted, of "'*mankind* as a whole'," can never be "proven" and thus no judgment ever formed. Responding to the strategic, permanently applicable miscue of deference to "'the God of Mercy'" perversely "aver[red]" in the "postwar statement of the *Evangelische Kirche in Deutschland*," she writes:

> It seems to me that a Christian is guilty before the God of *Mercy* if he repays evil with evil, hence that the churches would have sinned against mercy if millions of Jews had been killed as punishment for some evil they committed. But if the churches shared in the guilt for an outrage pure and simple, as they themselves attest, then the matter must still be considered to fall within the purview of the God of *Justice*.
>
> This slip of the tongue [substituting mercy for justice], as it were, is no accident. Justice, but not mercy, is a matter of judgment, and about nothing does public opinion everywhere seem to be in happier agreement than that no one has the right to judge somebody else. What public opinion permits us to judge and even to condemn are trends, or whole groups of people – the larger the better – in short, something so general that distinctions can no longer be made, names can no longer be named. Needless to add, this taboo applies doubly when the deeds or words of famous people or men in high position are being questioned. This is currently expressed in high-flown assertions that it is "superficial" to insist on details and to mention individuals, whereas it is the sign of sophistication to speak in generalities according to which all cats are gray and we are all equally guilty ... The charge against Christianity in general, with its two thousand years of history, cannot be proved, and if it could be proved, it would be horrible. No one seems to mind this so long as no *person* is involved....[308]

In contrast with public "opinion," Arendt makes as clear as Kant does that the exercise of the "power of judging" judges, in each instance, an individual, nonsubsumable object or event, a singularity in that, by definition, it is unsubordinated to general conceptualizations, unknown. Insisting that Eichmann, the individual, be judged, she also insists, in similarly Kantian mode, that to judge any object is to apply one's understanding and imagination to the individual phenomenon or "case" one perceives before one. In the case of Eichmann this means precisely to attend to, rather than gloss over or ascribe to any general conception the "details" of individual actions, and to listen with the attention of the unpreconceiving to the individual words composing the verbal actions that are his

---

308. *Ibid.*, pp. 296–97.

testimony, the extraordinary convention according to which acts performed in language are judged alongside matters of fact, with the weight of law.[309]

Arendt does not hesitate to draw the stark consequence of such an individually based analytic judgment when it comes to Eichmann in particular. For, to employ understanding with imagination so as to *judge* rather than pre-judge him, to relate the words with which Eichmann describes and accounts for his actions to those actions themselves, was to judge someone, who, by evidence of those words, was entirely devoid of the capacity for judgment, someone in whom the linchpin that is that power is lacking, in whom the abyss between cognition and moral action thus gaped unfathomably, never to be spanned. Up to and including "the grotesque silliness of his last words" – "'After a short while, gentlemen, *we shall all meet again*'" – Eichmann demonstrated *not* that the "evil" of his actions was commonplace, but that his own *inability to judge* those actions led inexorably to his own open, ongoing embrace of – and equation of evil with – "banality."[310]

It is for this reason that, quite apart from what others may think of his actions, what *Eichmann* thought about his actions could never be communicated by him, not because his views were so heinous as to be unutterable but because, at the time of those actions and in all the time succeeding them, what he thought – if he thought – of them remained in the realm of the merely material, void of content, because incapable of grasping any distinction or other than rote relation between meaning and verbal form, let alone moral distinction between action and mechanics. Contrary to the assumptions of the judges at his trial, Eichmann's apparently "'empty talk,'" Arendt suggests, rather than "feigned," was indeed empty in truth, through and through; his very real "inability to *think*" made him "genuinely incapable of uttering a single sentence that was not a cliché."[311] By speaking about the nearly unimaginable in "clichés" alone, Eichmann, Arendt argues, is not concealing his own private thoughts but making manifest, in the public form of sworn testimony, an "inability to speak" "closely connected with an inability to *think*" in the first place, the same inability that had made the actions he conceived and served seamlessly feasible for him, and now made him view himself, insofar as his own person was assigned any individual responsibility for those actions, as subject not to public judgment but to his own, merely personal misfortune, that of having "'had no luck.'"[312]

That Eichmann could not imagine or understand the extraordinary content of his acts, found entirely ordinary their equation of humanity with insensate materiality, remained as unimaginable to those present at his trial as it did to the many readers whom Arendt's report from Jerusalem appalled. Yet even this is

---

309. See Austin's reference to his own debt to Kant in arguing, in his inaugural theory of performative speech, for the particular performativity of "'ethical propositions'" and that "Accuracy and morality alike are on the side of the plain saying that *our word is our bond*," in *How to Do Things with Words*, pp. 2–3, 12.

310. Arendt, *Eichmann*, p. 252.

311. *Ibid.*, p. 48–49.

312. *Ibid.*, p. 175.

so because the imagination required of Eichmann was – and herein lies Arendt's underlying, and indisputable, point – *not* exceptional but, rather, itself banal. It was neither an extraordinary personal disposition, but rather the absence of an ability of relative banality, which made Eichmann in action, and thus, in fact, "a monster."[313] For it was not an unknown form of life, the esoteric, unencountered or extraterrestrial, but the most readily imaginable, commonest quality available to judgment, the being human of other human beings, that Eichmann could neither imagine, nor understand, nor feel in life, and so could not communicate in word or action. The being human of other human beings was the undefined "object" of judgment for which this subject of judgment possessed no language, knew or encountered no words that were not clichéd banalities, which is to say, no words that communicated anything to anyone, including Eichmann himself. So monstrous, Arendt argues, is the absence of all commonplace imagination that it eradicates the understanding conveyed by words as well as deeds in any but a strictly mechanical sense. So monstrous indeed, we may argue, is the extraordinary lack of the ordinary, the total inability to see someone not yourself as some one, to imagine, that is, *not* the extraordinary but rather the *ordinary* otherness of others, that it replaces the "purpose-free" "common sense" perceptions on which imagination depends with the purposeful coventionalization of the extraordinary, its conversion to a "norm" by the very words used to speak of it: the invented euphemisms of a so-called "technical" terminology whose concrete meaning and moral or practical consequences are inevitably expressed in time-worn cliché. Only in the absence of the ordinary, Arendt argues, can the total objectification, or dehumanization, of the human into pure materiality be conceived of as ordinary, as "business" (including "the business of war") "as usual," as if, to all intents and purposes – to quote Kant, writing of the human body employed as material canvas – "it were not a human being" ("... nicht ein Mensch wäre") upon whom one acted and of whom one spoke; "as if only" ("wenn es nur ...") a human being were not one.

For, Kant's (remarkably commonsensical) argument goes, unlike wall coverings and all purely decorative surfaces whose appearance to the eye can serve no purpose but to please and engage the mind in free play, the superficies of human beings is never pure of its telos, the purpose of enabling and sustaining individual life. Thus it is that, unlike the decoration of a wall that has never lived, the tattooing of human beings, in crossing the line between judgment and practice, between an undefined "field" of aesthetic "objects" and the fully self-defining realm of the "free" "subject," may come to serve the opposite purpose of reducing individual life to mere material givenness, i.e., to the surface of a foreign corporality lacking any imaginable, and thus conceivable, interiority. Furthermore, such conflations of subjects with objects to the point of nondistinction can and will mirror themselves, as mere surfaces, infinitely, so that total objectification (among which, the

---

313. *Ibid.*, p. 246: "'I am not the monster I am made out to be,' Eichmann said, 'I am the victim of a fallacy';" cf. pp. 276, 288.

routinized slaughterhouse tattooing of humans) may be used, in turn, to mark numerically the otherwise undistinguished living, thereby facilitating their final conversion into corpses, the ultimately indistinguished dead. And thus it is that human exteriority used by any subject as if merely another among its possible objects – another canvas to delineate or mark at will, a truly ineluctable medium of décor – may find its logical extension in the implementation of the skin of others for home furnishings, the absolute subversion of the non-subordinating "power" of judgment into a unilateral expression of totalizing utilitarianism, a monstrous conflation of cognitive limits with unlimited practices from which no object and no subject is free. This is the monstrousness of viewing and using all superficies as one, and of reducing all things to superficies as if materiality were everything, or, rather, things were "everything," and formative actions of any kind, from perception, to cognition, to feeling, to judgment, to the active constructions of "real things" (including unpredetermined events) from "no-thing" – in short, history – never indeed occur, or, in Kant's words, as if in sense perception and all the actions relating to it, there were never "anything that there appeared."[314]

Eichmann's inability to imagine any other *is* monstrous in that, along with actual, phenomenal perception, it cuts judgment quite out of the picture, thereby conflating the very ability to reason with "solution"-driven practicality, perverting by leaving no gap between Kant's First and Second Critique. What Arendt recognized was that while Eichmann's trial and testimony did not and could never indicate what "pure" "evil" looked and sounded like in human form, they did indicate that monstrosity, in the form of the failure to perform the simplest act of imagination, may indeed take the form (words and persona) of a banal bookkeeper or file clerk, "information" "processor" or bureaucrat, and that the result of such an absolute lack of imagination must be *the absolute inability to judge any object or action* in a manner neither sanctioned nor prohibited by pre-existing law or belief – an inability which, before Kant, may have seemed of no real consequence in itself, a matter either of personal disposition or "aesthetics" alone. In analyzing Eichmann's "banality," the real depth of his self-evident superficiality, Arendt thus effectively reveals the hidden radicality of judgment in Kant, the way in which the inability to imagine, and thus to judge, that which it is easiest to imagine and to judge, results not in a momentary lapse of mind or manners but in a lack unable even to conceive of itself as such, a truly unbridgeable chasm dividing delimited knowledge from moral action and language from that which language alone can

---

314. "At the same time ... it will be maintained, that we must at least be able *to think*, if not *to know*, these same objects also as things in themselves. Otherwise there would follow the principle without rhyme or reason, that an appearance were without something which there appears" ("Gleichwohl wird ... doch dabei immer vorbehalten, dass wir eben dieselben Gegenstände auch als Dinge an sich selbst, wenn gleich nicht erkennen, doch wenigstens müssen denken können. Denn sonst würde der ungereimte Satz daraus folgen, dass Erscheinung ohne etwas wäre, was da erscheint") (Kant, *KrV* B XXVI–XXVVII, III:30–31).

communicate, the commonplace combination of sensory imagination and understanding constituting the unsuspected depths of *common* sense.

These comments may appear to take Kant's seemingly frivolous reflections on wallpaper far afield. Yet it was the seeming frivolity, the lack of seriousness attributed to Arendt's analysis of Eichmann as a being void of any and all imagination that can begin to indicate the real extent of the wilderness that is the territory of judgment in Kant. For even its partial qualification as "aesthetic" proves insufficient to contain and domesticate – if not, indeed, as further evidence of – that wilderness itself. In a little-remarked comment in the preliminary version of the Introduction to the Third Critique, Kant notes that the "expression of an aesthetic mode of presentation always remains unavoidably ambiguous" ("Es bleibt also immer eine unvermeidliche Zweideutigkeit in dem Ausdrucke einer ästhetischen Vorstellungsart") in that the term, "aesthetic," may be used, so to speak, "generically," to denote any and every sense perception of an object issuing in a cognition, or, as it is the burden of his Third Critique to argue, it may instead be limited in meaning to specific experiences of feeling (pleasure or displeasure) in the act of perceiving an unknown object, experiences of a subject rendered "communicable" with and "for every" subject by their third-person articulation in the "general voice" of the verbal judgment of an object. In a side commentary later re-enacted nearly *verbatim* by Saussure with reference to the enduring ambiguity of the term, "sign," and preceded by Lessing's analogous note in *Laokoon* regarding the misleading use of the single German term, "Gemälde" to refer equally to "poetic" and "material paintings," Kant both remarks on the practical "ambiguity" of the term, "aesthetic," and states his *Critique of Judgment* will continue to employ it, due to a want not of intellectual clarity regarding what his *Critique* means to say but of the verbal means available with which to say it: "because we lack another expression" ("weil uns ein anderer Ausdruck mangelt").[315] Rather than invent a neologism, Kant (like Lessing and Saussure) retains a single common term whose ambiguity in context compels the encounter with its critical function again and again.

In his "Transcendental Aesthetic," foundational First Part of the First Critique, Kant indeed uses "aesthetic" in its pre-modern, exclusively perceptual sense, overtly criticizes Baumgarten's modern (in Kant's words, "German") confusion of the "beautiful" defined in "aesthetic" treatises with the rule-derived, aesthetic (i.e., sensory) objects of a cognitive "science," and, noting the "lack" of "another expression" for that inherently "ambigu[ous]" term, suggests that the central operative concept (and its respective "faculty" or "power") at the basis of his

---

315. See Kant, *KrV* B 36, III: 70n, for Kant's critique of Baumgarten and suggested division of the term "aesthetic" into separate "transcendental" and "psychological" (or perceptual-cognitive) "sense[s] or "meaning[s];" on the "ambigu[ity]" of the term see also Kant, *KU*, X: 35. See Saussure, *Cours*, p. 99; see Lessing, *Laokoon*, Chapter XIV, and Chap. XIV, note 1, in G. E. Lessing, *Werke*, 5 vols. (Berlin: Aufbau Verlag, 1978), III: 242, 242n.

Critique performs a double duty as well.[316] For, just as "aesthetic" is shown immediately in the "Transcendental Aesthetic" to pertain not only to the judgment of the beautiful and the sublime, so the "power of judgment" is shown from the very outset of the *Critique* to pertain not only to the aesthetic. In the Preface to the first edition of the First Critique, Kant gives a brief outline of the recent history of "metaphysics," "queen of all the sciences." That history leads from "despotic" dogmatists, to "nomadic" "skeptics," to the "physiology" of Locke, whose fatefully mistaken ascription to metaphysics of a genesis from physical experience alone (at least on Kant's account) "would have had rightfully to become suspect" ("mit Recht hätte verdächtig werden müssen"), since the very conception of such a "genealogy was in fact falsely fictionalized onto [metaphysics]" ("weil diese Genealogie ihr in der Tat fälschlich angedichtet war").[317] The fall of empiricism gave rise, Kant continues, to apparent "indifference" toward metaphysics on the whole, and it is this very moment, when a "falsifying fictionalization" of its "genesis" is said to make metaphysics seem an object of least intellectual interest, or "indifference," that Kant recasts as the *intervention of "judgment" into "fictionalization"* (or "mere seeming knowledge") and basis of the reinvention of metaphysics his *Critique* is about to undertake:

> This indifference is, however ... a phenomenon, which deserves attention and reflection. It is obviously not the effect of frivolity or unseriousness but rather that of the mature *power of judgment** of the age, which no longer lets itself be taken in by mere seeming knowledge, and it is a challenge to reason to take upon itself the most difficult of all its occupations anew, namely that of self-knowledge, and to set up a court of law which would ensure it in its justified claims, just as, by contrast, it would allow it to dispatch readily with all groundless pretentions not through pronouncements of power but according to its eternal and unchangeable laws, and this is none other than *the Critique of Pure Reason*.
>
> [Indessen ist diese Gleichgültigkeit ... doch ein Phänomen, das Aufmerksamkeit und Nachsinnen verdient. Sie ist offenbar die Wirkung nicht des Leichtsinns, sondern der gereiften *Urteilskraft** des Zeitalters, welches sich nicht länger durch Scheinwissen hinhalten last, und eine Aufforderung an die Vernunft, das beschwerlichste aller ihrer Geschäfte, nämlich das der Selbsterkenntnis aufs

---

316. Kant, *KrV*, B 36, III: 70n; *KU*, X: 35: "There always remains therefore an unavoidable ambiguity in the expression of an aesthetic mode of mental presentation, when, on the hand, one understands it to refer to something that excites a feeling of pleasure or pain, and, on the other, to refer to our basic cognitive faculty insofar as it is the sensory perception that allows us to cognize objects as appearances" ("Es bleibt also immer eine unvermeidliche Zweideutigkeit in dem Ausdrucke einer ästhetischen Vorstellungsart, wenn man darunter bald diejenige versteht, welche das Gefühl der Lust und Unlust erregt, bald diejenige, welche bloss as Erkenntnisvermögen angeht, sofern darin sinnliche Anschauung angetroffen wird, die uns die Gegenstände nur als Erscheinungen erkennen lässt.)
317. Kant, *KrV*, A X, III: 12.

neue zu übernehmen und einen Gerichtshoff einzusetzen, der sie bei ihren gerechten Ansprüchen sichere, dagegen aber alle grundlose Anmassungen, nicht durch Machtsprüche, sondern nach ihren ewigen und unwandelbaren Gesetzen, abfertigen könne, und dieser ist kein anderer als *die Kritik der reinen Vernunft selbst*.[318]]

A footnote denoted by an asterisk follows immediately upon this first naming of the "power of judgment" within the tripartite *Critique*, a verbal account of judgment occurring not in the last and Third Critique named for it but, rather, in the inaugural *Critique of Pure Reason*. In the text of that footnote Kant contests contemporary "complaints" ("Klagen") about the inadequacy of the "mode of thinking" ("Denkungsart") of "our time" ("unser Zeitalter") by turning them on their head, stating that "indifference" and "doubt" ("Zweifel") are "rather proofs" of the exercise of an "exacting mode of thinking" ("vielmehr Beweise einer gründlichen Denkungsart").[319] Apparent "indifference" is thus the ambivalent, at once positive and negative indication of a "mode of thinking" that has no positive mode of expression of its own, but through which, "and finally" ("und, endlich") following from which, "strict critique" ("strenge Kritik") can first occur.[320] Thus it is in the context of a footnote not to contemporary polemics but to a negatively expressive "indifference" to these, a "mode of thinking" he has called, for the first time, "the power of judgment," that Kant names, also for the first time, the "age" or "time" to which that "power" properly pertains. The next sentence in this footnote, relating "the power of judgment" to an "indifference" to current, falsely premised debates, categorically states: "Our age [or time] is the actual [or proper] age of Critique" ("Unser Zeitalter ist das eigentliche Zeitalter der Kritik"[321]). "The power of judgment" that takes the form of "indifference" in the face of "falsifying fictionalization" is interpreted *critically* by Kant to indicate the "actual[ity]" at "our" or any apparently "indifferent" "time" of the activity that is "critique." This "Phänomen" of seeming "indifference" to "mere seeming knowledge" is not only appropriate to, but indeed definitive of what Kant calls "our age," or "time," which is to say, every "time" in which the "phenomenon" of "indifference" is neither "frivolous" nor "unserious" but the expression of the positive discovery of a negative: that which we are missing, or lack. For "indifference" may be the mere but no less necessary appearance of an already critical, intellectual distance, the "doubt" and "challenge to reason" we "must be able" to pose and undergo when, "indifferent" to the spell of metaphysical or empiricist fictions alike, we exercise in the present our "power of judgment," i.e., the power to critique, rather than merely adopt or discard, accounts of how and what we can know.

318. Kant, *KrV*, A X–XI, III: 12–13.
319. Kant, *KrV*, A X, III: 12.
320. *Ibid.*
321. Kant, *KrV,* A XI–XII, III: 13

Few accounts of the operation of judgment are more instructive of Arendt's. For, at work in her apparent indifference to the "monstrosity" of Eichmann was an analysis of the monstrousness of the inability underlying *his refusal to judge himself*, the absolute lack of "imagination" and "common sense" that rendered commonplace judgment perhaps the sole action of which he was and remained incapable, or to which, one might say, he took exception. "Genealogically" speaking, the indefensible "case" of Eichmann originates in that specifically nonsensorily generated lack. For the inability to "think from the standpoint of somebody else" that permitted Eichmann to "defend" himself as the "victim of a fallacy" and accuse his captors of a logical mistake was the same that allowed him both to act upon numberless other beings as he did and escape, in mind as in body, any and all sense of the content and consequences of his actions, even onto the final "cliché," declaiming the inescapable brevity of life, to which he sentenced his judges upon hearing himself sentenced to die for his inestimable crimes. Like Kant's introductory analysis of judgment enacted in the guise of apparent "indifference" (to philosophical "schools"), and its inverse, the seemingly incontrovertible, because apparently purely empirical evidence of guilt or innocence that works to preclude judgment and relegate language to the status of a mere formality (the same appearance of certainty contested in Kleist's "Duel," as analyzed in the next Chapter), Arendt's fundamentally "critical" account of Eichmann, in the "universal," specifically "Kantian," rather than (in her view, uninstructively) *ad hominem* sense of the term, renders the centrality of "imagination" to the capacity for "judgment" and of judgment to all human understanding and action conspicuous by demonstrating, in the most elemental terms, the truly unimaginable consequences of its apparently "banal" absence. In so doing, she more alarmingly reveals "the monstrous" as neither singular nor unimaginably foreign but as inhering in any state of mind to which the most common employment of "the power of imagination" – of seeing another neither as no one but yourself, nor as nothing – remains utterly foreign, and in which, as a result, "the power of judgment" plays no part.

Unlike a disastrous inability to judge, confused by its inherently delusional subject with a purely mechanical logical "fallacy," apparent "indifference" to falsifying accounts of cognition, whether these be of the "mystifying," "dogmatic," or "skeptical" "physiological" kind, "is" itself nothing less, Kant proposes, than the phenomenal appearance of a "power" that makes all the difference: not the power to know anything *per se* but to perform upon all knowledge what Kant calls, in the Second Preface to the First Critique, "a revolution in mode of thinking" ("eine Revolutions der Denkart"[322]). "The power of judgment," neither cognitive nor moral in itself, is not only the necessary link between these two distinct, strictly limited and strictly unlimited capabilities of reason, respectively, that Kant, for the first time in the history of philosophy, brings to independent expression and so enables us to think. It is also, as this, its initial appearance as a negative affect

---

322. Kant, *KrV*, B XI, III:22. See Chap. One, this study.

requiring interpretation, posits, the necessarily occluded origin of the critique that produces those distinct practices of reason themselves.

"Judgment," that "power" without a "realm proper" or "objects of its own," may be nothing less than the "phenomenon" constituting the perceptible aspect, or "mode," of "thinking" ("Art des Denkens," "Denkungsart") for Kant, the appearance of an ability and activity that themselves know no critical bounds. For, while empirical knowledge must be mediated by formal limits if it is to be unassailable by doubt, "I can *think* what I *will*" ("aber denken kann ich was ich will"[323]), Kant asserts, in the same sense that, in the Second Critique, we "can" "will" ourselves the ability to act in "freedom" from the limits of self-interest, or morally. The power of judgment to articulate a "feeling" arising in the perception of an unknown object as a predication of that object, *rather than a personal feeling* – an impersonal, inherently "communicable" statement "free" of qualification other than the "condition" of communicability Kant calls "common sense" – may also be the power to perceive *as illusion* ("Scheinwissen") all "metaphysical" equations of knowledge with immaterial "Forms," no less than all exclusively sense-based negations of the possibility of forming any knowledge, or indeed of undergoing any experience, at all. Even before being submitted to "critique," the "power," rather than "reason," of "judgment" appears here, at the very outset of Kant's project, as a "mode of thinking" and therein articulating not only the "aesthetic" "forms" and "nonforms" of the beautiful and sublime, but the "forms" and "nonforms" of "thinking" that are the aesthetic appearance and articulation of "critique" whose defining "mode" and moment are "our" "own." For, the mode of professed indifference to falsifying intellectual fictions proves to be not so much misleading as a refusal to give itself, its own real difference, away: an impersonally "communicable" appearance of thinking, or critical "phenomenon," that Kant "expresses" as judgment in action.

---

323. Kant, *KrV*, B XXVIII, III: 31.

3. The Schema and the Language of Poetry

Subreption: [Hidden snatching]: the suppression of truth or facts with the view to acquiring a dispensation, a faculty; a false or misleading representation aimed at the acquisition of a power or faculty; a want of expression.

—*OED* [1971, II: 3125]

The activity Kant calls judgment is a power that lacks a proper object. Neither the phenomenal objects that are the limited representations of things as we perceive, conceive and know them, nor the noumenal object of the pure reason of moral action – the Good, "free" of personal interest, that is made rather than known – is the "objective field" or "realm" ("Feld der Gegenstände als sein Gebiet") that defines the exercise of judgment.[324] Directed toward no specific object or cognitive or moral purpose, judgment is at the same time the most "critical" power espoused in the *Critique*. Its very lack of an object-appropriate "reason" makes judgment both the necessary "middle link" ("Mittelglied") and "bridge" ("Übergang") between the First and Second Critiques and *the* subjective power or mental faculty without which, according to Kant, there could be no *Critique,* the "challenge to reason" whose undefined exercise defines its time as "our time," "the Age of Critique."[325]

Consisting either "in the free play of imagination and understanding" ("in dem freien Spiele der Einbildungskraft und des Verstandes"[326]) during the perception

---

324. Kant, *KU*, B XXII–XXIII, X: 85 (emphasis in text); see n.294, Section One, this Chapter.

325. Kant, *KU*, B VI, XXII, X: 85; *KU*, B XXI, X:84. In the *Logic*, Kant similarly attributes the genesis of all cognitive "error" [*Irrtum*] – as "difficult" in itself "to conceive" [*schwer zu begreifen*] as the "shying" of a "power from its own essential laws" ("wie irgend eine Kraft von ihren eigenen wesentlichen Gesetzen abweichen solle") – to the failure not to think, or to perceive, but "to judge:" "the basis for the arisal of all error ... must be sought, solely and alone, in the unnoticed influence of sensory perception upon understanding, or to speak more precisely, upon judgment. This influence, namely, brings us ... to mistakenly exchange the mere seeming appearance of truth for the truth itself" ("Der Entstehungsgrund alles Irrtums wird ... einzig und allein in dem unvermerkten Einflusse der Sinnlichkeit auf den Verstand, oder, genauer zu reden, auf das Urteil gesucht werden müssen. Dieser Einfluss nämlich macht, dass wir im Urteilen ... den blossen Schein der Wahrheit mit der Wahrheit selbst verwechseln") (*Logik* A 76, VI: 480).

326. Kant, *KU*, B 29, X: 132,

of the beautiful, or in the experience of "violence done to the imagination" ("gewalttätig für die Einbildungskraft"[327]) by "ideas of reason" exceeding "sensory form" in the perception of the sublime ("for the sublime proper cannot be contained in any sensory form but rather touches only upon ideas of reason" ["denn das eigentliche Erhabene kann in keiner sinnlichen Form enthalten sein, sondern trifft nur Ideen der Vernunft"[328]], judgment remains "actual," reaches no conclusion, nor could it. The free play of the senses and the mind, and violence done to the senses by the mind, entail instead "feelings" – of "pleasure and pain" ("Lust und Unlust"[329]) – that are, by definition, as unavailable to the architectonic laws of logic and phenomenal limits of representation that make cognition possible as to the self-legislating rule of freedom from all ruled cognition that instead makes possible moral action. Judgment has no "realm of its own" ("kein eigentümliches Gebiet") – what it perceives are not conceptual objects but forms or (in the sublime) their absence, "formlessness" ("Formlosigkeit") – and judgment, which is neither the knowing of some thing as it appears to us nor the doing of something in itself, similarly possesses no proper rules of exercise.[330] As such it is also singularly "indifferent," Kant writes, to the false claims or false representations that *have* ruled metaphysics, an indifference, however, that has the further effect of freeing the mind to think its own difference from givens. For, in grounding the power of judgment negatively, in "indifference" to past metaphysical (*or* anti-metaphysical, purely physiological) determinist precepts, Kant maintains the possibility of the subject's "will" to "think" critically, i.e., in independence from man-made and natural causality alike. It is to such "free" acts of the will whose possibility the entire project of the *Critique* aims at proving irrefutable, at deducing as no illusion but real, that no subject, in Kant's self-legislating sense of the term, can be "indifferent."

As thinking remains unprescribed by Kant, defined only as a function of the freedom that defines the will,[331] so judgment, that "Phänomen" that appears as the outer side of thinking, remains lacking in specific content even while

---

327. Kant, *KU*, B 76, X: 166.
328. Kant, *KU*, B 77, X: 166.
329. Kant, *KU,* B XXIII, X: 85.
330. Kant, *KU*, B XXI, X: 84; B 179, X: 168.

331. Kant may have been the first to pronounce the maxim, long both commonplace and disputed, "[The]will is free" ("[der] Wille sei frei"). However, unlike his innumerable successors, he did so while defining "the will" as only one among many, architectonically interrelated and delimited intellectual faculties, and logical and causal operations and functions, that are not "free" – self-defining or "pure" – but "applied" to the world, or, in the case of the "imagination *a priori,*" as discussed in this Chapter, to the "schema[tic]" "use" of the world. See Kant, *KU*, B XXVII, III: 31, *KrV* B 74–76, III: 97–78; see also *KrV* B 752–53, IV: 621; see also Chapter Two, Section Nine, this Study.

interacting with the world. Kant's "Analytic[s] of the Beautiful" and "the Sublime" break down received notions of aesthetic taste to arrive at a counter-definition of aesthetic judgment. Their step-by-step critique of taste affirms that judgment *is* what taste is *not*, i.e., equally independent of the transitory claims of private subjectivity and personal enjoyment, and supposedly impersonal and immutable pedagogic or religious goals and doctrines. Yet Kant's negative procedure leaves open the question of how, aside from the purely analytic definition of its constitutive qualities, this particular *power* can be said, positively, to work.

For, unlike knowledge constituted of delimited representations conjoined on the basis of categorical logical rules, and unlike those acts Kant calls the practical products of pure reason in that they are free to rule themselves, Kant's negative definition of judgment – as a faculty that follows no rules and has no proper realm of objects – directs itself as much against rules of taste as against prescriptions of aesthetic content. At once a "phenomenon" in itself and undetermined by either our cognition of, or pure freedom from, phenomenality, judgment is instead a *coordination* of faculties: of imagination and understanding in free play, or reason and imagination in conflict. The "power" of judgment – "meditating link" or "bridge" between the First and Second Critique – is thus, *in its own internal composition*, also such a bridge. For, understood in its function rather than as a spatial figure of unification, a "bridge" is a supplement enabling interactions between truly distinct givens whose outcomes it does not ensure. In Kant's tripartite *Critique*, those givens are the faculties of understanding, applied reason and sense-related imagination that compose cognitions as described in the *Critique of Pure Reason* or First Critique, and those of pure reason and a will "free" of all sensory self-interest, that, working together, engender moral action in the *Critique of Practical Reason* or Second Critique. Likewise, as Kant defines it, the "bridge," *Critique of Judgment* or mediating Third Critique between these, divides, with an eye to each side of the "abyss" it spans, into two interconnected halves: the "Analytic of the Beautiful" in which, rather than composing cognitions, understanding and imagination (acting in the absence of reason) engage each other in the "pleasurable" "free play" of "aesthetic" (rather than representational, cognitive) perceptions; and the "Analytic of the Sublime" in which sense-related imagination and the faculty of pure reason (acting in the absence of understanding) come into "painful," violent conflict. There is thus not one kind of aesthetic judgment, but two, just as there are separate, grounded terminations of every "bridge," across the countervailing forces of whose extension away from those groundings and toward one another the bridge itself is made, holds itself in place.

Similarly, rather than merely restating prescribed views of prescribed objects – and Kant's panoply of every such possible object makes clear that, when it comes to occasioning aesthetic judgment, for Kant (unlike any other theorist of the aesthetic of his time and well before the surrealists, hyperrealists, pop-artists, situationalists, conceptualists, installationists and performance artists of our own), *any object or "dynamic" appearance will do* – it is instead in allowing the interaction of the faculties to *play out* that we compose the statement judging an object to be "beautiful" or "sublime."[332] For, if judgment operated according to known rules and objects, it would constitute, in Kant's terms, a "grammar," rather the central mediating activity of the *Critique*.[333]

In its critical ability to coordinate rather than subordinate distinct intellectual capacities within us no less than to mediate between Kant's own structurally divided First and Second Critiques, the "power" of judgment fundamentally resembles the most essential, and enigmatic, of Kantian linkages or *Mittelglieder*, the "schema." As discussed in the preceding Chapter, the schema is introduced in the *Critique of Pure Reason* as the link that "must" necessarily join the two "heterogeneous" "sources" of cognition and their respective theoretical domains: the *a priori* or universal bases of sensory experience described in the "Transcendental Aesthetics" and the conceptual formalization of these analyzed in the "Transcendental Logic." But it is in the context of the analysis of aesthetic judgment in the Third Critique, and the particular practical examples Kant gives of imagination acting in freedom from cognition, that the workings of the "schema" come most clearly, if indirectly, into view.

Kant introduces the "Analytic of Basic Principles" of his "Transcendental Logic" with a discussion of the most principal among them, namely, that the rules of logic, while separate from, must be "united" with those governing our ability to perceive sensory objects:

---

332. Indeed, the closest proponent to Kant of the *necessarily* open field of judgment may be Mallarmé. In an acid denunciation of all official arbiters of taste written a century after the publication of the *Critique of Judgment*, Mallarmé critiqued the false appeal to "judgment" made by "juries" of the Salons so as to mask their exercise of a purely institutional power interested solely in censoring "systematically" all painting whose production they could neither understand nor control. Mallarmé notes that the only "mandate" of "judgment" free of such "bad faith" derives instead from "the public," "the multitude that demands to see with its own eyes," and who "with rare prescience, dubbed [these painters*] Intransigent, which in political language means radical and democratic" (*"les refusés" or "impressionist" artists denied admission to the Salons). The exercise of judgment, like that of the eye itself, according to Mallarmé, can never be appropriated and abrogated by officiating "bodies" empowered to decide for every other eye what it can and will see, but is rather an activity reserved for all such others, or the viewing "public" as such, whose right it is "to demand to see *everything there is*." Of the strategy of delaying the inevitable – the viewing, by all who wish to see it, of what "there is" – Mallarmé states presciently: "To gain a few years on M. Manet, what a sad [or pathetic] politics! ("Gagner quelques anneés sur M. Manet: triste politique!"). See Mallarmé, "The Impressionists and Edouard Manet" (first published in English, translated from the lost French original, in *The Art Monthly Review*, Sep. 1876) and "Le Jury de Peinture pour 1874 et M. Manet" (first published in "La Renaissance Artistique et Littéraire," 12 April 1874), both reprinted in their entirety in Penny Florence, *Mallarmé, Manet and Redon: Visual and Aural Signs and the Generation of Meaning* (Cambridge: Cambridge University Press), 1986, pp. 11–21.

333. Cf. Kant's comparison of the rule-governed parsing and organization of experience with a "grammar" in the *Prolegomena* (Kant, *Prolegomena* A 118, V: 192).

Our knowledge springs from two basic sources in the mind, the first of which is the faculty of receiving representations (the receptivity of impressions), the second, that of cognizing an object by way of these representations (the spontaneity of concepts); through the first, an object is *given* to us; through the second, it is *thought* in its relation to that representation (as mere determination of the mind). Perception and concepts thus make up the elements of all our knowledge, so that neither concepts without a perception that corresponds to them in some way, nor a perception without concepts, can constitute cognition....

Let us name the *receptivity* of our mind to receiving representations, insofar as it is in some way affected, *sensibility* [or sensory ability]; so is the contrary ability, to produce representations oneself, or the *spontaneity* of knowledge, *understanding*. Our nature is such that *perception* in us can never be other than *sensory*, i.e., it can only contain the mode in which we are affected by objects. By contrast, the faculty of *thinking* the object of a sensory perception is *understanding*. Neither of these inherent faculties is to be preferred to the other. Without the sensuous faculty no object would be given to us, and without understanding none would be thought. Thoughts without content are empty, [sensory] perceptions without concepts are blind ... Nor can these faculties, or capabilities, exchange their functions. The understanding senses nothing and the senses cannot think anything. Only in their uniting with each other can cognition arise. For this very reason we may not confuse their contributions, but rather have great cause to separate and distinguish the one from the other carefully. Thus we distinguish the science of the rules of sense perception in general, i.e., the Aesthetic, from the science of the rules of understanding in general, i.e., Logic.[334]

---

334. Kant, *KrV* B 74-77, III: 97-98: "Unsere Erkenntnis entspringt aus zwei Grundquellen des Gemüts, deren die erste ist, die Vorstellungen zu empfangen (die Rezeptivität der Eindrücke), die zweite das Vermögen, durch diese Vorstellungen, einen Gegenstand zu erkennen (Spontaneität der Begriffe); durch die erstere wird uns ein Gegenstand *gegeben*, durch die zweite wird dieser im Verhältnis und jene Vorstellung (als blosse Bestimmung des Gemüts) *gedacht*. Anschauung und Begriffe machen also die Elemente aller unserer Erkenntnis aus, so dass weder Begriffe, ohne ihnen auf einige Art korrespondierende Anschauung, noch Anschauung ohne Begriffe, ein Erkenntnis abgeben können.... Wollen wir die *Rezeptivität* unseres Gemüts, Vorstellungen zu empfangen, so fern es auf irgend eine Weise affiziert wird, *Sinnlichkeit* nennen: so ist dagegen das Vermögen, Vorstellungen selbst hervorzubringen, oder die *Spontaneität* des Erkenntnisses, der *Verstand*. Unsere Natur bringt es so mit sich, dass die *Anschauung* niemals anders als *sinnlich* sein kann, d. i. nur die Art enthält, wie wir von Gegenständen affiziert warden. Dagegen ist das Vermögen, den Gegenstand sinnlicher Anschauung zu *denken*, der *Verstand*. Keine dieser Eigenschaften ist der anderen vorzuziehen. Ohne Sinnlichkeit würde uns kein Gegenstand gegeben, und ohne Verstand keiner gedacht warden. Gedanken ohne Inhalt sind leer, Anschauungen ohne Begriffe sind blind ... Beide Vermögen, oder Fähigkeiten, können auch ihre Funktionen nicht vertauschen. Der Verstand vermag nichts anzuschauen, und die Sinne nichts zu denken. Nur daraus, dass sie sich vereinigen, kann Erkenntnis

The strict "separ[ation]" of our sensory "receptivity" from our "production" of "representations" "in relation" to "concepts" is both required by Kant's critical theory of cognition and requires its own mode of relation if knowledge based in the "function" of each is to "arise" from it. In the "Analysis of Principles" of the "Transcendental Analytic" that follows the expositions of the "Transcendental Aesthetic" and "Logic" (and precedes the analysis of scholastic "dialectics" as a "logic of mere seeming appearances" ["*Logik des Scheins*"] in the "Transcendental Dialectic"), Kant lists the three "higher intellectual faculties" – "Understanding, Power of Judgment and Reason" – delineated by the architectonic "plan" ("Grundrisse") upon which the "logic" of his *Critique* is "built" ("erbauet"), situating the subject of the *Third Critique* in second, mediating position.[335] He suggests the "designation," "a *Doctrine of Judgment*," serve to name the "canon" of logical "principles" that would "instruct" the "power of judgment" "to apply the concepts of understanding" "to [phenomenal] appearances," and attributes our ability to coordinate logic with perceptible sensuous objects to a "Transcendental Power of Judgment in General."[336] "Transcendental," here, it must be stressed, means not the exceptional but the universal; yet, "judgment," alone among the "higher faculties," is such a "transcendental power" that exceptions to it are not only evident to us but are themselves evidence of what Kant, most unusually, defines in a footnote as "what we call stupidity," an inability to discern even a single "case" "*in concreto*" to which a general rule of logic "*in abstracto*" applies:

> *The lack of the power of judgment is properly that which we call stupidity, and such an affliction cannot be helped. A dull or constricted mind only lacking in a proper level of understanding and concepts may well be outfitted through instruction, even to the point of learnedness. Yet since it is the wont of such persons to miss something there, too, so it is not uncommon to meet learned men who, in the use of their science, often betray the lack they will never ameliorate.
>
> [*Der Mangel an Urteilskraft ist eigentlich das, was man Dummheit nennt, und einen solchen Gebrechen ist gar nicht abzuhelfen. Ein stumpfer oder eingeschränkter Kopf, dem es an nichts, als an gehörigen Grade des Verstandes und eigenen Begriffen desselben mangelt, ist durch Erlernung sehr wohl, so gar bis zur Gelehrsamkeit, auszurüsten. Da es aber gemeiniglich alsdenn auch an jenem (der secunda Petri) zu fehlen pflegt, so ist es nichts Ungewöhnliches, sehr entspringen. Deswegen darf man aber doch nicht ihren Anteil vermischen, sondern man hat grosse Ursache, jedes von dem andern sorgfältig abzusondern, und zu unterscheiden. Daher unterscheiden wir die Wissenschaft der Regeln der Sinnlichkeit überhaupt, d. i. Ästhetik, von der Wissenschaft der Verstandesregeln überhaupt, d. i. der Logik.'

335. *Ibid.*, B 170, III: 183.
336. *Ibid.*, B 171, III: 184. See also Kant, *Logik* A 9, VI: 437: "Logic is thus more than mere critique: it is a canon which later serves critique, i.e., serves as principle for the judging of all uses of the understanding as such" ("Die Logik ist also mehr als blosse Kritik; sie ist ein Kanon, der nachher zur Kritik dient, d. h. zum Prinzip der Beurteilung alles Verstandesgebrauchs überhaupt").

gelehrte Männer anzutreffen, die, im Gebrauche ihrer Wissenschaft, jenen nie zu bessernden Mangel häufig blicken lassen."³³⁷]

Unlike the other, strictly cognitive "faculties," "the *power* of judgment" is at once "transcendental" *and* individual, in that it enables us to discern, rather than constitute, *a priori*, realizations of the "abstract" in the "concrete." Unlike the other "faculties," too, it is available but not given to every subject, and its absence results, to borrow Kant's own structural terms, in an "unbridgeable gulf" between the faculties themselves. Given his excursus on the "irremediable" "lack" of judgment no amount of instruction can conceal, the discussion of the so-called "Transcendental Doctrine" of judgment that follows his brief "Introduction" to "Transcendental Judgment in General" appears to represent just such a piece of "learned" "stupidity" on Kant's own part: a retreat from the concretely informative "power of judgment" to an abstract organization of categories and concepts of experience, which, as described in the preceding Chapter, Kant, repeating a *topos* of the mechanics of ancient metaphysics, entitles "schematism." The first section of the "Analytic of the Principles" of the "Transcendental Doctrine of Judgment" introduces the notion, adverse to the general critical principles entailed by Kant's "revolution" in metaphysics, of a "Schematism of Pure Conceptions of the Understanding" ("Von dem Schematismus der reinen Verstandesbegriffe") defined *not* by the production of "*a priori* synthetic judgments" whose "possibility" it is the central aim of the *Critique* to demonstrate,³³⁸ but by the contrary principle of conceptual subordination or "subsumption." The ground-laying discussion of the "schematism" particular to "the power of judgment" begins:

In all subsumptions of an object under a conception, the representation of the object must be homogeneous with the conception; in other words, the conception must contain that which is represented in the object to be subsumed under it, for that is precisely what the expression – an object is [or, is said to be: *sei*] contained under a concept – means. Thus is the empirical concept of a *plate* homogeneous with the pure geometrical concept of a *circle*, in that the rounding that is thought in the first can be intuited in the second.

[In allen Subsumtionen eines Gegenstandes unter einen Begriff muss die Vorstellung des ersteren mit der letztern gleichartig sein, d.i. der Begriff muss dasjenige enthalten, was in dem darunter zu subsumierenden Gegenstande vorgestellt wird, den das bedeutet eben der Ausdruck: ein Gegenstand sei unter einem Begriffe enthalten. So hat der empirische Begriff eines *Tellers* mit dem reinen geometrischen eines *Zirkels* Gleichartigkeit, indem die Rundung, die in dem ersteren gedacht wird, sich in letzteren lässt.³³⁹]

---

337. *Ibid.*, B 172–175, III: 184–86, "On the Transcendental Power of Judgment in General" ("Von der transzendentalen Urteilskraft überhaupt"); for the footnote defining "stupidity" as an "irremediable" "lack" of judgment, see B 173, III: 185n.
338. *Ibid*, *KrV*, B 20, III: 59.
339. *Ibid.*, *KrV*, B 176, III: 187.

"Judgment" and the Genesis of What We Lack 175

This introductory definition of "conceptual subsumption" as dependent ("muss") upon the homogeneity ("gleichartig sein") of the representation and conception of an object is offered as a self-evident rule of logic without further comment by Kant. The logical difficulty that both the principle of "subsumption" and Kant's exemplification of it in the "purely geometrical" and "empirical concept[s]" of "circle" and "plate" raise by implication, however, is that the "nominal," "discursive knowledge" defined by Kant as the "negative" product of the *Critique* can avail itself of none of the fully formal and thus "homogeneous" "principles" and "concepts" constitutive of "real" – "mathematical" or "moral" – knowledge and action, as these are described in Kant's *Logic*.[340] Whereas the rules of geometrical "construction"[341] determine, *a priori*, the very objects named by their "concepts," "the pure concepts of understanding," as Kant describes them in his expository *Prolegomena*, "serve only, so to speak, to spell out appearances, in order to render them legible as experience" ("die reine Verstandesbegriffe ... dienen gleichsam nur, Erscheinungen zu buchstabieren, um sie als Erfahrung lesen zu können").[342] Whereas geometers, in other words, need neither "spell" nor "read experience," in that the objects they describe are not first given to them, *a posteriori*, by the senses, but rather produced and governed, *a priori*, by the mathematical rules that define them, anyone aiming to describe "how" we "can read experience" in such a way as to constitute a coherent epistemology must grapple instead, as Descartes first made plain, with the necessary discursivity of – or "spelling of appearances" by – method.

Kant, who fully rejected purely nominal, conceptual syllogisms and all other scholastic techniques for "proving" foregone conclusions, knows that the "principle" he has just elaborated, that of the "contain[ment]" of an "object" by its "concept," is easier to stipulate than to demonstrate, easier said than done. Contrary to the principle of an *a priori* "homogeneity" between concept and object upon which a circularly constituted "subsumption" of empirical experience would have to depend, the central question for a specifically *critical* rather than syllogistic theory of understanding remains as it was, for Kant, to begin with: "how" is empirical knowledge, and thus, the "subsumption [of an object by a concept] possible?" How, that is, can logical conceptions and categories be rendered "homogeneous" with, and so "appli[ed]" properly to, sensuous perceptions and phenomenal representations defined as categorically different – in kind, source and mode of apprehension – from them in the first place? As quoted in Chapter Two, Section Nine, with regard to the origin or formation of language in general, but merits repeating here with regard to the "Analytics" of aesthetic judgment, and, as we shall see, to poetry in particular, Kant continues:

---

340. See Kant, *Logik*, §106, VI: 446, A 221–222, VI: 576; *KrV*, B XXIV, III: 29; cf. n. 121, Section Five, Chap. Two, this study.
341. Kant, *KrV*, B XII, III: 22.
342. Kant, *Prolegomena*, A 101, V: 180–81.

Now, pure conceptions of the understanding, in comparison with empirical (or indeed any sensuous) perceptions[343], are entirely dissimilar or heterogeneous, and never can be found in any intuition [or perception]. How then is the *subsumption* of the latter under the first, including the *application* of the categories to phenomenal appearances, possible, since no one will say: this [category], for example, causality, can also be perceived through the senses and is contained in the appearance. This so natural and monumental question is the real cause that makes a transcendental doctrine of judgment necessary, namely, so as to show how it is possible that *pure concepts of understanding* can be applied to appearances at all. In all other sciences, in which the concepts through which an object is thought in general are not so different and heterogeneous from those that represent the object *in concreto*, as it is given, it is unnecessary to give a special explanation to account for the application of the former to the latter.

[Nun sind aber reine Verstandesbegriffe, in Vergleichung mit empirischen (ja überhaupt sinnlichen) Anschauungen, ganz ungleichartig, und können niemals in irgend einer Anschauung angetroffen werden. Wie ist nun die *Subsumtion* der letztern unter die erste, mithin die *Anwendung* der Kategorie auf Erscheinungen möglich, da doch niemand sagen wird: diese, z.B., die Kausalität, könne auch durch Sinne angeschauet werden und sei in der Erscheinung enthalten? Diese so natürliche und erhebliche Frage ist nun eigentlich die Ursache, welche eine tranzsendentale Doktrin der Urteilskraft notwendig macht, um nämlich die Möglichkeit zu zeigen, wie *reine Verstandesbegriffe* auf Erscheinungen überhaupt angewandt werden können. In allen anderen Wissenschaften, wo die Begriffe, durch die der Gegenstand allgemein gedacht wird, von denen, die diesen in concreto vorstellen, wie er gegeben wird, nicht so unterschieden und heterogen sind, ist es unnötig, wegen der Anwendung des ersteren auf den letzten besondere Erörterung zu geben.[344]]

The purely logical operation of "subsumption," in other words, is introduced and defined by Kant in order to indicate, by way of negation, the central, "natural and monumental question" to which it *cannot* pertain. The rule of logical "subsumption," solely applicable to a homogeneous field, makes the introduction

---

343. On this more accurate rendering of Kant's use of the word, "Anschauung," to designate the ability to "look at" ("anschauen"), or, by any other means, perceive external phenomena, regardless of the content of the perception, which is to say, to mean the near opposite of what we understand by its conventional English translation, "intuition," see Section One, this Chapter, n. 289.

344. Kant, *KrV*, B 176–177, III: 187 (emphasis in text). See also Chapter Two, Section Nine, n. 242.

into reason of a nonlogical or impure mode of agency capable of acting upon the heterogeneity of object and concept "necessary." Having demonstrated logically that the rules of logic cannot apply to such a mode, in order to account for our critically fundamental capacity to apply the "cognitive faculties" given to us "in abstracto," to the sensory objects given us by experience "in concreto," Kant introduces the "rule" of a "mediating" "third something" that, neither "experiential" nor "intellectual" in origin, and neither an "image" ("Bild") of an object nor additional "faculty" or "power," is itself both (formed) "product" and (formative) "procedure" of the already hybrid – sensing and shaping – power of "imagination" ("Einbildungskraft"). Kant deduces the necessity for this main element, or "mediating imagined representation" ("vermittelnde Vorstellung") of the "transcendental doctrine of judgment" underlying the very possibility of empirical knowledge as follows:

> Now it is clear, that there would have to be some kind of third thing which on the one side is homogeneous with the category and homogeneous with the phenomenon on the other, and so makes the application of the former to the latter possible. This mediating imagined representation must be pure, without anything empirical about it, and so, on the one side, *intellectual*, while on the other side, *sensual*. Such a representation is the *transcendental schema* . . .
>
> The schema is in itself at all moments a product of the power of imagination; but in that the synthesis of the latter aims not at a single sense perception ["Anschauung"] but at unity in the determination of sensibility, so the schema must be distinguished from the image. Thus, when I set five points one after another:. . . . this is the image of the number five. By contrast, if I simply think a number in general, which can well be five or a hundred, so is this thinking more the imagined representation of a method for imagining a certain concept corresponding to an amount (for example, a thousand) in an image, than it is this image itself, which in this last case could only be seen at a glance and compared with the concept with difficulty. This imagining, then, of a general procedure of imagination for furnishing a concept with an image, I call the schema of this concept.
>
> In fact, it is not images of objects but schemata that lie at the basis of our pure sensory concepts. No image would ever be adequate to the concept of a triangle in general . . . Even less does an object of experience or image of the same attain to the empirical concept, but rather relates itself at every moment immediately to the schema of the power of imagination as a rule for the determination of our sensory perception ["Anschauung"] according to a certain general concept. The concept of a dog signifies a rule according to which my imagination registers [or "notes," "marks," or "documents:" "verzeichnen"] the figure of a four-footed animal in general without being limited to a single particular figure provided me by experience or any possible image that I can represent *in concreto*. This schematism of our understanding, in view of phenomenal appearances and their mere form, is a hidden art in the depths of the human soul, whose true hand

grips [or, levers of operation: "Handgriffe"] we will only with difficulty ever divine from nature and expose unveiled before our eyes.[345]

"Now" whether or not one indeed finds all this "clear" ("Nun ist klar …"), or whether Kant's introduction, in the mode of the hypothetical subjunctive ("there would have to be" ["es … geben müsse"]), of a "necessary" notion of the "schema" unlike any other in the history of philosophy, appears, instead, inherently self-referential – since, given the conditions of delimitation upon which his critical epistemology is predicated, "some third thing," or "schema," that is *not* unilaterally delimited, indeed there "must be" – one thing that will be clear to any reader of the *Critique* as a whole is that Kant's formulation here is directly echoed in the Introduction to the *Critique of Judgment*, in which Kant explains, *in the indicative*, why "there must thus be" ("also muss es doch geben") *this* "third," a

---

345. *Ibid.*, B 177–81, III: 187–190:

Nun ist klar, dass es ein Drittes geben müsse, was einerseits mit der Kategorie, andererseits mit der Erscheinung in Gleichartigkeit stehen muss, und die Anwendung der ersteren auf die letzte möglich macht. Diese vermittelnde Vorstellung muss rein (ohne alles Empirische) und doch einerseit *intellektuel*, andereseits *sinnlich* sein. Eine solche ist das *transzendentale Schema* … Das Schema ist an sich selbst jederzeit nur ein Produkt der Einbildungskraft; aber indem die Synthesis der letzteren keine einzelne Anschauung, sondern die Einheit in der Bestimmung der Sinnlichkeit allein zur Absicht hat, so ist das Schema doch vom Bilde zu unterscheiden. So, wenn ich fünf Punkte hinter einander setzte . . . . . ist dieses ein Bild von der Zahl fünf. Dagegen, wenn ich eine Zahl überhaupt nur denke, dre nun fünf oder hundert sein kann, so ist dieses Denken mehr die Vorstellung einer Methode, einem gewissen Begriffe gemäss eine Menge (z. E. Tausend) in einem Bilde vorzustellen, als dieses Bild selbst, welches ich im letztern Falle schwerlich würde übersehen und mit dem Begriff vergleichen können. Diese Vorstellung nun von einem allgemeinen Verfahren der Einbildungskraft, einem Begriff sein Bild zu verschaffen, nenne ich das Schema zu diesem Begriff. In der Tat liegen unsern reinen sinnlichen Begriffen nicht Bilder der Gegenstände, sondern Schemata zum Grunde. Dem Begriffe von einem Triangel überhaupt würde gar kein Bild desselben jemals adäquat sein. … Noch viel weniger erreicht ein Gegenstand der Erfahrung oder Bild desselben jemals den empirischen Begriff, sondern dieser bezieht sich jederzeit unmittelbar auf das Schema der Einbildungskraft, als eine Regel der Bestimmung unserer Anschauung, gemäss einem gewissen allgemeinen Begriffe. Der Begriff vom Hunde bedeutet eine Regel, nach welcher meine Einbildungskraft die Gestalt eines vierfüssigen Tieres allgemein verzeichnen kann, ohne auf irgend eine einzige besondere Gestalt, die mir die Erfahrung darbiete, oder auch ein jedes möglich Bild, was ich in concreto darstellen kann, eingeschränkt zu sein. Dieser Schematismus unseres Verstandes, in Ansehung der Erscheinungen und ihrer blossen Form, ist eine verborgene Kunst in den Tiefen der menschlichen Seele, deren wahre Handgriffe wir der Natur schwerlich jemals abraten, und sie unverdeckt vor Augen legen werden.

Third Critique. Just as judgment is described in the "Transcendental Analytic" of the First Critique as a "transcendental" power mediating between the "abstract" and the "concrete," so the *Critique of Judgment* analyzes the "passage" provided by aesthetic judgment across the otherwise unbridgeable "chasm" separating the "realms" in which, within a single, empirical world, we operate alternately: on the one hand, the "supersensory" "realm" of the (practically) pure reason of freedom, and, on the other, the phenomenal "realm" of sensory objects to which we "apply" the (practically) impure reason of cognition.[346] Like judgment, the schema coordinates otherwise incommunicable realms, and like judgment it has "no realm of its own" ("kein eigentümliches Gebiet");[347] its basis is the very *Critique* which could not cohere without it – an architectonic structure whose own explicit requirement of mediation echoes, again, the self-structuring necessity of the schema to cognition.

Yet, rather than view Kant's own logical procedure here as hopelessly circular – the hypothesis of something as necessary with regard to something already hypothesized as possible – we can view it instead as an act of subreption, as described in the definition of the term cited in the epigraph to this Section: a representation made, on no other basis than that of necessity, with a view toward "the acquisition of a power or faculty" one cannot properly identify in that identifying it would require it, the very power one positively "lacks." Kant, indeed, comes as close as the logic and language of the *Critique*, or, more precisely, as the *reliance of logic upon language that defines the Critique*, allows, to defining, as the nonlogical result of an action, the hybrid form of mediation the very logic of the *Critique* requires, proceeding from what may appear a pure product of logic to another, strictly illogical kind of product, one that, by its own definition, can have neither "proper" logical status nor "realm" within the "architectonic" structure of the *Critique*. In so doing he further suggests that in order for any architectonic, logically interrelated structure not merely to cohere within itself but to *act upon our understanding critically* it must contain, at its core, an illogically produced principle. Given by neither the senses nor the intellect, and so, like "the concept of freedom," unavailable to derivation by the "discursive" logic of the *Critique* itself,[348] the notion of the "schema" Kant's philosophical system compels him to invent, itself *represents* the necessity of that invention. For, rather than a discursive concept, a hypothetical *a priori* "form" (for perceiving phenomena), or a supposed mental

346. Kant, *KU* B XX–XXI, X: 84.
347. Kant, *KU* B XXI, X: 84.
348. On the "discursive" nature of the logic employed in the production of phenomenal knowledge, see Kant, *Logik* A 23, VI: 446: "herein ... mathematics has an advantage over philosophy, in that the cognitions of the former are intuitive, those of the latter, on the contrary, only *discursive*" ("hierin hat also ... die Mathematik einen Vorzug vor der Philosophie, dass die Erkenntnisse der erstern intuitive, die der letztern hingegen nur *discursive* Erkenntnisse sind"). Cf. Béatrice Longuenesse, *Kant and the Capacity to Judge. Sensibility and Discursivity in the Transcendental Analytic of the Critique of Pure Reason*. (Princeton: Princeton University Press, 1996), esp. 324ff.

"faculty," the "schema," Kant remarkably submits, is "a product and, as it were, a monogram of the pure imagination *a priori*" ("ein Produkt und gleichsam ein Monogramm der reinen Einbildungskraft a priori"[349]).

"Now," given the fact that imagination in Kant's *Critique* is never "pure" but always related to sensory perceptions, and never "*a priori*" to, but coincident with, empirical experience, Kant's "schema" is, "as it were," so deeply fundamental to the *Critique* as to be fundamentally at odds with it, so deeply internal to it as to stand quite outside it, which is, indeed, nothing less than to say, "a monogram, as it were, of the pure imagination *a priori*." A "monogram" or initializing sign of some thing or power, "pure" and "*a priori*," that stands and acts quite apart from that thing or power itself, indicating without identifying, without "spelling out:" this unusual if not unparalleled lexical usage in Kant expresses that for which Kant wants – indeed, in his own terms, "must" want – expression, the originary imprint, in an abbreviated signature, of imagination on the mind. Unlike the experiential notion of sensory "impressions" upon or mimetic "copies" of "sensations" within the intellect redundantly theorized in earlier empirical philosophy, by which sensation and knowledge merely circularly reflect each other, the schema – abstractly identifying delineation, mark, or "monogram" of the imagination upon the mind itself – first allows the mind to *be mind*, i.e., to coordinate its faculties or abilities. At the same time – which is to say, the "*a priori*" time of a "pure," or nonexperiential "imagination" that, unlike the operations of conceptualization or logic, leaves the sensuous, temporal trace or abbreviated signature of itself behind it within the mind – the schema, "product and, as it were, monogram of pure imagination," exceeds and so is incommensurate with the critical limits of reason, as of imagination to empirical perception, that Kant himself so consistently applies.

Performing an analogous coordinating function to that of the mediating schema, "the power of judgment" is the central, mediating, "higher faculty" of the *Critique*, and its practice, the defining activity of "the Age of Critique." Yet, unlike the schema, judgment is never produced by a "pure imagination" acting "*a priori*," in independence of experience itself. Instead, it must always be occasioned by the perception of an empirical object, however conventional and otherwise negligible or unconventionally, even violently striking, the distinct matter bearing the form (or absence of form) perceptible in that object may be. All perceptible objects, natural and made, may be "judged" in an aesthetic sense, depending on their effect upon us, Kant contends (and his highly unorthodox sampling of the objects of aesthetic experience amply demonstrates). Yet, not all objects of aesthetic judgment are made equal, he no less suggests. In analyzing the distinct "values" ("Werte") of individual artforms at the close of the "Analytic of the Sublime," Kant arrives, almost surreptitiously, at the single artform that, by dint of its peculiar relationship to its own medium, he judges to be of the "highest rank" and most sublime.[350] In §53 of the *Critique of Judgment*, he writes:

---

349. Kant, *KU* B 860–879, IV: 695–709.
350. Kant, *KU,* B 215, X: 265.

Of all the arts *poetry* (which owes its origin almost entirely to genius and wants least to be guided by precept or example) maintains the highest rank. It expands the mind in that it sets the imagination into a state of freedom and presents, within the limits of a given concept, that form which, among the unbounded variety of possible forms according with it, links the representation of this concept with a fullness of thoughts for which no verbal expression is fully adequate, thus raising itself aesthetically to Ideas.

[Unter allen behauptet die *Dichtkunst* (die fast gänzlich dem Genie ihren Urpsrung verdankt, und am wenigsten durch Vorschrift, oder durch Beispiele geleitet sein will) den obersten Rang. Sie erweitert das Gemüt dadurch, dass sie die Einbildungskraft in Freiheit setzt und innerhalb den Schranken eines gegebenen Begriffe, unter der unbegrenzten Mannigfaltigkeit möglicher damit zusammenstimmender Formen, diejenige darbiete, welche die Darstellung desselben mit einer Gedankenfülle verknüpft, der kein Sprachausdruck völlig adäquat ist, und sich also ästhetisch zu Ideen erhebt.[351]]

Poetry is that artform which knows the limits of its medium, "verbal expression," and the limits of that medium's own products, "given concepts" or conceptual discourse; *and* poetry is that artform which, "least guided by precept or example," "sets the imagination in freedom" from those limits by formally "linking" its conceptual medium to "a fullness of thoughts" for which "no expression of language is fully adequate." Poetry, in other words, is the highest artform because it practices the art of subreption, of wanting expression, itself as good a definition as any imaginable for the "Ideas" to which it "raises itself," the things in themselves, rather than things of experience, whose necessary want of commensurate expression is the very basis, indeed the very reason for being of Kant's *Critique*. Poetry cannot faithfully represent transcendental "ideas" to us, principle among these the critical idea of "freedom" itself – nothing and no artform can provide a representation adequate to that idea. Yet the "art of poetry" alone uses conceptual discourse in such a way as to indicate its relationship to "ideas," which is to say, to an ability "to think" to which any "given concept" and "verbal expression" remain "inadequate."[352]

That the practical identity of poetry consists in its ability to "link" necessarily "inadequate verbal expression" to "a fullness of thoughts" brings poetry closest to the two central, practically *and* theoretically necessary capabilities elaborated in Kant's tripartite *Critique*: the ability of judgment "to speak," "for every person," *a priori*, in a "general voice" articulating "common sense;" and the ability of the "schema," calling card or "monogram" left in the mind by a "pure power of imagination *a priori*," to "link" the heterogeneous givens of sensory experience and conceptual understanding in a way that mutually exceeds the limits of each.[353]

---

351. Kant, *KU*, B 215–216, X: 265.
352. Kant, *KrV*, B XXIX, X: 32.
353. See Chapter Two, Sections Eight and Nine, this study.

As if in acknowledgement of the structural link among the individual abilities, as among the individual *Critiques*, he describes, Kant's extraordinary focus on poetry does not end here, but rather includes an analysis of poetic practice directly linking what poets do to the "Transcendental Analytic" of the First Critique. The positive art of indicating a negative, that of the "inadequacy" of any "verbal expression" to "the fullness of thought" to which it may be "linked," poetry, according to Kant, does not present itself as either representing or even interested in such thoughts: neither the mind nor the "imagination" it "sets into freedom" is the object of whose "verbal expression" poetry, Kant states, must fall short. Rather than dream the possibility of a mind untethered to language, a new and no less mythological Promethean power uncriticized or unbound, or imagine an "imagination" "free[d]" once and for all from the necessary inadequacy of any conceptual representation to the "fullness of thoughts," Kant reverses any such "idealist" speculative tendencies by suggesting that the relationship of poetry to judgment may itself compose a monogram of another kind. "True to form," as the commonplace "inadequate expression" goes ("inadequate," since, in the *Critique*, as in poetry, to be "true to form" is already, or *a priori*, to be true to content), Kant continues his analysis by proceeding in the opposite sense, now considering "the art of poetry" not as it relates to imagination but, rather, to the given empirical world, and this is where Kant's theory of poetry becomes, in the fundamental terms of his moral theory, "really" (rather than merely phenomenally) "interesting," or – to use his own explicitly euphemistic disclaimer for any attempt to describe that which, by definition, can never be adequately described – where poetry itself, as Kant describes it, becomes, "*as it were*" ("gleichsam"), "really" "Good." His analysis of the conceptual limits of the artistic medium that "sets the imagination in freedom" describes the way in which its practitioners make us "feel" able to "judge:"

> [Poetry] strengthens the mind in that it allows it to feel its free, self-actuating capability, independent of determination by nature, for regarding and judging nature as a phenomenon from viewpoints it does not of itself present, either to sense or understanding, in experience, and thus of using nature on behalf of, and, as it were, as a *schema* of the supersensible.
>
> [(Die Dichtkunst) stärkt das Gemüt, indem sie es sein freies, selbsttätiges und von der Naturbestimmung unabhängiges Vermögen fühlen lässt, die Natur, als Erscheinung, nach Ansichten zu betrachten und zu beurteilen, die sie nicht von selbst, weder für den Sinn noch den Verstand in der Erfahrung darbietet und sie also zum Behuf und gleichsam zum Schema des Übersinnlichen zu gebrauchen.[354]]

"The art of poetry" allows the mind "to feel its faculty" – "free, self-actuating, and independent of determination by nature" – for "regard[ing]" "nature" not as

---

354. Kant, *KU*, B 215, X: 265.

the unfree, causally determined and phenomenally delimited "appearance" it "itself" "presents" "to our senses and understanding in experience," but, rather, as it can be "used" to relate to, or act "on behalf of," something with which nothing determined by nature can ever be commensurate, "the supersensible." Poetry allows us to "feel" our own capability for "judgment," which is to say, "to feel" the "faculty" for "feeling" (pleasure and pain) even while "feeling itself free" (from cognition and interest).[355] Yet this means that, following the very logic of the *Critique* from which Kant's formal establishment of the central intellectual and sensory interaction he calls "judgment" stems, and on which its own, critically original definition depends, poetry allows us to "feel" in such a way that only the application of the general predicates, "is beautiful," "is sublime," can properly designate and, in their abstraction from all particular content, adequately express. It permits us to "regard" "nature" not as a cognitive object as conducive of personal emotion, opinion, and employment as of scientific research, but rather as that impure form most fundamental to cognition, "the schema," "monogram of the imagination *a priori*." Turning nature, "so to speak," inside out, freeing our ability to cognize the sensory world as delimited, logically interrelated phenomena, into one of "using" it to bring to mind the "supersensible," poetry "strengthens" the "free and self-actuating" "ability" of the mind to "judge:" to predicate in undefined words ("beautiful," "sublime") an unknown object made of words, to "feel oneself free" in an act of speech whose linguistic condition is that it "speaks for everyone." In so doing, poetry allows us not merely to "feel" something whose occasion we cannot identify with a natural object, but to "use" "nature" itself as a "schema" for something we can neither "feel" nor perceive in itself, something less like any thing than the "freedom" "to think:" "the supersensible."

The relationship between poetry and judgment, then, is symmetrical and mutual: judgment of poetry *as* poetry is based in a feeling, and poetry allows "the mind" to "feel" it possesses the capacity "to judge." The interactive nature of that relationship makes it as difficult to maintain and separate its two agents as to decide with which of them it begins: whether it is our encounter with poetry that (first) makes us "feel" able to judge, or our capacity for judgment that allows us to encounter poetry in the way we do. Just as Kant notes in his discussion of the "free" exercise of "imagination" in "genius," that "poetry" is the only such exercise "actually capable of showing the full measure of aesthetic ideas," in that it "finds no examples" for its "representations" (whether of "ideas" or "experience"[356]) "in nature," so "the art of poetry" "strengthens" our "ability" to "say" something that does not constate something else (whether a piece of conceptual knowledge, a moral precept, or an individual feeling or interest) but rather responds, in the form of an impersonal statement about an object, to the "feeling" we as subjects experience in perceiving

---

355. Kant, *KU*, B 14–18, X: 122–125.

356. Kant, *KU*, B 194–201, X: 250–55; for Kant on the historic productivity of "genius," see. n. 366, Section Four, this Chapter.

either a "freely delineated," "dynamic form," or "formlessness."³⁵⁷ *Judgment and poetry, then, interact as acts of language do*, and the comparability of their activities is directly inserted into his "General Remarks" on the First Section of the Analytic by Kant:

> although, in the perception of a given object of the senses, [the imagination in judgments of taste] is tied to a definite form of this object and to that extent has no free play (as it does in the making of poetry), still one can easily conceive that the object could furnish it with such a form as ... the imagination, if it were left free to itself, would design.
>
> [ob (im Geschmacksurteile die Einbildungskraft) zwar bei der Auffassung eines gegebenen Gegenstandes der Sinne an eine bestimmte Form diese Objekts gebunden ist und sofern kein freies Spiel [wie im Dichten] hat, so lässt sich doch noch wohl begreifen: dass der Gegenstand ihr gerade eine solche Form an die Hand geben könne, ... wie sie die Einbildungskraft, wenn sie sich selbst frei überlassen wäre.³⁵⁸]

"Tied to a definite form of [an] object," the "play" of "perception" enacted in judgment is not as "free" "as in the making of poetry," Kant states, and, arising in the context of the section of the Analytic devoted to judgment of the "beautiful," this parenthetical, differential comparison of "judging" and "poetry-making" appears as reasonable as it is easy to overlook. Similarly, on the other end of the affective spectrum of experience from "play," "the feeling of the sublime in nature" is compared to "the mood of the mind" in experiencing the real practice of "the moral," i.e., the "exclusively *negative* satisfaction" we feel in the "violence" inflicted upon our "sensibility" by an "imagination" put to work "as an instrument" of "reason:"

> In fact, a feeling for the sublime in nature cannot well be thought without joining it to a mood of the mind similar to the moral. And though the immediate pleasure in the beautiful in nature likewise requires and cultivates a certain *liberality* of mode of thought, ... in aesthetic judgments of the sublime the violence [done to sensibility by reason] is presented as exercised through the imagination, working as an instrument of reason, itself.
>
> The satisfaction in the sublime in nature is also thus only *negative* (while that in the beautiful is *positive*), namely, a feeling of the deprivation of the freedom of imagination through [imagination] itself, because purposefully determined according to another law than that of its empirical use.

357. On judgment as the act of "say[ing]," see *Ibid.*, B 7, X: 117, and Chapter Two, Section Five, this study. On aesthetic experience as an apprehension of "free" and "dynamic forms" to the "formless," see Kant, *KU*, B XLIX, 49–50, 79–82 X: 103, 146–47, 168–170.

358. The comparison between "the imagination in judgment" and "in poetry" appears at the opening of the General Remarks to the First Section of the Analytic; see Kant, *KU*, B 69, X: 160.

[In der Tat last sich ein Gefühl für das Erhabene der Natur nicht wohl denken, ohne eine Stimmung des Gemüts die der zum Moralischen ähnlich ist, damit zu verbinden; und, obgleich die unmittelbare Lust am Schönen der Natur gleichfalls eine gewisse *Liberalität* der Denkungsart ... voraussetzt und kultiviert ... im ästhetischen Urteile über das Erhabene diese Gewalt durch die Einbildungskraft selbst, als einem Werkzeuge der Vernunft, ausgeübt vorgestellt wird.

Das Wohlgefallens am Erhabenen der Natur ist daher auch nur *negativ* (statt dessen das am Schönen positive ist), nämlich ein Gefühl der Beraubung der Freiheit der Einbildungskraft durch sie selbst, indem sie nach einem andern Gesetze, als dem des empirischen Gebrauchs, zweckmässig bestimmt wird[359]].

This analytic operation of identifying, so as to compare, otherwise mutually exclusive – "negative" and "positive" – outcomes is a familiar constituent of the "architectonic" plan of its "building" "sketched" at the very outset of the *Critique*.[360] Rather than fitting them to a dialectical exposition of givens or an organon-like design, Kant organizes the interacting operations of the intellectual faculties he analyzes into a free-standing, self-defining "system" by elaborating and constructing a kind of equilibrium of forces between them.[361] Whether resulting in limited knowledge of phenomenal objects, a feeling of pleasure or pain in perceiving the form of an object in the absence of knowledge, or the freedom to act morally, i.e., in the absence of both knowledge and affect, the operations that one individual *Critique* posits, another one takes away. The same organizing principle of exchange maintains the cohesion of the internally divided mediation provided by the Third Critique itself. Just as the beautiful affords "positive," the sublime affords "negative satisfaction," and the "free play" (of imagination and understanding) in the former compares with the "violen[t]" "deprivation" of "imagination" through "imagination itself" in the latter – this last operation further subdividing a single faculty, "imagination," into the comparable, negative and positive functions of subject and object of action respectively.

Such an architectonic method of coordinating comparable activites across the *Critique* does not obtain, however, in the section of the Analytic describing the necessarily incomparable, because non-objectifiable perceptual experiences we

---

359. Kant, *KU.*, B 117, X: 194–95 (emphasis in text).
360. Kant, *KrV,* B 27, III: 65; cf. Kant, *Logik,* A 143, VI: 523.
361. While Kant's creation of a formal "system" for understanding empirical experience may seem anachronistic when viewed from the momentary standpoint afforded by changing historical and cultural – including philosophical – norms, its permanent analogue remains Saussure's equally groundbreaking theory of language *as* "language" (*langue*), i.e., as neither an "organic" nor accidental product of physical and "social" history as it "appears ... at first sight," but, at any moment of its operation, as it is in its "true nature," an internally coherent and self-sustaining "system" allowing its objects, "signs," to be "exchanged" as "values" (Ferdinand de Saussure, *Cours de linguistique générale*, "Introduction," pp. 26, 34–5, *et passim.*).

judge "sublime." Abandoning any attempt to balance negative with positive, Kant instead describes the "naming" of the "sublime" by conjoining the acts of judging and poetry-making into a single mandatory, simultaneously experiential and moral action. What we read in this wrenching juxtaposition of descriptions is a word-for-word cancellation of the analogical perspective required for analytic comparisons in the first place: discrete phenomena replaced by dimensionless surfaces, the position of sensing, knowing subject destroyed by forces perceived but unknown. The absolute identification of the language describing "how the poets see" with the detailed relation of the "sight" described – language here describing not the content of a visual object but rather that of something we might call "sight" – condenses the acts of poetry-making and judging into a unilateral, modal assertion predicated by the single most arresting descriptive passage in the entire tripartite *Critique*. Having explained that, "when we name the sight of the starry sky sublime," "we must" not "lay at the foundation" of that "judgment" "concepts" of the "worlds" and "suns" the sky contains, "but merely how we see it, as an extensive vault that touches all," Kant continues:

> Just so, must the sight of the ocean [not be judged sublime] according to the way that we, enriched with miscellaneous bits of knowledge (which are, however, not contained within immediate perception), *think* it ... but rather merely as the poets do it, according to that which the appearance in [or appearance on the surface of] the eye shows – approximately, when it is regarded while quiet, as a clear mirror of water which is merely bounded by the sky, but when it is unquiet, as an abyss threatening to devour all – must we still be able to find [the ocean] sublime.
>
> [Eben so den Anblick des Ozeans nicht so, wie wir, mit allerlei Kenntnissen (die aber nicht in der unmittelbaren Anschauung enthalten sind) bereichert, ihn *denken* ... sondern man muss den Ozean bloss, wie die Dichter es tun, nach dem, was der Augenschein zeigt, etwa, wenn er in Ruhe betrachtet wird, als einen klaren Wasserspiegel, der bloss von Himmel begrenzt ist, aber ist er unruhig, wie einen alles zu verschlingen drohenden Abgrund, dennoch erhaben finden können.[362]]

To judge an appearance sublime is to "see" it and "name" it as such. In order, however, to see it as such we "must" regard it as "the poets do," as an appearance without recognizable contours, seen as if not with but rather as it appears "in" or "upon the eye" ("Augenschein"). Similarly, the act of speaking what they see is the condition of the poets seeing *as* poets, just as the act of "nam[ing]" it defines our judgment of the sublime. Both poetry-making and judgment are acts of language, in which "nature," available to us only in experience, is "used" as a "schema," available to us only in language; yet the nature represented in this conflation of

---

362. Kant, *KU* B 118–19, X: 196 (emphasis in text).

judgment, "seeing," and poetry-making is linguistic through and through.[363] A "schema for the supersensible," it is still sensible, like a "monogram;" "a product of the pure imagination *a priori*," it still perceives something external to the viewer, if in a distinctly nonphenomenal way.

In violently equating, rather than exchanging, the mode and object of "sight" in poetry and judgment alike, Kant makes clear that judgment, too, never merely reports on the known. Instead of representing either "nature" or the "feeling" of the subject "so speaking" ("so sprechen"), it predicates, as if for the first time, the object that occasions that feeling, making "it" the subject of a verbal equation with a quality ("beautiful," "sublime").[364] Neither based on nor aimed at the acquisition of scientific knowledge, but rather articulating the basis of the mind's "power" to "feel" itself "free" of "conceptual constraints," such acts of speech are the linguistic condition of the "self-actuating" practice of poetry defined by Kant, its "independence" from both "the determination of nature" and our "natural" or phenomenal and causally determined selves. This same independence, moreover, constitutes our ability "to judge," and poetry in particular "strengthens" it. Poetry, then, is as much an object of judgment, assigned by Kant's theory of judgment the "highest rank" among all the arts, as it is the artform that "allows" the mind "to judge" to begin with, to "regard" "nature" in a way distinct from either our cognitive representation or instrumental use of it. Yet poetry does something more than offer us a different, "aesthetic" view of the natural world. It allows the mind instead to "use" that world as poetry itself does, "at the behest" of some thing or power "independent" of perception that Kant calls "the supersensible."

For both poetry and judgment, that "use" is verbal. What poetry composes, judgment reads, but this is to say that poetry is the aesthetic object whose particular "experience," that of reading or hearing words, rather than intuiting or perceiving objects, is "use[]d" by the "mind" it "strengthens" in the same way it itself "uses" "nature" – not as delimited phenomenal representation, or unrepresentable transcendental Idea, but as "schema," or delimited and indelible signature, of a "pure imagination *a priori*," independent of any particular sense perception. As put to verbal "use" by poetry – its composition *and* its reading – the unfree "appearance[s]" "present[ed]" to us by "nature" are turned into "schemata" for the freedom to so use them, the "free, self-actuating" capacity of the mind to imagine, *and* to "judge" them as such.

In the "art of poetry," in other words, it is not counterbalancing faculties of experience but *language and nature "themselves"* that *exchange places* according to Kant, the latter put into the service of the former, not for personal or cognitive representational purposes but "at the behest" of the "supersensible." The language of poetry "uses" "nature" to do for the "inadequate expression" of the "fullness of

---

363. As discussed in the supplementary work to this study, this loss of perspective, as of all recognizable figures, defining the activity of seeing it represents, defines the openly "prosaic" diction and subject matter of Wordsworth's poetry and poetics. See *Words' Worth*.

364. Kant, *KU*, B 18, X: 124; see Chapter Two, Section Eight, this study.

thought" that is conceptual discourse what the "schema" does for cognition of nature: serve as "monogram" of a power of the mind it cannot itself represent. Poetry uses "nature" as a "schema" to express that which any representation *of* nature can itself only inadequately express and, in that "natural" representation of its own inadequacy, attains the rank of highest artform, which is to say, that which shows itself most inadequate to the immeasurable task it alone can perform. Poetry is the highest artform because it represents its own utilization of nature both as necessary and as necessarily inadequate; and *because* poetry is that artform inherently lacking in adequate "expression" for its real content – the reality that is the independence from natural conditions, or "freedom" of "thought" – its "use" of nature expresses or externalizes the most "internal" medium, the schema. The peculiar representational medium that is the language of poetry appears to hold a mirror not to nature but to the "hidden" "monogram" of "pure imagination, *a priori*," to present to us the signs of that *a priori* power, now not as abstract monogram but an undelimitable verbal content, in descriptions of scenes of nature that "appear" to us not natural but "sublime."

In representing "the sight of the ocean" not as a function of but in abstraction from knowledge, as something without phenomenal limitations that we nonetheless perceive, the language of poetry displays – as if it were, "so to speak," "the ocean" – both the "depth" and "extension" of thought informing Kant's *Critique*, endowing the internal cognitive form of the schema with the external identity of visible, material nature. Yet, it "uses nature, as it were, as a schema" not for the purpose of representing either schema or nature – of rendering the former concrete and the latter, verbal, and thereby fulfilling or fully "expressing" the reality either of internal form or external world. Rather, "poetry uses nature, as it were, as a schema" because it is the only way in which it can be neither schematic nor natural, but "poetry," which is to say, the only way it can represent, in the appearance of the very opposite or negation of the same, the supersensible that is *its* content, the "fullness of thoughts." Representational language that does not represent its content is the inherently "inadequate" language of poetry, the artform in which "external" and "internal," "nature" and "schema," "appear" to take on each other's identity. Yet this is to say that nothing in poetic language – neither the apparently concrete and abstract terms it uses, nor its necessary, or grammatical, and conventional, or stylistic forms – "is" "as" it "appears" to be: like a "schema" that "must" be both active and imperceptible, buried "in the depths of the soul," in order to function as such, the true content of poetry must be "hidden" from view. For, rather than represent each other, the things Kant calls "schematism" and "nature" – the "art" ("Kunst") whose readymade availability to enactment ("Handgriffe") allows for perception, and the objects that "art" allows us to perceive, respectively – remain categorically distinct from each other, thus allowing us "to think" the possibility of that which we cannot perceive, and that Kant calls, for that reason, "the supersensible." Just as acts of judgment remain divorced from cognitions of objects, and divide the "feeling" of the speaking subject from the qualitative predication of objects they perform, so "the art of poetry" maintains the "art" of the "schema" without which perception and "feeling," cognition and its occlusion, could themselves not be thought.

4. Poetry and the Judgment of Critique

Kant may use the notion of the schema to make possible our knowledge of nature, to make nothing less than science and philosophy themselves possible. The schema, he states, is, "so to speak, a monogram of pure imagination *a priori*" – something, in other words, that Kant cannot properly express within the limits of his own conceptual discourse, yet, nonetheless, does not simply dream up. Yet, according to Kant's philosophy it is not philosophy but "the art of poetry" that "uses" nature "as a schema for the supersensible:" as sign of the freedom of thinking to use representations *as* representations, a means of articulation unbounded by natural sensory limitations (itself imagined here as "a monogram"), and of the freedom, from even the most elemental determinations of nature, of imagination (theoretically imagined here as "pure") itself. At once signpost, avenue, and sole appearance of freedom, hovering between subject and object, as between the capacities of language and perception, and so strictly identifiable with neither, the *schematic* use of nature by poetry recognizes, as Kant recognizes with regard to his critical project, that any either purely "natural" *or* fully nonreferential (or, to use Kant's terms, not merely "fictional" but "*falsely* fictional"[365]) means of expression must be inadequate to the representation of nonrepresentational activity it wants to express. When poetry represents natural phenomena not as objects but as the effect of "seeing as the poets do," it thus does so in the manner Kant calls "genius," not because it has no use for such phenomena but precisely because, in the act of using them, it can take no "example" found in "nature" as its lead.[366] Poetry, on

---

365. See n. 317, Section Two, this Chapter.

366. See Kant, *KU*, B 180–182, 201, X: 241–42, 255 for his profoundly complex, because *practical* (rather than ideational-ideological) account of "genius" – closely presaging Wordsworth's in the *Preface to Lyrical Ballads* – as the *production* of, instead of subservience to "determined rules," a praxis in which the limited cognitive abilities and unlimited "free" action of speech analyzed separately in the First and Third Critiques effectively intersect (what Kant calls "the exemplary originality of the natural gift of a subject [making] *free* use of his cognitive faculty"). Perhaps most importantly, Kant's conception of "genius" includes its essential capacity to *produce history*. For while the particular productivity that Kant calls "genius" must be "lost" to every attempt to mime or "imitat[e]" it, its singular historical effectivity is to "awaken" future negations of imitation, the "revolutions," breaks or discontinuities in the reproduction of cultural norms that, arising with "the feeling of [their] own originality," provide the example of a *temporally* productive "freedom from rules" in "another genius in posterity."

Kant's account, takes nature much as it takes language, the discursive "world" of expression itself: indeed, from the practical point of view of poetry, natural and linguistic determinations are equivalent, which is to say, not equally inadequate but equally *useful* in their inadequacy – as either merely representable *or* mere representation – to that which they are purposed to express.

The "use" of such inadequacy, the expression of such lack, can give the mind some idea of its own "purposive" "occupations," Kant continues.[367] Yet it does this in the only "produc[tive]" way that representational language can: not by proffering grounds for moral actions and consequences but rather their near opposite, "mere play." Kant states: "[Poetry] plays with mere [or illusory] appearances, which it produces at its pleasure, or will, without thereby deceiving, for it declares its activity [or occupation] to be mere play, one which, however, can be purposively used by the understanding and its activities [or occupations]" ("[Die Dichtkunst] spielt mit dem Schein, den sie nach Belieben bewirkt, ohne doch dadurch zu betrügen; denn sie erklärt ihre Beschäftigung selbst für blosses Spiel, welches gleichwohl vom Verstande und zu dessen Geschäfte zweckmässig gebraucht werden kann"[368]). "Play with mere [or illusory] appearances" that declares itself as such does not "deceive" us unless we assume "mere play" and its "purposive" use "by understanding" to be opposed, which is to say, unless we have not read the foregoing *Critique*. But in that case we would also be unable to understand either "poetry" or "judgment" themselves, the way in which and, moreover, *why* their own identities are both practically and conceptually interdependent in Kant. For, just as "judgment" alone is capable both of defining "poetry" and "judging" it "the highest art," in that, instead of taking its "example[s]" from nature," it "uses" "nature" as a "schema" for (rather than truly illusory representation of) "the supersensible," so "poetry" alone provides "judgment" with exemplary descriptions of how and what one must "see" in order to be able to "judge," i.e., transcriptions of the sensory world "as it appears to the eye," unmediated by *a priori* cognition, that only the active language of "poetry" can provide.

As the "schema" is not only a necessary form of "linkage" between our capacities for sense perception and intellection, but one whose usage indicates that "imagination" acts *a priori* or "before" them, judgment is the critical, "middle link" ("Mittelglied") relating the necessarily distinct yet overlapping activities in which we share: those of logical and conceptual "understanding;" of sensory, or *a posteriori*, and nonsensory, or *a priori*, "imagination;" and, finally, of "feeling" "free" enough not only to feel but to "speak" not for one's self but "for every" self. To speak this way is to speak in the language of a "general voice," in which "general" means nothing less nor more than to speak as speech must always be spoken in order to be speech, the singularly "common," irreducibly abstract mode of enacting "sense." In direct contrast to any sensation, this is a "sense" never limited to any individual moment or piece of space, just as it is never its temporary speaker's alone, in that its articulate production depends *a priori* on an external social form. And that formal externality

---

367. Kant, *KU*, B 216, X: 265–266.
368. *Ibid*.

reflects no predetermined mode of conformity or empirically derived rule or "norm," but rather the inherently social "possibility" of "free" agency itself, i.e., the only purely other-directed, which is to say, "moral" ability to "think." And if judgment is the outer side of the "supersensible" act of thinking, a nonprescriptive, critical faculty for coordinating, rather than being unilaterally defined by, the limitations of both applied (or discursive) and pure (or non-discursive) reason, then poetry turns the *Critique*, which posits and defines those faculties, outside in, "freely" making the external side of reason, that of "nature" *as* we perceive and cognize it, into the internal "schema" of its own purposes, foremost among these that of allowing the mind to "feel" its critical "ability" "to judge." Poetry uses nature as that necessarily inadequate "schema of the supersensible" which allows the discursive representation of nature by understanding to serve the purpose of presenting understanding with that which it can never quite understand. If in aesthetic judgment we see no particular thing or object but "feel" something defined only by its universal "communicability," poetry communicates to us nothing but our universal ability to "judge" things and so see them differently. For the "nature" of which poetry makes its own articulate "use" presents to understanding neither a theoretically determined faculty of mind nor a cognitively determined representation of the world but rather, and in place of these, our ability to think in such a way that will always want expression, to think even the possibility of just such a wanting of expression. This expressive lack ensures "the fullness of thoughts" by inscribing articulation into the very basis of thinking while stripping it of discursive conceptualization, which is as much as to say, by expressing nothing less nor more than a "monogram of pure imagination" at work.

That is the subreption, the subterfuge of poetry: to "appear" to be "mere play" while performing – indeed, in order to perform – the most critically consequential kind of action within the mind. As for the basis or grounds of that subreption, the very notion is a contradiction in any event, as Kant, just before coining his own singularly thought-provoking expression for the schema – that of a "monogram" or stamp of the imagination previous to all experience – deceptively, indeed, nearly poetically, asserts. While denying that the *a priori* or *a posteriori* basis of the explicitly linguistic "condition" of a uniquely "*common* sense" could or even should be "researched,"[369] in describing "the schematism of our understanding in the viewing of appearances and their mere form" as "an art hidden in the depths of the human soul," Kant posits the existence not of a grounding principle or cause but of a *techne* concealed within us, "the nature of whose readymade mechanisms we will only ever with great difficulty discover and lay unconcealed before our eyes."[370] The *a priori* "art" of the schema first allowing the otherwise incommunicable

---

369. Cf. n. 57, Section One, Chapter Two, this study.

370. Kant, *KU*, B 182, III:190: "Dieser Schematismus unseres Verstandes, in Ansehung der Erscheinungen und ihrer blossen Form, ist eine verborgene Kunst in den Tiefen der menschlichen Seele, deren wahre Handgriffe wir der Natur schwerlich jemals abraten, und sie unverdeckt vor Augen legen werden."

capacities of sense perception and conception to communicate with each other[371] is enacted in the *a priori* "communicability" of the specifically verbal medium of judgment in Kant, even as its empirical and conceptual operation, in mediating sensory experience by discursivity, reveals to us, in the "deepest," i.e., most immeasurable sense, the world.

Revealing nothing by revealing that one is concealing everything; revealing everything by concealing nothing, including that which one cannot express, Kant both offers the "art" of the schema for us to "judge" and buries it "in the hidden depths" of that for which, no expression being adequate to it, we call, "the human soul." Lacking "imagination," in the conventional, *a posteriori* sense of sensuous images for the "hidden art" of which the schema is the *a priori* imprint or monogram; and lacking the art of poetry his critical theory of judgment defines as the "the highest of the arts," in that, using sensible "nature" as "schema for the supersensible," its language can communicate nature "as the poets see it" – as some unknown thing of infinite extension, duration, or depth – what more effective expression of the inseparable relation of judgment and poetry at the core of his *Critique* than Kant's own open, verbal burial of the *techne* or "art" they share. The "play[ful]," verbal "use" that the poet makes of "nature," as "schema" for something or some power unavailable to our temporally and spatially delimited perceptions of nature, must be found wanting in a critical philosophy whose theory of knowledge is based on the limiting presupposition of the schema. Yet, the "art" of the "schema," Kant suggests, is also one that, like the poets, every subject must "use" in order to perceive, "feel," *and* judge, rather than "know."

In relating "judgment," sole "power" to mediate between the necessarily noncommunicating "realms" of his *Critique* that he more or less invents, to its own central model for conceiving and enacting that power, the verbal "seeing" known as "poetry," Kant expresses – exposes and buries – the "art" for which there is "no example in nature" at the basis of his *Critique*: not poetry, certainly, but, perhaps, a stroke of genius, which is to say, a judgment that, based on the "communicability" of a *techne*, must lack a proper object – a judgment of critique.

---

371. Cf. n. 345, this Chapter, Section Three.

Chapter 4

KLEIST'S MERE FORMALITIES

1. Kant and Kleist: Representation and Irony

Whether or not Kleist truly grasped the architectonic impasses and structural limits written into Kant's hypothesis that all human cognition is necessarily, or *a priori*, representational in nature, no other writer, not even Nietzsche, more accurately represented, *a posteriori*, the representational limits of objective knowledge first theorized by Kant's *Critique*, nor, for that matter, the annihilation of those limits by the kind of acts that Kant called "free," and that his *Logic* defined as not merely "nominal" or "discursive" objects of knowledge but "real."[372] Kleist's

---

372. See Kant, *Logik* A 221–222, § 106, "Nominal- und Real-Definitionen," VI: 575–76. Cf. Chapter Two, Section Five, n. 120, this study, and, for Diderot's similar view, Chapter Two, Section Seven, n. 195, n. 201, n. 205, this study. Gauging the degree of Kant's direct influence upon Kleist is (to recall Kant's turn of phrase regarding the "research" of "common sense") neither a feasible nor desirable task. More significant, this study argues, than any purported causal relation between them is that both philosopher and author understand cognition as a discursive activity requiring representation and subordinated, *as* discourse, to critical limitations. In Kant, the central division between delimited, causally structured cognition and noncognitive, free (moral) action is at once enacted and reflected in the theoretical and structural division between the First and Second Critique. In Kleist, the collision of narratively incompatible instances of cognition and freedom composes the occasion and progress of the narrative itself. The critical relation of each to its ostensible subject matter – "history"/"story" ("Geschichte") in the case of Kleist, and causality in the case of Kant's representational epistemology – is brilliantly observed by Carol Jacobs, in "The Style of Kleist," *diacritics*, Vol. 9, No. 4 (Winter 1979): 47–61: "One suspects then that no "Geschichte" can escape its own disruptive repetition from history to story, and perhaps this means that it is impossible to have a text that does not thereby ultimately become critical in the Kantian sense of the word (reason undertaking the task of self-knowledge [Smith, p. 9], and critical even beyond the limits of sense" (59; see 55–59). See also Brodsky, "Kant and Narrative Theory," Chapter 2 of *The Imposition of Form*, pp. 21–25, esp. An historical account of the relationship is provided in Ludwig Muth, *Kleist und Kant* (Köln: Kölner Universitäts-Verlag, 1954).

distinctive stylistic approach to the problem of representation – unlike, and unmistakable for, any other in German letters – made him Kant's literary *Doppelgänger* whether Kleist willed that twinship or not. True to the double philosophical constraints of Kant's *Critique* – that of knowledge theorized as indeed achievable, but only by way of representation, and that of free action theorized as not only possible but necessary, yet only *without* the intervention of representational knowledge – Kleist, like Kant, would have found nothing to be gained but further mystification of the possible (what Kant called the "mystical illumination" preached by "monarch[ic]" "mystagogen"[373]) by attempts to replace the mutually critical limits of our capabilities with absolute fictions of either positivist-empiricist or idealist persuasion, whether such fictions are literary or philosophical in vocabulary. The spectrum of agents and sufferers of action narrated and staged by Kleist's stories, anecdotes, and dramas extends freely from the spiritual to the prosaic, the regal to the accidental, the whimsical to the literally earth-shattering, and the mythological to the involuntary and mechanical. Among all these (and more), however, transcendent figures do not figure, precisely in that they would "appear" by way of discourse to transcend discourse in the mode of divinities. Indeed, using the impersonal negative version of a verbal phrase often employed narratively by Kleist in a personally alienating, if grammatically positive sense – that of persons reduced, *marionettenhaft*, to "playing roles"[374] excluding freedom of movement along with consciousness from their performance – we may say that, in Kleist's own fictions, the fiction of unconditional transcendence, in the form of any figure, *spielt gar keine Rolle*.

Unlike Kant's *Critique* for the most part,[375] however, Kleist's understanding of the limits of discourse and discursive logic faced an additional *a priori* limit: the added constraint, and complication, of representing experiential knowledge in a medium that is itself representational and discursive to begin with, that is, of representing the very limits of cognitive experience in the already inherently representational discourse of fiction, language always at a self-reflexive remove from the "real" it represents. Perhaps it was that hall-of-mirrors-effect, of fiction representing the experience of representational experience, one set of representational limits

---

373. See Kant, "Von einem neuerdings erhobenen vornehmen Ton in der Philosophie" ("On a newly elevated superior tone in Philosophy") *Werkausgabe, op.cit.* VI: 386, 383n, 388.

374. See "Die Marquise von O . . .," in Heinrich von Kleist, *Sämtliche Werke und Briefe* 2 Bde., Hrsg. Helmut Sembdner (München: Deutscher Taschenbuch Verlag, 1987), II: 106, 112, 139. All further quotations from Kleist are from this edition, and denoted by volume and page no.

375. The most significant exception to this rule would be Kant's own introduction of narration into his deduction of the origin of the "concept of freedom" in the Second Critique. See Kant, *KprV*, A 54, VII: 140, and Chapter Two, Section One, n. 45, this study. I have analyzed the equivocal status and critical necessity of this narrative turn in Kant, in *The Imposition of Form*, pp. 81–86, esp.

mirroring, *ad infinitum*, the other, that, understandably, drove Kleist to distraction. Yet just as, at the end of the dialogue narrated in "On the Marionette-Theater," Kleist offers the most effective (which is to say, regressive) representation of this effectively infinite regression, in the image of a "concave mirror" whose own illusory imaging of unfathomable depths is both the merely mechanical effect of *lumens* ricocheting between inter-"facing" surfaces and a canny, visual representation of every – material or mental – force that, invisibly "hitting" or confronting a surface, effects a division between immediacy and "reflection," so Kleist's stories compel us to traverse the arc of the mind delineating and holding these two separate realms of experience in place. And what emerges at the other "end" of that traversal – the result to which the airtight construction and pointed impenetrability of these stories representing representational experience tend – are individual, at once externally determined and self-reflexive "realizations" of the fact that fictions of narrative and dramatic action are both the only way and, necessarily, the always misleading way to represent experience in any "real" sense at all.

From and reflecting this condition of fiction – of a knowledge of experience not hypothetically theorized, as it is by Kant, but rather *represented,* both lexically and diegetically, as limited by experience *a priori* – the peculiar slant of the literary discourse that Kleist employs extends. For, whether spoken in the first or authorial third person, the words of Kleist's works appear to glance off the depth of the events they represent like light off a theatrical scrim, their illumination angled to skim the surface of a fabric pulled so taut and thin as to become, at any moment that angle is altered, translucent, rather than visible as a fabric at all. Kleist's textual simulations of a purposefully fabricated, superficial perspective – his training of discourse so as to conceal, and, at another moment, reveal a pivotal scene already "there," already "taking place" behind a central screen, rather than kept waiting, like an omnipotent *deus ex machina* or circumstantial *dénouement,* off in the wings – could hardly be more in keeping with Kant's theoretization of all the things of experience as merely phenomenal, but no less consequential appearances, the vertiginous, simultaneous sense of the surface and unstated, noumenal depth of experience that every line of Kant's own discursive project conveys.

Thus, whatever the *real* as opposed to theoretical conflict between our cognitive mediations of experience, on the one hand, and the reality of the things and events we experience, on the other, as Kleist himself is said to have experienced during his "*Kant-Krise,*" it is fair to say that whenever no such crisis or even critical interest regarding the formalization required for any actual cognition, let alone all communicability of experience, to take place – when the representational relation of knowledge to experience, and suspension of representation in judgment, appear, instead, eclipsed by their conflation, as if the artifice of representation that we not only know and reason, but, increasingly, live and die by, could simply be occluded or *theoretically* suspended by paradoxical assertions of an entirely passive, "purely" sensory reception of a phenomenality somehow without phenomenality, or appearance of any kind – then Kleist, no stranger, in theory or practice, to eclipses of reason and other natural disasters, may offer the most timely, because untimely, critique of such nonreflective practices. For, unlike all deadly confusions nonsensically equating "language" with a variety of nonlanguages – pictures, bodies, magically sensate matter, purely sensory "non-sense" or, for that matter, materially transcendent "mathematics" (the list does not so much grow as cycle through itself repetitively) – and identifying words and any formal sign operative within any linguistic system as such with the realm of purely materially given and thus essentially *non*verbal, *Empirie* or 'stuff,'[376] Kleist's writing does not substitute a selective *découpage* and assemblage of verbal snippets for thinking. The conspicuously crafted semantic ambiguity of the very mechanics of Kleist's prose, its freighting of the essential sequentiality of syntax with the full weight of discrete alongside narrative meaning, reveals both the critical difference between representation and whatever object, state, or action is represented, and "succeeds" in relating these in an at once clearly meaningful and immediately opaque, unrecognizable way. Indeed, Kleist may be most meaningfully read whenever sterile monisms prevail instead, precisely because, for its active readers no less than its actor-characters, Kleist's prose achieves the contrary: recognizing, in a supremely dialectical fashion, its "success" is "failure,"

376. The facile use and figural abuse of the term, "archaeology," as a kind of *passe-partout* replacement for critical historical analysis of the complex bases and content of humanly composed objects and practices, popularized by Foucault's depiction of "history" as a series of static scenographies of domination, has come to stand for such reifying tendencies of late. Of the many incisive critiques, informing the history of philosophy and theory, that take aim at such doubly reductive, i.e., not merely thought-free but thought-annihilating compilations of human products, as if merely empirical extants, under arbitrary "taxonomic" themes and names, none may surpass Hegel's early exposé (*Phenomenology* [1807]) of the tiresome "trick" of the "method," passing off "lifeless determinations" for "wisdom," of "labeling" "natural and intellectual forms" alike as one does "boxes or cans in a grocer's stall" or "a skeleton with scraps of paper glued to it:"

> The knack of this kind of wisdom is as quickly learned as it is easy to practice; the repetition of it, once familiar, becomes as insufferable as the repetition of a conjuring trick already seen through... What results from this method of labeling everything in the heavens and earth, every natural and intellectual form, with a few determinations of a general schema so as better to order them... is namely a [taxonomic] table resembling a skeleton with bits of paper glued to it or the rows of sealed boxes or cans with stickers stuck on them in a grocer's stall ... lifeless determinations ... of an understanding as dead as such cognition is external. [Der Pfiff einer solchen Weisheit ist so bald erlernt, als es leicht ist, ihn auszuüben; seine Wiederholung einer eingesehenen Taschenspielerkunst.... Was diese Methode, allem Himmlischen und Irdischen, allen natürlichen und geistigen Gestalten die paar Bestimmung ... aufzukleben und auf diese Weise alles einzurangieren, hervorbringt, ist ... nämlich eine Tabelle, die einem Skelette mit angeklebten Zettelchen oder den Reihen verschlossener Buchsen mit ihren aufgehefteten Etiketten in einer Gewürzkrämerbude gleicht [...]leblosen Bestimmungen ... eines gleich toter Verstand ... und gleich äusserliches Erkennen. (G.W.F. Hegel, *Phänomenologie dies Geistes*, in *Theorie-Werkausgabe*, XX Bde., Hrg. E. Moldenhauer and K. M. Michel [Frankfurt: Suhrkamp, 1969-71], III: 50-51).

Kleist lucidly represents the relationship of representation and represented as elusive – as difficult as it is necessary to the very possibility of *acting* to ascertain.

The ways in which Kleist enacts that difficulty are legion and deservedly well known.[377] Prosaic, representational and grammatical; narrative, spoken, and interpolated, rather than overtly speculative: the shifts in meaning, as between tragedy and comedy, that *we* experience in reading Kleist's language convey an underlying sense of language itself as appearance or "Schein," just as they convey experience itself as communicable only through a kind of formalism, the "regular"[378] relation of events on which any account of experience depends. Easily and nonetheless accurately, one speaks of Kleistian "irony" – that all in Kleist is never as it seems. Yet the variety of formal and lexical ways in which Kleist writes – to quote Goethe on discursive mediation – "mit Ironie,"[379] make evident that no other medium than discourse could so convincingly state *and* question its own sense, enact its own self-evidence and concealment of evidence as richly and apparently obliviously, as significantly and insouciantly, comedically and disastrously, or with such lucidity and opacity, at every comprehensible and mysterious turn.

---

377. See esp. Lilian Furst, "Double-Dealing in the *Marquise von O* . . .," in *Echoes and Influences of German Romanticism,* ed. M. S. Batts, A. W. Riley, and H. Wetzel (New York: Peter Lang, 1987), pp. 85–95; Bernd Fischer, "Irony Ironized; Heinrich von Kleist's Narrative Stance and Friedrich Schlegel's Theory of Irony," *European Romantic Review*, Vol. 1, No. 1 (1990): 59–74; Helmut Schneider, "Standing and Falling in Heinrich von Kleist," *MLN*, Vol 115, No. 3 (April 2000): 502–18; Bianca Theisen, "Simultaneity: A Narrative Figure in Kleist," *MLN*, Vol. 121, No. 3 (April 2008): 514–21. See also my "Whatever Moves You: 'Experimental Philosophy', 17–43 (40–43 esp.).

378. As described in *Words' Worth,* this is Wordsworth's term for the condition, conveyed equally in poetry and prose by meter, that allows writing and reading to proceed past the "overbalances" of which experience is composed.

379. Johann Wolfgang von Goethe, "Vorwort zur Farbenlehre," *Werke*, Hamburger Ausgabe, XIV Bde., Hrsg. E. Trunz, et. al. (München: dtv, 1982), XIII: 317.

2. What happened: Misrepresentation and Missed Representation in "Die Marquise von O …"

The best – and least – well "known" example of the transparent obscurity of Kleist's prose occurs in the infamous sentence near the opening of the *Marquise von O …*, that, hiding the story's pivotal action in plain, narrative sight, *at once enacts and represents* the inaccessibility of its buried content to actors and readers of the story alike. The single sentence upon which the celebrated suspense of the story will hinge itself hinges upon a sign so literally self-effacing as to involve no semantic denotation at all. Standing for a break in representational content – an ostensible marking of a *lack* of sense – that sign is the dash or "Gedankenstrich" appearing just after the story's imperceptibly telling sentence begins: "Hier – traf er, da bald darauf ihre erschrockenen Frauen erschienen, Anstalten, einen Artzt zu rufen; versicherte, indem er sich den Hut aufsetzte, dass sie sich bald erholen würde; und kehrte in den Kampf zurück."[380]

Like the very event it both does and does not represent, Kleist's most famously confounding sentence turns conventions on their head even in the act of complying with their formal norms. Following syntactic prescriptions and employing commonplace turns of phrase, the sentence nonetheless renders its own sequential understanding, and thereby, any translation or paraphrase of it inaccurate *per force*. For the sense of Kleist's utterance bifurcates between the syntactically deferred and idiomatic, and immediate and literal meaning of a single verb: "traf" ("struck," "hit," "met"). A rendering of the sentence in English that reproduces the obligatory syntactic position of the verb in the original would literally translate the opening of the sentence as follows: "Here – struck he …". Yet the further development of the sentence reveals that "traf," its principal active verb, may mean something else entirely, as defined by its postponed predicate complement,

---

380. Kleist, II: 106. See ref. n. 386 for a necessarily disjointed, because syntactically *and* lexically literal English translation of this sentence, whose regular German syntax cannot be rendered in regular English syntax except through a series of smoothing transpositions. Directly re-attaching to the conjugated verb "traf" ("met," "struck," "hit") its long postponed, formulaic complement, as composed by Kleist, these literally "trans-lating" transpositions, moving the contents of one end of Kleist's sentence to the other, dispense with both the diacritical "dash" directly preceding that active verb and the deictic "Here" the "dash" immediately succeeds, thereby destroying by burying all access to the verb's literal meaning.

"Anstalten" ("preparations," "measures,"). Read with that complement already in mind, which is to say, retrospectively rather than sequentially, the main clause of the sentence would have to be re-translated as follows: "Here – he took...measures to call a doctor ...". Like the *a priori* spatial form of all cognitive phenomenal perception hypothesized by Kant, the sequencing integral to every syntactic utterance is determined by *a priori* grammatical rules. The subordinate clause intervening between the main active verb and its complement, itself introduced by the ambiguous (either co-temporaneous or causal) conjunction, "da" ("while;" "in that;" "since") – "da ihre erschrockenen Frauen bald darauf erschienen" ("while [or "in that;" "since"] her frightened women appeared soon thereafter") – has the progressive effect of effacing the immediate, physical meaning(s) of "treffen" ("hit," "struck," "met") with which the sentence begins, and replacing these recursively with the contrary, secondary and idiomatically specific meanings, "take," "make," that its delayed predication by "Anstalten" ("preparations;" "measures") dictates.

Cloaked in conventionality, the first, apparently inconsequential verb of a single sentence inconspicuously productive of the entire story to come will first be recognized as such after and apart from its having been read, when its duplicitous significance is revealed to the reader externally, either by word of mouth or the work of philology. In this it puts the reader in the "position" of the Marquise herself, subjected to an "unwitting conception" on which all subsequent conceptions depend.[381] Like the apparently saving gesture by which the Graf – at first reading – rescues the Marquise from violation, Kleist's sentence demonstrates that any single word, even one of apparently straightforward transitive significance like "treffen" ("meet," "strike"), and any even apparently meaningless or gratuitous sign, such as a "Gedankenstrich," a "line," "stroke" or "dash" taking the place of "thought," can confound all understanding of the "story" of which it is a part.

The problems for understanding that Kleist's sentence reveals relate not only to secondary problems of "translation." For, while their syntactic and grammatical norms distinguish the operations of linguistic systems from one another, their positive, practical constitution occurs on the level of each sentence and subject of which a language is capable. Language first produces subjects by linking them verbally, both to each other and to non-subjects, composing, in so doing, an articulated world of action and interaction wholly dependent in its origin and existence upon those relations. Yet the creation of grammatical subjects requires acts of predication that, just as systematically, project our attention away from them, both conceptually and syntactically. Just as the subject of a sentence only "is" insofar as it "does" (including the doing of being done to, i.e., defined or modified in some way), every sentence, every act of predication, is, in small, an act of narration. And while narration, by definition, incorporates that which is different from the subject it names, its specifically *verbal* delineation of the constitutive relations in which any subject is engaged may prove either immediately to be, or retrospectively to have been, a forking path. Not only the most celebrated

---

381. Kleist, II: 124.

Gedankenstrich in literature,[382] but the entire sentence in which it originally occurs (and appears "originally" to operate *only* syntactically), enacts the loss of a single representable sense in the course of predication itself: the inability of a purely graphic, nonrepresentational symbol or linear "stroke" ("Strich") - "—" - to coincide, linguistically and spatially, with the representational meaning of the deictic adverb that immediately precedes it, "Hier."[383] As its own temporal "encounter" by any reader demonstrates, no "—" can be "here" at one and the same moment in time: in order to be intelligible as such, a purely graphic and a verbal deictic indicating a single location can never coincide in space. Similarly, the conjugated transitive verb ("traf") whose position, abutting a dash succinctly demarcating and separating it from the directional, "here," conveys "at first blush" (to use another characteristically Kleistian *double-entendre*[384]) the sense of a target directly and purposefully "*struck*" - "Hier - *traf* er" - only to undergo the total alteration in meaning brought about by its grammatically postponed completion, one, no less semantically equivocal, subordinate clause later, by the formulaic object, "Anstalten" ("Hier - traf er.... Anstalten:" "Here ... he took ... measures"). Any single reading (let alone

382. For a compelling discussion of the critical equivocal status of Kleist's mischevious, apparently gratuitously inserted dash, whose "narrative context ... deliberately misleads the reader into ignoring [it]," see Dorrit Cohn's excellent "Kleist's 'Marquise von O ...': the Problem of Knowledge," *Monatsheft* Vol. 67, No. 2, 1975 (129–44): 129. While underscoring the imperceptible technical role of the dash in leading the reader of the story down the garden path, Cohn views the Marquise's failure to make the proper identification of the subject and transitive action for which it stands in realist, psychological terms, concluding that "Kleist endowed the Marquise with an unconscious form of knowledge unacknowledged by her conscious self," an "erotic knowledge" that, entailing a "frantic shutting out" that "paradoxically betrays the presence of the knowledge within the self" (133), echoes the self-deceiving psychology of all Kleist's characters: "Kleist so rarely provides insider views of his characters because their psyches are usually subject to such violent and conflicting emotions that words are powerless to describe them" (140). This study argues, by contrast, that what Cohn views as the Marquise's repression of powerful "emotions" may have never been objectifiable to begin with. On an epistemological level, then, the event simultaneously represented and buried by Kleist's "silent" (129) dash would be as incompatible with its "conscious," narrative representation as the appearance of natural "grace" in motion effected by their manipulation is known to the wooden limbs of Kleist's "marionettes," its enactment attributed, as they are ultimately by the Marquise, to the superhuman powers of "Angel" or "Devil" instead.

383. Kleist, II: 106.

384. In the course of the narration of the "Marquise von O ..." - story of an immediately indecipherable physical act as uncontemplated by its subject as its object - the involuntary physical act of blushing (variously, "becoming red," "embarrassed," "heated," or "glowing") seen to transpose an unspoken, internal excitement to the face, accompanies nearly every conscious meeting and inquiry regarding the relation between that subject and object. See Kleist, II:106, 107, 110 (2x), 112, 116, 122, 125, 128, 130, 135, 136 (2x), 140. See also II: 110 and 113, in which a related "loss of color" (in the Graf's face) is noted instead.

translation) of this most majestically misleading of sentences must indeed mangle its meaning, and, in so doing, further conceal the content of its effectively exclamatory, at once semantic *and* spatial indication ("Here—") of a specific action, removing, through their double, graphic and semantic representation, both the mystery of the story and its "solution" equally undetectably from view.

Including and occluding the answers to the central referential and causal questions of any narrative – who, what, where, how, and when? – Kleist's sentence renders these no more available to the reader than to the "unconscious" ("bewusstlos") Marquise herself, unrepresented object of a transitive action ("traf" ["met/struck"]) that, while originating in a distinct subject, "he," ("er"), ends instead in vaguely designated "measures" ("Anstalten") whose own purely formal, periphrastic sense contradicts the literal physical sense of the verb it complements, effectively shrouding not only our own but that subject's consciousness of what "he" has done.[385] Still, mangling English syntax instead of German semantics, so as to reproduce the critical syntactic position of each element in the original and juxtapose the alternative meanings that the crossing paths of its syntax and grammar suggest, a literal, grammatical rendering of the sentence, viewed retrospectively, might be graphically represented like this: "Here – struck/met/hit he, in that/since/because shortly thereafter her terrified ladies appeared, measures to call a doctor; assured, in that/while/because he put his hat on, that she would recover soon; and turned back into the battle."[386]

An additional consideration, however, renders the corrective aspirations of even that ungainly syntactic imitation moot, or, worse, misleading, in that it, too, remains, strictly speaking, beside the point. For, while a *Gedankenstrich* is a mark neither in need of nor available to direct lexical translation, Kleist's placement of it ("—") directly *after* the word, "here," makes "here" mean not, or not only, "here" but there, where "there" is no word of deixis, no verbal indication of a position in space, but a purely graphic *or* nonverbal linear stroke, a marking of somewhere *or* something else than "here" that is another here in itself. In the tapestry of *double-entendres* that compose this text – threads compiled into scenes whose subjects, actions, and object, upon closer inspection, can no longer be identified – Kleist's "dash" is terrifically easy to read past. Yet, still more troubling than the questions first raised by its perception after the fact, is the fact that this particular "dash" is, in narrative as well as syntactic terms, a mistake, a diacritical marking consistent with neither the content nor the grammar of the sentence in which it appears. Unrequired – indeed, rendered erroneous – by its immediate context, this dash (or

---

385. *Ibid.*, II: 106.

386. Ibid; see ref. n. 380 for German original. The additional, decorously obscene *double-entendre*, of the Graf's "assuring" others, while/in that he "put his hat back on" (*after* doing the undefined deed immediately designated by "traf"), that the Marquise will recover nicely, is also masked by the syntactic and diacritical (near) disappearing act this sentence performs on the Graf's main reported action ("traf er"), as are the sexual allusions of later repeated references to the Graf and his either "förmlich" ("polite") or practical (prophylactic) repositionings on his head of his hat.

"stroke" of a pen) may be judged to be either an irregular, graphic insertion on its author's part *or* to perform a very different, nongrammatical and non-narrative semantic function: that of rendering irreducibly present its own aberrant intrusion upon the regular, past-tense recounting of events in which it appears, and thereby enacting *in* representing or standing in for, in any present of its encounter, the mistaken occurrence of aberrancy itself. For, even were we instead to refer the dash within Kleist's sentence back to the deictic it succeeds, we would remain just as unable to say where (or what) "here" is, to know, in short, what we were reading.

The immediate purpose of any "Gedankenstrich" – the complex German word for a simple graphic mark whose yoking together of "thought(s)" and "stroke" renders its own "literal" meaning no less uncertain[387] – may be to leap, as it were, to a subsequent, associated, but unsubordinated thought, spontaneously leaving another behind, or, equally, to mark the extension of one's thinking in two different directions at once. Kleist's grammatically gratuitous, apparently semantically vacuous, syntactical dash does both, referring the narrative verb and subject that follow it (" – traf er" [– struck/hit/met/encountered he]) *back* to the adverbial deictic ("Hier—") that immediately precedes it, so as to convey an already completed, direct transitive action, *and* directing that same transitive verb *away from* the indicated location of its enactment, ("here") to a formulaic complement ("measures" or "preparations" ["Anstalten"]) at once delayed and overshadowed by intervening dependent clauses rife with their own ambiguous conjunctions and double-entendres: "ladies" who either "appeared *terrified*" or "*appeared* terrified;" "assurances" given either "while" or "because" the Graf, either literally or euphemistically speaking, "put his hat on his head;" and the "return" of the Graf "into the battle" (again, literally or euphemistically meant).

Just so, word after word, *treffen* after *treffen*, each syntactically and semantically *untreffend* ("here," and not "here;" direct and all but direct in their sense), the equivocal verbal representation and graphically marked occlusion of predication composing a single, apparently negligible, narrative sentence conceals ("here—") in the smallest discursive space, and without the slightest legible ripple, the central act whose identity and agent generate the entire story of "Die Marquise von O . . ." *as a story*.[388] Furthermore, even as the ostensible causal mystery of that story, a modern

---

387. When spelled out literally, the elided genitive or prepositional construction connecting "Gedanken" to "Strich" yields all of the following meanings: "a line of," "a line (standing) for," or "a line struck through and cancelling thought(s)."

388. Perhaps the best extensive gloss on the irresoluble, historically productive tension between agent and action, event and structure, and other incommensurate components of the "double vision" written into all of Kleist's stories is Steven Howe's excellent study of the political thinking underlying their composition in comparison with that of the theorist and literary author Kleist most resembled, Rousseau. See Steven Howe, *Heinrich von Kleist and Jean-Jacques Rousseau. Violence, Identity, Nation* (New York: Camden House, 2012): "In exploring the limitations of knowledge, the relation between agency and structure, and the necessary expedients of war against imperial tyranny, [Kleist] adopts a 'Dialektik der Aufklärung' that was not discovered by Adorno and Horkheimer in the 1940's but had

classic of the "whodunit" genre originating in the tragedy of Oedipus, appears resolved in the manner of a comedy of mistaken identity, the narrative representation of the titular Marquise's experience remains true to its entitling ellipses ("von O ...") and foundational *Strich*. Beginning with a personal advertisement of ignorance – a published inquiry into the empirical history of one's most intimate relations – and ending with the perpetuation of ignorance in future editions of those same relations, the "ganze Reihe von jungen Russen" ("whole series of young Russians"[389]) that follow upon the first, every intervening act related by its narrative appears, on one level, public or common knowledge, and, on another, imperceptible to its agents and readers alike.[390] Indeed, in Kleist's narrative world no real difference

---

rather been uncovered contemporaneously by its leading thinkers of the age and then given new and dangerous inflections by the experience of the Revolution and its wars" (204); on the clarity of Kleist's and Rousseau's "double vision," see in particular Chapter 1, "Kleist, Rousseau and the Paradoxes of Enlightenment," pp. 12–55.

389. Kleist, II: 143.

390. By direct contrast, leaning heavily on a presumed homology of fiction with "information," and systems and data theory, Jake Fraser's "Kleist's Secrets. Nachrichtenverkehr in *Die Marquise von O ...*" (*Deutsche Vierteljahrsschrift* [2017] 91: 254–296) employs the notion of "intelligence" gathering and concealment (or "secrets") to relegate even the possibility of conflict between sensory experience and understanding, of the kind every subject in Kleist encounters, to a critical past best replaced by a freshly informed awareness of both the (somehow) autonomous ability of "information" to "locate" "knowledge in non-knowledge" "ontologically," and our own continuous "submission" "to the material constraints" of "the event that exists only and through the medium of information" whose "conduits" we are (272). Whatever "knowledge in non-knowledge" can mean in a non-rhetorical sense, and wherever and however the "medium of information" and "the event that exists ... through it" are themselves enacted are not questions, on their author's view, but rather givens, as is the independent will of "information" to "locate" anything, let alone an oxymoron in space. While attempted erasures of experience by replacements granting "ontological" priority to mysteriously autotelic "information" may be viewed merely to extend to "secret" surveillance "services" the unselfconsciously transcendental-metaphysical substantivizations of "media" that have made the resuscitation of a regressive, neo-Aristotelian focus on "Being" inevitable, Fraser's chosen literary context (or, in his terms, that for which he serves as "conduit") raises the obvious question: what would the pregnant, not simultaneously non-pregnant Marquise think? For unlike Descartes' famous use of the phrase in his early *Cogitationes Privatae* to describe his mode of entry into the *mundi teatrum*, the emblem of "'*larvatus prodeo*'" that Fraser's study bears in epigraph is most accurately considered a mask itself, in that the "secret" of which, it argues, the Marquise's story (or, as René Girard similarly argued decades ago with regard to all stories) is the "operational" "effect" is itself neither "open" (to cite Anne-Lise François' instructive term) nor the temporally contingent "effect" of "thinking" described by Descartes, but, rather, "empty" – thus begging the question of what constitutes "information" in the first place. As the ever-ripening irony of literary history would have it, however, by locating the "proof" of

seems to distinguish the actors represented from the readers of their representation: both do not so much overlook the "big picture" conveyed by the story told, as forget that it is composed, of necessity, of innumerable brushstrokes, each apparently insignificant, each, logically speaking, equally critical.

Thus it is no criticism to state that, like Kant's epistemology of causally related, representational phenomena, Kleist's narratives "appear" at once inevitable and superficial: indicative not of any "thing in itself" but of the limited, refractive nature of our empirical perceptions, compounded in literature by their further representation. Always intimating that something they are not stating (or rather, are and are not stating) is actively afoot, steadily if imperceptibly advancing the unpredictable causality of their plots, the perfect coherence of these fables of implacable events presents the representations they enact – whether of a father whose wife joyfully watches through a keyhole as he kisses their daughter "just like a lover,"[391] or of the circulation in "newsprint" by that widowed daughter of her wish "to make the acquaintance" of her "child's father"[392] – with unwavering, impersonal equanimity, as if their thoroughly unverisimilar, yet no less recognizable content were itself indistinguishable from the formal discursive rules of its recounting. The detached, descriptive idiom of Kleist's distinctive narrative voice coolly strings together improbabilities in the manner of a speaker for whom the commission of the very act of narration is merely to reiterate accepted forms of expressions, conventional statements as extraneous to the experience they articulate as the discursive surface they weave is opaque. Even as their mimetic narrative content retains its wildly unconventional character without ever slipping into the recognizably absurd, the narrative sentences that convey those thoroughly unpredictable actions, scenes and events proceed with the kind of formal order that characterizes the successful performance of norms.

If literary "style" in general consists in a kind of authorial imprint – the distinctive, individual shaping of a common medium – Kleist's verbally inimitable style of narration, conflating the unmistakably individual with general rules of decorum, and spontaneous actions with their rote enactment, is its own perfect, prosaic imitation, the polite removal and repositioning of a "hat" capping and reproducing the "real" actions (in Kant's sense of the word) they hide in plain sight. Conveying with carefully wrought syntactic elegance their own fidelity to freedom, combining self-constraining discipline with gratuitous motivation, the orderly style of Kleist's stories resembles the props or material support of the at once

---

a Kleistian "information" theory in a single, openly satirical reference by Kleist, in the hilarious "Lehrbuch der Französischen Journalistik" (1809), to a "secret archive" in which this mock-Napoleonic manual for world domination through propaganda-"journalism" is reported hidden, Fraser helpfully re-introduces us to Kleist's own prescient account of the all-too actual consequences of granting to exclusively mediatized, imperial ambitions metaphysical rather than fictional priority.

391. Kleist, II: 138.
392. Kleist, II: 104, 131.

conventional and extraordinary "encounter(s)" they relate, a perfectly sentential mode that makes order itself appear not orderly but out of place, as displaceable and indispensable to the narration of action as its punctuation, a kind of verbal "hat" whose positioning demarcates actions, allowing them to begin and end.[393]

393. In the exquisitely literal cinematic rendering of the "Marquise von O ..." by Eric Rohmer (1976), in which the text of eventful narrative passages is reproduced preceding changes of scene on the screen, the diacritical function of his hat is placed squarely on view whenever the enigmatic "Graf," "performed" with perfectly sincere opacity by the great Bruno Ganz, enters into respectful proximity with the "unwitting" Marquise. Proof of its enduring transferability to any context, Kleist's practical employment of this piece of masculine haberdashery as "out-fitting," the punctuating, diacritical mark of disguised attempts both to "make good on" and mask ill-fitting actions, is perhaps nowhere more effectively carried forward than in Joel and Ethan Coen's masterful *Miller's Crossing* (1990). The densely layered, rapid-fire exchanges of dialogue, bullets and blows that together compose the "war" between smalltime gangsters comprising the main plotline of the Coens' film, one whose motivations remain as purposefully diegetically unclear as the causal laws its characters put into motion and manipulate remain steadfast, make its distinctively individually mannered (while never wooden) characters appear alternately puppeteers and marionettes. The mournful gravity with which the main protagonist, "Tom," brilliantly played by Gabriel Byrne, carefully attends from start to finish to his fedora, makes the Kleistian significance of "mere" props or trappings to this purposefully appointed, stylized film hard to miss, the choreography of its characters' casual capacity for violence, by a reversal on the "Marquise ...," placed squarely on the surface, Tom's oft-entreated "heart," hidden. Even had the Coens not stated that their conception of the film originated in the image of a fedora being blown through the woods, nor closed the film with the dark brim of Tom's fedora being lowered, like closing brackets or a casket cover, over eyes that, having first shown sorrow, had looked directly, in a sole and last close-up, at no one but the viewer, before being veiled in a dirge-like procession of receding frames, the insistence of the hat, in Byrne's eloquent hands, speaks volumes within the Coens' plotting of an irreparable faultline, the never clarified "misunderstanding" or "mix-up" its bearer always knew to be permanent. In the hands of the Coen Bros., the fearful prospect of an element of male décor, as conventional as "gangsterdom," blown pell mell across a forest whose named "crossing" point no winds respect, is represented in a story in which just the opposite transpires, and its wearer ends up lost *because* the hat, so to speak, sticks.

With or without the happy coincidence of a punctuating hat, few compositions, including Frank Stella's great "Marquise von O" series (1998–2000), enact the crafted density and lucidity of Kleist's writing – its polish, pathos, air-tight plotting, violence and humor – as effectively as the Coens' film, and, by no coincidence, no other verbal composition comes close. Small wonder that, like Kleist, the Coens are as often admired as criticized for their conspicuous use of eccentric objects and generic markings rather than recognizable motivation to support the extra-ordinary stories of the apparently ordinary they tell, or, what comes to the same, the sense of what does and does not meet the eye that their precisely scripted, verbal and visual narratives convey: light beaming through bullet holes in a debut "film noir;" tracks of blood and tires revealed from a God's eye perspective to snake across "innocent-as-the-driven"

And, like any object set into motion, the "merely" formal acts that Kleist's particular style of narrative sentence appears to relate prove to be causally effective as well. The singular "striking" of a sexual target that, narratively disguised as a polite "taking of measures," results in a "marriage contract" denying the "spouse" conjugal "rights," and ascribing all wealth and sovereignty to mother and offspring in "Die Marquise . . .;"[394] the war of a "righteous" Michael Kohlhaas against all after his arbitrarily disfigured property in not fully restored;[395] the divided outcome of a "duel" stipulated to decide truth "divinely" in "Der Zweikampf" ("The Duel"):[396] all are indecipherable actions and events that, unavailable to judgment, take on the cast of conventionality, even as the causal chain they unleash in reality proves ironclad. Catalysts of irreversible change, these pivotal Kleistian acts reveal the dormant active verb, *verbinden* ("to bind"), at the root of the term for rote social forms, *Verbindlichkeiten* ("obligations," "forms of courtesy"), whose many verbal variants compose a kind of standing lexicon in Kleist.[397] For, in the "world" of Kleist's compositions, both actions *and* their verbal representation rest explicitly on social and linguistic conventions, "binding" formalities whose following crosses the very line between form and content they draw. This is to say that not only gestures of polite social intercourse, but obligatory discursive and grammatical forms become narrative in effect once employed, i.e., as eventful, even physically consequential, as the metaphorically "binding" power of moral "obligation."

Such doubly binding terms inform Kleist's justly celebrated, structural (or, in Kant's terms, "architectonic") "irony" as well. Enforcing "formality" in both the discursive and social *and* epistemological and moral sense – that of a socially constituted "condition" originating in what Kant describes as a necessarily *linguistically* enactable "common sense," and that of a formalism of faculties entirely "free" from or *a priori* to any individual network of social conventions and norms – irony permeates Kleist's narratives from their syntax to turns of plot. Undergirding and accompanying them from beginning to end, it at once binds and divides the "roles" or "parts" played by discourse and action in the stories, making of narration itself a two-sided form of communication. In this (one might

---

Midwestern snow; weird, immobile hairstyles and signature bowling gear; regional and archaic speech patterns and music; conspicuous classical and biblical figures; detailed set design and stylized cinematography; and, yes, a wildly out-of-place pregnancy. In the immortal words of the proudly do-nothing character and least likely narrative vehicle of all, who insists on being called by a generic masculine moniker (become *au courrant* ever since among males of every occupation and description, indeed, so generically expressive a marker it is now used by all genders) and whose proper name in fact sets his terrifically mixed-up tale of woe in motion: each of these decorative elements is the "rug" that "pulls the whole [room] together," the "hat" keeping agent and action from falling apart.

394. Kleist, II: 142–143.
395. Kleist, II: 10, 14, 15.
396. Kleist, II: 261.
397. Kleist, II: 105, 110, 112, 117, 118, 130, 143, *et passim*.

well say, ironically) irony in Kleist most resembles not the falling apart but the necessary mediating link ("Mittelglied"[398]) of knowledge and freedom that is for Kant the "power of judgment." For, like Kleist's Janus-faced stories, Kant's capacity for judging, unbound by either cognitive or moral forms, provides a "bridge" or basis of relation between them, generally intelligible or "common" forms of communication ("Mit-*teil*-ung"[399]) that first enable acts of "participation" ("*Teilnehmen*") – that "taking part" of which, ironically, one becomes the medium or part taken, part of some thing or activity that, in itself unavailable to conscious perception, one cannot state in an appropriate way.

The way Kleist uses irony to "bridge" the division between cognition and action his stories represent appears especially pronounced in "Die Marquise von O . . .," a tale of ignorance and knowledge conspicuously pregnant with the fruits of their "encounter." Not only the quandary of visibly "altered circumstances"[400] that appear to dictate the story from beginning to end – from their publication in newsprint to their involuntary resolution in a second physical act, as the "obligatory forms" ("Verbindlichkeiten") that bind Marquise and Graf *postfactum* find their "release" in an "Ent-bindung" ("birth" or "delivery;" literally, "unbinding")[401] duly prefaced by the signing of contractual bonds – but each duplicitously knowing narrative sentence seems to serve as stand-in for a single, inexplicable[402] and, as it turns out, singularly productive act of "binding," one literally uniting otherwise isolated bodies to compose a new body, the non-narrative origin represented within the story by the graphic sign of its omission. Everything that follows narratively from, frames and precedes that discretely uninterpretable sign indicates that, no less than the Marquise, her author cannot decide whether the agent of the action it stands for is "angel," or "devil,"[403] or, perhaps more disturbingly, a kind of *Gedankenstrich* or bridge between the two. Author of the same act of violation from whose commission he had just defended the Marquise, the Graf seems to embody the pure viability of any mediating medium, a materiality of formation unrelated to peception, and, as such, inaccessible to judgment itself.

Just the opposite appears the case in another of Kleist's narrative fictions, whose story and plot structure function within his *corpus* as a kind of bookend to "Die

398. Kant, *KU* B V, X: 74.
399. Kant, *KU* B 65, 67, X: 157–58.
400. Kleist, II: 104.
401. Kleist, II: 143.
402. As if commenting on the contemporary concept of "enlightenment" ("Aufklärung"), Kleist weaves the word (along with its close verbal relations, "Erklärung" and "erklären" ["explanation," to explain"]) into the fabric of his story of a subject in search of "enlightenment" as to her own "inconceivable alteration of form" ("unbegreifliche Veränderung ihrer Gestalt" [119]) with a frequency approached only by the permutations of "verbinden" he employs, often in tandem with these. See Kleist, II: 105, 111 (3x), 112 (3x), 117 (3x), 118 (4x), 120, 129, 133, 142, *et passim*.
403. Kleist, II: 143.

Marquise von O . . .". The founding action of "Der Zweikampf" ("The Duel) is also an act of intimate violation: a striking or hitting literally reported to "pierce" ("durchbohr[en]"[404]) its target. Yet that definitive corporal transgression is instead represented with syntactically heightened directness. Rather than buried in narrative parts unknown, it emerges suddenly and abruptly out of an intricate web of subordinate clauses stemming not from its agent but its target, the subject named in the story's first words. The encasing of that subject in layers of syntax unfurling skeins of contextual information, both within and alongside each other, in the story's hyper-hypotactic first sentence, proves no more effective a bulwark against its breach than a "chestbone" against arrow. Rather than effectively buried under a diacritical mark, this "hit" hits the reader, too, with the sudden clarity and force proper to the physical event. Not the identity of that event itself, its what, how, where, and when, but its who, its doer, alone remains unaccounted for, and the judgment of what becomes a moving target of culpability, on the basis of sworn yet equivocal testimony, identifiable but misattributable physical evidence, and the entailment and displacement of all of these by other disputed events, compose the entire body of the narrative thereafter. In "The Duel" (literally, the "combat of two, or "Zwei-kampf"), the mediating function of judgment acts not as a nonrepresentational bridge (or dash) spanning two mutually exclusive experiential realms and modes (such as the "angel"/"devil" that "is" the "saving" *and* target-"striking" "Graf"), but as the unraveling of experience itself. For, "The Duel" tells a story of "encounters" that, in contrast with the unswerving blow that gives rise to them, only appear, or appear only temporarily to meet their mark, a series of misleading, mistaken, false, or simply missed signs that follow upon the direct hit they nearly cast into oblivion, effectively replacing it, by accumulated misdirection, as central subject of the story itself. For the issue in dispute in the eponymous "duel" is not, in fact, that of the proper identity of a successful assassin, agent of the undisputed offense of murder committed against a member of the landed gentry, but a purported failing or flaw of female virtue – first and most reliable substitute (as Kleist all too effectively, ironically demonstrates) for the judgment of men by men. The duel toward which the story builds sidelines the graphically described, concrete crime with which it began in favor of a dispute over the rectitude of an honored woman, as the object of judgment slides from the capital crime of murder to a notional lack of chastity and the mode of judgment slips from human discourse to sacred event, the latter supposedly embodied in the life or death of dueling combatants.

Yet, *like* the discursive murder investigation and trial that it first displaces then replaces, and ensuing narrative development of the story that bears its name, even the duel-to-the-death itself, supposed to play a *post factum* evidentiary role in defending not the "honor" of one of its participants but the veracity of a woman's virtue, turns out to be inconclusive in effect, and thus ends up turning, too, on questions of *judgment*, its own bases and demonstrable *bona fides*, rather than any

---

404. Kleist, II: 229.

decisive blow or "hit." In short, how one judges the unknown proves just as elusive in the narrative course of actions and detours from judging those actions comprising the story, "The Duel," as it does in the duel to which those actions, including the enactments of these detours, "lead." For, only in Kleist (or, perhaps, also, in his closest narrative successor, Kafka) would a purely physical action, institutionalized as substitute for judgment, fail to "do the job" (of killing) as well, as even the "might makes right" mode of non-reasoning – simple sensory rhyme nonsensically applicable to any bodily conquest – of this "combat of two" finds itself compelled to switch its stated subject and object. Rather than confirm its viewer's ability to identify not only who, in the duel, possesses might and who, right, but on which side of the slogan might and right themselves in fact reside, the duel's apparently incontrovertible, because plainly visible dubiety of outcome brings the need for the act of judgment itself, long consigned to oblivion, "so to speak," (as Kant might write) back from the dead.[405]

---

[405]. On Kleist's improbable achievement of uncertainty by causal, narrative means, cf. Achim Aurnhammer, "Im Horizont der Ungewissheit: Unzuverlässigen Erzählen in Kleists Novellen," in *Heinrich von Kleist: Neue Ansichten eines rebellischen Klassikers*, Hrsg. Werner Frick (Freiburg, i. Br.: Rombach, 2014), 101–128.

3. Contesting "Judgment" in "The Duel"

In the context of a *Critique* aimed at proceeding *beyond* the limits of both empiricist and idealist accounts of them, understanding and action are mediated not by operations of literary – representational and narrative – "irony," but by *Urteilskraft*, a discursive "power of judgment" whose analogous lack of cognitive and causal determination produces a singular ability to perceive sensuous objects not through *a priori* formal means, as synthetic, conceptual representations, but as unknown embodiments of dynamic forms whose equally dynamic experience we undergo as feelings. Subject only to their predication as "beautiful," these perceptible forms may be chasms as well as wall coverings, pictures as well as picture frames, landscapes as well as flowers in a vase, just as, in our apprehension of a sensuous object so apparently dynamic as to surpass any boundaries we can imagine, the "sublime" destruction or upending of all formal delineation and dimensionality that Kant calls "Unform" can be experienced by us anywhere our reason – here, the kind of "pure reason" whose operation is not delimited by specific objects – comes into conflict with our sensuously configured imagination (or imagination operating *a posteriori*).[406] Although Kant attributes to "judging" ("Urteilen") the general capacity for renewing philosophy, and with philosophy, science – equating it, in the First Preface to the First Critique, with the "Age of Critique" defining "our" and thus any "age" in which it is enacted[407] – he distinguishes the ability to judge ("Urteilskraft") in the Third Critique, by contrast, as the "power" to mediate between the otherwise incommunicable "realms" of limited knowledge and unlimited action described in the First and Second Critiques respectively, the very domains of experience and practice whose incommunicability Kleist's every text describes.

While there is nothing we might choose to call "ironic" about the exercise of the power of judgment Kant describes, like irony, it may operate anywhere at any time, turning any object, no matter how apparently negligible, into the basis for "feeling" precisely because it unsettles the content as well as context of an object, its "realm." A mere "bridge," or "Übergang," between "domains," or "Gebiete," of human endeavor separated in practice, the power of judgment called "aesthetic" is "free"

---

406. Kant, *KU* B 49, B XLIX, B 79, X: 146, 103, 168.
407. Kant, *KrV*, A X–XI, III: 12–13n; cf. Chapter Two, Section One, n. 46; Chapter Three, Section One, n. 321.

not to determine, govern, or regulate a demarcated "territory," or "Boden," of its own.[408] Grounded instead on the "condition" of the shared or "common sense" first produced by articulate speech, the power of judgment speaks on the second-hand or reported basis that is the communal property of articulation itself: to participate in the "common sense" of judgment, according to Kant, is, specifically, "to say" of some object, not that "it is," but that "it is [*said to be*[409]] beautiful" ["zu sagen, es *sei* schön"] [*Analytik des Schönen*, §2]), in other words, to constate, in speaking, the performance not of one's own but others' ability to speak.[410]

Thus, like irony, judgment, too, can be said to speak "in quotation marks,"[411] i.e., at once affirmatively and as if in an impersonal voice, even as it brings different aspects of language to the fore. "Irony" combines affirmation with negation by proffering propositions available to equally viable, opposing interpretations, whereas judgment is defined less by the content of what it says than what it does and does not do, brings to consciousness and suspends. "Contemplative"[412] rather than pragmatic, the power of judgment enables us to communicate a "feeling" as an adjective qualifying the object that occasions it, in the form of a statement already "presupposed"[413] to be understandable and constatable by all. Unlike irony, judgment neither says this *and* that, nor this and *not*-this, but, like irony, it says this is what I say "it" is without saying "I" say this, even while indicating that, in the place of "I," everyone else does or would: that what any subject of judgment says in predicating an object speaks for every

---

408. Kant, *KU* B XX–XXI, X: 83–85; cf. Chapter Three, Section One, n. 293, this study

409. Kant's use of the first subjective, "sei," to articulate the copular of judgment both conforms to the grammatical rules regarding reported or second-hand speech and substantiates his theory that all judgments speak not merely for their speaker but for all speakers, just as they issue not from an individual but what he calls a "common sense." Composed nearly entirely of discordant strings of speech acts committed pursuant to the sudden act of murder narrated in the indicative preterite in its first paragraph, perhaps more than any other story by Kleist, the entirety of "The Duel" after that first paragraph might well have been written in the first subjunctive.

410. Kant, *KU* B 6, 65–68, X: 117, 157–59; see Chapter Two, Section Three, n. 113, this study.

411. Cf. young Marcel's memorable description of the disturbingly "ironic tone" used by Swann, whenever "speaking of serious things" – "emit[ting] a judgment about a work, about a way of understanding life"—as a speech spoken "as if . . . in quotation marks," i.e., already conscious of others' use of language to emit judgments *not* their own, or not their own alone. It is the story of Swann that he himself narrates – one best defined as related entirely "between quotation marks" in that it occurred long before his own birth – that, Marcel "later" recognizes, provided the model not only of his "own" experience of life, but of his (circularly projected) *livre à venir*, i.e., the very long story of a life he has already written. See *A la recherche du temps perdu* 3 vol (Paris: Bibliothèque de la Pléiade, 1954), I: 97–98, 210–211.

412. Kant, *KU* B 15, X: 122.

413. See Chapter Two, Section One, n. 41, Section Eight, n. 219, this study.

("jedermann"[414]) subject's experience of that object in precisely the way that language itself – and perhaps language alone – is a pure (in Kant's terms, "real" and "concrete") construction of commonality. Furthermore, "contemplative" rather than cognitive, judgment suspends the influence of conceptual knowledge, personal opinion and all interest upon experience, including the impersonal interest definitive of moral action. Like cognition, judgment is always "related to" some sensory object, "something outside the self" ("auf etwas ausser mich bezogen").[415] Yet, unlike cognition and like the pure or moral use of reason, judgment is also "free" to regard objects without regarding them either as unknowable "things-in-themselves" or as cognitive "phenomena." Its own "feeling" of "free[dom]"[416] frees imagination to "play"[417] on equal footing with understanding in experiences of "pleasure" in the beautiful, and frees reason to "do violence"[418] to imagination by violating the boundaries of sense perceptions in the painful experience of the sublime.

---

414. See Kant, *KU* B 20, X: 126, cf. Chapter Two, Section Six, n. 167: "Denn er muss es nicht *schön* nennen, wenn es bloss ihm gefällt . . .; wenn er aber etwas für schön ausgibt, so mutet er andern eben dasselbe Wohlgefallen zu: er urteilt nicht bloss für sich, sondern für jedermann" ("For [a subject] must not name [an object] *beautiful* when it pleases merely him; but when [a subject] pronounces something beautiful so he attributes to others just the same pleasure: he judges not only for himself, but for everyone"); see also Kant, *KU* B 26, X: 130 (emphasis in text), Chapter Two, Section Eight, n. 233 this study:

> Ob ein Kleid, ein Haus, eine Blume schön sei: dazu lässt man sich sein Urteil durch keine Gründe oder Grundsätze beschwatzen. Man will das Objekt seinen eigenen Augen unterwerfen, gleich als ob sein Wohlgefallen von der Empfindung abhinge; und dennoch wenn man den Gegenstand alsdann schön nennt, glaubt man eine allgemeine Stimme für sich zu haben, und macht Anspruch auf den Beitritt von jedermann, da hingegen jede Privatempfindung nur für ihn allein und sein Wohlgefallen entscheiden würde.
>
> Hier ist nun zu sehen, dass in dem Urteile des Geschmacks nichts postuliert wird, als eine solche *allgemeine Stimme* . . .

> [Whether a dress, a house, a flower would be ("sei") beautiful: no one lets his judgment be cajoled by reasons and principles of reason to that conclusion. Some people want to submit the object to their own eyes, just as if their pleasure depended on the sensation; and nevertheless, when one names an object beautiful, one believes one has a general voice, and makes claim to the accession of everyone, since otherwise every private sensation would decide only for him and his pleasure alone.
>
> Here we can now see that in the judgment of taste nothing is postulated other than such a *general voice* . . . .]

415. Kant, *KrV* B 38, III: 72.
416. See Chapter Two, Section Three, this study.
417. Kant, *KU* B 29, X: 132.
418. Kant, *KU* B 77, X: 166.

Now, the conflict between representational cognition and noncognitive action – which is to say, Kant's conflict – may be the central story of all Kleist's stories, its presence imperfectly represented in the prosaisms of his irony, its absence, the grace presented in the perfectly empirical, sense-able and senseless movements of marionettes. Yet, just as Kant hypothesizes the ability of the "power" he calls judgment to mediate the conflict between cognitive limits and unlimited moral actions, so Kleist attempts, in "The Duel," to *represent such mediation* itself. His "Zweikampf," or "Conflict of Two," narrates, in the representational hypothetical form of fiction, how the enactment of judgment – as critical for Kant to the feasibility of his fundamental distinction between "applied" and "pure" operations of reason as is the suspension (in both senses of the term) of the binding logic and conflicting, phenomenal and moral grounds of these by the "bridge"-like ability to "feel oneself free" – manages illogically, indeed, in this story, "willy-nilly," or despite both human oversight and contrivance, to span the "chasm" between the two, and, in so doing, take on its *own* appearance in the world. Rather than analyze how a supposed "power" or capacity for judgment within us "communicates" itself externally through "free" articulate acts of qualitative predication, Kleist's story seeks judgment everywhere the eye can look, its explicitly juridical motif serving to underscore rather than obviate the question: how do we know "judgment" is not "misjudgment" or mistake?

For, rather than entitling this tale of the social mediation between mere appearances and moral reality, "The Judgment," Kleist, who, consistent with his own representational narrative mode, preferred referential to conceptual titles generally, names it for the decisive physical action aimed at rendering all need for internal judgment and discursive mediation moot: "The Duel" or combat ("Kampf") of two ("Zwei"). While "Michael Kohlhaas" tells the story of a just war waged against a casually unjust world to effect nothing less than the reversal of material cause and effect – the physical rectification of a self-evident wrong or "Unrecht" to a state of integrity to which questions of justice need not and do not apply – "The Duel" tells a story of diverging paths taken to ascertain the right subject and object of complaint, diversions of focus occurring not in spite of but on the basis of evidence. Replacing judgment of the person or persons culpable of a multiply witnessed capital wrong, first, with an inquiry into the parties to sexual relations aleatory to the event, followed by questions as to the nature of evidence capable of "proving" those relations in fact took place and, finally, by which means, human or "divine," and, moreover, at what moment, that or any proof should be considered definitive,[419] "The Duel" represents no universal capacity for judgment,

---

419. Assumed to be the last story he wrote, shortly before his suicide in Nov. 1811, at the age of 34, "The Duel" may be viewed – in the very sense of the inconclusive bases of judgment it presents – as Kleist's fictive embodiment and recapitulation of his own literary *corpus*, the narrative representation of its author's uncertainty as to whether the blows sustained by his "body" of work will prove, at some undetermined point in time, to have been merely apparently fatal, and the judgment and justice due it – if due it – ultimately make

in either the normative or Kant's critical sense,[420] but rather the potential extermination of such a "power" by assumptions of self-evidence based in either pure sentience or godly omniscience. In Kleist, as in Kant, judgment requires critique of perception – a practical fact of which every inevitably mis-taken representation undertaken in the prosaic proceedings of Kleist's fictions is Exhibit A. Whether fortuitously or by design – an opposition the ostensible "plots" of those

themselves known. Unwittingly befitting its title, the posthumous reception of "The Duel" has been sharply divided between readers who consider it the weakest – least passionately compelling – of Kleist's stories, and those who view it as his strongest and most profound. Reviewing the story's reception-history, James G. McGlathery attributes the roughly 50-year period of its (mostly) positive evaluation to an "existentialist period in literary criticism" beginning with Gerhard Fricke's *Gefühl und Schicksal bei Heinrich von Kleist. Studien über des innern Vorgang im Leben und Schaffen des Dichters* (Berlin: Junker und Dünnhaupt, 1929) and extending to Denis Dyer's *Stories of Kleist. A Critical Study* (New York: Holmes and Meier, 1977). With the exception of Horn's 1978 study and Brown's 1998 assessment of the complete literary works (see Secondary Bib.), the late twentieth-century renaissance of interest in and early twenty-first century bicentennial commemorations of Kleist's narrative work in particular have neither favored nor disfavored, but, rather, paid relatively scant attention to the story. See James McGlathery, "Kleist's 'Der Zweikampf' as Comedy," in *Heinrich von Kleist Studies*, ed. Alexej Ugrinsky (New York: AMS Press, 1980), pp. 87–92.

420. While Kant recognized the irresoluble conflict between public honor and internal human dignity resulting in the legalized state of nature – or murder – enacted in duels, and refused to condemn the individual's attempt to reconcile public and private selves by making his own being both ethical "means" and "end," he was also critical of the mere "show" or appearance of honor duels can be employed to effect, contrasting these, much as Kleist's story does, with a duel engaged in for "love of honor[ing]" virtue itself. See his *Anthropology from a Pragmatic Point of View*, § 74, "On timidity and bravery" ("Von der Furchtsamkeit und der Tapferkeit," Kant, *Anthropologie*, BA 213, XII: 588). For Kant's views on dueling see the section on "punishment and clemency" in, "Theory of Law," Part One of the *Metaphysic of Morals*, AB 1950205, VIII: 452–59. Cf. the contemporary debate regarding those views and their larger implications for post-Kantian political theory, in Alex Livingston and Leah Soroko, "From Honor to Dignity and Back Again. Remarks on LaVaque-Manty's 'Dueling for Equality," *Political Theory* Vol. 35, No. 4 (2007: 494–501), their response to Mika LaVaque-Manty, "Dueling for Equality: Masculine Honor and the Modern Politics of Dignity," *Political Theory*, Vol. 34, No. 6 (2006: 715–740); see also Michael Vloytinsky's compelling deduction of the case for viewing Kant's well-known endorsement of capital punishment in cases of murder as a regulative principle regarding the value of human life rather than an actual law either accountably or universally applicable in the sensory world, in "The Kantian Case Against the Death Penalty," published on-line at *academia.edu/2469736/*; and Rudolf A. Makkreel's expansion upon Vloytinsky's argument to include the notion of "reflective judgment" articulated in the Third Critique, in "Relating Kant's Theory of Reflective Judgment to the Law," *Washington University Jurisprudence Review*, Vol. 6, No. 9 (2013: 147–60).

fictions prove particularly hard to place – in entitling his final story for a "duel" whose outcome is inconclusive, Kleist encapsulated the experience plotted by all his fictions: no narratives, not even Kafka's, challenge our ability to identify the casual relation of their representations more skillfully. "Judgment" ("Urteil") – to quote Kant in his inaugural Preface to the First Critique – of the "real effects" ("Wirkungen") of *aesthesis,* in the perceptual sense, is one, Kleist implies, each "reader" and "judge" ("Leser" und "Richter") must make.[421]

As if to induce in every reader and judge the singular impact from which it stems, Kleist's story of judgment opens, as described above, with the most extensive, densely layered descriptive sentence in all of German-language narrative, a seamless fiction of seemingly endless contextual subordinations ending in a single punctual, indeed, in this case, literally puncturing event:

> Herzog Wilhelm von Breysach, who had been living in enmity with his half-brother, Graf Jakob the Redbeard, since his secret marriage with a countess named Katharina von Heersbruck from the House of the Alt-Hüningen, who appeared to be under his rank, returned, around the end of the fourteenth century, as the night of Saint Remigius began to fall, from a meeting held with the German Kaiser in Worms, in which he, lacking children by marriage, all of whom had died, had effected the legitimation of Graf Philipp von Hüningen, a natural son engendered with his wife before their marriage. Looking into the future with more joy than at any time during the whole run of his government, he had already reached the park, which lay behind his castle: as suddenly an arrow broke forth out of the darkness of the bushes, and pierced his body just below the breastbone.

> [Herzog Wilhelm von Breysach, der, seit seiner heimlichen Verbindung mit einer Gräfin, namens Katharina von Heersbruck, aus dem Hause Alt-Hüningen, die unter seinem Range zu sein schien, mit seinem Halbbruder, dem Grafen Jakob dem Rotbart, in Feindschaft lebte, kam gegen das Ende des vier-zehnten Jahrhunderts, da die Nacht des heiligen Remigius zu dämmern began, von einer in Worms mit dem deutschen Kaiser abgehaltenen Zusammenkunft zurück, worin er sich von diesem Herrn, in Ermangelung ehelicher Kinder, die ihm gestorben waren, die Legitimation eines, mit seiner Gemahlin vor der Ehe erzeugten, natürlichen Sohnes, des Grafen Philipp von Hüningen, ausgewirkt hatte. Freudiger, als während des ganzen Laufs seiner Regierung in die Zukunft blickend, hatte er schon den Park, der hinter seinem Schlosse lag, erreicht: als plötzlich ein Pfeilschuss aus dem Dunkel der Gebüsche hervorbrach, und ihm, dicht unter dem Brustknochen, den Leib durchbohrte.[422]]

What follows *not* from an apparently gratuitous "dash" ("—") standing in for an unperceived act of bodily transgression (as in "Die Marquise von O . . ."), but from

---

421. Kant, *KrV,* A xvi, III: 15.
422. Kleist, II: 229.

another punctuating diacritical mark, a full colon (":") introducing, into the life of a soon to be defunct, extensively described subject, the "sudden" "outbreak" of a "shot" out of the "dark," as unanticipated by its target as by the reader of "the whole," hundred-word "run" of more than a dozen grammatically "govern[ed]" descriptive and subordinate clauses packed into the single, roughly 10-line, overarching clause that precedes it,[423] is an approximately thirty-page story embedded instead with unverified assertions and declarations, or "Aussagen:" true, false, and equally false and true statements, suspicions, oaths, testimonies, verdicts, and sacraments, including the all-"decisive" "judgment" of God, supposed to be "spoken," through the rule of the duel, in the inevitable befalling of "death" to the dueling party that spoke falsely.[424] From a single arrow that meets its mark in the breast of the Herzog,

---

423. Like the grammatically ordinary, apparently unremarkable sentence within which the violation of the Marquise is at once hidden and stated, the grammatically extraordinary compounding of multiply layered dependent clauses into which the report of an apparently perfectly targeted collision of arrow and vital organ, "under the breastbone," intrudes into the opening sentence of "The Duel" makes its translation into any language less rich in the ability to accommodate virtually unlimited layers of perfectly regular, syntactic embedding a particularly ungainly task. While I have tried to maintain the syntax of the original in the version provided above, standard English translations of the sentence tend to level out the vertical accumulation of clauses in the original that, bringing different segments of "background" information forward onto the same narrative "plane," compel the reader to store, or "shelve," its temporally and causally dependent bits of data before reading further. Attempting to ease the mental effort the sentence requires of its readers to keep the different pieces of its "back-story" present, even while proceeding to the pointed, contextually "piercing" narrative event and final transitive verb with which its near mis-en-abîme of information (within information) abruptly ends (in being violently forced to a final full-stop), such facilitating renderings take the liberty of dividing Kleist's elongated first sentence into two, smoothly legible sentences, the second beginning roughly at the mid-point of the former, after the designation of the location of the Kaiser in Worms. See, for example, *The Marquise of O—and Other Stories*, trans. David Luke and Nigel Reeves (London: Viking, 1978), p. 287, for one of the most widely circulated simplifying versions of the sentence in English.

424. Kleist, II: 244, 251, 253, 254, 259. In "'Die Stunde der Entscheidung': Ordeal and Uncertainty in Kleist's 'Der Zweikampf'" (*Monatshefte* Vol. 101, No. 4 [2009]: 469–82), Brian Tucker views the story as a whole as a representation of "decisionism" – "the exceptional decision inherent in every application of the law" (477). The present study argues, by contrast, that the validity of any decision – including those universally supposed to speak on "divine" authority – is instead directly questioned, on an explicitly *temporal* basis, by Kleist's story, in which the voice of decisiveness believed to express itself definitively in the formal performance of a "contest" between truth and falsity, or innocence and guilt, proves instead merely another captive to the inconclusive vagaries of judgment. For, rather than befalling the judged once and for all, as the assassin's arrow felled the Herzog, one "exceptional" or "divine" "decision" replaces another in "Der Zweikampf" from one hour to the next, just as the subjects under scrutiny seem to replace each other on a moment's notice. Finally, the

punctuating and shattering, in the speed of a single transition from verb to object, a verbal carapace spun of interdependent familial, legal and intentional circumstances, an entire narrative mirroring the maddeningly ongoing period of its opening sentence ensues.[425] Just as gradual in its accretion of context and as kaleidoscopic in rhetorical effect, the interconnected series of declarations, feints, doubts, suspicions, dissimulations and proofs following from that sentence effectively extenuates the single decisive act the sentence reports and that the remainder of the story at first seems motivated to account for. These include, in sequential order, the cautious display of friendship to her brother-in-law and rival for the realm, Graf Jakob von Rotbart, by the Herzog's widow; the oath and

formal addition of a fresh amendment to the divine law of the duel necessitated by the inconclusive results of dueling witnessed in the story now predicates duels' decisiveness not upon "God's will" but on *whether* God "wishes" to will anything ("*Wenn* es Gottes Wille ist ...") – to judge any individual action or agent – in the first place. That temporal qualification of the "rendering" of divine, or extra-temporal, verdicts ("wie es der Spruch des höchsten Gottes ... entschieden hat") puts even all apparently conclusive decisions into question by destroying the alleviating notion of the decision as event that "divides" ("scheidet") not only the guilty from the innocent but what was from what is now. Not *what* is decided, but *whether* a decision *has been* rendered has itself been rendered permanently inconclusive by Kleist. The entirely open-ended verbal caveat with whose words the story ends – "When it is God's will" – puts all the signs of exceptional "decisionism" precluding the necessity of judgment into doubt (Kleist, II: 254 [emphasis added]). On Kleist's narrative representation of the temporal condition his story amends to "the outcome of any duel" hereafter, cf. John M. Ellis, "Kleist's 'Der Zweikampf,'" *Monatshefte*, Vol. 65, No. 1 (1972): 48–60, esp. 58: "once it is allowed that in some cases we may not know right away what the truth is, it follows that we cannot know for certain in any case. It will never be possible again to look at the outcome of any duel and say simply: there is the truth." Cf. Wolfgang Wittkowski's observation, in "'Die heilige Cäcilie' und 'Der Zweikampf': Kleists Legenden und die romanitische Ironie," *Colloquia Germanica* No. 5 (1972): 17–28, of the simultaneously motivating and anihilating effect of a statute whose own actual occurrence of application remains in doubt (46). It is for just this reason, Wittkowski cannily remarks, that Kleist's Von Trotta can continue to maintain the authority of the statute even while questioning the relation of its "truth" to any temporal demands we may place on its "express[ion]:" "Where lies the obligation of the highest divine wisdom to indicate and express the truth *in the moment* of its summoning by the believing?" ("Wo liegt die Verpflichtung der höchsten göttlichen Weisheit, die Wahrheit *im Augenblick* der glaubensvollen Anrufung selbst, anzuzeigen und auszusprechen?").

425. The complexly extensive opening sentence of "The Duel" provides a prime Kleistian, which is to say, simultaneously mimetic and ironic representation, of the principle of the "gradual composition [or fabrication] of thinking in speaking" on which Kleist wrote. See Kleist, II: 319–24. For an excellent analysis of the institutionally and culturally critical dimension of the essay, see Jill Ann Kowalik, "Kleist's Essay on Rhetoric," *Monatshefte*, Vol. 81, No. 4 (1989): 434–446.

evidentiary defense of his innocence presented in tribunal by Rotbart; the affirmation of her own innocence of intimacy with Rotbart by the woman he names as his lover and alibi at the time of the crime, Frau Littergarde von Auerstein; the defense of Frau Littergarde and public oath taken to prove her innocence "in God's judgment before the world" sworn by Herzog Friedrich von Trotta, when, on the strength of evidence presented as "the most decisive proofs"[426] of his purported tryst with Littergarde, Rotbart is acquitted – "freigesprochen" – of murder by the Kaiser and Littergarde accused of perjury in his place.[427] This extensive concatenation of verbal acts finally appears on the point of culminating in the performance of the bodily act for which the story is named, when Rotbart, employing an idiomatic, formulaic (or "förmlich"[428]) variant of "treffen" reminiscent of its duplicitous use by the narrator of "The Marquise . . ." with regard to another widow of famed virtue ("Hier – traf er . . . Anstalten"), declares he will "prove" the "truth" of his statements "with regard to Frau Littegarde" ("Frau Littegarden betreffend"), and therein his own innocence of the crime of murder regarding which he was summoned to testify to begin with, effectively substituting one object of "regard," one target of "treffen[d]" for another, through the "'honest, chivalric contest of a duel.'"[429]

The result of the duel, however, proves as inconclusive and equivocal, its true meaning as "mysterious" or "hidden" ("geheimnisvoll"[430]) as duels to the death can only prove in Kleist. Performed to express, once and for all, the "judgment of God," this staged "contest of two" yields not neatly opposing but changing results, not one singular and self-evident but a developing, internally divided "truth." Even the most empirically determinable condition – the presence or absence of life – gradually proves indeterminate after the duel is completed, as executor and victim of what had appeared a single mortal blow gradually exchange internal physical states. Rotbart, author of that wound and declared victor of the duel, finds himself, no less sensibly than incomprehensibly, dying over time; von Trotta, subjected to Rotbart's piercing stroke of the sword, and the agent, for his part, of a mere "skin" wound to his opponent and ostensible slayer, finds himself, no less incomprehensibly, progressively healed, fully alive.[431] As the "divine judgment" believed to have first been rendered by the duel remains in force in the minds of all those privy to it (and von Trotta and Littegarde, deemed guilty of deception, are imprisoned), the refutation of its verdict by mounting physical evidence produces considerable internal, intellectual conflict in those it directly affects. In nearly the same breath, Littegarde passionately exclaims she is as "pure of guilt . . . as the breast of a newborn child, . . . the body of a nun," and, in the very act of asserting her innocence,

426. Kleist, II: 241
427. Kleist, II: 242
428. For Kleist's uses of "*förmlich*" to describe verbal actions, see Kleist, II: 236, 242.
429. Kleist, II: 242.
430. Kleist, II: 248.
431. Kleist, II: 243.

chides von Trotta for "'believing what my mouth says,'" posing of her defender the single decisive question she herself considers to have been already answered definitively, and thus merely a "rhetorical" one: "'Has the divine judgment of God not decided against me?'"[432] The wounded von Trotta asserts in response that he has been "given ... life again" by Littegarde's "words" of innocence and urges the lady for whom he would have died willingly to "think" the "more comprehensible" of the "two" – contradictory – "thoughts" produced by that singular judgment, i.e., that, given the sensible fact of his living, he should be deemed the duel's winner: "Of two thoughts, which confuse the senses, let us think the more comprehensible, more conceivable, and before you believe yourself guilty, rather believe that, in the duel I fought for you, I won!" ("Lass uns, von zwei Gedanken, die die Sinne verwirren, den verständlicheren und begreiflicheren denken, und eher du dich schuldig glaubt, lieber glauben, dass ich in dem Zweikampf den ich für dich gefochten, siegte!")[433] As much a "believe[r]" as any in the infallibility of "divine judgment," von Trotta reasons it can be no fault of "divine wisdom" itself if the verdict it "indicates" and "expresses" is not delivered *at the same "moment" it is "summoned"* by those in mortal need of it: "'In what lies the obligation of the highest, divine wisdom to indicate and express the truth in the moment of its summoning by those who believe in it?'" ("Wo liegt die Verpflichtung der höchsten göttlichen Weisheit, die Wahrheit im Augenblick der glaubensvollen Anrufung selbst, anzuzeigen und auszusprechen?"[434])

Unfortunately for him and his beloved, the imperial tribunal does not share von Trotta's enlightened hermeneutical bent. Despite his advancing recovery from his adversary's blow, and the latter's ongoing deterioration, von Trotta remains officially "condemned," along with Littergarde, to die.[435] Other revelations, unconnected to the event of the duel, render the "divine" nature of the "judgment" "expressed" by it more troubling still. The deception of Littegarde's chambermaid is discovered (she impersonated Littegarde), and the fact made evident (the chambermaid is demonstrably pregnant) that her seduction-in-disguise of Rotbart calls the content (if not the form) of his alibi, "Frau Littegarde betreffend," into question: Rotbart, it seems, was indeed occupied elsewhere as an assassin's arrow "pierced" the Herzog's "breast," but the body being *betroffen* by his own at that moment was not in fact Littegarde's. Despite the vindication of Littegarde's virtue and, with it, von Trotta, that this new evidence brings, the Kaiser declares himself ruled immutably by "the holy judgment" first spoken through the duel.[436] It is the dying Rotbart, who, upon learning he had mistaken the identity of his sexual conquest and alibi, orders himself carried to the scene of execution to declare von Trotta and Littegarde "unschuldig" ("innocent"), announcing, moreover, that all

432. Kleist, II: 253.
433. Kleist, II: 254.
434. *Ibid.*
435. Kleist, II: 254.
436. *Ibid.*

appearances to the contrary, this had been "God's sentence" all along. Even though it had then been von Trotta who emerged from the duel gravely wounded, and, thanks to "a special stroke of heavenly good fortune," was now in the "bloom" of health; and even though, bringing their mutual reversal of fortunes full circle, it is now he, Rotbart, who, having been barely wounded in the duel and declared blameless, lies dying before the healthy man condemned to death, it is not only to acknowledge the "innocence" of the condemned that he orders himself brought to the place of their execution. For in addition to confessing his own guilt ("I am the murderer of my brother, the noble Duke Wilhelm von Breysach"[437]) and exonerating von Trotta and Littegarde, Rotbart pronounces that, all evidence to the contrary, "'the sentence of the highest God'" "'spoken before the eyes of all gathered'" "'on that portentous day'" remains the same as when it was *first* "decided" ("'wie es der Spruch des höchsten Gottes, an jenem verhängnisvollen Tage, vor dem Augen aller versammelten ... entschieden hat!'"[438]).

In Rotbart's dying declaration, the meaning attributed to a divine judgment is contradicted even as its autonomous formal terms are emphatically maintained, and, in contrast with the failure of demonstrative empirical evidence to result in any alteration of the original verdict rendered, the sheer extravagance of Rotbart's purely verbal, interpretive fiat works to singular effect. The previously unmovable Kaiser, (ironically) described as "frozen like a stone by [Robert's] words,"[439] reverses rather than confirms his sentence and bids von Trotta and Littegarde no longer be burned at the stake. Rotbart expires, but not without reminding us of the single purposeful object "The Duel" has labored, by a labyrinthine casting of doubt on every word spoken within it, to make us forget: the arrow that, unlike every other assertion of will in the story, and most unlike a "contest of two" conducted in public view, emerged unilaterally, from invisibility, to hit *its* mark to begin with, the target, basis and conclusion of the maze-like opening of the narrative itself. Early in the story it is noted that the distinctive workmanship and "engraved" marks of the arrow allowed its ownership to be traced.[440] "Five months" after the murder of the Herzog, an arrowmaker in Strassburg had recognized it as one he had made for Rotbart and it was his "statement" clarifying that fact, the "Erklärung"[441] made by a thing's maker who had no particular interest in the purpose to which it was put, which led to the summoning of Rotbart before the Kaiser's court in the first place. It was there that Rotbart testified, and others freely corroborated his testimony regarding another collateral matter: that during the night of his brother's murder he was otherwise engaged, with no less than the most virtuous widow in the land, and so, by implication, could not have caused his brother's death.

The shock of Rotbart's salacious revelation overshadows the question immediately at hand, moving his interlocutors to focus their attention on a

437. Kleist, II: 260.
438. Kleist, II: 259.
439. *Ibid* (emphasis added).
440. Kleist, II: 231.
441. *Ibid*.

reputedly virtuous woman's imputed hypocrisy, and so to take their eyes from the proverbial "ball" set in motion by the arrow's fatal course – in this case, the relaying of undisputed evidence of Rotbart's proprietary relation to the arrow itself. Yet also overlooked during Rotbart's startling confession – not to murder but to a tangential liaison with Littegarde or, as it turns out, with someone herself bearing only a tangential relation to Littegarde – was the appositive term and apparently merely formal disclaimer or testimonial "formality" included in the midst of Rotbart's testimony as to "why" his "participation in the murder of [his] brother" was "improbable," if not impossible: "'why it is neither probable nor even possible that I, *whether personally or indirectly* [or "by any external means," literally, "through any form of mediation": *mittelbar*] participated in the murder of my brother'" ("'warum es weder wahrscheinlich, noch auch selbst möglich sei, dass ich an dem Mord meines Bruders, *es sei nun persönlich oder mittelbar,* Teil genommen...'"[442]).

The ensuing conclusion of this sentence describing his own whereabouts at the time of the murder – logically speaking, its premise – is, to Rotbart's knowledge, true: as far as he knew at the time of his testimony, he had indeed spent that night in Littegarde's arms. But the opening of the sentence – logically speaking, its conclusion – declaring it is neither "probable nor even possible" that he could have "either personally or indirectly" participated in the murder, is, to Rotbart's knowledge, false, a fact that he admits only with his last breath, after realizing his own death is imminent and that he himself had been deceived.[443] Everything that

---

442. Kleist, II: 235 (emphasis added).

443. Contrast this with Ellis's opening observation that Rotbart, the single character in the story he views in singularly positive terms – "the Count," Ellis states, is "human, colorful, attractive, forceful, resourceful, and thoroughly impressive," in all ways "more credible and understandable, and more likeable" than the "weak and irresolute simpleton" von Trotta – "is not in fact guilty of the lie of which Friedrich accuses him" ("Kleist's 'Der Zweikampf,'" pp. 54, 59, 48). Consistent with his objection to the amendment undermining the "immediate" quality ("unmittelbar") of divine law, Ellis ignores the formulaic appositive, "or by any other means" ("mediately") ("oder mittlebar"), constituting the lie of Rotbart's testimony. The general neglect of the phrase within the story and its reception alike suggests that it may indeed take a "simpleton" – someone whose courage derives from the, for him, unquestionable honesty of another – rather than a "resourceful," "likeable" character like Rotbart, to recognize the words of a lie when he or she hears them. Like Ellis, Peter Horn fails to recognize the lie at the center of Rotbart's declaration, focusing his attention instead on what Rotbart believes to be the truth of his alibi (Horn, *Heinrich von Kleists Erzählungen* [Königstein/Ts.: Scriptor Taschenbuch, 1978], pp. 206–7), even while recognizing its logic to be mere "casuistry" and criticizing what he calls Rotbart's "literalist" reading of the prohibition against murder as failing to include the causative: "'You should not have [or, cause to be] killed'" (210). For an opposing view underscoring the decisive effect of von Trotta's actions upon the narrative – principally, that of granting it the "necessary time" to change course – see Hilda Meldrum Brown, *Henrich von Kleist. The Ambiguity of Art and the Necessity of Form* (New York: Oxford University Press, 1998), p. 131. While Meldrum

Rotbart had said, and everything that others had said about Rotbart; everything that Littegarde had said and that von Trotta had said about Littegarde (and that her mother had said to her about him); and everything that the Kaiser said God had said in the *Zweikampf* itself, in a string of *Aussagen* productive of still others, all prove to have been mere distractions, no less fatal for being distractions, from the lie, spoken in the form of a mere formality, that both set the stage for and prefigured the unreliability of a supposedly dispositive "contest of two." For, once Rotbart claims, both in "good faith" and by mistake, to have been intimately occupied "elsewhere" on the night of the murder, which is to say, in immediate proximity to the person of the otherwise virtuous Littegarde, and once that inflammatory alibi is challenged by von Trotta, and Littegarde's honor, defended in a duel, the apparently purely conventional technical term, "mittelbar," uttered within Rotbart's sworn iteration of the technical disclaimer, "es sei nun *persönlich oder mittelbar*" ("whether personally or indirectly [or mediately]"), is, at first, immediately and then retrospectively forgotten, if ever it was heard at all – including by the simultaneously mechanically reciting, openly lying Rotbart himself.

Yet it is that apparently merely *förmlich*,[444] or formal, aside – "oder mittelbar" – that had already rendered Rotbart's or any "alibi" indifferent to the matter at hand. For one can present all the sensory alibis, every *alius*, "otherwise" or "elsewhere" engaged, dreamt or demonstrated under heaven, and still the "probability" inherent in the "possibility" of "mediated" action will remain undeterred, untouched, for any action enacted not "personally" but through any of innumerable "other" means all enabled by the purely "formal" forms that *are* the forms of communication are always impersonal and personal at once. So, in this story, the positive denial of such communication – of any and all "participation" via any "means:" "oder mittelbar" – is at once publicly uttered and uncommunicated, unconsidered and undiscussed, and the resulting story we read is the wrong story, itself a screen for another wrong story, itself the screen for a non-story, i.e., the conclusion that was instead obvious from its first sentence, and that the focus of his listeners (and readers) on the "personal," to the exclusion of the "merely" formal content of his sworn statement made disappear from view as soon as Rotbart's licentious declaration, itself as deceived as it was duplicitous, was made. In "The Duel," one act gets substituted for another act, one object of judgment for another, as soon as judgment begins.

Brown importantly points to the ease with which an illicit alibi comes to replace a material arrow in the minds of the tribunal members, stating, "[the case against Rotbart is] readily set aside when he produces his ailibi – despite the damning 'Indizenbeweis' or piece of concrete incriminating evidence ... to the effect that the murder weapon, namely a specially designed arrow, actually belonged to [Rotbart]" (129), she, too, fails to note the lie already present in the apparently "merely" formal terms of Rotbart's initial declaration: a mere verbal formality whose blithe utterance in actual contravention of the truth the dying Rotbart recognizes to have indeed been the basis of the "divine judgment" against him after all.

444. See n. 428, this Section, this Chapter.

No duel can decide this error in judgment, this tendency to miss the obvious in the course of seeking the truth. Rotbart's final confession returns us to the act whose mediated authorship we, like all the witnesses to the duel, had forgotten to remember to seek – the truth of "mediation" hidden behind an initial lie. For, as Rotbart discovers and, discovering, attributes to a judgment divine, the lie committed in an apparently merely *förmlich* articulation of innocence hiding behind a "personal" truth, itself hides another truth Rotbart himself did not know was *itself* both "persönlich" *and* "mittelbar," immediately "personal" in the closest, most physically intimate, "first-hand" sense, *and* mediated through intentionally misleading signs accepted by him at face value, which is to say, an act of deception that, unknown to Rotbart, underlay his own deceptive, apparently merely technical utterance of an alibi, similarly accepted at face value by the tribunal.

Given the contradictory layers of meaningful speech in this story – of truth and falsity presented, credited or entirely missed – it is little wonder that the conditional caveat, "when [or: if] it is God's will" ("Wenn es Gottes Wille ist"), would ultimately be amended to a statute originally ordering that *aesthesis* transcend judgment, i.e., that immediacy of perception must trump all "mediat[ed]" forms of communication in judgments deemed "divine," and divinity seen to make itself evident in a present in which "guilt comes immediately to light" ("dass die Schuld dadurch unmittelbar ans Tageslicht komme"[445]). The compounding of the irony of the story by the addition of a supplemental inscription literally enshrining the temporal and causal uncertainty on which all contests of the very kind it narrates are to be predicated henceforth – a kind of mitigating footnote to divine will and escape clause from mundane error serving to codify not the demonstrability of guilt or innocence but validity of indecision, by anticipating that, at any time, the divine may "wish" to remain silent, to refuse to make its "judgment" known – is wonderfully, humorously plain. Like the conclusion of "The Marquise von O . . .," with the exception of the dead Herzog whose initial naming, elaborate historical contextualization, and targeted murder gets the narrative underway, "The Duel" ends happily for all who seem to merit such deserts, and, for all others, with some measure of assurance, in the form of an amending conditional clause, that some measure of adjustment, if not of justice, could be applied to all future appearances of "divine will." Much as the marriage and inheritance contracts signed and presented by the Graf to the present and future mother of his offspring mitigate the contradictory possibility of his appearing alternately "angel" and "devil" again, the written caveat that divine knowledge of truth, God's own judgment, will appear to us in "decisive" form only if God so wills, ensures that differing presentations and temporal interpretations of evidence may henceforth be permitted to mitigate possible assassinations of the innocent by the state.

Less evident, however, is Kleist's insistence, in closing a narrative entitled "The Duel" with the citation of an amendment inscribing into law the uncertain validity of all such contests, that judgment on earth, *like* a narrative, is never ruled by divine

---

445. Kleist, II: 261.

signs, even and especially those it represents and cites; that the signs it may fail to consider, in deciding what constitutes a just conclusion to any action, may also appear, at any moment, words empty of meaning, formalities without sense – merely verbal terms "hitting" (*treffen*) upon nothing "regarding" (*betreffend*) the matter at hand. Unlike divine judgment, Kleist's *story of judgment* indicates that blindness, whether willed or involuntary, to the binding nature of "mere" formalities will issue in mystifications of the "possible" – "das möglich[e]" – of the very kind at which Rotbart's many maneuverings aimed, a self-interested disabling of the common critical capacity for judgment disdainfully dubbed anti-philosophical "philosophisizing," or "mystagoge[ry]"[446] by Kant. In Kant, such mystification pretends to transcend the necessity of form to thought, indeed, to replace thinking itself by an unlimited self-sufficiency and immediacy of sense believed imitative of divine omniscience. Just as such travesties of thought rely at every step on the inherently comparable, individual concepts (such as "divine," "absolute," "truth," "directly," "revealed," "senses"[447]) whose very significance they purport to supersede, so in Kleist's story an intended mystification of others' critical ability to judge, rather than "transcend" evidence, is accomplished through the deceptive articulation of a lie *as* mere form.

By leaving the lie of "mediation" as "mere form" unperceived by those it immediately misled – the tribunal, before whom it is presented, that neglects or forgets its actual, "probable or possible" meaning, as well as all present and future readers of this, Kleist's final text, who regularly fail to read it, its textual appearance resembling "only" another *Gedankenstrich* pregnant with meaning we ignore – and concluding with an amendment permitting such errors to continue even as, in retrospect, they remain open to question, the judgment that both the duel and "The Duel" are intended to render remains, on Kleist's account, inconclusive, the contest between the evident and the non-evident undecided, just as Kant's critical conflict, between the modes of cognition and moral action, remains irresolvable by either of these alone. Yet, it is just such a structural – permanently reciprocal (rather than dialectically transformable) – conflict or "contest" that, first exposing the pure, critical utility of negation, constituted the basis of the "power to judge" to begin with: an impersonal "power" whose "necessary" "possibility" Kant hypothesized, rightly, to be undeniable by other means, in that, like the ungrounded, empirically nonreferential "faculty of common sense" at its foundation, it itself never occurs

---

446. Kant, "Von einem neuerdings erhobenen Ton in der Philosophie" ("Of a Newly Elevated Tone in Philosophy"), *Werkasugabe* VI: 388 (A 409); cf. Chapter Two, Section One, n. 50, this study. On the "political aesthetic" of Kleist's representations of contrived appearances in its relation to Rousseau's, see Steven Howe, *Heinrich von Kleist.*, Chapter One, "Kleist, Rousseau, and the Paradoxes of Enlightenment" (pp. 12–55) and "Conclusion" (pp. 195–228).

447. Kant, "On a Newly Elevated," VI: 388 (A 409); cf. n. 50, n. 53, ChapterTwo, Section One.

in *propria persona,* such that the only positive "proof" of its ability and activity occurs in the *alius* of speech. If ever proof could be rendered, in the representational world to which Kant limits cognition, of the theory of a nonrepresentational power of judgment based in the inherently mediating medium of discourse that his Third Critique describes, such evidence would itself have to be representational, causal and *a posteriori* – in short, as conclusive and inconclusive, "probable," "possible," and mistaken as the extenuating, referentially fictional events *and* really referential, "merely formal" lies composing Kleist's story.

For, just as Rotbart's testimony lies when it "formally" denies its speaker's participation in verbal "mediation," the impersonal mode of action that turns out to be the content of "his" crime in that it communicates its commission to the hands of another, so Kant's theory of judgment provides the answer to the question that the tribunal "hearing" Rotbart's case fails to pose, *the* question whose terms his own testimony provides. Like a "dash" or *Gedankenstrich* "bridg[ing]" and so holding together two separate realms of action never legible at the same time, the double function of judgment, as *critical because discursive* form of mediation, in Kant, is to transpose Rotbart's appositive declaration of an apparently merely formal disclaimer – *"noch mittelbar"* ("nor by any other means [of mediation]") – into the diacritically altered form of a question: *"noch mittelbar?"* ("still [or yet] available to mediation?"). Lest we, too, like Rotbart's tribunal, distractedly forget how full of truly, because practically critical meaning, all "personal" disclaimers notwithstanding, the merely formal or *förmlich* may turn out to be, that question, which is no less than the central question posed by Kant of his own *Critique* – "*can this yet be mediated?*" – enacts for us the very "possibility" (if not mimetic "probability") of discursive mediation that is its own double and reply. For the very posing of Kant's essential critical question and "revolution in mode of thinking" that, in defiance of pointless, perennially attractive dualisms *and* monisms, asks instead whether mediation as such remains possible, must by definition cross *a posteriori* with *a priori,* just as its answer, already contained in the ability to seek it, is a "pure" speech act available to all speakers, i.e., every subject "free[d]" from empirical and fictive conditions to speak – upon the specifically linguistic condition of "feeling one's self free" – not only "personally," but for "every other," which is to say, on the necessarily heterogeneous, *a priori and a posteriori* "condition" defining all use of language as such. As if merely "formally" constating what must misleadingly appear, *a posteriori,* "mere" "common sense" and is the *a priori* "communicability" of mediation itself, like Kant's theory of judgment, Kleist's story of judgment answers the question whose centrality to judgment – and thus to the "critical" ability "to think" in "freedom" from determination that judgment alone has the "power" to articulate – makes both question and answer, once articulated, appear equally to go without saying: "noch mittelbar"?; aber doch.[448]

---

448. Roughly: "But of course;" "you said it!"

BIBLIOGRAPHY

Primary Bibliography

Adler, H. G. *Eine Reise*. Vienna: Zsolnay Verlag, 1999 [orig. pub. 1962].
Arendt, Hannah. *Eichmann in Jerusalem. A Report on the Banality of Evil*. New York: Viking, 1963.
Arendt, Hannah. *Lectures on Kant's Political Philosophy*. Ed. Ronald Beiner. Chicago: University of Chicago Press, 1982.
Aristotle. *The Basic Works of Aristotle*, Ed. Richard McKeon. New York: Random House, 1941.
Arnauld, A. and P. Nicole. *La Logique ou l'Art de penser*. Ed. P. Clair and F. Girbal. Paris: Librairie Philosophique J. Vrin, 1981 [orig. pub. 1662].
Austin, J. L. *How to Do Things with Words*. Cambridge, MA: Harvard University Press, 1962.
Baudelaire, Charles. *Oeuvres complètes*. Ed. Marcel A. Ruff. Paris: Editions du Seuil, 1968.
Condillac, Etienne Bonnot de. *Essai sur l'origine des connaissances humaines, ouvrage où l'on réduit à un seul principe tout ce qui concerne l'entendement humain*. Ed. C. Porset. Intro. J Derrida. Paris: Editions Galilée, 1973 [orig. pub. 1746].
Derrida, Jacques. *L'origine de la géometrie*. Paris: Editions de Minuit, 1962.
Derrida, Jacques. *De la grammatologie*. Paris: Editions de Minuit, 1967.
Derrida, Jacques. *Marges de la philosophie*. Paris: Editions de Minuit, 1972.
Descartes, Renée. *Oeuvres philosophiques*. 3 Vols. Ed. Ferdinand Alquié. Paris: Garnier, 1963, 1967, 1973.
Diderot, Denis. *Ouevres complètes*. 25 Vols. Ed. Herbert Dieckmann, Jean Fabre, Jacques Proust, with Jean Varloot. Paris: Hermann, 1975–.
Goethe, Johann Wolfgang von. *Werke*. Hamburger Ausgabe. XIV Bde. Hrsg. E. Trunz, et. al. München: Deutscher Taschenbuch Verlag, 1982.
Habermas, Jürgen. *Theorie des kommunikativen Handelns*. Frankfurt: Suhrkamp, 1981.
Habermas, Jürgen. *The Theory of Communicative Action*, 2 Vol., Trans. Thomas McCarthy. Boston: Beacon, 1984 [orig. pub. 1981].
Habermas, Jürgen. *Der philosophische Diskurs der Moderne*. Frankfurt: Suhrkamp, 1985.
Hegel, G. W. F. *Theorie-Werkausgabe*. XX Bde. Hrsg. E. Moldenhauer and K. M. Michel. Frankfurt: Suhrkamp, 1969–71.
Hegel, G. W. F. *Vorlesungen über die Ästhetik*. 3 Bde. Hrsg. E. Moldenhauer and K. M. Michel. Frankfurt: Suhrkamp, 1970 [orig. (posthumous) pub. 1835, based on Hegel's lecture notes, Gustav Hotho, Editor, Berlin, 1820–1829]
Heidegger, Martin. *Vorträge und Aufsätze*. Pfullingen: Neske, 1954.
Heidegger, Martin. *Identität und Differenz*. Frankfurt: Klostermann, 1957.
Hobbes, Thomas. *Leviathan*. London: Viking Penguin, 1985 [orig. pub. 1651].
Hume, David. *A Treatise of Human Nature*. Oxford: Oxford University Press, 1978 [orig. pub. 1739–40].
Husserl, Edmund. "Die Frage nach dem Ursprung der Geometrie als intentional-historisches Problem." Ed. Eugen Fink. *Revue internationale de la philosophie*. 1939.

Husserl, Edmund. *Die Krisis der europäischen Wissenschaften und die transzendentale Phänomenologie*. Ed. Walter Biemel. The Hague: Martin Nijhoff, 1954.
Husserl, Edmund. *The Crisis of European Sciences and Transcendental Phenomenology*. Trans. David Carr. Evanston, Ill.: Northwestern University Press, 1970.
Husserl, Edmund. *Philosophie der Arithmetik*. *Husserliana*, Bd. 12. Hrsg. Lothar Eley, Berlin: Springer, 1972.
Kant, Immanuel. *Werkausgabe*. XII Bde. Hrsg. Wilhelm Weischedel. Frankfurt: Suhrkamp, 1974.
Kleist, Heinrich von. *Sämtliche Werke und Briefe*. 2 Bde. Hrsg. Helmut Sembdner. München: Deutscher Taschenbuch Verlag, 1987.
Kripke, Saul. *Naming and Necessity*. Cambridge, Mass: Harvard University Press, 1972.
Kripke, Saul. *Wittgenstein on Rules and Private Language*. Cambridge, Mass.: Harvard University Press, 1984.
Lessing, G. E. *Werke*. 5 vols. Berlin: Aufbau Verlag, 1978.
Locke, John. *An Essay Concerning Human Understanding*. London: Viking Penguin, 2004 [orig. pub. 1689.].
Mallarmé, Stéphane. "The Impressionists and Edouard Manet." *The Art Monthly Review* (1876).
Moore, G. E. *Some Main Problems in Philosophy*. London: George Allen and Unwin, Ltd., 1953.
Nietzsche, Friedrich. *Über Wahrheit und Lüge im extramoralischen Sinne*. Stuttgart: Reclam. 2015 [orig. pub. 1896].
Proust, Marcel. *A la recherche du temps perdu*. 3 vols. Paris: Bibliothèque de la Pléiade, 1954 [orig. pub. 1913-27].
Rousseau, Jean-Jacques. *Discours sur les sciences et les arts; Discours sur l'origine et les fondements de l'inégalité parmi les hommes*. Introduction by Jacques Rogier. Paris: Flammarion, 1992 [orig. pub. Paris: Plissot, 1751; Geneva, 1755].
Rousseau, Jean-Jacques. *Du contrat social; ou, Principes de droits politiques*. Paris: Garnier Flammarion, 1966 [orig. pub. 1762]
Rousseau, Jean-Jacques. *Essai sur l'origine des langues, où il est parlé de la mélodie et de l'imitation musicale*. Ed. Charles Porset. Paris: Nizet, 1969 [orig. pub. 1781; written 174?; 175?; 176?].
Rousseau, Jean-Jacques. *Essai sur l'origine des langues, où il est parlé de la mélodie et de l'imitation musicale*. Ed. Jean Starobinski. Paris: Gallimard, 1990.
Rousseau, Jean-Jacques. *Rousseau, juge de Jean-Jacques*. Ed. C. A. Fusil. Paris: Plon, 1923 [orig. pub. 1782].
De Saussure, Ferdinand. *Cours de linguistique générale*. Ed. Charles Bally, Albert Sechehaye, Albert Riedlinger. Paris: Payot, 1971 [orig. pub. 1916].
De Saussure, Ferdinand. *Cours de linguistique générale*. Rev. ed. Ed. Tullio de Mauro. Paris: Payot, 1978.
Spinoza, Baruch. *The Ethics and Selected Letters*. Trans. Samuel Shirley. New York: Hackett, 1982 [orig. pub. 1677].
Wordsworth, William. *The Prose Works*. Ed. W. J. B. Owen and Jane Worthington Smyser. 2 vols. Oxford: Clarendon, 1974.
Wordsworth, William. *The Fourteen-Book Prelude*. Ed. W. J. B. Owen. Ithaca: Cornell University Press, 1985 [orig. pub. 1805, 1850].
Wordsworth, William. *The Thirteen-Book Prelude*. Ed. Mark L. Reed. Ithaca: Cornell University Press, 1990.
Wordsworth, William. *Lyrical Ballads and Other Poems, 1797-1800*. Ed. James Butler and Karen Green. Ithaca; Cornell University Press, 1992.

Secondary Bibliography

Aarsleff, Hans. *From Locke to Saussure. Essays on the Study of Language and Intellectual History*. Minneapolis: University of Minnesota Press, 1982.
Agamben, Giorgio. *The Sacrament of Language. An Archaeology of Oath*. Trans. Adam Kotsko. Stanford: Stanford University Press, 2010 [orig. pub. 2008].
Agamben, Giorgio. *The Kingdom and Theology. For a Theological Genealogy of Economy and Government*. Trans. Lorenzo Chiesa with Matteo Mandarini Stanford: Stanford University Press, 2011 [orig. pub. 2007].
Agamben, Giorgio. *Opus Dei. An Archaeology of Duty*. Trans. Adam Kotskol. Stanford: Stanford University Press, 2013 [orig. pub. 2012].
Aurnhammer, Achim. "Im Horizont der Ungewissheit: Unzuverlässigen Erzählen in Kleists Novellen." In *Heinrich von Kleist: Neue Ansichten eines rebellischen Klassikers*, Hrsg. Werner Frick. Freiburg, i. Br.: Rombach, 2014.
Azmanova, Albena. *The Scandal of Reason. A Critical Theory of Political Judgment*. New York: Columbia Press, 2012.
Barthes, Roland. *Mythologies*. Paris: Editions de Seuil, 1957.
Barthes, Roland. *Mythologies*. Trans. Annette Lavers. New York: Farrar Straus and Giroux, 1972.
Benjamin, Walter. *Illuminationen*. Frankfurt: Suhrkamp, 1977.
Blanchot, Maurice. *L'espace littéraire*. Paris: Gallimard, 1955.
Blanchot, Maurice. *The Space of Literature*. Trans. Ann Smock. Lincoln: University of Nebraska, 1982.
Boulter, Stephen. *Rediscovery of Common Sense Philosophy*. London: Palgrave, 2007.
Brodsky, Claudia. *The Imposition of Form. Studies in Narrative Representation and Knowledge*. Princeton: Princeton University Press, 1987.
Brodsky, Claudia. "Architecture and Architectonics. The Art of Reason in Kant's *Critique*. Canon. *The Princeton Journal of Thematic Studies in Architecture*. Vol. 3 (1988): 103–118.
Brodsky, Claudia. "Narrative Representation and Criticism: 'Crossing the Rubicon' in *Clarissa*. In *Reading Narrative: Form, Ethics, Ideology*. Ed. James Phelan. Columbus: Ohio State University Press, 1989, 207–219.
Brodsky, Claudia. "Whatever Moves You. 'Experimental Philosophy' and the Literature of Experience in Diderot and Kleist." In *Traditions of Experiment from the Enlightenment to the Present. Essays in Honor of Peter Demetz*. Ed. Nancy Kaiser and David E. Wellbery. Ann Arbor: University of Michigan Press, 1992, 17–43.
Brodsky, Claudia. *Lines of Thought. Discourse, Architectonics, and the Origin of Modern Philosophy*. Durham, NC: Duke University Press, 1996.
Brodsky, Claudia. "From the Pyramids to Romantic Poetry. Housing the Spirit in Hegel." In *Rereading Romanticism*. Ed. Martha Heller. Amsterdam: Rodopi, 1999, 327–66.
Brodsky, Claudia. "Szondi and Hegel. The Troubled Relationship of Literary Criticism to philosophy." *Telos*. no. 146 (2007): 45–64.
Brodsky, Claudia. "Beyond the Pleasure of the Principle of Death. Goethe's *Werther* and Goldsmith's *Vicar of Wakefield*. In *Einsamkeit und Geselligkeit um1800*. Ed. S. Schmid und R. Emig. Hamburg: Carl Winter Verlag, 2008, 29–40.
Brodsky, Claudia. *In the Place of Language. Literature and the Architecture of the Referent*. New York: Fordham University Press, 2009.
Brodsky, Claudia. "Remembering Swann." In *Swann's Way*. Norton Critical Edition. Ed. Susanna Lee. New York: Norton, 2014, 470–92.

Brodsky, Claudia. *Words' Worth: What the Poet Does*. New York and London: Bloomsbury, 2020.
Brown, Hilda Meldrum. *Heinrich von Kleist. The Ambiguity of Art and the Necessity of Form*. New York: Oxford University Press. 1998.
Campbell, Sally Howard. *Rousseau and the Paradox of Alienation*. Plymouth, UK: Lexington Books, 2012.
Carter, Christine Jane. *Rousseau and the Problem of War*. New York: Garland Press, 1987.
Cascardi, Anthony. *Consequences of Enlightenment*. Cambridge: Cambridge University Press, 1999.
Chomsky, Noam. *Cartesian Linguistics*. Cambridge, Mass.: MIT Press, 1966.
Chomsky, Noam. *Language and Mind*. New York: Harcourt Brace Javonovich, 1968.
Chouillet, Jacques. *Diderot. Poète de l'énergie*. Paris: Presses Universitaires de France, 1984 [orig. pub. 1964].
Charles, C. C. *Romantic Paradox. An Essay on the Poetry of Wordsworth*. London: Routledge & Kegan Paul, 1962.
Cohn, Dorrit. "Kleist's 'Marquise von O . . .': the Problem of Knowledge." *Monatsheft* Vol. 67, No. 2 (1975): 129–144.
Colletti, Lucio. *Ideologia e società*. Bari: Universale Laterza, 1975.
Crawford, David. W. *Kant's Aesthetic Theory*. Madison: University of Wisconsin Press, 1974.
Deleuze, Gilles. *Mille plateaux*. Paris; Editions de Minuit, 1980.
Deleuze, Gilles. *Le Pli. Leibniz et le baroque*. Paris: Collection critique, 1988.
de Man, Paul. *Blindness and Insight*. Minneapolis: University of Minnesota Press, 1983 [orig. pub. 1971].
de Man, Paul. "The Epistemology of Metaphor." *Critical Inquiry* Vol. 5, No. 1 (1978): 13–30.
de Man, Paul. "The Temptation of Permanence." In *Critical Writings. 1953-1978*. Trans. Dan Latimer, Ed. Lindsay Waters. Minneapolis: University of Minnesota Press, 1989, 30–40 [orig. French pub. *Monde Nouveau*, Oct. 1955].
Danby, John. *The Simple Wordsworth*. London: Routledge & Kegan Paul, 1971 [orig. pub. 1960].
Dugan, C. N. and Tracy B. Strong. "Music, Politics, Theater and Representation in Rousseau." In *Cambridge Companion to Rousseau*. Ed. Patrick Riley. Cambridge: Cambridge University Press, 2001, 329–64.
Dyer, Denis. *Stories of Kleist. A Critical Study*. New York: Holmes and Meier, 1977.
Eilenberg, Susan. *Strange Power of Speech. Wordsworth, Coleridge and Literary Possession*, New York: Oxford University Press, 1992.
Ellis, John M. "Kleist's 'Der Zweikampf.'" *Monatshefte* Vol. 65, No. 1 (1972): 48–60.
Empson, William. "'Sense' in the *Prelude*." In *The Structure of Complex Words*. Cambridge: Harvard University Press, 1989 [orig. pub. 1951], 289–305.
Fischer, Bernd. "Irony Ironized: Heinrich von Kleist's Narrative Stance and Friedrich Schlegel's Theory of Irony." *European Romantic Review* Vol. 1, No. 1 (1990): 59–74.
Florence, Penny. *Mallarmé, Manet and Redon: Visual and Aural Signs and the Generation of Meaning*. Cambridge: Cambridge University Press, 1986.
Forguson, Lynd. *Common Sense*. London: Routledge, 1989.
François, Anne-Lise, *Open Secrets. The Literature of Uncounted Experience*, Palo Alto, Ca.: Stanford University Press, 2007.
Fraser, Jake. "Kleist's Secrets. Nachrichtenverkehr in *Die Marquise von O . . .*". *Deutsche Vierteljahrsschrift* (2017) 91: 254–296.
Fricke, Gerhard. *Gefühl und Schicksal bei Heinrich von Kleist. Studien über den inneren Vorgang im Leben und Schaffen des Dichters*. Berlin: Junker und Dünnhaupt, 1929.

Furst, Lilian. "Double-Dealing in the *Marquise von O . . .*" In *Echoes and Influences of German Romanticism*. Ed. M. S. Batts, A. W. Riley, and H. Wetzell. New York: Peter Lang, 1987, 85–95.
Gregoric, Pavel. *Aristotle on the Common Sense*. Oxford: Oxford University Press, 2007.
Guyer, Paul. *Kant and the Claims of Taste*. Cambridge; Cambridge University Press, 1996.
Hartman, Geoffrey. *Wordsworth's Poetry. 1787–1814*. New Haven: Yale University Press, 1975.
Heffernan, James A. W. *Wordsworth's Theory of Poetry*. Ithaca: Cornell University Press, 1969.
Horn, Peter. *Heinrich von Kleists Erzählungen*. Königsteins/Ts.: Scriptor Taschenbuch, 1978.
Howard, Dick. *The Politics of Critique*. Minneapolis: University of Minnesota, 1988.
Howe, Steven. *Heinrich von Kleist and Jean-Jacques Rousseau. Violence, Identity, Nation*. New York: Camden House, 2012.
Jacobs, Carol. "The Style of Kleist." *diacritics* Vol. 9, No. 4 (Winter 1979): 47–61.
Jameson, Frederic. *Valences of the Dialectic*. New York and London: Verso, 2009.
Jones, Mark. *The "Lucy Poems": A Case Study in Literary Knowledge*. Toronto: University of Toronto Press, 1995.
Jarvis, Simon. *Wordsworth's Philosophic Song*. Cambridge: Cambridge University Press, 2007.
Kalar, Brent. *The Demands of Taste in Kant's Aesthetics*. London: Continuum, 2006.
Kelleher, Paul. "'The Man Within the Breast': Sympathy, Deformity, and Moral Subjectivity in Adam Smith's *The Theory of Moral Sentiments*." In *Inventing Agency. Essays on the Literary and Philosophical Production of the Modern Subject*. Ed. C. Brodsky and E. LaBrada. New York: Bloomsbury, 2017, 173–200.
Kleist, Heinrich von. *The Marquise of O— and Other Stories*. Trans. David Luke and Nigel Reeves. London: Viking, 1978.
Kowalik, Jill Ann. "Kleist's Essay on Rhetoric." *Monatshefte* Vol. 81, No. 4 (1989): 434–436.
Kulenkampff, Jan. *Kants Logik des aesthetischen Urteils*. Frankfurt a. M: Klostermann, 1978.
LaVaque-Manty, Mika. "Dueling for Equality. Masculine Honor and the Modern Politics of Dignity." *Political Theory* Vol. 34, No. 6 (2006): 715–740.
Lemos, Noah. *Common Sense*. Cambridge: Cambridge University Press, 2004.
Livingston, Alex and Leah Saroko. "From Honor to Dignity and Back Again. Remarks on LaVacque-Manty's 'Dueling for Equality.'" *Political Theory* Vol. 35, No. 4 (2007): 494–501.
Longuenesse, Béatrice. *I, Me, Mine: Back to Kant, and Back Again*. Oxford: Oxford University Press, 2017.
Longuenesse, Béatrice. *Kant and the Capacity to Judge. Sensibility and Discursivity in the Transcendental Analytic of the Critique of Pure Reason*. Princeton: Princeton University Press, 1996.
Lukács, Georg. *Die Theorie des Romans*. Berlin: Cassirer, 1920.
Lukács, Georg. *Theory of the Novel*. Trans. Anna Bostock. Cambridge: MIT Press, 1971.
Manders, Dean Wolfe. *The Hegemony of Common Sense. Wisdom and Mystification in Everyday Life*. New York: Lang, 2006.
Makkreel, Rudolf A. "Relating Kant's Theory of Reflective Judgment to the Law." *Washington University Jurisprudence Review* Vol. 6, No. 9 (2013): 147–160.
Marchant, Robert. *Principles of Wordsworth's Poetry*. Swansea: Brynmil Publishing Co., 1972.
Marken, Kenneth. *John Locke and English Literature of the Eighteenth Century*. New Haven: Yale University Press, 1936.

McGlathery, James. "Kleist's 'Der Zweikampf' as Comedy." In *Heinrich von Kleist Studies*. Ed. Alexej Ugrinsky. New York: AMS Press, 1980.
Morgenstern, Mira. *Rousseau and the Politics of Ambiguity*. University Park, Pa.: The Penn Sate University Press, 1996.
Murray, Robert. N. *Wordsworth's Style. Figures and Themes in the Lyrical Ballads*. Lincoln: University of Nebraska Press, 1967.
Muth, Ludwig. *Kleist und Kant*. Köln: Kölner Universitäts-Verlag, 1954.
Negri, Antonio. "The sacred dilemma of inoperosity. Giorgio Agamben's *Opus Dei*." Trans. Jason Francis McGimsey, Ed. Matteo Pasquinelli. UniNomade. Sep. 9, 2012.
Negri, Antonio. "Il sacro dilemma dell'inoperoso. A proposito di Opus Dei di Giorgio Agamben," In *Uninomade*, Feb. 2, 2012.
Panagia, Davide. *The Political Life of Sensation*. Durham, NC: Duke University Press, 2009.
Petscher, Iring. "Jean-Jacques Rousseau. Ethik und Politik." In *Rousseau und die Folgen*, Hrsg. R. Bubner, K. Cramer, R. Wiehl. Göttingen: Handerhoeck & Ruprecht, 1989, 1-23.
Rancière, Jacques. *La chair des mots. Politique de l'écriture*. Paris: Galilée, 1998.
Rancière, Jacques. *Flesh of Words. The Politics of Writing*. Trans. Charlotte Mandell. Stanford: Stanford University Press, 1998.
Rancière, Jacques. *Malaise dans l'ésthétique*. Paris: Galilée, 2004
Rancière, Jacques. *Aesthetics and Its Discontents*. Trans. Steven Corcoran. Cambridge: Polity Press, 2009.
Reich, Klaus. *Rousseau und Kant*. Tübingen: Verlag J. C. B. Mohr, 1936. Reprinted in *Rousseau und die Folgen*, Hrsg. R. Bubner, K. Cramer, R. Wiehl. Göttingen: Vandenhoeck & Ruprecht, 1989, 80-96.
Rescher, Nicholas. *Common Sense. A New Look at an Old Philosophical Tradition*. Milwaukee, Wis.: Marquette University Press, 2005.
Rosenfeld, Sophia. *Common Sense. A Political History*. Cambridge: Harvard University Press, 2011.
Saurette, Paul. *The Kantian Imperative: Humiliation, Common Sense, Politics*. Toronto: University of Toronto Press, 2005.
Savi, Marina. *Il concetto di senso commune in Kant*. Milano: Franco Angeli, 1998.
Schneider, Helmut. "Standing and Falling in Heinrich von Kleist." *MLN* Vol. 115, No. 3 (April 2000): 502-518.
Segrest, Scott Philip. *America and the Philosophy of Common Sense*. Columbia, Mo.: University of Missouri Press, 2010.
Séguin, J. P. *Diderot. Le Discours et les choses*. Paris: Librairie Klincksieck, 1978.
Shell, Susan Meld. *The Embodiment of Reason*. Chicago: University of Chicago Press, 1996.
Stebbing, L. Susan. *Logical Positivism and Analysis*. London: Oxford University Press, 1933.
Striker, Jacques. *A History of Disability*. Trans. William Sayers. Ann Arbor: University of Michigan Press, 1999.
Stroll, Avrum. *Moore and Wittgenstein on Certainty*. Oxford: Oxford University Press, 1994.
Terada, Rei. *Feeling in Theory. Emotion after the "Death of the Subject."* Cambridge: Harvard University Press, 2001.
Theisen, Bianca. "Simultaneity: A Narrative Figure in Kleist." *MLN* Vol. 121, No. 3 (April 2008): 514-521.
Todorov, Tzvetan. *Frail Happiness*. Trans. John T. Scott and Robert D. Zaretsky. University Park, PA: Pennsylvania State University Press, 2001 [orig. French pub. 1985].
Trachtenberg, Zev. *Making Citizens. Rousseau's Political Theory of Culture*. New York: Routledge, 1993.

Tucker, Brian. "'Die Stunde der Entscheidung': Ordeal and Uncertainty in Kleist's 'Der Zweikampf,'" *Monatshefte* Vol. 101, No. 4 (2009): 469–82.

Twilley, Nicola. "Sight Unseen." *The New Yorker* May 15, 2017.

Vaihinger, Hans. *Die Philosophie des Als Ob*. Leipzig: Felix Meiner Verlag, 1911.

Van Holthoon, Fritz. "Common Sense and Natural Law. From Thomas Acquinas to Thomas Reid." In *Common Sense*. Ed. Fritz van Holthoon and David R. Olson. Lanham, Md.: University Press of America, 1987, 99–114.

Venturi, Franco. *Jeunesse de Diderot (1713–1750)*. Trans. Juliette Bertrand. Paris: Albert Skira, 1939.

Vloytinsky, Michael. "The Kantian Case Against the Death Penalty." *academia.edu/2469736/*.

Vossler, Otto. *Rousseaus Freiheitslehre*. Göttingen: Vandenhoech & Ruprecht, 1962.

Wardle, Huon. "Cosmopolitics and Common Sense." *Open Anthropology Cooperative*, Working Paper Series No. 1, ISSN 2045–57L.

Wardle, Huon. "Kingston, Kant, and Common Sense." *Cambridge Anthropology* Vol. 18, No. 3 (1995): 40–55.

Weingart, Brigitte. "Contact at a Distance." In *Rethinking Emotion*. Ed. R. Campe and J. Weber. Berlin: de Gruyter, 2014, 73–100.

Wenzel, Christian Helmut. *Introduction to Kant's Aesthetics. Core Concepts and Problems*. London: Blackwell, 2005.

Wittkowski, Wolfgang. "'Die heilige Cäcelie' und 'Der Zweikampf': Kleists Legenden und die romantische Ironie." *Colloquia Germanica* No. 5 (1972): 17–58.

Wokler, Robert. *Rousseau, The Age of Enlightenment, and Their Legacies*. Princeton: Princeton University Press, 2012.

Wolfson, Susan. "Wordsworth's Craft." In *The Cambridge Companion to Wordsworth*. Ed. Stephen Gill. Cambridge: Cambridge University Press, 2003.

INDEX

Adler, Hans, vi
Adlon, Percy
   Céleste of, 18
Adorno, T. W., 62
Aeschylus
   tragedy of Cassandra in, x
Agamben, Giorgio
   "mute" "incarnation" of the "sacred" in, xi–xiin
   "Opus Dei" of, xi–xiin
agency
   as ability to alter an apparently "natural" "state of things," in Locke and Rousseau, xiii
   as basis for equalizing social conventions and contracts in Rousseau, xiii
   as differentiation and departure from *aesthesis,* xx
   "free," in Locke and Rousseau, xiv, 86, 109–10n
   and freedom from phenomenality in Kant, 156, 190–1
   and judgment in Kant, xv, xvii, 56, 84
   and language in Wordsworth, xviii
   linguistic condition of, 138
   mistaken in Kleist, xvii
   relation to structure of, in Steven Howe's analysis of Kleist's political thought and "standing," xiii–xiv
   and "revolution(s) in thinking," 18n
Arendt, Hannah
   on Adolf Eichmann speaking "on the stand", xvi–xvii
   Eichmann in Jerusalem by, 157–67
   on Kant's undefined *sensus communis,* 37n
Aristotle, 25n, 34n, 124–5
Arnauld A., and P. Nicole, 101n
Austin, J. L., 90n

automata and *hommes-machines*
   desire for total noncontingency they embody, xii
   as fantasy of a superhuman ability to fabricate the "animate" absence of experience as such, xi–xii
Azamanova, Albena, 115–16n

Balzac, Honoré de
   "Chez d'œuvre inconnu" of, 12
   death by desire for the lifeless represented by, xii
Baudelaire, Charles
   negative condition of lyric in, x, 62
Beck, Ulrich, 36n
"being in time" ("Dasein in der Zeit")
   first conception of, by Kant, 73n
Benjamin, Walter, xii, 62
Borges, Jorge Luis
   and Ovidian theme of death by *aesthesis,* xii
Boucher, François, xii
Boulter, Stephen, 25n, 38n
Brodsky, Joseph
   and Ovidian theme of death by *aesthesis, xii*
Bronzino, Agnolo di Cosimo, xii
Browning, Robert, xi
Burke, Edmund, 59
Byrne, Gabriel, 205n

Carnap, Rudolf, 31n
Carter, Christine Jane, 79n
Cascardi, Anthony, 37–8n, 65n
Celan, Paul, x, 62
Chomsky, Noam
   on Descartes' account of language, 108n
Coen, Joel and Ethan ("the Coen Bros.")
   cinematic style of, in comparison with Kleist's narrative prose, 205–6n

filmic equivalent of diacritical marks in the works of, 205–6n
Miller's Crossing, of, 205n
use of mannered and regional speech patterns, "generic" and idiosyncratic physical props to represent "character" externally by, 205–6n
Cohn, Dorrit, 200n
Condillac, Etienne Bonnot de, xi, 64, 82n, 82–3n, 101, 101n, 108n
consent
founding notion of verbal act of, in Locke, xiii
Crawford, David W., 67n

Daedalus, xi
Davidson, Donald, 33–4n
Deleuze, Gilles, xin
Delibes, Léo, xi
de Man, Paul, 81n, 98n, 115n
Derrida, Jacques
L'origine de la géometrie, trans. of Husserl, by, 8n
on Rousseau, 60–1n, 81n, 98n, 101n
Descartes, Renée
accounts of distinctive capacities of human language by, 24n, 82, 82–3n, 83n
Discours de la méthode of, 24n, 83n, 98
discursive conception of *cogito* by, 108, 108n, 136n
Geometry of, 98
integration of algebra with geometry by, 98, 99n
problem of "method" in, 124, 175
"*larvatus prodeo*" motto, in *Cogitationes Privatae* of, 203n
portrayal of, in Rosselini's "*Cartesius,*" 17–18n
Diderot, Denis
account of "origin" of language by, xv
accounts of forms of representation and communication invented by the sensorily deprived of, xiii, xv, 2–3, 10–18
on "bonnet blanc" controversy regarding "inversions" of a supposed "natural" order of language, 14, 101–5
comparison of poetic discourse with "a stack of hieroglyphs" by, 15–17
De l'interprétation de la nature of, 11
"double light of metaphor" in, 11, 17, 95, 97, 100
his "Saunderson," 3, 10–12, 16–17, 98–9
hypothetical conception of an "homme horloge," by, xi
"Lettre sur les aveugles" of, 10–11, 16–17
"Lettre sur les sourds et muets" of 10–18
literary production of, 60n, 103n
logical and historical precedence of adjective theorized by, 14, 103–4
logical-hypothetical description of infinite diversity of natural formations by, 10–12, 17
"Molyneux Problem" in, 99–100, 103
notion of "decomposition" as theoretical method of, xi, 12–13, 105
Pensées philosophiques of, 11
on poetry, 12, 15–17
"real" limit of perception in, xviii, 10
Donizetti, Domenico, xi
Dryden, John, xii
Dugan, C. N., 109–10n
Dvorák, Antonin, xi

Eichmann, Adolf
Arendt's account of the absence of all commonsensical conception of the general, and thus of violence, in, 158
his "clownishness" as symptom of a lack of "common sense," 157–8, 166
his own equation of "evil" with "banality," 160
the relation of his platitudinous speech to the commission of genocide, 157–61
Einstein, Albert, 26n
Ellis, John M., 216–7n
Euripides, tragedy of Cassandra, in, x

Feuerbach, Ludwig, 62
Fichte, Johann Gottlieb, 47
Fischer, Bernd, 197n
Florence, Penny, 171n
Forguson, Lynd, 33–4n
François, Anne-Lise, 203n
Fraser, Jake, 203–4n
Freud, Sigmund
    his structural economy of pleasure and pain first formulated in Kant's Third Critique, 34–5n, 62
Fricke, Gerhard, 213–14n
Furst, Lilian, 197n

Ganz, Bruno
    perfect performance of the role of "role-playing" played by Kleist's "Graf," in Rohmer's *Marquise von O*, of, 205n
Geertz, Clifford, 36n
Girard, René, 203–4n
Gittings, Robert, 140n
Goethe, Johann Wolfgang von, 60n
    advocacy in his *Color Theory* (*Farbenlehre*) of discursive mediation enacted "mit Ironie," 197, 197n
    early romanticism of, 62
    master-slave opposition conceived by his Faust, 135
    Werther, of, 61n
Goldsmith, Oliver, 60n
Goya, Francesco, xii
Gramsci, Antonio, 36n, 38–9n
Gregoric, Pavel, 24n
Guyer, Paul, 36–7n, 50n

Habermas, Jürgen, 38n, 115–16n
    antecedents of his theory of "communicative action" in Kant's and Schiller's concepts of aesthetic "play," 154–5n
    his concept of the "public sphere," contrasted with the architectonic function of Kant's Third Critique, as necessary "bridge" between his First and Second, 113, 113n
Hamann, Johann Georg, 64

Hawthorne, Nathaniel, xii
Hegel, G, W, F., 25n
    account of his correlation of the origin of thinking with the architectural origin of the aesthetic in *Words' Worth*, xviii
    the alternating absence and presence of specific "faculties" within the intellectual actions analyzed in Kant's three Critiques as antecedent of his temporal delineation of the dialectic, 134–5
    best known adage of, concerning mental death by indistinction, in relation to Kant's combinatory cognitive "art" of the "schema," 130n
    "false consciousness" in, 39–40n
    his and Kant's use of the term, "Anschauung" to signify "perception" rather than "intuition," 149n
    his scathing critique of the "lifeless" leveling of all mental and natural "forms" by "compartment[alizing]" thematic and taxonomic "method(s)," 196n
    Kant's analysis of the positive and negative experiences of the beautiful and sublime in relation to his dialectic, 34–5n, 62
Heidegger, Martin, 62
    and "anti-Enlightenment" theory, 64
    his critique of the everyday conventionalization of metaphor in *Identity and Difference*, 97–8n
    his differential account of "Being," 135
    the evacuation and reversal of his "ontological" critique of metaphysics by Agamben's notion of a "coming" "utopia," xi–iin
    his use of architectural terms, 115n
Hephaestus, xi
Herder, Johann Gottfried, 18

Hobbes, Thomas
   and "anti-Enlightenment" theory, 97–8n
   his attribution in *Leviathan* of "discourse" to "the mind," 108n
   his recognition of the conventionalization of metaphors in both philosophy and everyday speech, 97–8n
Hoffmann, E. T. A., xi
Hölderlin, Friedrich
   critique of Heidegger's commentary on, by Paul de Man, 115n
   negative condition of lyric in, x, 60n, 62
Homer
   death by *aesthesis* in, xii
   sirens of stupefaction in, x
Horkheimer, Max, 62, 202–3n
Horn, Peter, 213–14n, 221n
Howard, Dick
   his analysis of Rousseau's specifically temporal accounts of a hypothetical "state of nature," of "man," and of "revolution," 52n
   on the key role of "feeling" in Kant's Third Critique, 61–2n
Howe, Steven
   on the political thinking informing Kleist's stories, in relation to Rousseau's, 202–3n, 224n
Hume, David
   adoption by "new" (i.e., old) "ontological" "materialisms," of the radical mental passivity prerequisite to his skepticism, 122n
   as basis of Paul Guyer's backwards rejection, as insufficiently imitative of, of Kant, whose "critical" "revolution" arose explicitly to negate the skeptic's usurpation of mental action by sensation, 36–7n, 50n
   defense of, by Kant, against "commonsensical" dismissals of the challenge to all knowledge and possibility of moral action he raised, 40–1n, 41n
   degradation of all causal logic to a temporary product of custom, "habit," or "association" by, 51–2n
   Diderot's account of the demonstration, by the sensorily deprived, of every mind's intellectual productivity, in relation to his limitation and replacement of all such productivity by empirical impressions, 94n
   emphasis on passive "sensibility" in *Enquiry* of, 59
   his equation of "Understanding" with purely habitual inferences from impressions, 97–8n
   skeptical account of all knowledge in favor of "feeling" of, 59, 94n
   theory of mind of, compared to the myopia of the sighted, as these are described by Diderot's "Saunderson," 16, 94n
   recognition of the conventionalization of metaphor in both philosophical and everyday discourse by, 97–8n
   stated debt to, by Kant, 51, 51–2n, 94n
Husserl, Edmund, 62
   his account of the origin of geometry in comparison with Kant's, 8, 8n, 95n
   his account of "writing" as the required external means of transmitting, repeating and reenacting the "original" conception of geometry, 9
Hutcheson, Frances, 59

James, Henry
   death by *aesthesis* portrayed by, xii
Jameson, Frederic
   his opposition of the logical "contradictions" exposed by Rousseau's "historical reasoning" to caricatures of "Enlightenment Reason," 73n

his redefinition of Rousseau as "impossible founder" of "the dialectic itself," comparable in its "structural" epistemological scope to Kant's "transcendental antimony" of time, 73n

Kafka, Franz, 62
  and Kleist, 209, 215
Kalar, Brent, 36–7n
Kant, Immanuel
  account of "genius" by, 4, 4n, 181, 183, 183n, 189, 189n
  account of origin of geometry by, 5–6, 8–9, 16, 18, 95n, 122
  acknowledgement of debt to Rousseau by, 51–2, 51n, 73–4n
  "ambiguity" of term "aesthetic" noted and disambiguated by, 163–4
  "Answer to the Question, What is Enlightenment?" ("Beantwortung der Frage …") of, 148n
  Anthropology from a Pragmatic Point of View of, 24n, 214n
  "Augenschein" ("appearance upon the eye") of nature seen "as the poets do," distinguished from its phenomenal appearance, by, 186
  "being in time" ("Dasein in der Zeit") first conceived and formulated by, 7, 74, 133, 133n, 143
  "communicability" constituting verbal act of aesthetic judgment, defined by, 36n, 37n, 66–7, 71, 90, 109, 115, 116n, 120, 147, 154–5, 154n, 167, 191–2, 225
    contrasted with Habermas' "communicative action," 154–5n
  "Copernican turn" enacted and described by, 9, 9n, 16, 17, 18, 25, 61n, 121
  critical correction of "ambiguity" of his previous use of the term, "practical," by, 42–6
  demonstration, on the basis of hypothetical verbal actions, of the "possibility" of ("moral")
  "free" action, by, xv, xvii, 28–30, 36, 38
  distinction between objects of nominal and real definition and knowledge in his *Logik,* xv, 69, 69n, 90, 142, 175, 193, 193n
  employment of the German *Gemeinsinn* ("common sense") in sharp distinction from Scottish "Common Sense" Philosophy, commonplace German notions of "healthy" or "common human understanding" ("gesunder" or "gemeiner Menschenverstand"), and conventional notions of a "logic of common reason" ("Logik der gemeinen Vernunft") that "is actually no logic but an anthropology" ([die] eigentlich keine Logik sondern eine anthropologische Wissenschaft ist"), 23–4, 24n, 25n, 26, 26n, 31, 35, 40n, 45n, 47n, 119, 154
  exposition of the basis and explanation of the role of "synthetic judgments *a priori*" in his *Critique* by, 110–12
  "feeling," in his theory of judgment, xvi, xviii, 24, 32, 34n, 35, 37, 50, 56, 58–9, 61–3
  on "feeling free" in act of aesthetic judgment commensurate with "free delineation" perceived in its objects, 55–6, 64–5, 68, 109–10, 113–15, 113n, 120, 148
  "free agency" in, 16, 19, 58–9
  "general voice" ("allgemeine Stimme") of speech required to enact aesthetic judgment, theorized by, 109–10n, 117–21, 128, 143, 147, 163, 181, 190, 212n
  "grammar" of cognition in, 171, 171n
  grounds for hypothetical reasoning deduced by, xv, 7, 9, 9n, 10, 16, 26–9, 34, 36–7n, 38, 47, 50, 50n, 55, 50, 61–2n
  Grundlegung der Metaphysik of, 42, 42n

"Herumtappen" ("groping around in the dark") defining millennia of pre-Euclidean mathematics, described by, 3, 5, 6, 7, 8, 8n, 16
"heterogeneity" of cognition theorized by, xvi, 6–7, 59, 65, 123–4, 127–8, 133–4, 149, 171, 176, 181
interpretation of "apparent indifference" to philosophy by, 53n, 164–5, 169
Metaphysik der Sitten of, 77n
"monogram of imagination *a priori*" in First Critique of, xvi, 63, 126–30, 133, 135–6, 179–83, 187–92
on "mystagogery" of antidiscursive "sensers of truth" that "pretend to the throne [of philosophy]" 184, 224
on "nomadic skeptics," 164
notion of the "fortuitous notion" ("glücklicher Einfall") in, 5, 6, 8, 8n
notion of "free play" (of faculties) in, 26–7, 36n, 40, 44, 54–5, 55n, 63, 71, 90, 107, 119, 153–5, 161, 168–70, 184–5, 212
"On a Newly Elevated Tone in Philosophy" ("Von einem neuerdings ...") of, 31n, 32n, 194, 194n
on poetry, xvi, 181–92
poets' "use" of "nature" described by, xvi, 182–3, 187–92
on "the power of judgment" as definitive of any "Age of Critique," 29, 29n, 164–5
Prolegomena of, 25n, 40–1, 41n, 51n, 52n, 147, 171n, 175, 175n
relation of agency to speech described by, xiv
relation between feeling and language described by, 128n
"revolution(s) in mode of thinking" described by, xii, 3, 3n, 4, 5, 6, 7, 8n, 9, 10, 13, 16, 18, 24, 27, 37, 37n, 49, 50, 94, 111, 121, 121n, 143, 148, 149, 166, 174, 225

"schema" described by, as "art [of cogntion] buried in the soul," in distinction from ancient Greek usage, xvi, 63, 120–8, 125, 125n 130, 135, 177–9, 188, 191–2
Second Critique (*Critique of Practical Reason*) of, 27–9, 36, 54, 56, 58, 59, 65, 112, 113, 115, 116, 148, 149, 150n, 162, 167, 168, 170, 171, 193, 194, 210
"Second Preface" to First Critique of, 3, 5, 7, 38, 74n, 121, 133, 166
"self-legislation," concept of, and Rousseau's, 58, 62
on sonoric illusion of spiritual "harmony," 56–7
Streit der Fakultäten (*Conflict of the Faculties*) of, 18n
"stupidity" ("Dummheit") defined as "lack of any power to judge" by, 173
subject of judgment conceived as agent of otherness, by, 142
"subreption" in, 179, 191
Technik ("technology"), *techne*, and "technical," in contradistiction to "moral" "imperatives," described by, 42–9, 45n, 46n, 47n, 54, 64n, 65n, 70–1, 95, 114n, 122, 124
unconventional critical use of the hybrid notion, *sensus communis*, by, 23, 24, 25n, 37n, 47, 67n
"Unform" ("nonform") and "Formlosigkeit" ("formlessness"), theorized by, 153, 155, 167–9, 184, 210
"violent" experience of the "sublime" described by, 169–70, 184
"wallpaper" ("Papiertapeten") opposed to "tattoos" by, 154–6, 161, 163
Keats, John, 62
death by *aesthesis* represented by, xii
negative condition of lyric represented in, x
opposition between paradoxical self-memorializing epitaph he composed and those posthumously composed for

him and erected by others, 140,
140n
material "symbols" of Diderot's
sensorily deprived contrasted
with thoughts said feared to
"sink to nothingness" by, 106
Kelleher, Paul
analysis of "dis-ability," as universal
temporal condition, within the
context of Smith's *Theory of
Moral Sentiments,* by, 15n
Kleist, Heinrich von
"Aufklärung" ("enlightenment"),
ambiguous references to, in his
fictions, 207n
"blushing" and other external
appearances of otherwise
invisible emotion named in his
fictions, 200n
causality and freedom combined in the
distinctive discursive "style" of
his works, xviii, 193n, 204
death by desire for the lifeless
represented by, xii
dialectical relationship of success and
failure in his works, 196, 224
"The Duel" of, xvii–xviii, 206–9,
213–25
"Erklärung" ("explanation") of the
apparently self-evident, in, 220
"formalities," merely conventional, or
"polite," yet "binding,"
("Verbindlichkeiten"), in, 201n
"hat(s)" and other diacritical props and
accoutrements in, 204, 205n
"Kant-Krise" ("Kant-crisis") of, 195
"marionette-like" ("marionettenhaft")
"role-playing" ("Rolle spielen")
ascribed to the actions of
characters in his narratives,
194
"The Marquise von O . . ." ("Die
Marquise von O . . .") of,
xvii–xviii, 194, 197–207
"Gedankenstrich" ("dash") at its
foundation, 198–203
"the means of mediation" ("mittelbar")
stated and ignored in his works,
221–4

"Michael Kohlhaas" of, 206, 213
prose syntax of his narratives, 196,
198n, 201, 206, 208, 216n
relation of his causal fictions to Kant's
epistemology and moral theory,
192–3, 193n, 195–7
representational fiction and
representational cognition in,
195–7, 204
unfathomably motivated causality
and prominent signs of
demarcation defining the
widely differing contents of
all his stories, compared
with the individual verbal and
visual signatures integral to each
similarly divergently themed
film of the Coen Bros., 205–6n
Kripke, Saul, 91n
Kulenkampff, Jan, 36n

La Méttrie, Julien Offray de, xi
Latour, Bruno, 36n
LaVaque-Marty, Mika, 214n
Lefebvre, Henri, 39n
Lemnos, Noah, 50n
Lessing, G. E.
Laokoon of, 163
Lévi-Strauss, Claude, 62
Livingston, Alex, and Leah Soroko,
214n
Locke, John
account of "framing" of human
language, in distinction to
animal mimesis, in *Essay
Concerning Human
Understanding* of, 83n, 108n,
164
agency described in *Second Treatise* of,
xiii–xiv
founding concept of "consent" in,
xiii
Longuenesse, Béatrice, 108n
on Descartes' *cogito* as antecedent of
the active, "I think,"
accompanying all judgment in
Kant, 136n
Louis, Morris, ix
Lukács, Gyorgy, 39n

McGlathery, James G., 213–14n
Makkreel, Rudolf A., 214n
Mallarmé, Stéphane
  differential and dialectical relations composed in the poetry of, 62
  Kantian advocacy of an unprescribed "public" realm of aesthetic judgment by, 171n
  negative lyric condition in, xi
Manders, Dean Wolfe
  on "potentiality for critical thought," 39–40n
Mandelstam, Osip, xii
Marcuse, Herbert, 62
Marx, Karl, 62
  importance of language to his (Hegelian) critique of "false consciousness," 39–40n
  and "new," "post-Marxist" and "post-historical," "ontological" "materialisms," xi, xiv
  the relation of his structural thought to Kant's structural economy of pleasure and pain, and negative generation of value, 34–5n
  and Rousseau, 73–4n, 79n
Moore, G. E., 25–6n, 31n, 33–4n
Morgenstern, Mira, 74n
Muth, Ludwig, 193n

Narcissus and Echo, xi
Negri, Antonio
  "On Giorgio Agamben's *Opus Dei*" by, xi–xiin
neo-Platonic
  aesthetic theory, 34
  mysticisms, xi
Nietzsche, Friedrich, 64
  "On Truth and Lie in an Extramoral sense" ("Über Wahrheit und Lüge im aussermoralischen Sinne") by, 14

Offenbach, Jacques, xi
Ovid
  death by desire for the lifeless reflection of a self-projection in, xi–xii

Pascal, Blaise, 64
Pinter, Harold, xvii, xx
  "The Room," by, x
  speech patterns in the plays of, x
Plato
  and Aristotelian Scholasticism, 124–5
  "Ideas" in aesthetic theory of, 40
  and Kant's "schema," 125
  theory of *anamnesis* of, 37–8n
Porset, Charles
  annotation of first standard edition of Rousseau's posthumously published "Essai sur l'origine des langues" by, 81n
  on the probable date of composition of the "Essai," 81n
Proust, Marcel
  account of the "real horizon" of experience by, xviii–xix
  and Céleste Albaret, author of *Monsieur Proust* (1972) and subject of Percy Adlon's *Céleste*, 18
  "ironic tone" of the speech of Swann, original "author" of his life, as observed by the fictive narrator of his *A la recherche du temps perdu*, 211n
Pygmalion and Galatea, xi–xii

Rameau, Jean-Philippe, xii
Rancière, Jacques, xiin
  Aesthetics and Its Discontents of, xiin
  "Aesthetics as Politics" of, xiin
  The Flesh of Words of, xixn
  and Wordsworth, xixn
Rawls, John, 116n
Reagan, Ronald, 39–40n
Reich, Klaus, 51–2n
Reid, Thomas, 25–6n, 33–4n
Rescher, Nicholas, 32n
Richardson, Samuel
  and literature of "feeling," 60n
Rilke, Rainer Maria, 62
Rohmer, Eric
  film, *Die Marquise von O . . .*, of, 205–6n
Rosenfeld, Sophia, 39n

Rossellini, Roberto
  film, *Cartesius*, of, 18
Rousseau, Jean-Jacques
  "agency," "free," human capacity for
    ("en sa qualité d'agent libre"),
    conception of, by, xiv, 83–5,
    109–10n
  Confessions of, 132n
  Du contrat social of, xiii, 59–60, 84n,
    89–90, 109–10n, 131
  death by *aesthesis* represented by, xii
  *Discourse on whether the Arts and
    Sciences Improve the Morals of
    Men* ("First Discourse") of, 72–3,
    72n
    account of "man's departure from
      nothingness" in its opening
      sentence 71–2, 72n, 77n, 84n
  *Discourse on the Origin and
    Foundations of Inequality among
    Men* ("Second Discourse") of,
    xiv, 59–60, 60n, 74–81, 77n, 79n,
    83–5, 89–91, 131–2
    account of necessary substitution of
      abstract formal signs for
      gestures, 76–8
    distinction of animal from human
      language in, 84–5
    verbal creation of referent of
      spatial demarcation composing
      the act of appropriation,
      narrated in, 75n, 77n, 78–80,
      79n, 91, 91n
    distinction of human language
      from the non-"divers[ifying],"
      "unchanging" "languages" of
      "automata" and "animals" in
      Discours de la méthode of, 82–3,
      82n, 83n
  "Essay on the Origin of Languages" of,
    74n, 81–3, 81n, 82n, 83n, 85–90,
    88n, 91n
    account of "trope" as first word in,
      82–91
  host of Hume, 51
  hypothetical reasoning of, xiv, 52, 60–1,
    61–2n
  Kant's acknowledged debt to, 51–2,
    51n, 73–4n

  on origin of language, 72–4, 76–84,
    89–91, 91n, 85–6, 100, 106
  paradoxical historical status as
    "anti-Enlightenment" founder of
    the Enlightenment, 61n, 64
  "real" limit of experience indicated by,
    xviii
  Rêveries d'un promeneur solitaire of,
    132n

Saurette, Paul, 38n
Saussure, Ferdinand de, 143
Savi, Mariana, 24n
schema
  Kant's conception of, as "monogram of
    imagination *a priori*, xvi, 63,
    126–8, 129n, 130, 133, 135–6,
    180–3, 187–9, 191–2
Schiller, Friedrich
  adoption of Kant's notion of "free play"
    by, 154n
  death by *aesthesis* in, xvii
  early romanticism of, 62
Schmitt, Carl
  "absolute utilitarianism" and "nihilism"
    of, critiqued by Negri, xiin
Scottish School of Common Sense
  Philosophy, 25–6, 25n, 31n, 32n,
  33n
Segrest, Scott Philip, 25n
Shaftesbury, Lord and 7th Earl of
  "good sense" in, 25n
  "sensibility" in, 59
Shakespeare, William
  death by desire for the lifeless in, xii
  Merchant of Venice of, xx
Shaw, George Bernard
  death by desire for a projection of the
    self in, xii
Shell, Susan Meld, 36n
Shelley, P. B., 62
Socrates, 48
Spinoza, Baruch, 135n
"standing" and agency, xiii–xiv, xvii
  as social access to "rights," x
  as subject-position in relation to
    possibility ("chance"), x
  and verbal action, xx
Stebbing, Susan, 31n

Stella, Frank
    "Marquise of O" series, 205n
Striker, Jacques, 15n
Stroll, Avrum, 31n
Strong, Tracey B., 109–10n

tautology
    conversion, via redundancy, of *verba* into empirical givens by, 32–3
    Kant's critique of, 31n
    as usurpation of thinking and "death of philosophy" described in Kant's "On a Newly Elevated Tone in Philosophy," 32, 32n
Terada, Rei, 61n
Theisen, Bianca, 197n
Todorov, Tzvetan, 85n
Trachtenberg, Zev, 72n
Tucker, Brian, 246n
Twilley, Nicola, 97–8n

Vahinger, Hans, 113n
Vico, Giambattista, 64
Virgil
    tragedy of Cassandra in, x
Vloytinsky, MichaelL 214n
Von Holthoon, Fritz, 25n
Vossler, Otto, 60n

Wardle, Huon, 36n
Wenzel, Christian Helmut, 36–7n

Wittgenstein, Ludwig, 31n, 64
Wittowski, Wolfgang, 216n
Wokler, Robert, 73–4n
Woolf, Virgina
    Cassandra figure in, x
Wordsworth, William
    accounts of the "real" limit of experience in, xv, xviii
    on "communicability," xx
    on dependance of "the state of public taste" on mutual interactions of language and mind 134n
    "Essay on Epitaphs" of, 141
    geometrical delineation in, xx, 139
    "Gondo Gorge" passage in *The Prelude* of, xviii
    "A Guide through the District of the Lakes" by, 138n
    "Lucy Poems" of, xviii, 144
    most widely circulated, severely truncated definition of poetry of, 141n
    "Power" of "Imagination" referenced by, 129n, 134n
    "Preface to *Lyrical Ballads*" of, xx
    on "real language" vs. "poetic diction," xviii–ix, xiiin, 80n, 138–9
    "The Sublime and the Beautiful" of, 138n
    viewed as "nature poet," xviii
    viewed as poet of "feeling," 60–1n, 62

www.ingramcontent.com/pod-product-compliance
Lightning Source LLC
Chambersburg PA
CBHW062127300426
44115CB00012BA/1837